War and Society
in Habsburg Spain

I. A. A. Thompson

War and Society
in Habsburg Spain

Selected Essays

VARIORUM

Published by VARIORUM

Ashgate Publishing Limited
Wey Court East
Union Road
Farnham, Surrey
GU9 7PT England

Ashgate Publishing Company
110 Cherry Street
Suite 3-1
Burlington
VT 05401-3818
USA

ISBN 978-0-8607-8328-2

A CIP catalogue record for this book is available
from the British Library and the US Library of Congress.

Transferred to Digital Printing in 2014

Printed and bound in Great Britain
by Printondemand-worldwide.com

COLLECTED STUDIES SERIES CS376

CONTENTS

This volume consists of xii + 353 pages

PUBLISHER'S NOTE

The articles in this volume, as in all others in the Collected Studies Series, have not been given a new, continuous pagination. In order to avoid confusion, and to facilitate their use where these same studies have been referred to elsewhere, the original pagination has been maintained wherever possible.

Each article has been given a Roman number in order of appearance, as listed in the Contents. This number is repeated on each page and quoted in the index entries.

It has not been possible to reproduce all the illustrations originally included in these articles.

PREFACE

The articles on war and society reprinted here represent two of the channels of investigation which have flowed both directly and tangentially out of the research I began into Spanish military administration in the reign of Philip II thirty years ago. My interest in the historical study of war, inspired by Michael Roberts's seminal essay on *The Military Revolution 1560-1660*,[1] and directed towards early-modern Spain by John Elliott, was not so much military, as in war as a social and economic phenomenon and as a problem of organization, procurement and finance. This latter set of problems, following up some of the issues raised by Roberts and by the Catalan historian, Jaime Vicens Vives, in an equally celebrated and seminal paper,[2] led to an enquiry into the interconnections between war and the development of government, the early-modern state, and absolutism. The former, influenced by Sombart and Nef,[3] looked to the sociology and economics of war and to the social and economic effects of the associated development of state institutions and finances. It is largely this second line of enquiry which is reflected in the present collection.

If there is a common theme running through these essays it is a more or less overt assessment of the effectiveness of Spanish government in its military, administrative and financial operations, and in its interventions in the social and political order. Given the apparent precocity of government growth in Spain in the sixteenth century, the volume as a whole might therefore be seen, in a more general guise, as a commentary on the operational capabilities of the early-modern, so-called absolutist state.

With three exceptions the articles are reprinted as they were first published. Chapters IV and XII, originally in Spanish, appear here in English versions. Chapter II was circulated in typescript for the "War, State, and Economic and Social Structure" Theme at the VIIIth International Economic History Congress in Budapest in 1982, and is now published for the first time, though in a slightly revised and updated form. Since 1982 a good deal of work has been done on sixteenth- and seventeenth-century Castilian finances, and although J.I.Fortea and L.M.Bilbao, in particular, have produced more informed

---

[1] Belfast, 1956

[2] "Estructura administrativa estatal en los siglos XVI y XVII", *Rapports IV, XIe Congrès International des Sciences Historiques*, Stockholm, 1960.

[3] Especially, J.U.Nef, *War and Human Progress* (Cambridge, Mass., 1950).

and sophisticated analyses of the weight and incidence of taxation in Castile,[4] I have chosen to leave my data largely unaltered. Revenue figures are subject to considerable variation and margins of tolerance, as well as being susceptible to processing in a number of different ways. Not everyone would accept the case for the ruralization of taxation after 1590, for example, but the main thrust of my argument querying the standard perception of fiscal exhaustion in Castile, even at the end of the sixteenth century, has actually been reinforced by the recent calculations of L.M.Bilbao, and the second part of the paper dealing with the redistributive effects of taxation broaches an issue of profound importance which still remains without serious investigation.

The essays in Part II, though published over a twenty-year period, were in fact mostly written by the mid 1970s. Chapter VIII is in great part an elaboration of ideas previously adumbrated in "The Appointment of the Duke of Medina Sidonia" in 1969 (Chapter V) and in a paper read at a symposium held by the Council for Nautical Archaeology at the University of Kent in Canterbury in 1974. The claim that "The *first* task of the Armada was to parade, to sail up the Channel and beat its chest before England's gates" (unfortunately too often read as if I were saying that it was the Armada's *only* task) still seems to me not merely a nice conceit, but a useful view of the Armada's function, which makes sense of much that otherwise seems dysfunctional and in no way denies the weight that was and should be given to its other purposes. Though the essay is reproduced here as it was commissioned for the Armada Quatercentenary in 1988, without the full panoply of scholarly apparatus, much of the evidence it adduces can be found referenced in Chapters V and IX. Likewise, Chapter IX has its roots in a chronologically more ambitious paper read at a symposium on Mediterranean Warfare 1400-1650, held in the University of St Andrews in 1975.

It is to Colin Martin and his invitation to contribute to the Canterbury symposium on Archaeology and the Spanish Armada in 1974 that I owe my return to a subject that I had assumed to be exhausted. It was his queries concerning the guns which were being recovered from the wrecks he was examining that first drew my attention to a question which Michael Lewis seemed to have settled, and sent me back to Simancas to look again at the material I had previously noticed there. Chapters VI and VII are the results of that inspiration,

---

[4] José Ignacio Fortea Pérez, *Fiscalidad en Córdoba. Fisco, economía y sociedad: alcabalas y encabezamientos en tierras de Córdoba (1513-1619)* (Córdoba, 1986); L.M.Bilbao, "Ensayo de reconstrucción histórica de la Presión Fiscal en Castilla durante el siglo XVI", in E.Fernández de Pinedo (ed), *Haciendas Forales y Hacienda Real. Homenaje a: D.Miguel Artola y D.Felipe Ruiz Martín* (Bilbao, 1990), pp.37-62.

and though published thirteen years apart were originally conceived as twin aspects of a single study. Chapter X is reprinted here simply for what it was, a Quatercentenary *jeu d'esprit*; but behind the light fantastic there is perhaps a serious point about the counterfactual and counter-historical assumptions that are being made, generally without examination, whenever some historical event is said to have been important. A few essential footnotes have been added to the text that appeared in *Lloyds Log*.

The essays on crime, municipal office and nobility in Part III reflect more immediately my interest in the social relations of war and the socio-political implications of war financing. Chapter XI was something of a youthful digression from what is still planned to be a full-scale military sociology, utilizing, among other sources, the personal and geographical data in muster lists of the sort analyzed for the galleys. In retrospect, one might have been wiser to have persisted with the title originally proposed, "Condemned-Men on the Galleys of Spain: A Map of Crime in Sixteenth-Century Spain", and to have paid more attention to the likely effect on the figures of primary patterns of migration within Spain, especially from Galicia to Andalusia. Chapters XIII and XIV were also conceived as a pair, as two complementary ways of exploiting the same body of evidence, the one purely quantitative, the other an approach to a quantification of mentalities by a simple analysis of language and content. The conclusions of "The Purchase of Nobility in Castile" were subjected to a critical comment by J.S.Amelang in the *Journal of European Economic History* XI (1982), 219-26. On the basis of the very different experience of ennoblement in Catalonia, for which he presented some useful figures of his own, Amelang suggested that it was possible that data on sales by the finance departments left out of account the free grant of patents of nobility by the Crown as a grace, which in Catalonia were very numerous, and that therefore the role of the Crown in the expansion of nobility in sixteenth- and seventeenth-century Castile may well have been understated. The question was undoubtedly worth raising, but the processes of ennoblement were so different in Catalonia, where not only the proving of nobility in the courts was unimportant compared with Castile but the sale of nobility also seems not to have existed, as to deprive the argument from analogy of much force. Moreover, it is not the case that the sources I used did not include some free grants, but rather that there is no evidence in other sources, the complaints of the Cortes, for example, or the papers of the Cámara, which was the body where such grants would have been proposed, of any significant number of free grants such as would have caused me to modify my original argument. An average of less than two sales a year in a population of five or six million leaves plenty of margin for error.

Looking back, one can recognise in some of these pieces the influence of a typical 1960s "annalisme", with its preoccupation with serializable data, its concern with the quantification of mentalities, and its desire to go beyond the typical, "literary" social history and to base social analysis on "direct" sources. Some of these efforts succeeded better than others, or at least one came to feel less need to pile more significance on the material than it could reasonably carry, as perhaps was the temptation in one's earlier efforts. Nonetheless, and even allowing for the now fashionable, if often well-placed, criticisms of the Annales methodologies, the sources utilized in Chapters XI, XIII, XIV and II, registers of oarsmen on the galleys, recruiting lists, the analysis of royal privileges, private petitions, and council reports, and the accounts of commissaries, purveyors and paymasters, which survive in their thousands and tens of thousands in the archives, still have a great deal more to offer for the history of the economy, society and politics of Castile than scholars have so far got out of them.

Chapter I was co-authored with Geoffrey Parker to take into account some comments I made on a paper he originally presented at the 1971 Lepanto conference at the National Maritime Museum, Greenwich. It was reprinted in his *Spain and the Netherlands 1559-1659* (Collins, 1979), and I should like to thank him for permission to reprint it again here. My particular thanks are due also to Robert Smith, Chairman of The Manorial Society of Great Britain, for allowing me to reproduce Chapter VIII from *Royal Armada 400*; to the editors of Mariner's Mirror, The Historical Journal, Lloyds Log, The Economic History Review, and the European History Quarterly for Chapters I and VI, V, X, XI and XIV respectively; and to Tamesis Books, John Donald, and Basil Blackwell for Chapters VII, IX, and XV. Finally, I should like to thank Mark Steele not only for his very valuable comments on an earlier version of Chapter II, but also for his help and advice in the preparation of this volume.

Within each section it has seemed best to retain the chronological order of composition, not least because later pieces were written in the light of and assuming data and positions deployed in previous papers. Inevitably, there is a certain amount of overlap, both of argument and of material; one can only hope that it is no more than is understandable and forgivable in fifteen essays by the same author.

Keele, 1992   I.A.A. THOMPSON

NOTE ON CURRENCY, WEIGHTS AND MEASURES

maravedí, maravedís   the smallest monetary unit of account (abbreviated to *mrs*).

cuento   one million *mrs* (= 2,666.7 ducats).

ducado (ducat)   money of account, 375 *mrs*.

real   silver coin of 34 *mrs* (c.1600 £1 sterling = c.40 *reales*).

escudo   gold coin 22 carats fine, originally 350 *mrs*, but raised to 400 in 1566, and to 440 in 1609. In Castilian accounts, the *escudo* usually referred to was the *escudo de diez reales* worth 340 *mrs*.

arroba   as a measure of wine, the same as the *cántara*, c.16 litres, or 3½ gallons; as a measure of oil, c.12.5 litres, or 22 pints.

fanega   dry measure, c.55½ litres, or 1½ bushels.

quintal   weight, 100lbs. Castilian, c.46 kilograms, or 101½lbs.

vara   linear measure, c.84cms., or 33 inches.

tonelada   the *tonelada de carga* was a measure of ship's capacity equivalent to 1.38 cubic metres before 1590, and 1.51 cubic metres thereafter; the *tonelada de sueldo* was an accounting ton which allowed an extra 20/25 percent as a bonus.

I

THE BATTLE OF LEPANTO, 1571
THE COSTS OF VICTORY

by Geoffrey Parker and I. A. A. Thompson

IT is a commonplace that war was by far the greatest single consideration affecting the finances of the early modern state. Perhaps more
interesting, and less studied, is the question of the relative expense of
different forms of warfare and alternative military strategies. Without an
adequate costing of the available alternatives it is impossible fully to understand why policy decisions were taken or to make a valid assessment of the
fiscal consequences of any particular policy. What we are attempting to do
in this paper is to cost one such policy alternative, the adoption by Spain
and Venice in 1571 of an offensive strategy against the Turk in the Mediterranean after a generation during which their naval and military posture
towards Constantinople had been almost entirely defensive.

The Holy League signed between Spain, Venice, and the Papacy on
25 May 1571, called for a Grand Fleet of 200 galleys, 100 round ships,
50,000 infantry, and 4,500 cavalry, with the appropriate artillerymen and
pioneers, to campaign for six months. The cost of this armament was not
difficult for any courtier of 'moderate intelligence' to work out, and the
Duke of Sessa, one of Spain's foremost naval commanders, actually
undertook the calculation as a form of occupational therapy during a
period of bed-ridden and gouty idleness some two months before the
battle. Sessa put the total for the campaign at 2,700,000 *escudos*, which,
divided in the ratio 3:2 as stipulated in the alliance, would have cost Spain
about 1·6 and Venice about 1·1 million *escudos* – both very substantial
sums. In the event, however, they were never paid. The costs of the
Lepanto campaign were scaled down, re-distributed and in part repudiated,
so that ultimately it can be argued that in real terms, the battle itself cost
practically nothing at all.[1]

First there were reductions in time and numbers. The Grand Fleet was
only mobilized for five and a half months (1 June to 15 November 1571),
and although there were at least 211 Christian galleys and six galeasses in
the battle, only 26 ships (instead of 100) and only 40,000 soldiers (instead of
54,500) took part. In addition, the papal contingent (12 galleys and 3,000
men) was paid for by the Pope directly, with some help from Florence.
These economies brought the overall cost to be shared between Spain and

Venice down to about two million *escudos*. A statement of expenses drawn up by the Spanish officials aboard the Fleet on 14 November 1571, put Philip II's actual contribution at 1,226,241 *escudos*.[2]

The accuracy of this figure is, of course, questionable. The account of 14 November was as much a political as a fiscal document. It was drawn up very quickly and in very general terms as a statement of the king's position prior to the settlement of the allied account. It was avowedly an estimate – so many items had passed through the hands of local officials in Naples, Milan, Spain and Sicily, that it was really impossible at that stage to know what provisions and supplies had been allocated to the fleet, or how much they had cost – and it was an estimate unashamedly inflated in the king's favour. Even the treasury officials had scruples, scruples which were allayed only by the conviction that the Venetians were not to be trusted an inch either.[3] However, the Venetians accepted the Spanish estimate in broad outline and, by implication, they agreed to a contribution from the Republic of about 800,000 *escudos*. Probably this figure of two million *escudos* is as close as we can reasonably expect to come to the gross cost of the Lepanto campaign.

By any standard Philip II's 1·2 million *escudos* was a very large sum, approaching 40 per cent of Spain's available income. But Lepanto was not just a Spanish enterprise. The burden was spread among all the Mediterranean states of the Monarchy. Of Philip II's share nearly one-third of the men, 80 per cent of the galleys, and possibly one-third of the money came from Italy. The greater part of the preparations, the procurement of provisions and supplies, naval stores and munitions of all kinds took place in Italy. Without oars, cables, and hardware from Milan and Naples, the Spanish galleys could not have been fitted out, nor equipped so cheaply; without the wheat and biscuit from Naples and Sicily to supplement the bad harvest in Spain and the deficiencies of the Venetians, Lepanto could not have taken place.[4] Forty-five of the galleys and the two élite *tercios* of Don Pedro de Padilla and Don Diego Enríquez were maintained and paid for by the revenues of the kingdoms of Naples and Sicily.[5] In addition, the five unattached companies (*compañías sueltas*) from Sicily and the Italian regiments of Sigismondo Gonzago from Lombardy and the Count of Sarno from Naples were probably also paid by the Spanish dominions in Italy.[6] In all, Philip II's Italian states furnished about 443,000 *escudos* for troops and galleys alone, or 36 per cent of the total cost: 275,000 from Naples (22·5 per cent), 122,000 from Sicily (10 per cent), and 45,000 from Milan (3·7 per cent). Regarded as an imperial rather than as a purely Spanish enterprise, Lepanto was only a moderate burden – 1·2 million *escudos* representing only about 13 per cent of the 9 million or so which the king received each year from his Mediterranean possessions. Moreover, the burden was distributed more or less equitably in proportion to each province's share of the revenues.[7]

TABLE I: PHILIP II'S REVENUES, *c.* 1571

state	revenues in *escudos*	% of total	contribution to Lepanto in *escudos*	% of total
Spain	5,600,000	63	783,191	63.8
Naples	1,950,000	22	275,800	22.5
Sicily	690,000	7.7	122,250	10
Milan	650,000	7.3	45,000	3.7
Total	8,890,000	100	1,226,241	100

This table demonstrates the remarkable coincidence between the taxable strength of Naples and Spain and their contributions to the battle, in contrast to Milan which apparently paid less than its share, and Sicily which paid somewhat more. Nor does the 10 per cent share in the 'visible' Lepanto budget by any means measure the full extent of Sicily's participation in the activities of the Grand Fleet. Professor H. G. Koenigsberger's evidence on Sicily demonstrates that the years 1571–77 were a time of enormous strain on the island's finances. During the years 1571–73 Sicily contributed a total of 1·2 million *scudi* – quite apart from the loss of tens of thousands more in taxes waived on the grain supplied to the Fleet and to the Venetians under the terms of the League. The royal governor of the island, Terranova, was fully justified when he claimed that, in proportion to its size, no other kingdom had done as much.[8] For Naples too, the official figure of 275,000 *escudos* was certainly a bare minimum: in February 1571 the kingdom promised a donative of one million *escudos*, payable over two years, and by April the viceroy already had 900,000 *escudos* available for use on the fleet.[9]

These were all large sums, but they still left Spain to provide almost two-thirds of Philip II's share of the campaign costs. Fortunately the Pope came to the rescue. For most of the sixteenth century the King of Castile collected two important clerical taxes, the *cruzada* (the proceeds from the sale of indulgences in Spain) and the *subsidio* (a clerical income tax). These two taxes, together worth between 750,000 and 850,000 *escudos* annually, could only be collected with Papal authorization and had to be applied exclusively to the fight against the Infidel. In 1567 the Pope created a new tax on the Spanish church to help the king finance the war in the Netherlands, the *excusado* (the tithe of the third richest man in every parish).

However, Pius V's scruples over indulgences and Philip II's refusal to enter a League against the Turk, to which the Pope was passionately attached, in addition to serious jurisdictional conflicts and disagreements over foreign policy strained relations between them. The *cruzada* was suspended after 1566, the *excusado* was not collected, and the *subsidio* was due for renewal in 1571. When in March 1570, the Turkish attack on Cyprus led the Pope to approach Philip again about joining a League against the Sultan, the king made it clear that Spain's participation would be impossible without the 'Three Graces' (as these taxes were always called).[10] In July 1570, Pius issued the bulls authorizing the collection of the three taxes (the *excusado* on rather better terms than in 1567) and in return the king agreed in principle to the League. News that the 'Three Graces' were again conceded to the king had an immediate effect on his credit; bankers were at once willing to advance money against promise of repayment from one of the new taxes with a sure yield – 400,000 *escudos* were borrowed form the Genoese in May at low interest and were at once used to prepare the fleet.[11] The total annual yield of the 'Three Graces', something in excess of a million *escudos*, was substantially greater than the 783,191 *escudos* which was Spain's share of the Lepanto enterprise!

The cost of Lepanto to the Spanish monarchy was thus by no means an intolerable burden. Venice was not nearly so fortunate. Her share of the bill, perhaps 800,000 *escudos*, was smaller than Philip II's but her revenues were also far less.[12] The Republic's income in 1571 amounted to 2,000,000 Venetian ducats (or 1·75 million *escudos*), of which 700,000 ducats came from the city, 800,000 from the Italian mainland and 500,000 from Venice's seaborne empire.[13] Venice's overseas possessions were too small, too distant, and too poor to shoulder much of the burden of manning and equipping the Grand Fleet as Philip II's dependencies had done. On the other hand, the Pope offered some help. In March 1570, Pius confirmed the claim of the Seigneury to levy a tax on the landed property of the Venetian clergy – the *decimo al clero* – to further the Republic's naval construction. This appears to have been worth about 50,000 ducats a year, just over six per cent of the total cost of the Venetian fleet. Here again, Venice was left worse off than Spain. The conclusion is inescapable that in real terms the Republic paid far more for the victory of Lepanto than Philip II.

Even these modifications, far as they are from what had originally been anticipated, give a misleading impression of the true cost of the campaign. The allied battle fleet was not built for the occasion from scratch. On the contrary, both Venice and Spain maintained very considerable permanent forces for the defence of their Mediterranean possessions. Between 1545 and 1633 the Venetian navy always numbered a minimum of 100 light and

12 great galleys, to which six galeasses were added after 1565. This establishment number was often surpassed: over 130 Venetian galleys were involved in the 1571 campaign, while in 1581 the Republic had in its service 146 light and 18 great galleys. The cost of this regular defence force was enormous – 489,320 ducats in the uneventful year of 1587, over 600,000 in the more turbulent 1590s.[14] The greater part, perhaps 60 per cent, of the cost of Lepanto to Venice was thus a recurring charge which would have been incurred whether or not there was a battle fought; perhaps only an extra 300,000 ducats were required from Venice to convert defence into offence.

The position of the Spanish Monarchy was the same. The Venetian envoy in Madrid was right when he pointed out that Philip should not consider the galleys as costing him anything extra as they had to be paid for the whole year round.[15] It is true that the 96 or so galleys which the King was maintaining in October 1571 was the highest number that he – or possibly any king of Spain – had ever had in service, but this was largely independent of Lepanto. Philip II was committed to maintain a minimum of 100 galleys as a condition of the *subsidio* grant from as early as 1561, a number still not attained in 1571. Some 15 new galleys were indeed added to the squadrons of Sicily, Naples, and Spain during 1571, and new contracts were made with private owners, but the 1571 fleet was still only a point on the curve of recovery from the disasters of Djerba and La Herradura in 1560 and 1562; it was far from being a peak.

TABLE II: THE GROWTH OF PHILIP II'S MEDITERRANEAN FLEET, 1562–77

squadron	Nov. 1562	1567	17.3.1571	7.10.1571	1574	1576	1577
Spain: in Spain	7	10	} 24	18?	32	43	33
in Italy	7	15		14	14		
Naples	8	14	29	33	54	44	32
Sicily	10	10	11	10	22	22	14
Gian Andrea Doria	12	11	11	11	12	12	12
other contractors	11	19	10	10	12	11	11
Total fleet	55	79	85	96	146	132	102

The real 'extraordinary' burden of the Lepanto campaign for Spain lay in the troops aboard the fleet; yet only two-thirds of the 25,000 paid men provided by Philip II were raised specially for the campaign. The 9,700 Spanish infantry at Lepanto were divided into four *tercios*: the *tercio* of Naples under Don Pedro de Padilla, the *tercio* of Sicily under Don Diego Enríquez, a *tercio* under the command of Don Lope de Figueroa, known as the *tercio de Granada*, and a *tercio* raised mainly in the crown of Aragon under Don Miguel de Moncada. All four *tercios* had been serving in the war against the *morisco* rebels in Granada which finally petered out in the early spring of 1571, and without exception they were so depleted and in such poor condition that the companies had to be almost entirely re-recruited.[16] Thus, while the *tercios* of Figueroa and Moncada were in effect new *tercios*, those of Padilla and Enríquez were not, they were permanent and regular units, in normal circumstances based in Naples and Sicily and paid for out of Neapolitan and Sicilian revenues. They served outside Italy only during specific emergencies (like the *morisco* revolt) and they would undoubtedly have had to be reinforced and shipped back to Italy regardless of Lepanto. A document drawn up in May 1571, at the time of their embarkation for Italy, credits the *tercio* of Naples with 3,277 men and that of Sicily with 2,152 – some 54 per cent of the total number in the four *tercios*.[17] Besides these two regular units, each galley normally carried a special task-force of fifty soldiers, provided by the king, during the summer campaign season. These too would have been provided with or without Lepanto. The *tercios* of Naples and Sicily usually supplied the soldiers for the galleys of the Italian squadrons, but the 1,900 men required for the remaining 38 galleys and the 1,000 men of the five un-attached Italian companies from Sicily, who apparently served permanently with the galleys of Sicily, should also be added to the list of regular troops.[18] The recurring account for Philip II's Mediterranean fleet then stands as follows:

TABLE III: PHILIP II'S LEPANTO BUDGET: RECURRING COSTS

83 galleys	371,800
54 per cent of 9,700 Spanish foot	130,000
1,000 Sicilian infantry	21,200
1,900 other infantry	44,764
	567,764 *escudos*

Recurring costs thus represented about 64·3 per cent of Philip II's share of the expenses of the Lepanto campaign.

A final balance sheet of the 'visible' costs of Lepanto for the two principal Christian powers would thus show a net cost to Venice of about 300,000 ducats above her normal defence budget, partially offset by a papal grant worth 50,000; while Philip II spent about 660,000 *escudos* more than his ordinary outlay on defence, receiving in return papal concessions, payable in Spain, worth over a million. In addition, the victory brought the allies a booty of some 400,000 *escudos*, half of which went to Spain, half to Venice and the Papacy. The Christians captured 130 vessels, 390 guns, and 3,486 Turkish slaves; they lost 17 galleys of the Papal and Venetian fleets, and suffered a great deal of damage and the loss of many oarsmen. Net profit cannot have been less than 3,500 *escudos* per galley, the value of the bare hulls and the artillery. Although much of the booty must have been redistributed in rewards and gratuities, it should not be ignored in this account.[19]

But it is not enough to leave the matter here. There is a counter-factual problem also. Lepanto was not fought in a vacuum; it was merely the high point of half a century's confrontation between the Spanish and Ottoman empires. It was the Christian response to a period of the most intense Moslem military and naval pressure. There were, indeed, few years between 1551 and 1578 when Spain could be confident that the Turkish navy would not come west in force. More than 600,000 *escudos* had to be spent on the relief of Oran in 1563. The Sultan besieged Malta in 1565, and so terrified the West that Philip II's plans for the defence of the Mediterranean the following summer involved the levy of 30,000 men at an estimated cost of 1,400,000 *escudos* – well over double the extraordinary expenditure on the 1571 campaign. Similarly expensive preparations had to be undertaken by the Venetians during these crisis years. There followed a brief respite between 1567 and 1569, but with the fall of Cyprus to the Turks in September 1570, massive *defensive* preparations for 1571 would have been inevitable.[20]

Lepanto itself did nothing to increase the security of the West. Even in the mid-1570's, the persistent threat from the enemy fleet made it necessary for Philip to raise 9,000 men for the defence of Sardinia, together with all the victuals and munitions they required, and, in addition, to enlist 10,000 to 12,000 more as a special strategic reserve to be ready to go wherever they might be needed.[21] In the context of the general defence budgets of these years, therefore, even the 'extraordinary' expenditure of the League was a recurring charge. Lepanto was not so much an unusual burden as a redirection of resources. In the short term at least, it was a triumphant vindication of those who argued that attack was not only the best form of defence, but also the cheapest.[22]

Notes

Abbreviations used in these notes:

AGS	Archivo General de Simancas (Spain)
AGS CMC 2ª	ibid., Contaduría Mayor de Cuentas, segunda época, with *legajo* number
AGS E	ibid., sección de Estado, with *legajo* and folio
AGS GA	ibid., sección Guerra Antigua, with *legajo* number
BPU Ms Favre	Bibliothèque publique et universitaire, Geneva, collection manuscript Edourd Favre, with volume and folio number

I

1 For details of the treaty of the League and the Lepanto campaign in general, see L. Serrano, *Correspondencia diplomática entre España y la Santa Sede durante el Pontificado de San Pio V*, 4 vols., Madrid 1914, vols 3–4, and *La Liga de Lepanto entre España, Venecia y la Santa Sede (1570–73)*, 2 vols., Madrid 1919. For Sessa's estimate see M. Brunetti & E. Vitale, *La corrispondenza da Madrid dell' ambasciatore Leonardo Donà (1570–1573)*, Venice-Rome, n.d., I, pp. 342–3, letter of 1 Aug. 1571.

2 BPU, Ms Favre 62, ff. 37–47, 'Vilanço de las galeras, naos y infantería que servieron el año pasado 1571', and ff. 33–35v., 'Relación que han dado los oficiales de Su Magestad del gasto que se ha hecho en la armada', 14 Nov. 1571.

3 BPU Ms Favre 62, ff. 68–68v.

4 Brunetti & Vitale, I, pp. 180, 204, 228–9, 348.

5 The 31 galleys of Naples and the 11 of Sicily, plus the three of Stefano de Mari and Bendineli whose retainers were also assigned on Neapolitan revenues; BPU Ms Favre 28, ff. 83, 98, 101, two letters of Philip II to the duke of Sessa, 27 Dec. 1576; H. G. Koenigsberger, *The Government of Sicily under Philip II of Spain*, London, 1951, p. 128; AGS CMC 2ª, leg. 814, account of Juan Morales de Torres, 'Pagador General del Armada y Exercito de Su Magestad', for money received 1 June 1571 to 4 Jan. 1578, items 11, 12, 141.

6 José-María Gárate Córdoba, ed., *Los Tercios de España en la ocasión de Lepanto*, Madrid 1971, p. 266. (This book was kindly brought to our notice by Dr Henry Kamen of the University of Warwick.) For the *compañías sueltas*, Francisco-Felipe Olesa Muñido, *La Organización naval de los estados mediterráneos y en especial de España durante los siglos XVI y XVII*, 2 vols., Madrid 1968, II, p. 834. Sforza's *coronelía*, however, seems to have been paid by the Pagador General Morales, AGS CMC 2ª, leg. 814, item 5.

7 E. Albèri, *Le relazioni degli ambasciatori veneti*, 15 vols., Florence, 1839–, series I vol. 6, p. 385 (Spain 1572), vol. 5, p. 12 (Naples 1563), p. 15 (Sicily 1563); for Milan AGS E leg. 1240, f. 2, leg. 1244, f. 17.

8 Koenigsberger, pp. 54, 129–30; AGS E leg. 450, n.f., 'Relación del dinero que se deve en el Armada de Su Majestad', 10 Sept. 1574, puts at about 150,000 *escudos* the money owed for victuals and munitions procured by the duke of Terranova for Tunis and for the Fleet.

9 Brunetti & Vitale, I, pp. 207, 267. Naples also paid the 1,000 Italians raised in the Romagna in 1574 by *Coronel* Stefan Motino for example, AGS CMC 2ª leg. 814. item 139.

10 Serrano, *Correspondencia diplomática*, III, pp. 350–1; Brunetti & Vitale, I, pp. 199–200, 213, 255, 257.

11 Brunetti & Vitale, I. pp. 199, 207, 267, 277, 335, and I. Cloulas, 'Le "subsidio de las galeras", contribution du clergé espagnol à la guerre navale contre les Infidèles de 1563 à 1574', *Mélanges de la Casa de Velázquez*, III (1967), pp. 289–326, and on p. 302.

12 We have no direct figures for the exact cost to Venice, but the cost of the Venetian arsenal, the crews, and the rations of the galleys alone was over 600,000 ducats in 1594, and over 700,000 in 1602; more Venetian warships were mobilized in 1571 than in either of the later years. (Cf. R. Romano, 'Economic aspects of the construction of warships in Venice in the sixteenth century', in B. S. Pullan, *Crisis and change in the Venetian economy in the sixteenth and seventeenth centuries*, London, 1968, pp. 59–87, on p. 80.)

13 F. Besta, *Bilanci generali della Repubblica di Venezia*, Milan, 1912, p. 241.

14 Information in this paragraph is based on the excellent article of R. Romano in B. S. Pullan, *Crisis and change*, pp. 59–87.

15 Brunetti & Vitale, I, p. 348.

16 C. Douais, ed., *Dépêche de M. de Fourquevaux, ambassadeur du roi Charles IX en Espagne, 1565–1572*, 3 vols., Paris 1896–, II, pp. 306–7, 325 343, 350, 362; Brunetti & Vitale, I, pp. 137 187, 212–3, 260, 283, 310,

17 Gárate Córdoba, pp. 112–13.

18 Olesa Muñido, II, pp. 802, 834, 840.

19 Gárate Córdoba, p. 262 document 26; for the value of these prizes, *ibid*. p. 268 document 29.

20 One observer in Madrid did in fact think, for a time, that the preparations in 1571 were largely defensive, Brunetti & Vitale, I, p. 257.

21 BPU Ms Favre 28, ff. 97–101v, Philip II to the duke of Sessa, 27 Dec. 1576; AGS GA leg. 79, f. 93, Juan Delgado on 'Los puntos de lo que escrive Don Juan Çanoguera de Cerdeña'. Between 1572 and 1577 extraordinary expenditure averaged around 900,000 *escudos* a year, see AGS CMC 2ª, leg. 814.

22 For a very forceful statement of the view that the League would actually save the king money, see Serrano, *Correspondencia diplomática*, III, pp. 324–9, fray Luis de Torres to Philip II, 4 May 1570.

II

TAXATION, MILITARY SPENDING AND THE DOMESTIC ECONOMY IN CASTILE IN THE LATER SIXTEENTH CENTURY

The continuous financial burdens of war carried by the Spanish Monarchy in the 16th and 17th centuries were the source of widespread grievance among contemporary commentators and *arbitristas*, and almost all modern historians have followed them in taking it as axiomatic that Habsburg imperial policies were seriously detrimental to Castilian economic development by calling for fiscal and credit measures which destroyed incentive, investment and demand, and diverted capital and spending power from the domestic economy. A recent discussion of the problem writes of the 'debilitating haemorrhage of Spanish treasure and the virtual destruction of the Castilian economy in order to finance the war against the Dutch.'[1] In this process the last twenty-five years of the 16th century are generally regarded as critical. The Holy League against the Turk, the Revolt in the Netherlands, intervention in France, and the Armada against England led to spectacular increases in domestic consumer taxation (notably the more than doubling of the *alcabala* after 1575 and the introduction of the *millones* in 1590) which coincided with the checking of the long period of demographic expansion dating from the first quarter of the century. The peasant in Castile is portrayed as crushed under a weight of taxation heavier than anywhere else in Europe and urban demand choked by 'une déperdition énorme de capitaux, aux dépens de l'Espagne, au profit de l'étranger.'[2] Yet little consideration has been given to evaluating the *real* burden of taxation in Castile, and almost none to its social, geographical and sectoral incidence. Until that has been done any assessment of the economic impact of taxation can only be premature. Furthermore, with the exception of specie exports, there has been

---

[1] Geoffrey Parker, 'War and economic change: the economic costs of the Dutch Revolt', in J.M.Winter (ed), *War and economic development* (Cambridge, 1975), p.55.

[2] B.Bennassar, 'Consommation, investissements, mouvements de capitaux en Castille aux XVIe et XVIIe siècles', in *Conjoncture économique, structures sociales: hommage à Ernest Labrousse* (Paris, 1974), p.145.

no attention at all paid to the effects of government spending. The recycling of taxes by government spending represented a significant intervention by the state in the allocation of national resources, and the great bulk of that spending was for military purposes. This raises a number of important questions, concerning the contribution of the state and its preparations for war to economic prosperity, which have not been sufficiently discussed in the context of a territory which, though continually involved in wars, was at this time largely free of the immediate depredations of warfare.

Taxation

Total tax revenues in Castile (excluding 'voluntary' and transactional contributions) increased fourfold between 1557 and 1601.[3] The 2.5 million ducats of 1557, reached 4.4 million in 1567, 6.6 million in 1577, 8.0 million in 1591, 10.1 million in 1601. However, the increase is much less steep translated into constant values. Adjusted to the general movement of prices the 2.5 million of 1557 rises to 5.3 million in 1601, an increment of 112 percent instead of 304 percent.[4] Further, the unremitting increase of the nominal figures all but disappears. Even in nominal terms the relative increase was as great between 1557 and 1574 as between 1574 and 1601 (2.5 to 5.1 million; 5.1 to 10.1 million), and after the establishment of the new *encabezamiento* of the *alcabalas* in 1577, taxes remained almost static in real terms, being in 1601 (despite the 3,000,000 ducats of the *millones*) only 10 percent above 1577. Even this modified rise exaggerates the longer-term trend because the situation in the 1550s was exceptionally favourable to the taxpayer, after thirty years or so in which taxes had been outstripped by prices and population growth. Per capita real taxation was only about 25 percent higher in 1591 than in 1544. Segovia was in fact paying 15 percent less in

---

[3] It would be impossible here to document and explain individually each of the numerous calculations, estimates and judgements that have gone into this paper. For general fiscal data I have relied heavily on M.Ulloa, *La hacienda real de Castilla en el reinado de Felipe II* (Madrid, 1977); and for price data exclusively on E.J.Hamilton, *American Treasure and the Price Revolution in Spain 1501-1650* (Cambridge, Mass., 1934).

[4] On the basis of Hamilton's figures, I have deflated 1567 by 1.25 with respect to 1557 prices, 1577 by 1.36, 1591 by 1.55, and 1601 by 1.9. I also assume that population rose overall by perhaps 10% between 1557 and 1577, by a further 5% by 1591, and then fell by 5% by 1601. For population figures, A.Molinié-Bertrand, *Au siècle d'or. L'Espagne et ses hommes. La population du Royaume de Castille au XVIe siècle* (Paris, 1985).

3   TAXATION AND THE DOMESTIC ECONOMY IN CASTILE

real terms per capita in the 1580s than in the 1530s, and until 1575 the situation was no less favourable in Cordoba.[5]

The *alcabala* increase of 1575 marks a real divide not so much in the size of the tax-take, as in the nature of the tax system. Before 1575 just about half the tax increment had come from foreign trade taxes, whilst real per capita consumption taxes increased by only 6 per cent. After 1575 consumption taxes increased by nearly 5 million ducats, more than doubling their real per capita weight, whereas income from foreign trade taxes remained virtually unchanged. Pre-1575 tax increases, though quantitatively just as great as those after 1575, were relatively painless; in contrast, the increase in consumption taxes post 1575 was general and immediate in impact. Whatever the economic consequences of foreign trade taxes may be, as compared with domestic consumption taxes, there would undoubtedly have been a much greater sensitivity to the fiscality of the last quarter of the century. Nonetheless, the impact of even this shift was in part offset by the natural downward movement of real taxation in a period of inflation. Each leap was followed by a decade or more of steady real decline, refluxes of fiscality allowing the economy to recuperate (Table I). When, with the demographic disaster of 1596-1600 and the ending of the price rise, that reflux ceased to be automatic, taxes had to be reduced absolutely (the *millones* being cut to 2½ million in 1607, and to 2 million in 1611).

Table I: Tax Revenue in Castile 1557-1601 (in million ducats)

	1557	1567	1577	1588	1591	1598	1601
nominal revenue	2.5	4.4	6.6	6.7	8.0	7.1	10.1
index	100	176	264	268	320	284	404
'real' revenue	2.5	3.9	5.4	4.9	5.6	4.5	5.3
index	100	156	216	198	224	180	212

---

[5] A.García Sanz, *Desarrollo y crisis del Antiguo Régimen en Castilla la Vieja: economía y sociedad en tierras de Segovia 1500-1814* (Madrid, 1977), p.330; J.I.Fortea Pérez, *Córdoba en el siglo XVI* (Córdoba, 1981), p.414.

TAXATION AND THE DOMESTIC ECONOMY IN CASTILE   4

Insofar as it is possible to make any worthwhile estimate of Castilian GNP, taxation took about 4½-5 percent of national income in 1557, 6 percent in 1567, 8 percent in 1577, 9-9½ percent in 1591 and 9½-10½ percent in 1601.[6] However, to the direct take from taxation we also need to add the capital value of *juros* committed after 1557 (c.50-60 million ducats) and the proceeds of donatives, sales and other forms of voluntary taxation (perhaps 20 million ducats or more). The total revenue drawn out of the economy by the Crown between 1557 and 1609 can be calculated at something near 400 million ducats, c. 9 percent of national income at a reasonable estimate, or 7½-8 percent excluding foreign trade taxes from that figure. This is not too much out of line with the 5 to 8 percent that Cipolla thinks was the normal maximum in the early-modern period,[7] nor with other comparable examples. Measured in wheat (prices at the *tasa*), Castilian taxation reached its 16th-century zenith in the years 1591-6 with the equivalent of 3,673,000 hectolitres. Head for head this was much the same as has been estimated for France in the late-15th century, and only two-thirds of the figure for the mid-17th century.[8] At 6.15 ducats per *vecino* Castilian taxes in 1591-6 were the equivalent of 27 days of labour: in 1601 they equalled 37 days of labour. A level of taxation in late-15th century Normandy at least as high (26 days of labour 1461, 69 days 1483) had not inhibited growth, and it is unlikely that by itself it would have done so in late-16th century Castile.

The notion of a Castile crushed beneath the weight of taxation is belied by the enormous sums spent willingly by communities in their own interests, real or imagined, in litigation or on offices or judicial exemptions. In 1596

---

[6] GNP estimates: J.Gentil da Silva, *En Espagne, développement économique, subsistance, déclin* (Paris, 1965), p.92 (73.3 million ducats c.1570); A.Domínguez Ortiz, *The Golden Age of Spain* (London, 1971), p.198 (c.105 million 1590s); F.J.Vela Santamaría & A.Marcos Martín, 'Las grandes ciudades campesinas de Andalucía occidental en el siglo XVI. El caso de Jerez de la Frontera', *Andalucía Moderna (Siglos XVI-XVII)*, 2 vols. (Córdoba, 1978), II, 406, calculate per capita income in Jerez in 1590 at 5,248 *maravedis* (63 ducats/*vecino*), which would give c. 82 million ducats for Castile as a whole; F.Brumont, *Campo y campesinos de Castilla la Vieja en tiempos de Felipe II* (Madrid, 1984), p.188, comes up with an almost identical calculation for average 'riqueza'/*vecino* in La Bureba (Burgos province) 23,550 *maravedis* (62.8 ducats). For the mid 17th century, A.Domínguez Ortiz, *Política y Hacienda de Felipe IV* (Madrid, 1960), p.183, estimates Crown income of 20 million ducats at 11% of GNP (180 million ducats).

[7] C.M.Cipolla, *Before the Industrial Revolution* (London, 1976), p.47.

[8] P.Contamine, 'Guerre, fiscalité royale et économie en France (deuxième moitié du XVe siècle)', in *Proceedings of the Seventh International Economic History Congress* (Edinburgh, 1978), vol.2, pp.266-73.

5   TAXATION AND THE DOMESTIC ECONOMY IN CASTILE

the 933 *vecinos* of Logroño paid 52,267 ducats for the right to elect their own *regidores*, 26 times the amount they paid the king in taxes, according to one contemporary.[9] The *vecinos* of Valverde, near Madrid, borrowed 93 ducats each to buy their jurisdictional independence; interest charges came to over 6 ducats per *vecino*,[10] as much as the national average paid in taxes. The scores of examples of this kind point to a fund of resources available in Castile, even at the end of the 16th century, and suggest that the opportunity costs of higher taxation are to be seen first of all in the reduction of litigation and in the surrender of their jurisdictions or the abandonment of their constitutions by communities in the 17th century.[11]

High taxation is not, of course, necessarily depressive. It can induce a more productive use of resources, and there is some reason to believe that it did so in late 16th-century Castile. The renting out of municipal commons to pay the *millones*, the sale of wastes by the Crown, and even the sale of offices with administrative control of common pastures provided the occasion for more extensive, and sometimes more intensive, land use.[12] Fiscal pressure also provoked, or was the pretext for, the unfreezing of resources tied up in treasure, real property or entail. Nine titled nobles were given permission to raise 190,000 ducats against their *mayorazgos* to cover the costs of their military contingents in 1580; they asked for 380,000.[13] 'Services' to the Crown, therefore, helped counteract the 'thésaurisation' which Bennassar has seen as one of the constraints on investment in the 17th century.[14]

---

[9] Archivo Municipal de Logroño, Libro de Actas 8 (7 Aug.1596); Biblioteca Nacional, Madrid, Ms. 1749, f.351v.

[10] AGS (Archivo General de Simancas), CJH (Consejo y Juntas de Hacienda) 345 (473), 12 Jan. 1607.

[11] R.L.Kagan, *Lawsuits and Litigants in Castile 1500-1700* (Chapel Hill, N.C., 1981), chap.6; I.A.A.Thompson, 'El concejo abierto de Alfaro en 1602', *Berceo* 100 (1981), pp.319-20.

[12] García Sanz, *Desarrollo y crisis*, p.145; ACC (*Actas de las Cortes de Castilla*) vol.15, pp.655-7, 'las tierras son más que nunca han sido por las que de nuevo se han rompido que eran dehesas concejiles y baldíos' (26 Aug.1598).

[13] AHN (Archivo Histórico Nacional, Madrid), Consejos leg.4408, 1580 no.49.

[14] Bennassar, op. cit., p.146.

It is essential, in addition to the total tax-take, to know how taxation was distributed among classes, regions and sectors. In our present state of knowledge the first is impossible, except to point to the importance of direct ecclesiastical contributions on the one hand (the *subsidio*, the *excusado*, and the *tercias* were together worth about 1,250,000 ducats in the 1590s); and the military levies, 'loans', donatives and luxury taxes of the landed and the wealthy on the other. The *empréstido* of 1591-2 brought in 972,000 ducats, at least.[15] The problems of determining the final incidence and the equitableness of indirect sales and consumption taxes are complex. The theoretical difficulties, and there were arguments for both the regressiveness and the progressiveness of consumption taxes in the 17th century, are compounded in practice by the 'denaturization' of what were nominally sales or personal taxes as communities met their obligations in whatever ways best suited them. As for the rest, it is possible to estimate the regional and sectoral distribution of taxes only in the grossest way. It is nonetheless necessary to make the attempt. Grouping taxes into those levied on foreign trade, generally ad valorem import and export duties; those assessed on internal trade, preponderantly urban in incidence (*alcabalas*); and those which for convenience might be called 'per capita taxes' in that they were nominally either personal or charged on the consumption of basic comestibles, and hence were of general incidence and broadly proportionate to population (*servicios, millones, salinas, Cruzada*), the approximate share of total taxes deriving from each group is as follows:

Table II: Distribution of Tax Revenue by Type, 1557-1601

	1557	1567	1577	1591	1601
Foreign Trade	21.5%	27.5%	20.4%	17.2%	13.2%
Urban Trade	37.5%	29.1%	42.8%	35.1%	28.8%
General 'per capita'	26.8%	23.7%	19.4%	33.4%	44.0%

Against a steady fall in the tax return from foreign trade, the squeeze on urban demand reached its most intense after 1575. Thereafter, the stagnation of the *alcabala* and the introduction of the *millones* in 1590 and 1601 shifted the balance of the tax burden from the large urban centres to the country as

---

[15] IVDJ (Instituto Valencia de Don Juan, Madrid), envío 45, f.478.

7 TAXATION AND THE DOMESTIC ECONOMY IN CASTILE

a whole, and from trade to agricultural consumption. The city of Seville, to give an extreme example, paid 14.1 percent of the *alcabala*, 6.5 percent of the *millones*.[16] This reversal contributed greatly to the other major shift, the increasingly heavy per capita burden falling on Castile-León north of the Tagus, and on Old Castile in particular. The earlier demographic reflux and the lower price-table in Old Castile meant that from the 1560s the real, per capita tax-rate rose faster than in Andalusia. By 1590, the real burden per head of 'urban trade' and 'general per capita' taxes had risen 7 percent more in Old Castile than in Andalusia (index 125 and 117). With the addition of the *millones* in 1590, the gap widened to 31 percent (191 and 146). The readjustment of the *servicio* and *millones* rates by c. 15 percent in favour of Old Castile in 1594 and 1595 was promptly offset by further catastrophic population losses at the end of the century, and when the *millones* were reintroduced in 1601, at more than twice the previous level, they lifted the real, per capita increase in Old Castile to 277, 38 percent more than the corresponding figure for Andalusia.[17]

It was the scissors of long-term demographic decline and the inflation of taxes which made it impossible for communities to maintain their fixed obligations, and this was a phenomenon which, though first marked in the last decade of the 16th century, did not become generalised until the second quarter of the 17th century when within a decade taxes were tripled on a population perhaps down by a quarter on its sixteenth-century peak. Fiscal exhaustion, manifested in the widening gap between tax demands and tax returns, was really a problem of the mid-17th century, when the nominal tax-take must have exceeded 15 percent of national income, not the late 16th

---

[16] The *millones* were officially set at 440 *maravedis/vecino* in the cities, 327 in the country, ACC vol. 13, p.149 (7 Dec.1593); the *alcabalas* were commonly several times greater in the cities than in their *tierras*, some three times greater in Córdoba and Cáceres, for example: J.I.Fortea Pérez, *Fiscalidad en Córdoba* (Córdoba, 1986), p.133; J-L.Pereira Iglesias, 'Contribución fiscal del partido de Cáceres durante el siglo XVI: alcabalas y tercias', *Norba* I (1980): 253-78. For Seville, F.Morales Padrón, *La Ciudad del Quinientos* (Seville, 1977), p.238. The *repartimiento de millones of* 1611 in ACC vol.26, p.354: Guadalajara city, for example, paid 1,638,290, or 0.15% of *millones*, 0.36% of the *encabezamiento*; Valladolid city paid 11,101,326, or 1.46% of the *millones*, 1.84% of the *encabezamiento*.

[17] Regional distribution of *alcabalas*, *servicios* and *millones* in M.Artola, *La Hacienda del Antiguo Régimen* (Madrid, 1982), and A.Castillo, 'Population et "richesse" en Castille durant la seconde moitié du XVIe siècle', *Annales* 20 (1965): 719-33. Deflators for Andalusia and Old Castile for 1590/1591, 1601, on base 1560: for population, 125:95, 120:85; for prices, 154:143, 167:155.

century, when tax demands were still broadly met, and was more a consequence than a cause of Castile's economic and demographic downturn. Yet even a figure in excess of 15 percent, however high by sixteenth-century standards, was not out of line with the tax rates experienced in other West European states in the later 17th century (1695, England 15 percent, France 21 percent, Holland 38 percent).[18] In the context of the situation in Castile after 1640, when Spain was fighting a war with France and rebellion on her own borders in Catalonia and Portugal, Contamine's observation is very pertinent, 'La fiscalité la plus sévère était sans doute beaucoup moins catastrophique que la présence physique de la guerre.'[19]

Expenditure

400 million ducats of internal revenue was not of course 400 million ducats lost to the Castilian economy. The amount drained away to pay the costs of war in the Netherlands, the Mediterranean, France, subsidies to the Emperor, secret and diplomatic expenses, and bankers' charges and profits perhaps reached 150 million ducats -- the figure a treasury official in the 1630s claimed on the basis of *licencias de saca* had been spent on the Netherlands by 1612.[20] 80 million of this was met by the royal share of bullion imports from America, leaving some 70 million extracted from Castile, c. 1½ percent of national income. This is not an insignificant figure, not least because it represented a loss of silver and gold, but not quite the 'debilitating haemorrhage' of contemporary or modern assertion. Even in the period of peak foreign expenditures after 1585, the loss of spending power in Castile (even if it is assumed that it would not have been hoarded or transmuted into even higher prices) was the equivalent of a less than 3 percent variation in the price of wheat.

The remaining 80 percent plus of government income went back into the Spanish economy. About 160 million ducats (40 percent) was recycled at source to *juro*-holders. By the 1590s the local *encabezamientos* were allocated almost in their entirety to *juro*-holders, principally in the larger cities and provincial capitals with a large rentier class, rather than the smaller country towns, thus retaining coin within the local economy and transferring wealth

---

[18] C.Wilson, *Economic History and the Historian* (London, 1969), p.120.

[19] Contamine, op. cit., p.271.

[20] Biblioteca Nacional, Madrid, Ms. 6754, f. 74 (Domingo de Salcedo)

9   TAXATION AND THE DOMESTIC ECONOMY IN CASTILE

(in return of investment) from the country as a whole to the urban wealthy. Given the social imperatives of 16th-century consumption, the effects of this redistribution on demand in the secondary and tertiary sectors were probably positive. The increasing commitment of the *alcabalas* to the payment of *juros* must also have done something to mitigate the shift in the weight of taxation from foreign trade to local trade taxes which took place after 1575. But the massive redistribution of wealth effected by the *juro* remains almost totally unexplored by historians.[21]

The final 160-170 million ducats was fed back into the economy by way of government spending, perhaps 70 percent of which was on the military budget. Domestic military expenditure increased threefold during the course of the 1580s. From 750,000-1,100,000 in 1559-79, it ranged between 2.5 and 3.5 million ducats in the peak years 1586-97, and then fell back to 2-2.5 million under Phillip III.[22] The proportion of national income devoted to domestic military expenditure rose from c. 1 percent in 1559-79, to c. 2 percent in 1580-85, c. 3¼ percent in 1586-98, and c. 2 1/3 percent in 1599-1609.

Military Spending

The decade after 1580 altered not only the size but also the nature of military expenditure and brought an unprecedented increase of state intervention in the market and in industrial entrepreneurship. The Atlantic

---

[21] F.Chacón Jiménez, *Murcia en la centuria del quinientos* (Murcia, 1979), pp.227-8: in 1547 22% of the *alcabalas* and *tercias* of Murcia was assigned to *juros* (836,789 of 3,849,000); in 1595 95% (12,257,229 of 12,890,500). Some *juro* revenue went abroad, in the portfolios of the Genoese, and others; and a good deal was transferred from the localities to Court expenditure; but the fact that contemporaries, like Alamos de Barrientos, could take a somewhat Panglossian view of these recycling effects goes a long way towards explaining why such levels of taxation were accepted: see J.M.Guardia (ed), *Antonio Pérez: L'Art de Gouverner. Discours adressé à Philippe III* (1598) (Paris, 1867), p.62, 'Que verdaderamente, segun doctrina de los sabios y cursados en estas materias, lo que hace insufribles los tributos, es que lo procedido de ellos salga de los mismos que los pagan y de sus naturales; porque cuando anda y vuelve a ellos mismos, saliendo de unos y dando en otros de un mismo reino y provincia, por mucho que den, les queda mucho, pues torna a su poder lo que dieron; que si bien unos se empobrecieren, otros amigos y parientes y vecinos de aquellos se enriquecerán, cuya abundancia forzosamente se ha de volver a comunicar y extender a los demás, o ahora o muy brevemente: lo cual cesa pasando nuestras riquezas a los extranjeros, y no habiendo camino por donde puedan volver a nosotros, para que las tornemos a dar.'

[22] I.A.A.Thompson, *War and Government in Habsburg Spain 1560-1620* (London, 1976), p.289.

galleon carried more artillery and required supplies of timber, iron, canvas and other naval stores on a far larger scale than the Mediterranean galley. The formation of an Ocean Fleet doubled the ordnance in the Spanish war machine. The Atlantic navy in 1597 needed six times as much hemp as the entire Spanish and Portuguese squadron of thirty-two galleys. As masts, spars, timber, tar, pitch, tallow, non-ferrous metals, sailcloth and canvas linen, as well as a good deal of cordage, cable and powder had to be bought abroad, the expansion of the navy added considerably to Spain's foreign trading deficit. The response was an increase of state investment in mining, munitions and shipbuilding and an extension of government control over private arms manufacturing in order to ensure supplies and reduce dependence on foreign sources. Shot and armour manufactories were set up, state gunpowder production doubled, and expenditure on domestic manufactures of arms and munitions tripled, from 50,000 ducats a year in the early 1580s to 166,000 ducats in 1604.[23]

However, by far the largest component of the procurement budget was the victualling account. The needs of the navy increased the grain and victualling requirements of the commissariat two- to three-fold. At least twice as much was spent on victuals as on munitions, hardware and manufactured goods combined. Bread grains alone consumed three-eighths of total non-pay expenditures, and wine another one-seventh.

Who were the beneficiaries of the 3 million ducats, plus or minus, of military spending? The tax levied for military purposes was redistributed very unevenly across Spain. The recipients were the regions hosting garrisons and serving as bases for the navy. All were on the periphery - Catalonia, Navarre, Guipúzcoa, Aragon on the French frontier, Andalusia, Portugal, Galicia and the Cantabrian coast. Between 90 and 95 percent of the military budget was spent in these areas. The central mesetas of Old and New Castile were primarily dormitory areas for the horseguards and for transient companies of recruits. Periodic levies of grain from the Tierra de Campos took place after 1579, bringing in a nominal 75-100,000 ducats every second year or so, but, as with the board and subsidies given to troops in passage and in billet, full payment was rarely forthcoming. By 1594, the *vecinos* of Quintanilla and Calzadilla (Palencia) had been owed nearly 5 ducats each for twelve years, probably the equivalent of a year's taxation, and Castile as a whole was owed in excess of 1.6 million ducats, or so it was claimed in the

---

[23] Ibid. pp. 31-6, and chap. 9

11 TAXATION AND THE DOMESTIC ECONOMY IN CASTILE

Cortes in 1598.[24] The social and economic burdens of billeting were, therefore, added to the direct burdens of taxation and extended, by the passage of troops to Portugal and the Atlantic bases after 1580, to provinces previously little affected.

The permanent garrisons in the non-Castilian coastal and frontier provinces were, from one point of view, workhouses maintaining unemployed Castilians outside Castile. They undoubtedly brought increased income into those provinces, even if, as the locals complained, this was partly offset by the underpayment of the troops and by costs of billeting. The literature of complaint, however, needs to be treated with caution and was often political rather than economic in inspiration. The Galicians generally welcomed the troops, and in Cascaes, when a commander investigated the complaints of the Portuguese, he found that the townsmen regretted it when the soldiers left, because as they spent their wages there, 'bivían todos de aquel dinero'.[25] Moreover, in longer established garrisons, especially in Guipúzcoa, Navarre and Catalonia, the soldiers tended to become naturalised and the military establishment to merge into the local economy, with the soldiers working in the town or in the fields when not on duty. The influx of Castilian coin, therefore, not only boosted spending by c. 60,000 ducats in Guipúzcoa and Navarre, 85,000 in Catalonia, and 65,000 in Aragon (1600), but in towns like Fuenterrabía, Pamplona, Puigcerdà, Perpignan, etc., probably also produced a sizeable per capita increase in wealth.

The pattern of military spending after 1580, with the progressive run-down of the galleys and the expansion of the ocean fleet, reflected a shift of the axis of Spain's military effort from east to west. It involved a shift from Catalonia and Valencia, which had been the beneficiaries of the demand generated by the galleys and the despatch of recruits to northern Europe via Italy, towards Andalusia, Portugal, Galicia and the Cantabrian provinces. By the end of the 16th century galley construction in the Barcelona *atarazanas* was in marked decline, with an allocation of 15-50,000 ducats a year compared with 100,000 spent in 1561-2. The shift was relative only, not absolute, from c. 16 percent of 1 million ducats to c. 10 percent of 3½ million (partly because of the large new garrison in Aragon after 1591). Galleys and reinforcements still crossed from the Levante to Italy and back;

---

[24] AGS CJH 227 (325), 20 Mar. 1594; *ACC* vol. 15, p.759.

[25] AGS Guerra Antigua leg. 729, Consejo de Guerra 10 Sept. 1610.

TAXATION AND THE DOMESTIC ECONOMY IN CASTILE   12

expenditure on garrisons and fortification works was even greater than in the 1570s; and Catalan and Valencian merchants continued to play a major role in supplying the North African *presidios* and the galleys through the Cartagena commissariat. Though shallower after 1580, the 'geographical immersion' of Catalonia in Spain's international politics between 1570 and 1604/9 is probably rightly regarded by Ruiz Martín as one element in the Principality's economic recovery at the turn of the 16th century.[26]

Galicia and the Cantabrian provinces also benefited from the activity generated by the presence of the Ocean Fleet and the boost to shipbuilding in the years after the Armada. At least 40,000 *toneladas* of shipping were built for the Crown in Basque yards in 1588-99, at a cost of upwards of 1½ million ducats. In addition to freightage paid to Basque masters and wages to seamen (c. 250,000 ducats in 1590), 50,000 was regularly budgeted for shipbuilding, a figure which reached 200,000 in 1597. A rough calculation would suggest that as much as 20 percent of the entire region's income derived from Crown spending.

Galicia was the region perhaps most profoundly affected by the Atlanticisation of war. Almost entirely untouched by military spending in the 1560s and 70s, the region was maintaining a garrison of 700 or more in Corunna, Bayona and El Ferrol after 1580, costing nearly 100,000 ducats by the early 17th century. Two-thirds of this was met by the return of taxes, the rest by money from Castile.   The coast was refortified, and from 1588 Corunna and El Ferrol also became major naval bases.   270,769 ducats entered the coffers of the paymaster in Corunna for naval victualling and fortification works in 1589; 162,500 in March-April 1591; 166,000 in 1598, together with 132,000 ducats of grain. Galicia, the lowest per capita taxed area in Castile, cannot have been paying more than 400,000 ducats or so into the treasury at the same time. Despite problems of unpaid supplies and billets, rising inflation with the influx of specie, and the sacking of Vigo and Corunna by the English in 1585 and 1589, the benefits brought by military spending, both locally and through increased demand for Galician fish and forest products, especially barrel staves, and for Galician shipping, can be seen clearly in the buoyancy of the demography of coastal Galicia at the end of the 16th century compared with the inland regions. El Ferrol's population nearly doubled in 1587-94; the population of Bayona increased from 705

---

[26] F.Ruiz Martín, 'Juan y Pau Sauri: negociantes catalanes que intervienen en las empresas imperiales de Felipe II', in *Homenaje al Dr D.Juan Reglà Campistol*, 2 vols. (Valencia, 1975), I, 457-77, at p.477.

13 TAXATION AND THE DOMESTIC ECONOMY IN CASTILE

vecinos in 1579 to 947 in 1594, and both Corunna and Vigo recovered rapidly after their sacking by Drake. The positive effect, however, was not widespread and fluctuated considerably with naval activity. It created poles of development. Corunna grew by 50 percent between 1587 and 1652; its province declined by a fifth.[27] Military spending may have been able to slow the rate of deceleration general in northern Spain after the 1580s, but it was unable to alter the underlying trend of the economy, even in maritime Galicia.

Far more important centres of military and naval procurement were Seville and Lisbon. Lisbon was the channel for the import of goods from northern Europe. Seville was the centre of an Andalusian regional economy that increasingly was coming to serve as the 'granary of the fleets'. As much as a third of Spain's domestic military budget was spent by the various purveyors based in Seville and its outports. Military purchases in Seville rose from 3-400,000 ducats a year in 1576-7, to 600-1,000,000 in the 1580s and 90s, the equivalent of one-quarter to one-third of the demand generated from the New World. In peak years, the government was spending there nearly half the internal tax-take from the whole of Andalusia.

The Seville Commissariat 1576-81

I have tried to assess the impact of this expenditure on Andalusia by examining the accounts of the commissariat in Seville for the years 1576-81 for the provisioning of the galleys, North Africa, the Indies fleets, and the army of 35,000 men for the invasion of Portugal, the largest single force equipped in Spain in the Habsburg period. This was a critical moment in the expansion of military demand, and this demand, being met by the royal commissariat direct from suppliers in the (with some exceptions) open market, is analysable in a way that ceases to be possible with the spread of contracting at the end of the century.[28]

Altogether more than 1.6 million ducats was spent by the purveyor; over 1 million on victuals, 365,000 on material, and c. 250,000 on ancillary services (milling, packing, portering, carting, etc.). A further 200,000 ducats

---

[27] J.Ruiz Almansa, *La población de Galicia 1500-1945* (Madrid, 1948), pp. 289, 254, 227, 250, 208.

[28] Accounts of Diego de Postigo 1577-Feb.1580, Andrés Sanz de Portillo 1580-1, in AGS Contaduría Mayor de Cuentas, 2a época, legs. 556, 530, 558; and of Francisco Duarte, Factor of the Casa de Contratación in Seville, 1576-80, in Archivo General de Indias (Seville), Contaduría, legs. 312, 314 no.1, 315 no.12 (2), 323 nos.2-8, and Contratación, legs. 4311, 4312.

or so was spent independently by the Captain General of the Artillery on arms and munitions, though mostly outside Andalusia. Only one-quarter of total purchases was of non-food items. An average of c. 110,000 ducats a year was spent on manufactured goods and materials in the peak years 1579-80, but, as there was no significant local industry in Seville, 65 percent of that was in fact passing straight through Seville, 40,000 ducats to buy iron and timber in the Basque provinces and Galicia and cloth in Córdoba, 30,000 to buy linen, naval stores and non-ferrous metals from Brittany, England and northern Europe. This 70,000 ducats of military imports was 2.8 percent of one contemporary estimate of goods imported annually into Seville.[29] The remaining 40,000 ducats, only about three-quarters of the value of the *alcabalas* paid by Seville's local craft manufacturers (at perhaps 5 percent or so of turnover), could have paid the wages of no more than c. 700 workers in a population of 26,000 *vecinos*.

These are only very rough orders of magnitude, but it seems clear that even in Seville the boost to manufacturing from military demand was modest, within the range 2-4 percent. Certain crafts were of course much more affected, as can be seen by comparing the sums paid to them by the commissariat in 1576-81 with their *alcabala* commitments in 1596 (in *maravedis*):

Table III: Level of Demand of Seville Commissariat 1576-158 (selected manufactures)

	a) alcabala[30]	b) av. 1576-81	b/a	c) maximum year	c/a
sayaleros	235,000	2,250,000	960%	2,959,090 (1581)	1260%
toneleros	532,000	1,730,000	325%	2,874,338 (1580)	540%
esparteros	575,000	517,000	90%	1,458,935 (1580)	250%
zapateros	1,347,000	1,064,000	79%	3,867,500 (1579)	290%

Unfortunately, relevant data are lacking for these years to permit a comparison of specific price movements with the general trend, but, except in the case of cooperage which had particular problems, the absence of any extraordinary pull on prices suggests that even these levels of demand were well within the capacity of the local craft manufacturers. The following table

---

[29] A.González Palencia (ed), *La Junta de Reformación* (Madrid, 1932), p.45.

[30] *Alcabala* figures from Ulloa, op. cit., p.217.

15   TAXATION AND THE DOMESTIC ECONOMY IN CASTILE

presents some examples of the relationship between the prices paid and the quantities supplied.

Table IV: Impact of Military Demand on Prices in Seville 1576-81

	Iron Shot	Hempen	Shoes	Casks
1576		74 mrs 12,535 varas	112 mrs 6,880 pairs	40-44 reales 1,400,000 mrs value
1577	13 mrs 8,400 lbs	72,73,76 mrs 49,352 varas	108 mrs 2,000 pairs	23-25 reales 2,000,000 mrs value
1578	13.55 mrs 2,650 lbs	72 mrs 38,960 varas	102 mrs 1,000 pairs	23-27 reales 1,600,000 mrs value
1579	13.6 mrs 6,150 lbs	72,75 mrs 11,416 varas	110½ mrs 35,000 pairs	31-34 reales 2,000,000 mrs value
1580	12.1 mrs 20,560 lbs	72 mrs 39,375 varas	110½ mrs 3,200 pairs	37 reales 2,900,000 mrs value
1581		76.2, 80 mrs 35,868 varas		36 reales 500,000 mrs value

What should be noted is how shallowly the demand for manufactured goods penetrated, even into the local economy. Practically all purchases were made in Seville and in the feeder ports of Lower Andalusia, Ayamonte, Sanlúcar de Barrameda, Puerto de Santa María, Cadiz. The only substantial purchases made outside Seville were 20,000 varas of hempen (herbaje) in Zafra (Badajoz), valued at 3,200 ducats, and c. 7,000 varas of untailored cloth (paños catorcenos) in Córdoba, value c. 5,800 ducats, some 1.2 percent of Cordoban cloth output.[31]   Perhaps another 6 varas of woollen cloth in 3,000 military outfits ordered   also came from Córdoba, making a possible further 3 percent of output, but the source of the cloth is unspecified.   Apart from an insignificant 286 varas of cloth (204 ducats) bought in Antequera, and 350 yards of silk damask (698 ducats) bought in Granada, even the neighbouring cities and manufacturing centres of Andalusia remained

---

[31] Fortea Pérez, *Córdoba en el siglo XVI*, p.311: c. 16,000 pieces, value 500,000 ducats

untouched. As for New and Old Castile, the only Castilian manufactures specified in the accounts were 100 blankets from Valladolid (181 ducats) and 231½ *varas* of cloth from a merchant of Toledo (188½ ducats). Neither Segovia, nor Cuenca, nor any of the other textile or manufacturing centres of Spain was represented at all in these purchases, and only 162 1/3 *varas* of foreign woollens are known to have been imported.[32]

Three times as much was spent on agricultural produce and foodstuffs (c. 1,050,000 ducats) as on manufactured goods and materials. This demand was satisfied only by reaching into a much wider area. Beef, pork and fatstock came from Jerez de la Frontera, Ronda, Antequera, but also from as far afield as Almodóvar del Campo, 215 km. away; rice came from Valencia; cheese from Mallorca and 'Flanders'; fish from Portuguese, Galician, Asturian, French and English sources, as well as from the Andalusian coast; oil from the nearby Aljarafe; wine from Aljarafe, Cazalla and Jerez, but also in 1580 in some quantity from Catalonia. Nonetheless, a great deal of this expenditure also flowed back into Seville in payments to merchants, landlords, ecclesiastics and others with rights in harvests, vineyards and olive-groves. The citizens and hierarchy of Seville sold over 60 percent of the wine bought by the commissariat to the value of 140,000 ducats, nearly 90 percent of the oil, and 76,000 ducats of wheat. These agricultural sources brought twice as much of the commissariat's money into the city as did its manufactures and services.

The indications are that military demand put a real strain on the agricultural production of the region. This is exemplified in the case of wheat. The wheat bought in 1578, 1579 and 1580 amounted to no more than 2 percent of the probable grain output of Andalusia in an average year,[33] yet the area scoured for wheat stretched for 250 km. across the provinces of Córdoba, Granada and Jaén, as far as Baeza (232 km.), Ubeda (240 km.) and Quesada (258 km.). Even so Andalusia was able to provide only 67 percent of recorded purchases in 1578, and 53 percent in 1579. 29,000 *fanegas* were imported in 1578 and 68,000 *fanegas* in 1579, from Italy, France and

---

[32] That is not to say that other purveyors on other occasions did not buy in the Castilian market. In 1586, the Valencian, Josepe Berenguer, signed a contract in Cartagena for 14,000 ducats to supply the Oran garrison with clothing, 3,000 *varas* of which were from Cuenca and 100 from Segovia, AGS Guerra Antigua, leg. 190.

[33] The estimate is that of Don Juan Chacón de Narváez of Antequera, from an extensive correspondence in 1583, AGS Guerra Antigua, leg. 155.

England, at an average price 57 percent above that paid for domestic supplies. Grain levies, which by the later 1580s had risen to 4 percent or more of the average harvest in Andalusia, became less a stimulus than an additional fixed burden, exacted regardless of harvest fluctuations by an oppressive commissariat.   In the period 1582-96 the index of Andalusian grain prices, which had lagged behind in 1554-69, now led those of both New and Old Castile by a substantial margin.   Although it is difficult to isolate the effects of military purveyance from other factors affecting the price of grain, the demands of the commissariat cannot but have added to the inflationary pressures.

The 250,000 ducats of ancillary costs for milling, weighing, packing, loading, carting, and other services, was of particular importance in being fed more or less entirely into labour.   Over the five years 1576-81 it generated approximately 900,000 days of labour, spread fairly widely across the area of Seville's catchment, with a disproportionate multiplier effect on local spending.

The substantial recirculation of wealth into the Andalusian economy effected through the machinery of military spending on the Atlantic war, occurring when it did, may have done something to counteract the long recession in the Atlantic trade from 1571-83/4 by reversing the effects of 'la double mutation méditerranéenne et flamande de la politique espagnole au cours des années 70,' which Chaunu regards as having constituted 'un facteur décisif de ce long ralentissement, sur dix ans, de la pente ascensionelle des mouvements.'[34]   However, the full reflationary potential of military demand was to some extent counter-balanced by the actual methods of state intervention.   The involvement of government itself meant a degree of de-commercialisation of the economy, with the commissariat setting up its own milling facilities and bake-houses, fixing prices, stopping the trade in grain, and requisitioning merchandise in the ports.   The movement of produce was prohibited across an area stretching from Granada to Extremadura and north to León and the Tierra de Campos.   Wheat and barley were requisitioned at the *tasa* (the legal maximum price), and other produce at a price adjudged to be fair by the purveyors.   Both procedures entailed large book losses, and were in effect covert forms of taxation.   The wheat *tasa* (11 *reales* per *fanega* up to 1582, 14 *reales* from 1582 to 1605) was exceeded in 11 out of the 15 years between 1582 and 1600 for which Hamilton presents data.   In 1580,

[34] H. & P. Chaunu, *Séville et l'Atlantique* (1504-1650), 8 vols (Paris, 1955-9), VIII 2¹, 612.

1,942 *arrobas* of oil were requisitioned in Ecija and Jerez de los Caballeros at 7 *reales*, only 65 percent of the average price of 3,939 *arrobas* bought from other suppliers at 9, 10, and even 11 *reales*. Complaints of similar underpricing were made by foreign merchants whose goods were requisitioned, and it became necessary to grant exemptions in order to induce shippers to continue to come to Spanish ports. These conditions were aggravated by non-payment. In December 1584, no less than 454,000 ducats was owed for supplies, transport and labour contracted between 1574 and 1582 by the purveyor in Seville. These debts had still not been paid off by September 1586. The city of Jerez de la Frontera claimed to be owed 80-90,000 ducats for goods taken three years before.[35] Credits were being traded at 25 and 30 percent discounts, but when payment was eventually made the treasury refused to pay more than the discounted price. All this, which was peculiar to Andalusia only to the extent of the region's involvement with the commissariat, amounted to a form of secondary extraction the burden of which it is impossible to assess with any precision, but which clearly has to be offset against the benefit that was derived from government spending. The ultimate balance may not have been hugely positive, but despite the vociferous, special local pleading so widespread at the end of the 16th century, it was unlikely to have been negative. The impact of the exceptional demands made on Andalusia in the years after 1579 is not shown up in any differential movements in the regional all-price series. Not only was there an extraordinary stability in price levels everywhere,[36] but even in the years of maximum military demand, 1580 and 1587, the Andalusian index of general commodity prices (in contrast to the grain price index) was not only not out of line with those of the other regions, it was in 1580 below both New Castile and Valencia, and in 1587 it was the lowest of all four regions. It may be that the demands of the Armada kept Andalusian prices up in 1588 when they were falling in all the other regions, but this was the only year in the period 1584-95 when the Andalusian index was substantially above that of New Castile. It is true that Andalusian prices, which had been rising at only three-quarters of the rate of New Castilian prices between the 1550s and 1570s, rose

---

[35] AGS CJH 136 (197), 7 Nov. 1581

[36] Hamilton, op. cit., pp. 201, 203, 'The outstanding phenomenon is the almost incredibly close agreement among the regional index numbers of prices...less disparity appears among the price series from 1580 to 1600 than in the base period 1571-80, when they are artificially brought together.'

19 TAXATION AND THE DOMESTIC ECONOMY IN CASTILE

25 percent faster than New Castilian prices in the next twenty years, but so too did Old Castilian and Valencian prices which had risen even more slowly in the earlier period.

Conclusions

1.   Fiscal exhaustion was rather a 17th- than a 16th-century phenomenon. Before the 1630s the tax burden was neither unremittingly excessive nor, in the broad view, exceptional. Less than 9 percent of national income compares favourably with 17th-century rates, not only in Spain but in other European states as well.

2.   To the extent that military spending, in addition to any 'protection' value it may have had for domestic and foreign trade, redressed the specie outflow of taxation at the regional level, its effects can be regarded as positive.

3.   The weight of military demand fell on agriculture, and the capacity or otherwise of the agrarian sector to respond was of the greatest consequence for the economy as a whole.   With at least two-thirds of direct military demand directed into the agrarian sector it is unlikely that there was much, if any, net transfer of resources to manufacturing, as might have been imagined, or from the landed classes to the trading classes. Of 558,000 ducats spent on wheat in Andalusia 1576-80, 194,000 went to the aristocracy, gentry and ecclesiastical hierarchy.   That alone was more than 10 percent of total expenditure.   The stimulus war is generally believed to have given to the manufacturing sector was in reality rather marginal.   Whereas, on one estimate, the purchases of wine by the Seville commissariat amounted to some 40 percent of shipments to the Americas,[37] purchases of woollen cloth could not have exceeded 4½ percent of the output of the single city of Córdoba, and purchases of ironware 3 percent of total Basque exports.[38] The new Crown armour works established in Navarre in 1595 and appropriating c. 10 percent of the armaments budget, employed only 42 men.[39]   Conversely, the preponderance of agricultural produce in military demand meant that the

---

[37] E. Lorenzo Sanz, *Comercio de España con América en la época de Felipe II*, 2 vols. (Valladolid, 1979), I, 469, estimates that 20,000 *pipas* were despatched annually.

[38] E.Fernández de Pinedo, *Crecimiento económico y transformaciones sociales del país vasco 1100/1850* (Madrid, 1974), p.30, citing Pedro de Medina.

[39] AGS Guerra Antigua leg. 790, D.Pedro Pacheco, 25 Aug. 1613.

harvest was of far more importance for Spain's balance of payments than the limitations of her commercial and industrial base. Some 90,000 ducats of foreign merchandise was bought by the Seville commissariat in 1576-81, about one quarter of all purchases of non-food items; but no less than 178,000 ducats was spent on imported wheat, 60 percent of it imported in the bad year 1579, 47 percent of that year's requirement, compared with only 11.6 percent in 1580, a far better year.

5.   The role of the state was of crucial importance, not, as is generally claimed, because of its indifference to stimulating the economy, but because of the way it intervened in the market and because its attempts to promote expansion and self-sufficiency in the state-run or state-controlled arms industries were undermined by the very processes of state intervention. Monopsony regulations, low fixed-prices and the exclusion of the middle-man left the small-scale producer defenceless against a fluctuating demand and persistent underpayment, and the state-run manufactories repeatedly short of working capital.[40]   The result of state intervention was the increased penetration of the Spanish economy by foreign contractors and foreign supplies, even where there was plenty of potential domestic capacity, as for cordage, match, gunpowder, shot, cannon, barrel-staves, ships.[41] The cause was less the inability of the economy to supply than the inability of the state to pay.   The shortfall was made up by non-fiscal exactions on the very activities that most needed stimulation.   In that sense, it might be said that Spain was not taxed enough for the demands of its public sector to be translated into sustained economic benefit.

6.   It was constitutionally privileged and administratively or economically backward regions, like Aragon, Cantabria and Galicia, which were better protected against the state and probably showed the clearest gains. Andalusia's fortunes were uneven, but the net balance may still have been positive, at any rate relative to the Castiles. In effect, the tripling of military expenditures in the 1580s represented a major transfer of resources from centre to periphery, that is, in general, from high-rate tax-paying areas to exempt or low-rate areas. No more than 4 or 5 percent of regular military expenditure in the 1580s and 90s was spent in the interior provinces of Old and New Castile, which paid more than half the taxes, compared with c. 16

---

[40] For details, Thompson, *War and Government*, chap. 9

[41] AGS Guerra Antigua leg. 778, 'Los pertrechos que se traen de fuera del reino para provision y apresto de las Armadas', 13 Oct. 1613.

21 TAXATION AND THE DOMESTIC ECONOMY IN CASTILE

percent in the 1570s. Some 50 percent of military expenditure was going to areas which hardly contributed at all to the military budget (Crown of Aragon, Basque provinces, Portugal); Galicia got over half of its taxes back in military spending; and even Andalusia, contributing (with foreign trade taxes) perhaps 3.5 million ducats to royal revenues, saw about a third return via the commissariat. The 'debilitating haemorrhage' was not so much from Spain to Flanders and Genoa, as from the central Castiles to the frontier and coastal perimeter, and in particular from Old Castile, hit by both the changing terms of military expenditure and the changing terms of taxation. As Chaunu writes, 'On pourrait établir - sous forme de règle, sinon de loi - qu'un effort militaire est d'autant plus lourd, d'autant plus négatif pour l'unité économique qui doit le fournir, que les opérations auxquelles il aboutit se déroulent dans un éloigné ou, du moins, en dehors de l'espace géographique dans lequel ces puissances économiques ont coutume d'agir.'[42]   The pattern of military expenditure may, therefore, be one factor contributing to the diverging trends in the economies of Castile and the peripheries from the later 16th century.

---

[42] Chaunu, op. cit., VIII 2¹, 613.

III

The European Crisis of the 1590s:
The Impact of War

I

War was not a defining characteristic of the 1590s. Indeed, on one recent count the 1590s was the decade with the lowest incidence of new wars in the whole of the sixteenth and seventeenth centuries.[1] With the exception of the Ottoman front in Hungary and the complicated manoeuverings of the Poles, the Swedes and the Russians, war in the 1590s was really a phenomenon of Atlantic Europe. For almost all of Germany and Italy the period was one of peace, although Savoy was involved in plots against Geneva (1586, 1602) and in intervention in Provence in pursuance of claims against France; and Milan, Naples and Sicily were compelled to share the burden of Madrid's foreign policies. Even in the Low Countries there was less military activity during the 1590s than in the two previous decades. Holland and most of the Republic, apart from some border provinces, were largely free of fighting after 1576, and in the southern Netherlands the worst phase was over by about 1592. Only for England, with formal involvement in the Netherlands in 1585, intervention in France in 1589, and rebellion in Ireland after 1593, was open war a relatively new experience. For England, however, as for the United Provinces and for Spain (excepting a few unfortunate localities raided by pirates or enemy expeditions), war was experienced in the 1590s largely as a problem of provision. Only in France, among the leading states of Europe, was the direct experience of war in the final paroxysm of the Religious Wars, already a generation old by 1588, more extensive and more acute. Yet even in France war was being phased out in the 1590s – in Languedoc from 1592, in Picardy, Normandy, Maine, Anjou, Poitou and the rest of Aquitaine by 1594, in Champagne, Burgundy and Provence by 1595–6, and only in Brittany not until 1598.[2]

Nor was war greater in scale in the 1590s than it had been in earlier periods, though not since 1559 had so much of Atlantic Europe been involved simultaneously. The army of Flanders was no larger than in the 1570s. The Invincible Armada carried only half the numbers on the Christian fleet at Lepanto. Queen Elizabeth never had an army anything like as large as that of Henry VIII in 1544.[3] War was, however, different in kind.

In the first place, war became global in its implications. The Americas, Asia, Morocco, Algiers, Turkey, and Poland were all seen as part of a single struggle against what Pierre Vilar has called 'the Catholic, feudal empire of Philip II'.[4] 'There is to be seen no maner of hostillitie at this daie in anie part of Christendome, saving in Hungarie, but by his [Philip II's] great armies by sea or land', declared Elizabeth I in a proclamation of September 1597 prohibiting the shipping of strategic materials to Spain.[5] The singleness of the struggle pervaded the political consciousness of Europe, extending the impact of military events in the west into Italy, Germany, Poland and the Baltic. The Swedish constitutional crisis of 1593–8, for example, would not be comprehensible outside this context.[6] Consequently, even where war was not physically present, it was felt to be close. There was an enemy within (papist, Huguenot, *morisco*) and an overpowering fear of invasion from without which magnified and distorted the psychological impact of war in this period.[7]

This was the more particularly so because no state could satisfactorily provide protection for its territories from the sea. The extension of war into the Atlantic in the 1580s compelled governments to the construction of highly expensive coastal fortifications and the creation of high seas fleets, by their nature relatively capital-intensive and logistically demanding compared with armies (a development that in both England and Spain took place mainly after 1588).[8] It also led them to promote a more general militarisation of society as a whole in the interests of national defence, through rearming, retraining and the re-forming of local militias, with all the political, social and jurisdictional problems that that entailed.[9]

For Spain, the war against England meant a fundamental shift of priorities from east to west and a relocation of military bases to the Atlantic coast, with a gradual run-down of her Mediterranean galley defences. The shift from galley to galleon was a shift from a war of aristocratic dash to a war of professional seamanship, and from a war of men to a war of materiel. The Spanish Armada packed some eight to nine times the firepower of the Spanish galley squadron, doubling the entire ordnance stock of the Spanish war machine, and increased hemp and cordage requirements sixfold.[10]

Parallel changes were taking place on land. The Netherlands war was a forcing-ground for military innovation and a training-school for soldiers of all nations. Although it may be going too far to describe the reforms of Maurice of Nassau in the 1590s as the initiation of a 'military revolution', there were, in fact, crucial changes taking place in warfare which can be summed up as a shift from mass to line, from pike to shot, and, with increasing professionalism in war, a shift from prowess to proficiency and from ascription to achievement in military status.[11] It is not without significance that the Netherlands were the seat of this 'revolution'. What was taking place was a movement, if still a modest one, towards the 'production-line' warfare of an early industrial society.[12] The administrative tasks and skills required of governments, the commercial links and the industrial involvement necessary, were of an entirely new order. Governments were being drawn into an increasing intervention in the control of strategic materials and the promotion of strategic manufactures in the interests of military autarky.[13]

All these considerations are relevant to the nature of the demands made by the wars and their impact on the economies and societies that sustained them. The wars of the 1590s affected different countries in different ways and to different degrees, but it was only Ireland, the southern Netherlands and parts of France that suffered directly war's devastations.

II

Benedict and Greengrass have provided illuminating accounts of the more spectacular ravages of war in the French countryside.[14] The devastation wrought by Parma's campaigns in Flanders and Brabant in the 1580s was no less horrendous. The immediate impact of military events in these areas, particularly on the rural economy, but on the towns as well, is undeniable.[15] The question is, How general were those experiences and what were their long-term consequences? What were the mechanisms by which short-term damage could lead to structural change and how can we distinguish the impact of war from the impact of other factors? How resilient was the early modern economy to sporadic disaster? Was François de la Noue right in saying, admittedly of an earlier and less ferocious phase of the Religious Wars, that France was so prosperous and so fertile that what the war destroyed in one year could be restored in two?[16] The tithe figures for Normandy and Beaune suggest that things were back to normal by the first decade of the seventeenth century. The recovery of cloth production in Amiens was quite spectacular, regaining prewar levels by 1608. In Rheims, recovery in the 1590s, though less sustained, was even more spectacular.[17] The 1590s, therefore, cannot be seen as a period of unrelieved gloom. The war was being wound up in stages and, as Jean Meyer writes, 'comme toujours, destructions et reconstructions se superposent'.[18]

In the southern Netherlands, the decade of crisis was the 1580s; the 1590s was a decade of recovery. Almost all indices mark an upturn after 1589–92 from the extreme low points of the mid-1580s. Recovery, however, was uneven and incomplete. In a few cases the record levels of the prewar period were regained during the 1590s, but for the most part recovery was a slow process, taking twenty, thirty, or more years, and in some cases no substantial recovery took place at all.[19] But the exceptional severity of the late sixteenth-century crisis cannot be attributed solely to war. In some ways, it can be argued, war merely intensified existing endogenous trends towards crisis. The ravages of war in the countryside were exacerbated by the disastrous harvests of 1585 and 1586 which led to the most dramatic famine in over two hundred years, and the process of agrarian recovery was further hindered by another series of bad harvests in 1593–5.[20]

In Ireland, a ferocious war, waged with scorched-earth policies on both sides for much of the ten years 1593–1603, none the less left the country with no long-term economic scars. There was no widespread shortage of cattle or corn; Dublin's trade had collapsed, but more as a result of the coinage debasement of 1601–2, and trade soon revived with the development of new exports of timber and barrel-staves from Wexford, Waterford and Youghal, and beef from Cork. The first decades of the seventeenth century were in fact a period of exceptional buoyancy in the Irish economy.[21]

The immensely varied nature of local responses, both in the southern Netherlands and in France, is not something that can be explained simply by war. Recent studies by Gutmann[22] and by Friedrichs[23] have argued that it was not war alone but a combination of disasters that was necessary to change a region's underlying patterns of economic and demographic growth – war and bad weather and/or pestilence in the Basse-Meuse, a second wave of devastation during the process of recovery in Nördlingen. The evidence of Brittany gives support to Gutmann's central thesis that the impact of war depended not on the nature of the devastation but on the nature of the economy. Brittany's experience was very like that of the Basse-Meuse, and for some of the same reasons, most important, the diversified nature of its economy.

Moreover, on the broader than local perspective, war brought gains as well as losses. The military operations that ravaged the southern Netherlands and led to a massive flight of skill and capital positively benefited the north. Against the difficulties of Antwerp and Hondschoote we have to set the growth of Amsterdam, Leyden, Rotterdam, Haarlem and Delft. The Flanders crisis brought profits to the Liège armaments manufacturers and to the linen industries of Brittany and Normandy.[24] The disruption of the Netherlands trade did Burgos and London no good, but it certainly helped Valencia and Hull,[25] amongst others, whilst the Hanse's direct trade with Spain prospered greatly during the embargo on trade with the Dutch, both before and after the Truce of 1609–21.[26] The French Atlantic ports, Honfleur, Le Havre, La Rochelle, all prospered during the civil wars. There were even profits to be made from privateering, if organised in a businesslike way, to offset against the lost opportunities of England's

Iberian traders – opportunities which in fact were to prove illusory in 1604.[27]

In short, the direct impact of war was too ambiguous and the incidence of warfare too geographically limited to be related too closely to a general European crisis of the 1590s. There are structural shifts of real importance which can be traced to the end of the sixteenth century, but they can by no means be attributed simply to war. War, without doubt, played a major part in the process of economic introversion that was taking place in the southern Netherlands, a process marked by ruralisation, de-urbanisation and regionalisation, with urban capital turned to agrarian investment, a tendency to the concentration of landholding, and a market dominated by domestic demand.[28] But one is describing here a process that was characteristic of other areas where the impact of war was of a very different kind, or not important at all, as in Castile or the Veneto, or, indeed, that characterised the European economy as a whole in the 'general crisis of the seventeenth century'.[29]

The impact of war did not fall only on the areas in which fighting actually took place. The burden of billeting and purveyance, the loss of crops and animals, the levying of contributions in money and kind, and the stopping of trade by the commissariat could be enormously damaging in non-operational areas as well, because they fell selectively on the same military corridors and embarkation dormitory areas for prolonged periods, year after year, and could lead, in the same way, to the destruction of capital, communal indebtedness and peasant expropriation, the main channels through which, it is suggested, war damage might cause structural change.[30] In Spain, where perhaps these pressures were heaviest and most continuous, there is a plethora of complaint during the 1580s and 1590s precisely from those regions newly affected by fleet purveyance and the passage of troops to the Atlantic ports, all reporting a similar situation of abandoned lands, short-range migrations to the more protected larger towns and seigneurial jurisdictions, and communal indebtedness. By 1598, if a statement in the Cortes is to be believed, the villages of Castile were owed 1,600,000 ducats for victualling and billeting expenses, a fivefold increase in only twelve years.[31] Unfortunately, too much of the rather general information we have on these matters is protest-based, and without systematic comparisons it is impossible to say how important these burdens really were. It is perhaps indicative that when an inquiry was conducted into the decay of Castilian agriculture early in the seventeenth century only five of thirty-eight replies mentioned billeting and purveyance as of any significance.[32]

War was also a drain on manpower. Spanish writers, worried by the signs of demographic recession at the end of the sixteenth century, were quick to blame the recruiting officer. We should, however, be careful about giving too much weight to their opinions. Spain maintained no more than 3½ per cent of her adult males in the armed services and recruited, almost entirely on a voluntary basis, about one in a thousand of Castile's population every year.[33] In England, where the contemporary concern was rather with overpopulation, about 0·13 per cent of the population was recruited for foreign service annually between 1585 and 1603.[34] Without knowing the economic standing, the marital status or prospects, the mortality rate, or the length of absence of these soldiers, it is impossible to say what effect this military drain had. Overall, the demographic consequences were probably minimal, even at the local level and in a relatively heavily burdened county like Kent, where the recruiter took 0·38 per cent of the population every year. The recruiting figures that we have for Castile in the 1590s suggest that it was the size of the levy that was contingent upon the state of the population, not vice versa.[35] Cellorigo, for one, recognised that it was not so much the wars but deeper inadequacies in the economy that were responsible for Castile's demographic decline.[36] A comparison of the demographic history of Andalusia, Extremadura and Galicia, the regions most affected by the shift to the Atlantic in the 1580s and 1590s, with that of other parts of Castile, argues against putting too much emphasis on military factors.[37] The prosperity of front-line counties like Norfolk, Kent and Sussex in the earlier seventeenth century tells a similar story.[38] The war disturbed but did not dislocate underlying patterns of growth.

It was through taxation that the impact of war was felt most widely. In general, war doubled state expenditures during the 1590s. Elizabeth spent £4½ million on war in 1585–1603, doubling her prewar expenses. The military budget of the Dutch Republic rose from under 5 million florins in the early 1590s to 10 million florins a year in 1604–6, of which 90 per cent was raised internally. Spain's domestic military budget tripled between the late 1570s and the late 1580s to a peak of around 3½ million ducats. In addition 33 million florins were sent to the Netherlands in the 1570s, 60 million in the 1580s, and 90 million in the 1590s; at the same time, the loyal provinces contributed 7 million florins between 1577 and 1586, and 48 million between 1587 and 1599. By the 1590s Madrid's total annual expenditure stood about 75 per cent higher than in the 1570s, and that in turn was two and a half times as high as at Philip II's accession. By 1600 all governments were in debt, not necessarily, of course, for the first time. Even Elizabeth left about £330,000 owing at her death. The Dutch Republic had short-term debts exceeding a year's income. The capital value of Spanish *juros* increased by some 50 million ducats in the last quarter of the century, the equivalent of four years' gross revenues. In France the *rentes* totalled 50 million *livres* in 1588, 150 million in 1595, half the entire Crown debt.[39]

None the less, even in the 1590s the share of the national income spent on war could have amounted to only about 8 per cent in Castile, perhaps twice that in the United Provinces by the 1600s, and something under 4 per cent in England.[40] This takes no account of direct, local contributions which are almost impossible to assess, but which in England seem to have been considerable and in some cases equalled the value of several subsidies.[41] Compared with a hundred or even fifty years later, these levels were really rather modest.[42] The *per capita* tax burden in the 1590s was the equivalent of about six days of labour in Castile, just over two days in England, The fisc imposed a good deal less than the Church, or the landlord,[43] or indeed than the weather. Even in Castile, the *additional* domestic taxation levied in the 1580s and 1590s was the equivalent in its impact on spending to no more than a 5 per cent rise in the price of wheat. A harvest only 10 per cent below normal would, in theory, have increased grain prices six times as much.[44]

None the less, taxation was unpopular and politically sensitive. Only in conditions of virtual military dictatorship, as existed in France at the local level, could the tax-take be increased five- or sixfold within a decade (St Antoine, Dauphiné; Montpellier). In Castile, where taxes had already tripled between 1559 and 1577, it was possible to increase them by only 30 per cent during the 1580s and 1590s, barely in pace with inflation. In England less than half of expenditure was met by new taxation, which amounted to about 5d per head. Governments, reluctant to risk exacting the entire charge for war directly from existing taxes and unable to get consent for fundamental reforms of the fiscal system (subsidy reassessment, *medio de la harina*), settled for *ad hoc* solutions: borrowing, benevolences and a variety of forms of 'voluntary taxation' and other expedients, sales of offices, noble privileges, lands, jurisdictions, revenues, trading licences and monopolies, as well as forced loans and the exaction of personal and administrative services of different kinds. None of these measures was new, but they were given a new intensity and extension in the 1590s precisely as the traditional forms were becoming exhausted. It was these expedients, much more than the actual levels of extraction, that had profound social, political and economic implications.

The growth of the public debt, offering a still relatively secure alternative for investment, had obvious repercussions on the capital market and drew off funds from potentially more productive employment. The large number of patents of nobility sold by the French Crown was in part a symptom, but also a channel for an unprecedented social mobility.[45] The alienation of ecclesiastical lands effected a wholesale transfer of property to the benefit variously of the *noblesse* (sword and robe), peasant proprietors, and traders and farmers of *seigneuries*.[46] The more than £500,000 of Crown lands sold by Elizabeth between 1589 and 1602 may have had only a limited effect on the actual tenure of the land, but did it not, as James I's Lord Treasurer, Middlesex, believed, seriously weaken ties of obedience to the Crown in the counties?[47] There can be no doubt that Philip II's sales of township status and his extension of the sale of municipal *regimientos* to even the smallest towns and villages after 1581 resulted in the mass transfer of control over communal lands and the village economy from annually elected village councils to proprietary 'village tyrants'. Between 1581 and 1600 more than 400 populations were involved, forty-four of them within the jurisdiction of Seville alone.[48] The effect was to undermine the corporate dominance of the cities over their hinterlands and with it the security of their food supplies. We have here, perhaps, one aspect of the crisis of the cities to which other contributors have drawn attention. The transfer of the usufruct of communal lands and wastes to a narrow plutocracy, most often of pastoralists, dangerously narrowed the margin of subsistence for the population of Castile in the seventeenth century.

Military expenditure involved a transfer from the taxpayer to the soldiery, the supplier and the state creditor. As in the main the new taxation of the 1590s was not levied on commerce and manufacturing,[49] it is tempting to think of it primarily as an expropriation of agrarian resources. Certainly, agriculture does not seem to have been sufficiently compensated by the profits of increased military demand. This was partly because, in global terms, military demand was not very great, and partly because of government interference in the market. The grain purchases of the Spanish commissariat, at their peak of about 400,000 *fanegas*, double what had been required in the early 1580s, drew off perhaps 4 per cent of a normal harvest in Andalusia, which was the principal granary for the fleets.[50] That amount could have been grown twice over on the estates of the Duke of Osuna alone. Harvest fluctuations could have ten times the effect on the market, or more. Moreover, government-imposed price maxima tended to check the upward pressure of prices, as did, in England, the new grain-marketing regulations introduced in 1587, perhaps deliberately to enable victuallers to buy more easily and more cheaply.[51] Compulsory purchases at controlled prices in years of dearth, combined with non-payment or late payment and the discounting of bills, added up to a form of supplementary extraction further disadvantaging the agrarian sector and depressing rural demand.

This is not to say that the net effect of external war on the rural economy was necessarily negative. Locally, and in the short-term, military demand may have had a bullish effect on prices, as may have been the case in East Anglia and in Andalusia, for example,[52] and this would have been particularly beneficial to the agricultural producer in that it did not derive from reduced output. It may also be that the limited evidence of any sustained pull on prices attributable to military demand reflects an adaptation of agrarian production to new demands, fiscal even more than material. García Sanz's work on Segovia has shown how the war taxes of the 1590s were raised, at least in part, by bringing under-utilised land resources into cultivation.[53] This response to fiscal pressure is, of course, a common historical phenomenon, and an analogous process was operative in Ireland where, as Hayes-McCoy writes, 'It was said that Tyrone and Tyrconnell had never been so rich, and had never before produced so much food, as they did in the war years.'[54]

The requirements of the military victualler were, in the broad sense, substitutional. This was not the case with the demand for military hardware, and the manufacturing sector, or at least some branches of it, must have received some stimulus from government and private spending on war. Too much should not be made of this effect, however, nor of its putative implications for the development of capitalism.[55] Only one-third or one-quarter as much was spent on materiel as on victuals, and, despite the concentration of demand in the state and the changes in the nature of warfare, the scale and the demands of war in the 1590s were not substantial enough to be of profound significance at the macro-economic level. Individual industries clearly benefited. There was a lively demand for iron in the war years, and shipbuilders should have done well, not only out of government orders but also out of the accelerated losses caused by the wars, insofar as these outweighed the reduction of carrying capacity required for trade.[56] But it is doubtful whether military demand was sufficient or sustained enough to stimulate any industry as a whole, let alone any economy in which industry was only a small part of the whole. The output of iron guns and shot from the Kent and Sussex foundries increased by about 50 per cent to 800 or 1,000 tons a year between 1578 and 1600, but that was only about 5–7 per cent of England's iron production and probably no more than 1–2 per cent of the iron and steel output of western Europe.[57] In 1621 the royal cannon-founder, John Browne, claimed that the King's service would have occupied his furnaces for only ten days a year.[58] Even in the middle of the seventeenth century it can be calculated that the total productive capacity of cast-iron cannon in Europe could have absorbed only about 3 per cent of iron output.[59] The military demand for textiles was even more marginal. The value of the clothing (of all materials) supplied to the English forces in the Netherlands in 1589 was exceeded fiftyfold by the total value of shortcloth exports.[60] The woollen cloth purchased for the 35,000 men invading Portugal in 1580, one of the largest armies ever raised in Habsburg Spain, could not have exceeded 4½ per cent of the output of the single city of Cordoba.[61]

Moreover, the military supplier and the arms manufacturer suffered from government interference and indebtedness in the same way as the agriculturalist. The business of war did not, therefore, offer either a particularly broad or a particularly easy path to fortune or social advance. Though some achieved a spectacular eminence, rarely was this success lasting. The new noble dynasties were established by lawyers and administrators, not as a rule by government contractors and military profiteers, whose agreements were frequently dishonoured by treasuries and who paid severely for their compensatory malfeasances. Nearly all the most notable of Spain's military contractors were either disgraced or bankrupted within a few years (Pedro de Baeza, Juan Pascual, Gómez de Acosta, Núñez Correa). The Evelyns were one of the few families in England to make a name for themselves from the profits of war. Even Jean Curtius, who did enormously well when the arms industry of Liège benefited from the difficulties of Antwerp and Malines, was forced to move operations to Spain when military activity in the Low Countries died down in the early seventeenth century and to diversify into the manufacture of domestic ironware.[62] The state was too powerful, too dangerous and too unreliable a customer for the ordinary businessman, unless he had powerful protectors at Court.[63]

III

In other ways, however, war contributed to a crisis of the social order which, while neither initiated nor resolved in this period, was made more acute by the events of the 1590s. The exceptional social mobility during the French Wars of Religion, marked by sales of patents of nobility, lands and offices, both distorted and devalued traditional concepts of nobility.[64] In Castile, too, sales of hidalguía (few), regimientos (many) and señoríos closely followed the chronology of war;[65] while in England the inflation of honours under James I must be seen as a deferred legacy of the war years.[66] The fiscal privileges of nobility were beginning to be eroded by benevolences, forced loans and administrative burdens, and challenged in their essence by proposed universal, indirect taxes, like the millones or the flour tax in Castile.[67] At the same time, the increasing professionalisation of war was in danger of making traditional nobility a military anachronism.[68]

The wars were thus not merely a cause but also an aspect of the crisis. They were, in part, wars for the restoration of nobility and traditional noble values, wars to recoup fortune, credit and political influence. This is easy enough to see in France where the wars were wars against false nobles, financiers, venal officers, mignons, and what Huppert calls the 'gentry'.[69] In England, as well, the younger generation, arriving in France clad, to the astonishment of their hosts, like knights out of ancient tapestries, was elevating the cult of honour into a challenge to the old men of the gown who held power, patronage and influence.[70] Paradoxically, success, even in war, benefited the bureaucrats. Only in Spain, where the aged counsellors of Philip II's *junta secreta* could be held responsible for the failures of the 1590s, did the military nobility get their victory, with the accession in 1598 of a twenty-year-old king whose idol was the imperial knight, Charles V. In France, the victory of Henry IV was also the victory of the *noblesse de robe* in the King's councils.[71] In England, Essex, with all he stood for, was outmanoeuvred after Cadiz by Cecil's propaganda machine, and the 1590s, which began with the chivalric revival of the Accession Day tilts and the Garter ceremonies, ended with aristocratic treason and conspiracy.[72] Nobility was discredited by its own métier, its respect undermined and its image tarnished by brigandage, profiteering and incompetence.[73] The Duke of Medina Sidonia, returning to be jeered at by street urchins, was seen as the paradigm case of the unfortunate consequences of giving priority to 'precedency' over 'military valour' (Campanella).[74] Faced with the demand for promotion by merit and experience (Brantôme, Valdés, Isaba, Williams, Sutcliff), the nobility had to be rehabilitated by books and military academies, and access to nobility protected by labyrinthine genealogies and ancestral memories of valour.[75]

The nobility may in the end have done well enough economically out of the wars, as Russell Major argues; their local power may have been reinforced, or at the very least not seriously eroded, by the Crown's reliance on their authority; upward mobility may have been checked by 1600 and class lines rigidified with the fossilisation of noble values;[76] but this was achieved only at the cost of raising up the ogre of its own mirror-image. The growth of a distinctive 'bourgeois' consciousness that some historians have discerned about the turn of the sixteenth century[77] was both a reaction to the closing of noble ranks, which made a nonsense of mere titular ennoblement, either by sneering at it or by creating alternative hierarchies within it, and at the same time a recognition of the gulf between the military and the mercantile interest, brought home by the lean years of war which had dramatically straitened the passage through trade to wealth and fortune.[78] Once again, there is a precognition, no more, in the 1590s of the crisis of a later generation.[79]

IV

In his *Méditerranée* Braudel asks of the decade 1600–10, 'l'heure est-elle favorable aux États moyens?'.[80] A crisis of empires seems to be apparent in the 1580s and 1590s. It can be seen in the weakened hold of the Ottomans in north Africa and of the Iberians in north Italy and the East and West Indies, in the failure of Polish imperialism, in Russia's introversion after

Ivan the Terrible. The empires were posited on war. When war ceased to be able to sustain the Ottoman state, the empire fractured, and without the Ottomans the Catholic, Mediterranean empire of Spain that opposed it ceased to cohere.[81] By the late 1590s the Spanish position in north Italy was falling apart, to be saved only by the abandonment of French interests in Italy at the treaty of Lyons (1601).[82] This transformation was rooted in the changed nature of naval warfare in the 1580s and 1590s. With the cheap iron gun and the round-ship coming into the Mediterranean, making the individual corsair as viable an enterprise as he was in the Indies, and with Spain having to maintain an ocean fleet as well, the economics of protection turned against size.[83] The state was not an efficient supplier of protection on that scale, and as protection costs were forced up it was impossible for the state to compete on all fronts.[84] The Armada was fitted out at the expense of a severe tonnage crisis in the Indies trade in 1589–98.[85] The Americas could be protected only at great cost, with the sacrifice of shipping in Newfoundland and North Atlantic waters, and by making the monarchy dependent for its defence on its own enemies.[86] War at sea, therefore, offered the Dutch, 'the most advanced bourgeois nation', and the English both the opportunity and the means to challenge a Spanish imperialism that Pierre Vilar represents as the 'supreme stage of feudalism'.[87] As Wallerstein has written of the Thirty Years War, on the Hispano-Dutch front the concluding phase of the later sixteenth-century struggle, 'The war became one of the modalities by which reallocations of economic roles and intensifications of economic disputes occurred.'[88]

V

Can we also talk of a 'crisis of the state' in the 1590s? 'Already by 1590', Trevor-Roper writes of his Renaissance State, 'the cracks are beginning to appear.'[89] These stresses were largely the consequence of the burdens of war. The effectiveness of the machinery of government was put to the test by the size and the nature of the administrative tasks which war presented in the 1590s. New administrative agencies had to be created or old ones adapted (war secretariats, navy boards, military governors in Spain, Lords-Lieutenant, deputies, muster-masters in England, the Council of State, the provincial admiralties, the audit office in the United Provinces, the development of the secretaryship of state and the intendancies in France). The keynote was to be professionalism, regulation and central control. But military law, prerogative government and 'stranger' commissioners were seen to threaten customary and statutory rights and local interests, and at every level the desire to evade or the attempt to exploit fiscal and military levies and purveyance led to tensions and confrontations, setting communities against each other and reactivating long-standing conflicts of authority and jurisdiction. The administration of war was turned into a battlefield. Control over the militia was fought over by 'county gentry' and 'court gentry', JP and deputy lieutenant, magnate captain and professional muster-master.[90] In Castile the authority of the cities was challenged by the towns of their *partidos*, lords supported by the Council of War were taken to law by their vassals supported by the Council of Castile, and the militia was sabotaged as effectively by the civilian justices there as it was by the JPs in England.

The state, lacking in funds, in internal cohesion, in administrative discipline, in commercial knowhow, far from being strengthened by war was forced to retreat. In Spain the 1580s and 1590s see the most advanced administration in Europe beginning a withdrawal from direct involvement in the administration of war and having to turn from royal officials to contractors, municipalities and local magnates.[91] In England the experiment with direct administration of the customs collapsed and military supply became increasingly privatised.[92] The state had reached the limits of its administrative capacity. In Spain military contracting, the devolution of fiscal and military organisation to the cities and the reinforcement of seigneurial authority, the alienation of jurisdictions and the sale of exemptions that are the legacy of the 1590s, add up to a decentralisation of power and practical authority that is at the heart of the problems of the Spanish state in the seventeenth century. In England, too, the Crown's monopoly of military power was at best partial. Noble retinues continued to be both militarily and socially important, and the influence of the local magnate and gentry remained a real constraint on the appointment of lieutenants, deputies and militia captains.[93] Both Philip II and Elizabeth were forced by the exhaustion of alternative fiscal expedients into increased dependence on parliamentary taxation and into increasing compromises with their parliaments. The war years are critical for the development of parliamentary influence, and perhaps even more so in Castile than in England, where a new *pactismo* was established between *rey* and *reino* as a direct consequence of the *millones* grants.[94] In the United Provinces the centralisation of Leicester was defeated with the curtailment of the powers of the Council of State and its subordination to the States General (1588), the reorganisation of the Admiralty Board (1597), and the efforts of the States to control the armed forces.[95] In France, on the one hand, the reaction against the war strengthened the idea of monarchy; on the other, the postwar settlement built in limitations – the Edict of Nantes, the capitulations with the grandees, which cost more than 32 million *livres*, the concessions to municipal self-government, the *paulette*, the failure of Sully's *élections*.[96] Faced with a crisis of government which threatened to turn into a crisis of the constitution, princes were compelled to defer internal conflict by compromise or retreat if war was to be pursued or concluded satisfactorily. None of the issues raised during the 1590s was resolved. It was left to their successors a generation later to face up to the same issues in a more resolute way.

VI

War was undoubtedly one element in the epidemic of popular disturbances and discontents in the 1590s, but it was only one element, and opposition to the wars, as such, though not unknown, was not widespread. Protests against high taxes, the export of grain to the army and the depredations of the soldiery characterised the peasant rebellions in Upper Austria and Hungary, the Gautiers and Croquants in France, popular discontents in the southern Netherlands, and other isolated disturbances, like those in Ipswich in 1586[97]. A growing war-weariness, and even a rejection of basic policy aims, can be seen, but expressed usually in indirect and sometimes surprising ways: the reluctance of gentlemen and commoners to join up for the wars, the pro-Spanish utterances of ordinary people in Kent and Oxford,[98] the celebrated 'let them be damned' speech of the representative of Madrid in the 1593 Cortes,[99] the extraordinary resistance of Avila and other cities of Old Castile to the *millones*, the disaffection of the Portuguese, smarting at the pillaging of their empire and their shipping, which found one outlet in false Sebastians and another in the murder and mistreatment of the Spanish soldiers garrisoning Lisbon.[100]

In some ways it was the soldier, owed months of back pay and left starving by the incompetence or rapacity of the commissariat, who was the real sufferer in the 1590s, and it was the military mutiny that was the characteristic popular revolt of the decade.[101] The returned soldier, often sick, starving and maimed, clearly posed a problem for governments to which they responded with welfare policies, hospitals and pensions which went some way, at least, to meet the need.[102] But was the returned soldier the serious and widespread problem that the panic reactions of some contemporaries have led us to believe? Did war really turn young gentlemen, yeomen, artificers and other lusty young fellows into rogues and thieves, as Sir John Smythe thought, or were his opponents right when they claimed that the levies were 'the very scum, thieves, and rogues of England, and therefore have been very well lost, and that the realm, being too full of people is very well rid of them, and that if they had not been consumed in those wars they would have died under a hedge'?[103] Given the underlying social problems of the 1590s, it may be doubted whether war contributed as much to the problem of poverty or to the increase in vagrancy as is commonly said.[104] If it was overwhelmingly the landless, the unemployed, the marginal who went into the armies and navies, then the recruiter was doing the community a service by exporting vagrancy, or at least transferring the burden of poor relief from the locality to the exchequer and bringing some of the starving within the orbit of an organised procurement system with access to the international market. There is something to be said for the commonplace contemporary view of war as a social safety-valve – 'Foreign War serving', as Sir Walter Raleigh wrote, 'like a Potion of Rhubarb to waste away Choler from the Body of the Realm'.[105] The Turkish invasion of Hungary not only drew off the dangerous throng of unemployed soldiers in Istanbul, it also did a lot to check the growth of banditry, notably in Catalonia and the Romagna, that may be associated with the preservation of a formal peace in the Mediterranean after the 1570s.[106] One reason for the formation of a special Catalan galley squadron in 1600 was to divert the young from a life of banditry.[107] If the means did not exist to socialise the deviant, they had to be created.

In some sense, then, war had a conservative function in the 1590s, damping down discontents, deflecting internal hostilities against external enemies and domestic scapegoats (foreigners, *moriscos*, witches, gypsies),[108] and periodically reinforcing loyalty to the regime in response to victory, disaster or threat. It was the fate of the Armada that induced the Cortes to concede Philip II the *millones*, and the sack of Cadiz in 1596 that persuaded them to recommend its regrant after protracted resistance, just as in England it was the threat from Spain that underwrote the cult of Gloriana, completed the collapse of the Puritan opposition in Parliament, and sustained the sometimes prickly co-operation between Elizabeth and the Commons. It was left to James I to deal with the fiscal archaisms and the political and social frustrations papered over by the Elizabethan myth. The Bye Plot, the Gunpowder Plot, the disaffection of Raleigh were all, it has been argued, manifestations of a revolt of the 'mere gentry' against *peace.*[109] The legacy in England of the dissatisfactions of the 1590s was an expectation of reform with the peace that, unfulfilled, led to a growing alienation of the local community and polarisation between Court and Country.[110] So too, it was only with peace that the profound constitutional and religious differences within the United Provinces were released, and only after peace with Russia in 1595 that Charles of Sweden was able to turn inwards against Fleming in Finland. In many respects peace turned out to be rather more dangerous than war.

VII

Not the least of the crises of the 1590s was a crisis of war itself. The wars of the 1590s were wars which nobody really won. Reputations evaporated, even of the greatest (Essex, Parma, Medina Sidonia). Universal failure exposed the pitiless waste of resources. Even the wealth of the Indies could achieve nothing; nor could divine providence be relied upon to defend its cause. The interests of true religion seemed no longer to be forwarded by expensive and inconclusive butchery. The Sainte Union degenerated into brigandage and tyranny. There was a shrieking dissonance between means and ends. Anthony Wingfield bemoaned the paradox that the military profession was despised just at the moment when it was 'never so necessary' (1589).[111] Cynicism was everywhere. Old Sir John Smythe was convinced that the gentry of England were packing off their tenants to certain death in the wars in order to cash in on entry fines.[112] The captain and the colonel were condemned as callous profiteers of their men's lives.[113] The common soldier had to be forced to the wars. Any man with any substance would buy himself out. Even to be a soldier was coming to be shameful.[114] It was for this reason, above all, that the many attempts to bring about a general militarisation or re-militarisation of society for the purposes of national defence, through the reactivation or the reform of local militias, trained-bands, weapons practice, or horse-breeding, inspired by the invasion psychosis of the 1590s, proved to be largely ineffective. The glowing chivalric revival had burnt out. The '1590s' began with Philip Sydney; they ended with Don Quixote.

There is a spiritual crisis of the 1590s, a 'traumatisme de fin de siècle',[115] a loss of meaning and purpose, a debilitating dejection that one finds in surprising places, as in the letter written to a patron by Philip II's secretary of war, Esteban de Ibarra, a man who had worked with Alba in the golden days:'Everything is in such a state that it takes away one's will to work and serve just to see the way things are going.'[116] Perhaps it is this spirit which goes some way towards explaining the muted nature of the political crisis of the 1590s. Discontent and disillusion seem to channel themselves away from active opposition. Bitterness is turned into verse. Dissidence is displaced into *desengaño*. 'Melancholia', scepticism, atheism, withdrawal from the active world of politics and a picaresque rejection of established values, on the one hand, and, on the other, a 'moralizing puritanism', the revival of Augustinian salvationism, and neo-Stoicism have all been seen as responses to the wars.[117] For Lipsius and Quevedo, at least, the link was explicit.[118] But neo-Stoicism was important because it was much more than an escape. It offered a new social ethic and a rehabilitation of the military ethos. It civilianised the military virtues and pointed the way towards a new perception of the role of nobility in the service of the state.[119] It was to be one of the principal means by which the traditional social order overcame the 'crisis of the 1590s.'

Notes

1   F. A. Beer, *How Much War in History: Definitions, Estimates, Extrapolations and Trends* (Beverly Hills, Calif., 1974), pp. 12–15.
2   J. Meyer, 'Le paysan français pendant les guerres de la Ligue', in B. Köpeczi and E. H. Balázs (eds), *Paysannerie française, paysannerie hongroise, XVIe–XXe siècles* (Budapest, 1973), p. 66, for France. For Holland, A. Th. van Deursen, 'Holland's experience of war during the Revolt of the Netherlands', in A. C. Duke and C. A. Tamse (eds), *Britain and the Netherlands*, vol. 6 (The Hague, 1977), pp. 31, 34; and, for Flanders, E. Thoen, 'Warfare and the countryside: social and economic aspects of military destruction in Flanders during the late Middle Ages and the early modern period', *The Low Countries History Yearbook*, vol. 13 (1980), p. 25. On the campaigns of the 1580s and 1590s in the Netherlands, see G. Parker, *The Dutch Revolt* (London, 1977), pp. 208–35.
3   G. Parker, *The Army of Flanders and the Spanish Road, 1567–1659* (Cambridge, 1972), p. 271; C. S. L. Davies, 'The English people and war in the early sixteenth century', in Duke and Tamse, *Britain and the Netherlands*, vol. 6, p. 2.
4   P. Vilar, 'The age of Don Quixote', in P. Earle (ed.), *Essays in European Economic History, 1500–1800* (Oxford, 1974), p. 105; G. Parker, 'The Dutch Revolt and the polarization of international politics', in G. Parker, *Spain and the Netherlands, 1559–1659* (London, 1979), pp. 65–81.
5   J. Payne Collier (ed.), *The Egerton Papers*, Camden Society, 1st ser., vol. 12 (1840), p. 260, an attitude mirrored in Castile by the *procurador* for Murcia in the Cortes in 1593: *Actas de las Cortes de Castilla*, vol. 12 (Madrid, 1887), p. 463.
6   M. Roberts, *The Early Vasas* (Cambridge, 1968), pp. 333, 373.
7   P. Williams, *The Tudor Regime* (Oxford, 1979), p. 15; P. Benedict, *Rouen during the Wars of Religion* (Cambridge, 1981), p. 170; F. Braudel, *The Mediterranean and the Mediterranean World in the Age of Philip II* (London, 1973), vol. 2, p. 1223, for Spanish and Venetian fear of the Turk; and, for Spanish fears of *morisco* treachery, see *Actas de las Cortes* (hereafter *Actas*), vol. 9, p. 28, vol. 11, p. 542, vol. 13, p. 95, and F. Pérez Mínguez, *Don Juan de Idiáquez* (San Sebastián, 1934), p. 262.
8   C. S. R. Russell, 'Monarchies, wars, and estates in England, France and Spain, c.1580–c.1640', *Legislative Studies Quarterly*, vol. 7, no. 2 (1982), p. 210.
9   See L. Boynton, *The Elizabethan Militia, 1558–1638* (London, 1967); I. A. A. Thompson, *War and Government in Habsburg Spain, 1560–1620* (London, 1976), ch. 4. Proposals for national militia training were made in the United Provinces also but dropped in 1600 by the States as 'contrary to the liberty and character of these lands': Van Deursen, 'Holland's experience', p. 31.
10 P. W. Bamford, *Fighting Ships and Prisons: The Mediterranean Galleys of France in the Age of Louis XIV* (Minneapolis, Minn., 1973), pp. 24–5; Thompson, *War and Government*, pp. 32–3.
11 M. Roberts, 'The military revolution, 1560–1660', in M. Roberts, *Essays in Swedish History* (London, 1967), pp. 195–225; G. Parker, 'The "military revolution, 1560–1660" – a myth?', in Parker, *Spain and the Netherlands*, pp. 86–103; M. D. Feld, 'Middle-class society and the rise of military professionalism: the Dutch army, 1589–1609', in M. D. Feld, *The Structure of Violence: Armed Forces as Social Systems* (Beverly Hills, Calif., 1977), pp. 169–203; J. R. Hale, 'Armies, navies and the art of war', in R. B. Wernham (ed.), *The New Cambridge Modern History*, vol. 3 (Cambridge, 1968), p. 178. For parallel developments in the Ottoman army, see V. J. Parry, 'The Ottoman Empire, 1566–1617', in ibid., pp. 365–6.
12 The concept comes from Feld, 'Middle-class society', p. 179.
13 'In Western history war has always made it necessary, to a lesser or greater extent, for the governments which wage it to control or seize the sources of trade and production': J. U. Nef, *Western Civilization since the Renaissance: Peace, War, Industry and the Arts* (New York, 1963), p. 18.
14 See their contributions to this volume, and Benedict, *Rouen*, pp. 221–6.
15 See Thoen, 'Warfare and the countryside', H. van der Wee, *The Growth of the Antwerp Market and the European Economy (fourteenth–sixteenth centuries)* (The Hague, 1963), vol.

III

2, ch. 8, and the essays by Daelemans, De Wever, Jansen and Tits-Dieuaide in H. van der Wee and E. van Cauwenberghe (eds), *Productivity of Land and Agricultural Innovation in the Low Countries (1200–1800)* (Louvain, 1978). G. Parker, 'War and economic change: the economic costs of the Dutch Revolt', in J. M. Winter (ed.), *War and Economic Development* (Cambridge, 1975), pp. 49–71, surveys the data on the southern Netherlands at pp. 50–4.

16 J. Russell Major, 'Noble income, inflation, and the Wars of Religion in France', *American Historical Review*, vol. 86 (1981), p. 48; G. Livet, *Les Guerres de religion (1559–1598)* (Paris, 1962), p. 87: 'Si bien qu'on peut poser la question de l'interprétation de cette dépression finale (longue ou courte durée? guerre ou crise aiguë de subsistances?).'

17 Above, pp. 86–7. For Amiens, see P. Deyon, 'Variations de la production textile aux 16e et 17e siècles', *Annales ESC*, vol. 18 (1963), pp. 948–9. See Livet, *Guerres de religion*, pp. 85, 90, on the limited demographic effect of the war.

18 Meyer, 'Paysan français', p. 66. Rouen was recovering from 1594 (Benedict *Rouen*, p. 230), Marseilles from 1596 and Lyon in the 1590s (J. N. Ball, *Merchants and Merchandise: The Expansion of Trade in Europe, 1500–1630* (London, 1977), pp. 94, 77), while Languedoc in general escaped relatively lightly. E. Le Roy Ladurie, *Histoire du Languedoc* (Paris, 1967), p. 69, writes that after the final truce in 1596 'la reprise est rapide, générale, vigoureuse'; the crisis of the Religious Wars checked economic growth but did not reverse it and was nothing like as severe as that of the fourteenth century.

19 Thoen, 'Warfare and the countryside', p. 29 ('economic recovery . . . always occurred with amazing rapidity') and pp. 30–8 on the range of experiences; C. Verlinden, 'En Flandre sous Philippe II: durée de la crise économique', *Annales ESC*, vol. 7 (1952), pp. 28–9; Van der Wee, *Antwerp*, vol. 2, p. 271, vol. 3, p. 70; Van der Wee and Van Cauwenberghe, *Productivity of Land*, pp. 13, 48, 84–6; H. van der Wee, 'Typologie des crises et changements de structures aux Pays-Bas (XVe–XVIe siècles)', *Annales ESC*, vol. 18 (1963), p. 223, on the rapidity of agrarian and economic recovery after 1587 and 1588.

20 Van der Wee, *Antwerp*, vol. 2, p. 260; H. van der Wee, 'Structural changes and specialization in the industry of the southern Netherlands, 1100–1600', *Economic History Review*, 2nd ser., vol. 28 (1975), p. 218; C. Verlinden, J. Craeybeckx and E. Scholliers, 'Price and wage movements in Belgium in the sixteenth century', in P. Burke (ed.), *Economy and Society in Early Modern Europe* (London, 1972), p. 60.

21 T. W. Moody, F. X. Martin and F. J. Byrne (eds), *A New History of Ireland*, vol. 3 (Oxford, 1976), pp. 140–1.

22 M. P. Gutmann, *War and Rural Life in the Early Modern Low Countries* (Princeton, NJ, 1980).

23 C. R. Friedrichs, *Urban Society in an Age of War: Nördlingen, 1580–1720* (Princeton, NJ, 1979).

24 Van der Wee, 'Structural changes', p. 217, and *Antwerp*, vol. 2, p. 262.

25 R. Davis, *The Trade and Shipping of Hull, 1500–1700* (York, 1964), pp. 7, 11; E. Salvador, 'En torno al comercio y a la economía valenciana del quinientos', *Estudis*, vol. 1 (1972), pp. 36–40.

26 P. Dollinger, *The German Hansa* (London, 1970), pp. 350–1. England's Baltic trade also increased by 150 per cent between 1575 and 1595, but it was carried overwhelmingly in foreign bottoms after 1585: H. Zins, *England and the Baltic in the Elizabethan Era* (Manchester, 1972), pp. 274, 289.

27 K. R. Andrews, *Elizabethan Privateering* (Cambridge, 1964); H. Taylor, 'Price revolution or price revision? The English and Spanish trade after 1604', *Renaissance and Modern Studies*, vol. 12 (1968), pp. 5–32, and at p. 20: 'our countrymen exclaim and wish nothing but wars, alleging that no merchandise but victual is in any request to yield profit'.

28 Van der Wee, *Antwerp*, vol. 2, pp. 270, 279, 308, 397; Van der Wee and Van Cauwenberghe, *Productivity of Land*, pp. 14, 47, 85; Verlinden, 'En Flandre', p. 60; Van der Wee, 'Typologie', p. 222.

29 I. Wallerstein, *The Modern World-System*, vol. 2 (New York, 1980), pp. 14–16.

30 The impact in England is discussed by A. Everitt, 'The marketing of agricultural

produce', in J. Thirsk (ed.), *The Agrarian History of England and Wales*, vol. 4 (Cambridge, 1967), ch. 8, p. 523, and by Outhwaite, above, pp. 24 ff.

31 *Actas*, vol. 15, p. 759

32 Biblioteca Nacional, Madrid, MS 9372, fos 31–40v, reproduced in C. Viñas Mey, *El problema de la tierra en la España de los siglos XVI–XVII* (Madrid, 1941), pp. 215–26.

33 Thompson, *War and Government*, pp. 103–6.

34 C. G. Cruickshank, *Elizabeth's Army* (Oxford, 1966), pp. 290–1. This calculation assumes a population of c 4½ million for England and Wales or c 1 million households.

35 Thompson, *War and Government*, p. 104, table 4.1.

36 *Memorial de la política necesaria y útil restauración de la república de España* (1600), fo. 4, cited in M. Colmeiro, *Historia de la economía política en España*, vol. 2 (Madrid, 1965), p. 604.

37 For a survey of some of the recent demographic literature, see A. W. Lovett, 'The Golden Age of Spain: new work on an old theme', *Historical Journal*, vol. 24 (1981), pp. 739–49; for Andalusia, J. I. Fortea Pérez, *Córdoba en el siglo XVI: Las bases demográficas y económicas de una expansión urbana* (Cordoba, 1981), ch. 3; for Galicia, J. Ruiz Almansa, *La población de Galicia (1500–1945)* (Madrid, 1948); for Old Castile, L. A. Ribot García et al., *Valladolid, corazón del mundo hispánico – siglo XVI* (Valladolid, 1981), p. 76.

38 J. T. Evans, *Seventeenth-century Norwich* (Oxford, 1979), pp. 4–5, 19; P. Clark, *English Provincial Society from the Reformation to the Revolution: Religion, Politics and Society in Kent, 1500–1640* (Hassocks, 1977), ch. 10; A. Fletcher, *A County Community in Peace and War: Sussex, 1600–1660* (London, 1975), p. 21.

39 Williams, *Tudor Regime*, p. 75; Parker, *Dutch Revolt*, pp. 237, 249; Thompson, *War and Government*, pp. 69–71; F. Ruiz Martín, 'Las finanzas españolas durante el reinado de Felipe II (alternativas de participación que se ofrecieron para Francia)', *Cuadernos de historia: anexos de la revista 'Hispania'*, vol. 2 (Madrid, 1968), pp. 109–73; Braudel, *Mediterranean*, vol. 1, pp. 510–17, on the 1596 'bankruptcy' in Spain, vol. 2, p. 694, for a graph of *asientos*; R. Briggs, *Early Modern France, 1560–1715* (Oxford, 1977), p. 220.

40 For estimates of national income in Castile, G. Gentil da Silva, *En Espagne, développement économique, subsistance, déclin* (Paris, 1965), p. 92; A. Domínguez Ortiz, *The Golden Age of Spain* (London, 1971), p. 198. The Dutch and English figures are guesses extrapolated from wage rates on the basis of 400,000 families in the United Provinces and 1 million in England. Taking a soldier's pay of 130 florins a year in Holland (P. Zumthor, *Daily Life in Rembrandt's Holland* (London, 1962), p. 337, n. 6), and 8d a day in England (Cruickshank, *Elizabeth's Army*, p. 88), for comparability, a figure of 52 million florins is reached for the United Provinces and £12 million for England. For a justification of the method, see P. Bairoch, 'Estimations du revenu national dans les sociétés occidentales pré-industrielles et au XIXe siècle', *Revue économique*, vol. 28 (1977), pp. 177–208.

41 Williams, *Tudor Regime*, p. 75; Clark, *English Provincial Society*, pp. 225, 228; A. Hassell Smith, *County and Court: Government and Politics in Norfolk, 1558–1603* (Oxford, 1974), pp. 278–9.

42 C. Wilson, 'Taxation and the decline of empires, an unfashionable theme', in C. Wilson, *Economic History and the Historian* (London, 1969), p. 120.

43 N. Salomon, *La Campagne de Nouvelle Castille à la fin du XVIe siècle d'après les 'Relaciones topográficas'* (Paris, 1964), ch. 6, esp. pp. 234, 243.

44 B. H. Slicher van Bath, *The Agrarian History of Western Europe, AD 500–1850* (London, 1963), p. 118. Castilian wheat prices at the *tasa*.

45 D. Bitton, *The French Nobility in Crisis, 1560–1640* (Stanford, Calif., 1969), ch. 6.

46 Livet, *Guerres de religion*, pp. 91–5; H. Drouot, *Mayenne et la Bourgogne: étude sur la Ligue (1587–1596)* (Dijon, 1937), vol. 1, p. 45.

47 R. B. Outhwaite, 'Who bought crown lands? The pattern of purchases, 1589–1603', *Bulletin of the Institute of Historical Research*, vol. 44 (1971), pp. 18–33. Cranfield is reported to have told the King often that 'in selling land he did not only sell his rent, as other men did, but sold his sovereignty, for it was a greater tie of obedience to be a tenant to the King than to be his subject': M. Prestwich, *Cranfield: Politics and Profits under the Early Stuarts* (Oxford, 1966), p. 339.

48 Data from Archivo General de Simancas, Dirección General del Tesoro (Inventario 24),

legajo 323. *Actas*, vol. 18, p. 583, Alonso Muriel (Madrid). 'es poner en los regimientos tiranos perpetuos'.

49 This was probably not true of Holland, where the main tax, the *verponding*, was levied as a percentage of the rental value of real property: J. de Vries, *The Dutch Rural Economy in the Golden Age, 1500–1700* (New Haven, Conn., 1974), p. 210. In England, although the subsidy may have fallen more heavily on the towns and the merchants, the Book of Rates was unchanged since the reign of Mary, and the effective rate was very low: Williams, *Tudor Regime*, pp. 78–9.

50 The estimate of Andalusian grain output was made by Don Juan Chacón de Narvaez in 1583: Archivo General de Simancas, Guerra Antigua, *legajo* 155, fos. 46, 49, 53, 57, 62, 65, 66.

51 B. Pearce, 'Elizabethan food policy and the armed forces', *Economic History Review*, 1st ser., vol. 12 (1942), p. 41; Cruickshank, *Elizabeth's Army*, p. 82.

52 The data in E. J. Hamilton, *American Treasure and the Price Revolution in Spain, 1501–1650* (Cambridge, Mass., 1934), app. 6, pp. 390–2, support this conclusion, as does the generally high level of wheat prices in Norwich during the 1590s: see above, p. 28, and local complaints, like that of the mayor of Chester in March 1595, in Pearce, 'Elizabethan food policy', p. 45.

53 A. García Sanz, *Desarrollo y crisis del Antiguo Régimen en Castilla la Vieja: Economía y sociedad en tierras de Segovia, 1500–1814* (Madrid, 1977), p. 145; *Actas*, vol. 15, pp. 655–7: 'las tierras son más que nunca han sido por las que de nuevo se han rompido que eran dehesas concejiles y baldíos' (26 August 1598).

54 Moody et al., *New History of Ireland*, vol. 3, p. 125. See also W. W. Rostow, *The Process of Economic Growth* (Oxford, 1953), pp. 149, 153–4; De Vries, *Dutch Rural Economy*, p. 210; P. Deane, 'War and industrialization', in J. M. Winter (ed.), *War and Economic Development*, pp. 91, 98.

55 J. U. Nef, 'War and economic progress, 1540–1640', *Economic History Review*, 1st ser., vol. 12 (1942), pp. 13–48.

56 R. Davis, *The Rise of the English Shipping Industry in the 17th and 18th Centuries* (London, 1962), pp. 5, 7, on the ambivalent impact of war in the 1590s and the excessive emphasis on big ships. L. A. Clarkson, *The Pre-Industrial Economy in England* (London, 1971), p. 163, argues that the leather industry also benefited from military demand: 'government contracts were a forcing-house of entrepreneurship'.

57 C. Cipolla, *Guns and Sails in the Early Phase of European Expansion, 1400–1700* (London, 1965), pp. 39–40, for the Kent and Sussex figures. M. Oppenheim, *A History of the Administration of the Royal Navy and of Merchant Shipping in Relation to the Navy* (London, 1896), p. 159, gives a figure of 2,500 tons a year. For English iron output in the 1570s (*c.* 13,000 tons), D. C. Coleman, *Industry in Tudor and Stuart England* (London, 1975), p. 42, and for the European figures see Nef, *Western Civilization*, pp. 35, 80. See also Fletcher, *County Community*, p. 19.

58 Cipolla, *Guns and Sails*, p. 44.

59 Collating Cipolla's estimate for cannon production in ibid., p. 73, with Nef. Similarly for copper, the demand for coin after 1599 seems to have been much more important than the demand for guns, doubling copper prices between 1599 and 1610: Ball, *Merchants and Merchandise*, p. 120.

60 Cruickshank, *Elizabeth's Army*, p. 99; D. C. Coleman, *The Economy of England, 1450–1750* (Oxford, 1977), p. 64. See also Nef, *Western Civilization*, p. 101.

61 Calculated from the accounts of Diego de Postigo and Andrés Sanz de Portillo, 1577–81, Archivo General de Simancas, Contaduría Mayor de Cuentas, 2a época, *legajos* 556, 530, 558; Cordoba's output from Fortea Pérez, *Córdoba*, p. 311.

62 On Curtius, J. Lejeune, *La Formation du capitalisme moderne dans la principauté de Liège au XVIe siècle* (Liège, 1939), pp. 279–304; Alcalá Zamora y Queipo de Llano, *Historia de una empresa siderúrgica española: Los altos hornos de Liérganes y La Cavada, 1622–1834* (Santander, 1974), p. 82, On Evelyn, J. W. Gough, *The Rise of the Entrepreneur* (London, 1969), p. 206. According to L. Stone, 'The nobility in business, 1540–1640', in *The Entrepreneur: Papers Presented at the Annual Conference of the Economic History Society* (Cambridge,

1957), p. 19, Lord Robartes was the only peer who achieved his wealth and thus his title mainly as a result of industry (tin).

63 Nef, *Western Civilization*, pp. 98–9, for some general observations. Note the close ties between Pascual and Lerma, Núñez Correa and Franqueza, Cranfield and Buckingham. Conversely, the success of the Tripp family of Dordrecht took place in a state with a 'weak' court: Ball, *Merchants and Merchandise*, p. 120.

64 J. H. M. Salmon, *Society in Crisis: France in the Sixteenth Century* (London, 1975), p. 326; Benedict, *Rouen*, pp. 182, 225, 250; Bitton, *French Nobility*, p. 95; Ladurie, *Languedoc*, p. 68; Drouot, *Mayenne*, vol. 1, p. 45; J. H. Mariéjol, *Histoire de France illustrée*, ed. E. Lavisse, vol. 6, pt 2 (Paris, 1911), p. 3.

65 M. Ulloa, *La hacienda real de Castilla en el reinado de Felipe II* (Madrid, 1977), ch. 22; I. A. A. Thompson, 'The purchase of nobility in Castile, 1552–1700', *Journal of European Economic History*, vol. 8 (1979), pp. 313–60.

66 L. Stone, 'The inflation of honours, 1558–1641', *Past and Present*, no. 14 (1958), pp. 45–70, and his *The Crisis of the Aristocracy, 1558–1641* (Oxford, 1965), pp. 66–82.

67 It was precisely this that inspired the sedition in Avila in October 1591: A. Merino Alvarez, *La sociedad abulense durante el siglo XVI: La nobleza* (Madrid, 1926), p. 99. See also the Ligue manifesto of 31 March 1585: Salmon, *Society in Crisis*, p. 238.

68 Reflected in the hostile reactions to modern warfare of traditionalist apologists for nobility, like Sir John Smythe, *Certain Discourses Military*, ed. J. R. Hale (Ithaca, NY, 1964), or Sir Henry Knyvett, *The Defence of the Realme*, ed. C. Hughes (Oxford, 1906), as well as in the many contemporary expressions of the social futility of nobility, e.g. Ford's 'Ye're fat in no felicity but folly' or Raleigh's 'fools and therefore insufficient for charge, or cowards and therefore uncapable of lieutenancy': see W. Notestein, *English People on the Eve of Colonization* (New York, 1954), p. 40; H. R. Trevor-Roper, *The Gentry, 1540–1640*, Economic History Review Supplement, vol. 1 (1953), p. 38. For the decline of the French *noblesse* as a military class, J. Bérenger, 'Noblesse et absolutisme de François Ier à Louis XIV', in B. Köpeczi and E. H. Balázs (eds), *Noblesse française, noblesse hongroise, XVIe–XIXe siècles* (Budapest, 1981), pp. 20–1.

69 G. Huppert, *Les Bourgeois Gentilshommes* (Chicago, Ill., 1977), pp. 169–70; Salmon, *Society in Crisis*, pp. 237, 241; Mariéjol citing Robert Dallington (1598), *Histoire de France*, vol. 6, pt 2, p. 19; Drouot, *Mayenne*, vol. 1, p. 43.

70 A. Esler, *The Aspiring Mind of the Elizabethan Younger Generation* (Durham NC, 1966), pp. 93, 174, 108–11, 124. Essex's personal challenge to the duke of Villars, the governor of Rouen, was very much in the same vein: Benedict, *Rouen*, p. 218.

71 Salmon, *Society in Crisis*, p. 316; Bérenger, 'Noblesse et absolutisme', p. 18.

72 Esler, *Aspiring Mind*, p. 139. For the chivalric revival, see R. Strong, *The Cult of Elizabeth* (London, 1977), chs 5 and 6.

73 H. Kamen, *The Iron Century* (London, 1971), pp. 132–3; Salmon, *Society in Crisis* pp. 270–1; François de la Noue (as cited by Sir John Smythe, *Certain Discourses Military*, p. lvii) 'doth in terrible sort blame and disable almost the whole nobility of France of this time, imputing unto them many imperfections'; Bérenger, 'Noblesse et absolutisme', p. 21. Williams, *Tudor Regime*, p. 439, argues that the proletarianisation of war pushed the aristocracy to the exploitation of offices at Court, at the cost of both reputation and popularity.

74 Fray Jerónimo de Sepulveda, 'Historia de varios sucesos', in J. Zarco Cuevas (ed.), *Documentos para la historia del monasterio de San Lorenzo el Real de El Escorial*, vol. 4 (Madrid, 1924), p. 59.

75 J. R. Hale, 'The military education of the officer class in early modern Europe', *Renaissance War Studies* (London, 1982), pp. 225–46. For some of many government attempts to remilitarise the nobility, see Bérenger, 'Noblesse et absolutisme', p. 21, and A. Rodríguez Villa, *Ambrosio Spínola, primer marqués de los Balbases* (Madrid, 1905), p. 44.

76 Russell Major, 'Noble income', pp. 42–3; Salmon, *Society in Crisis*, pp. 323, 325. For some, of course, it was peace that was a financial disaster: see, for example, R. W. Kenny, *Elizabeth's Admiral* (Baltimore, Md, 1970), p. 265. For the ossification of noble values, see Huppert, *Bourgeois Gentilshommes*, pp. 18, 170; Drouot, *Mayenne*, vol. 1, pp. 44.

52–3; R. B. Grassby, 'Social status and commercial enterprise under Louis XIV', *Economic History Review*, 2nd ser., vol. 13 (1960–1), reprinted in R. F. Kierstead (ed.),. *State and Society in Seventeenth-Century France* (New York, 1975), pp. 200–32, on the revival of *dérogation* in the early seventeenth century at p. 201. For Spain, Thompson, 'Purchase of nobility', p. 354.

77 See R. Villari, 'Rivolte e coscienza rivoluzionaria nel secolo XVII', *Studi Storici*, vol. 12 (1971), Spanish trans. in R. Villari, *Rebeldes y reformadores del siglo XVI al XVIII* (Barcelona, 1981), at pp. 29–32; Huppert, *Bourgeois Gentilshommes* pp. 8–10, 21, 33, 173, on Loyseau; Salmon, *Society in Crisis*, pp. 323–4; Grassby, 'Social status and commercial enterprise', pp. 203–6; Drouot, *Mayenne*, vol. 1, p. 53.

78 Of all admissions to the chartered companies, 1575–1630, only 6 per cent date from 1585–1603: T. K. Rabb, *Enterprise and Empire: Merchant and Gentry Investment in the Expansion of England, 1575–1630* (Cambridge, Mass., 1967), p. 72. See also Prestwich, *Cranfield*, p. 52, and Benedict, *Rouen*, p. 182.

79 Villari, 'Rivolte e coscienza rivoluzionaria', *passim*.

80 F. Braudel, *La Méditerranée et le monde méditerranéen à l'époque de Philippe II*, vol. 2 (Paris, 1966), p. 46. The rendering in the English translation is '1600–1610: the comeback of the smaller state?' (vol. 2 (London, 1973), p. 701).

81 Braudel, *Mediterranean*, vol. 2, p. 1200; Parry, 'Ottoman Empire', pp. 351–2; A. C. Hess, *The Forgotten Frontier* (Chicago, Ill., 1978), ch. 6, 'North Africa in revolt', pp. 100–26.

82 Braudel, *Mediterranean*, vol. 2, p. 1219; J. L. Cano de Gardoqui, 'España y los estados italianos independientes en 1600', *Hispania*, vol. 23 (1963), pp. 524–55.

83 J. F. Guilmartin, *Gunpowder and Galleys: Changing Technology and Mediterranean Warfare at Sea in the Sixteenth Century* (Cambridge, 1975), ch. 6, on the decline of the 'Mediterranean system'. See also A. Tenenti, *Piracy and the Decline of Venice, 1580–1615* (London, 1967); G. Fisher, *Barbary Legend: War, Trade and Piracy in North Africa, 1415–1830* (Oxford, 1957), pp. 127, 176.

84 The 250–300 ships plundered in and out of Venice, 1592–1609, and insurance rates to the Levant of 25 per cent were symptoms of that: Braudel, *Mediterranean*, vol. 2, pp. 887, 880.

85 H. and P. Chaunu, 'The Atlantic economy and the world economy', in P. Earle (ed.), *Essays in European Economic History, 1500–1800* (Oxford, 1974), p. 119.

86 By 1598, 400,000 pesos (35 per cent of remittances to Seville) were being held back in Mexico for defence: I. Sánchez Bella, *La organización financiera de las Indias* (Seville, 1968), p. 59 and n. 155; Andrews, *Elizabethan Privateering*, pp. 224–6.

87 Vilar, 'Age of Don Quixote', p. 105.

88 Wallerstein, *Modern World-System*, vol. 2, p. 23.

89 H. R. Trevor-Roper, 'The general crisis of the seventeenth century', in T. Aston (ed.), *Crisis in Europe, 1560–1660* (London, 1965), p. 78.

90 J. Hurstfield, 'County government: Wiltshire, *c*. 1530–*c*.1660', in J. Hurstfield, *Freedom, Corruption and Government in Elizabethan England* (London, 1973), pp. 237–44; W. B. Willcox, *Gloucestershire: A Study in Local Government, 1590–1640* (New Haven, Conn., 1940), pp. 73–102; Hassell Smith, *County and Court*, pp. 242–6, 277, 280–93; Clark, *English Provincial Society*, ch. 8; Williams, *Tudor Regime*, p. 123.

91 Thompson, *War and Government*, ch. 10.

92 F. C. Dietz, *English Public Finance, 1558–1641* (New York, 1932), pp. 308, 312 n. 17, 325; A. P. Newton, 'The establishment of the Great Farm of the English customs', *Transactions of the Royal Historical Society*, 4th ser., vol. 1 (1918), pp. 129–55; Cruickshank, *Elizabeth's Army*, p. 85; Andrews, *Elizabethan Privateering*, p. 238.

93 Williams, *Tudor Regime*, pp. 128, 436–7.

94 C. Jago, 'Habsburg absolutism and the Cortes of Castile', *American Historical Review*, vol. 86 (1981), pp. 307–26; I. A. A. Thompson, 'Crown and Cortes in Castile, 1590–1665', *Parliaments, Estates and Representation*, vol. 2 (1982), pp. 33–4. For parallel developments in France during the Assembly of Notables, 1596–7, see Salmon, *Society in Crisis*, pp. 302–4.

III

The Impact of War　283

95 Parker, *Dutch Revolt*, pp. 242, 247; J. den Tex, *Oldenbarnevelt*, vol. 1 (Cambridge, 1973), pp. 61–5.
96 'Majestas major ab igne' (the motto on a royal medallion of 1604) sums up one side of this equation, with an accentuation of absolutist theory and the discrediting of the Estates, general and provincial; for the other side of the equation, see Salmon, *Society in Crisis*, pp. 301, 317–18, 320; *Cambridge Modern History*, vol. 3 (1907), pp. 665–6; Mariéjol, *Histoire de France*, vol. 6, pt 2, pp. 12–20.
97 Kamen, *Iron Century*, pp. 337–41; Livet, *Guerres de religion*, pp. 95–7; Salmon, *Society in Crisis*, pp. 277–91; Benedict, *Rouen*, pp. 172, 249; Parker, *Dutch Revolt*, p. 230 and, for anti-tax riots in the United Provinces, p. 237; Williams, *Tudor Regime*, p. 326.
98 B. Sharp, *In Contempt of All Authority* (Berkeley, Calif., 1980), p. 39; Clark, *English Provincial Society*, pp. 249–50.
99 *Actas*, vol. 12, p. 473: 'y que pues ellos se quieren perder, que se pierdan'.
100 *Calendar of State Papers, Venetian*, vol. 8, nos 327, 550, 616, 739, 790, 828; Museo Naval, Colección Navarrete, vol. 8, doc. no. 28, 'Relación de arbitrios propuestos para la defensa de la Monarquía de España . . . por Alonso Gutiérrez en el Consejo de Estado', Aranjuez, 1 May 1602, at fos 183–4; *Colección de documentos inéditos para la historia de España*, vol. 43, pp. 530, 538–9, Don Juan de Silva, Lisbon, June and July 1594.
101 G. Parker, 'Mutiny and discontent in the Spanish Army of Flanders, 1572–1607', in Parker, *Spain and the Netherlands*, ch. 5, pp. 106–21; P. van Isacker, 'Les mutineries militaires aux Pays Bas à la fin du XVIe siècle', *Annuaire*, University of Louvain (1909), pp. 469–80. There were more than forty mutinies in the Spanish Netherlands, 1589–1607. Kamen, *Iron Century*, pp. 337–41; Cruickshank, *Elizabeth's Army*, p. 79, on the Ostend mutiny of 1588, caused by poor victuals at high prices; Outhwaite, above, pp. 30–2, on the sufferings of the troops in Ireland and Berwick. Parry, 'Ottoman Empire', p. 371, revolts of janissaries 1589, spahis 1592 and 1603 over pay.
102 J. Pound, *Poverty and Vagrancy in Tudor England* (London, 1971), p. 5; Willcox, *Gloucestershire*, p. 106; C. Viñas Mey, 'La asistencia social a la invalidez militar en el siglo XVI', *Anuario de historia económica y social*, vol. 1 (1968), pp. 598–605.
103 Smythe, *Certain Discourses Military*, pp. 25–6; M. Lewis, *The History of the British Navy* (London, 1959), p. 188; 'the navy is for the greatest part manned with aged, impotent, vagrant, lewd and disorderly companions; it is become a ragged regiment of common rogues' (1608).
104 But cf. Pound, *Poverty and Vagrancy*, pp. 4–5: a band of 500 soldiers back from Portugal threatened to loot Bartholomew Fair; F. Aydelotte, *Elizabethan Rogues and Vagabonds* (London, 1967), p. 71 and n. 6, attributing the increase in vagabondage after 1588 to returned soldiers and sailors, and p. 170, citing Hext. However, it is clear from the six proclamations against vagrant soldiers, 1589–98, that many vagrants were pretending to be soldiers. In fact, poor relief paid by the corporation of Winchester through St John's Hospital *fell* between 1585 and 1592. In Warwick in 1587 only *c.* 10 per cent of the poor were in the age group 15–30, and in Ipswich in 1597 only 6 per cent. In neither town is there any indication of returned soldiers among the vagrants or the poor: A. Rosen, 'Winchester in transition, 1580–1700', and A. L. Beier, 'The social problems of an Elizabethan county town: Warwick, 1580–90', in P. Clark (ed.), *Country Towns in Pre-Industrial England* (Leicester, 1981), pp. 144–95 and 46–85, at pp. 159 and p. 63 respectively: Clark, *English Provincial Society*, p. 235.
105 For this and other quotations in similar vein, see E. Silberner, *La Guerre dans la pensée économique du XVIe au XVIIIe siècles* (Paris, 1939), ch. 2.
106 Kamen, *Iron Century*, pp. 341–6; Braudel, *Mediterranean*, vol. 2, p. 1199.
107 Archivo General de Simancas, Estado, *legajo* 1945, *consulta* of Consejo de Estado, 16 November 1600.
108 As Livet, *Guerres de religion*, p. 101, puts it: 'La foi remplace le pain.' In Valencia the upsurge of persecutions against the *moriscos* by the Inquisition in the years 1585–95 (coinciding with the fears of a Huguenot-*morisco* axis) is quite remarkable, with the numbers of *procesados* peaking in 1589–92 at 1,124, compared with an average of 60–80 up to 1585: R. García Cárcel, *Herejía y sociedad en el siglo XVI: La inquisición en Valencia, 1530–1609* (Barcelona, 1980), p. 211 and chart p. 210. In Essex the peak period for

witchcraft prosecutions coincides with the threat from Spain (A. D. J. Macfarlane, *Witchcraft in Tudor and Stuart England* (London, 1970), pp. 28, 70) and in France there is a direct connection between the prosecution of witches and the fortunes of the Ligue (A. Soman, 'The parlement of Paris and the Great Witch-Hunt (1565–1640)', *Sixteenth-Century Journal*, vol. 9 (1978), p. 39. In the Nord, on the other hand, the upsurge comes in the immediately postwar years, 1590–1620: R. Muchembled, 'Sorcières due Cambrésis: l'acculturation du monde rurale aux XVIe et XVIIe siècles', in M.-S. Dupont-Bouchat, W. Frijhoff and R. Muchembled, *Prophètes et sorciers dans les Pays-Bas XVIe–XVIIIe siècles* (Paris, 1978), p. 177.

109 Trevor-Roper, *Gentry*, pp. 37–40.

110 R. C. Munden, 'James I and "the growth of mutual distrust": King, Commons, and reform, 1603–1604', in K. Sharpe (ed.), *Faction and Parliament: Essays on Early Stuart History* (Oxford, 1978), pp. 43–8; Hassell Smith, *County and Court*, pp. 242, 275, 277, 333–4; Clark, *English Provincial Society*, pp. 256–7, 259, 265–6. For suggestions of a comparable court-country divide within the French nobility, see J. H. M. Salmon, *The French Wars of Religion* (Boston, Mass., 1967) p. 90.

111 R. Hakluyt, *Voyages*, vol. 4 (London, 1907), p. 352.

112 Smythe, *Certain Discourses Military*, pp. xxxiv, 21.

113 Knyvett, *Defence of the Realme*, p. 30.

114 Hakluyt, *Voyages*, vol. 4, p. 350; Knyvett, *Defence of the Realme*, p. 19: 'of late yeares all pryvate soldiers have bin so lightlie regarded, yea so uncharitablie and cruellie used as were it not for theire extraordinarie obedience and loyall love which they beare to yor most sacred Ma[ne] they would more willinglie be hanged at there dores then abyde shamefull martirdome with sundrie extremities abrode'; Smythe, *Certain Discourses Military*, pp. xxxviii, lxxx, 19, 22.

115 Meyer, 'Paysan français', p. 70.

116 Museo Naval, MS. 505, no. 91, Esteban de Ibarra to Don Pedro de Toledo, S. L. de El Escorial, 21 August 1597: 'y todo está de manera que quita la gana de travajar y servir, ver como y por donde se camina'.

117 Esler, *Aspiring Mind*, pp. 194–5, 208, 232 and 228, quoting G. B. Harrison: 'a . . . progress from romance to realism, from realism to satire, from satire to nausea': O. H. Green, *Spain and the Western Tradition*, vol. 4 (Madison, Wis., 1966), p. 363; Parker, *Dutch Revolt*, p. 204; Huppert, *Bourgeois Gentilshommes*, pp. 166, 169; M. Defourneaux, *Daily Life in Spain in the Golden Age* (London, 1970), p. 228; J. H. Elliott, 'Self-perception and decline in early seventeenth-century Spain', *Past and Present*, no. 74 (1977), p. 47; Salmon, *Society in Crisis*, p. 273; H. Ettinghausen, *Francisco de Quevedo and the Neostoic Movement* (Oxford, 1972), p. 8; and, for other penitential and devotional responses to war, Benedict, *Rouen*, pp. 191, 194, 202.

118 Ettinghausen, *Francisco de Quevedo*, pp. 21, 128–9.

119 For this interpretation, see, especially, G. Oestreich, *Neostoicism and the Early Modern State* (Cambridge, 1982).

IV

ASPECTS OF SPANISH MILITARY AND NAVAL ORGANIZATION DURING THE MINISTRY OF OLIVARES

The Programme

At the core of the criticism levelled by the new ministry in 1621 against the previous reign was a sense of shame and outrage at the loss of international respect for the reputation of Spanish arms. 'Le lastima mucho ver el descaecimiento a que ha venido en lo militar nación tan valerosa y belicosa como la española.'[1] The entire reform programme of Zúñiga and Olivares was, in effect, a blueprint for the restoration of Spain's military power.

The root of the problem was - it goes without saying - money, money, and yet more money. But money was not quite everything. 'A cuatro cabos se reduce lo sensible de la guerra: gente, dinero, órden y obediencia.'[2] That catalogue suggests a programme of military reform operating at two levels, one concerned with the basic procurement of physical resources - money, men, ships, munitions; the other with the establishment of certain principles of order and organization. Those principles are sometimes explicit, sometimes not, and the main purpose of the rather summary account of the procurement programme that follows is to draw attention to the principles of organization and government that inform them.

Four themes recur constantly throughout Olivares's writings: the need for leaders ('la falta de cabezas'); the need for a guaranteed supply of soldiers ('un medio con que se asegure el tener esta Corona treinta mil soldados perpetuos y efetivos'); the need for a powerful ocean fleet; and the need to provide the necessary resources on a permanent and a geographically and socially equitable basis.

For Olivares what was necessary was nothing less than the remilitarization of Spain. The aim was to restore honour and respect for the military in order to

---

[1] J.H.Elliott and J.F. de la Peña, *Memoriales y cartas del Conde Duque de Olivares*, 2 vols. (Madrid, 1978-81) [hereafter *MC*], vol. 2, p.66, 1 Aug. 1634.

[2] Olivares 1637, *MC* 2, p. 154.

2   SPANISH MILITARY AND NAVAL ORGANIZATION

animate vassals to serve their king. A prerequisite, clearly recognized by Olivares, was that soldiering must be voluntary, which was precisely what the Union of Arms, the 'dotación de presidios', and the other schemes for guaranteeing the regular payment of the soldiery were designed to achieve. Dragging men off to the garrisons in chains was both consequence and cause of the loss of 'honour military'. A series of royal decrees reaffirmed or extended the privileges and exemptions of the *fuero militar*. More radical was the idea of restoring the link between the military and Nobility by fabricating a ladder of honours, offices and titles, from 'limpieza' to 'rico hombre', through which the soldier and the sailor could rise by long or outstanding services.[3] Not the least of the implications of such a scheme was the equalizing of the military and naval careers. The idea was never seriously implemented, though substitutes serving for *caballeros* of the Military Orders were promised *hábitos* after two years service,[4] and in the later years of Olivares's ministry membership of the Council of War became very much an honorific title, awarded to both generals and admirals before they went to their postings.

The sense of a special military honour was increasingly associated with the sense of a specific military professionalism. The *Ordenanzas Militares* of 28 June 1632 codified the rules for promotion, set down in the previous reign, and established minimum qualifications for officers. One of the consequences of the so-called 'military revolution' was the need for training and discipline down to the lowest levels. The gap between the 'veterano' and the 'bisoño' seems to be increasing in the 17th century, and there is a clear recognition by Philip IV and his ministers of the need to bridge that gap by using the *presidios* as training-camps and to promote the training of artillerymen, gunfounders and mariners.[5]

The hope that the military career would again become the pathway to civil honour, as it had been in the time of the Orden de la Banda, was hardly compatible with the contradictory hope of 'turning Spaniards into merchants' or with the even more urgent emphasis on militarizing the aristocracy. Those

---

[3] J.H.Elliott, *The Count-Duke of Olivares. The Statesman in an Age of Decline* (Yale U.P., 1986), p.147 note 69.

[4] A.Domínguez Ortiz, 'La movilización de la nobleza castellana en 1640', *Anuario de Historia del Derecho Español* 25 (1955): 799-824, at p.808 note 22.

[5] AGS [Archivo General de Simancas] GA [Guerra Antigua] 3147, CCG [*consulta* of Council of War] 27 May 1621; *MC* 2, pp. 69, 106; J. de Salas, *Historia de la matrícula de mar y examen de varios sistemas de reclutamiento marítimo* (Madrid, 1879), ch. 9.

lacking *hidalguía* or who were 'indecente por sangre ni por ocupación mecánica' were categorically excluded from standing in for *caballeros* of the Orders.[6] Olivares's preoccupation with the 'falta de cabezas' was essentially rooted in the unspoken conviction that leadership was the preserve of the nobility. It was their supposed failure to go to the wars that Olivares wanted to remedy by giving them preferential treatment in military promotion (1632) and by educating their youth in obedience, discipline and the military arts.

Whether there was either a solution or a problem here is to be doubted. The de-militarization of the aristocracy was a theme of fashionable head-shaking in the 17th century that has since gained a much too easy acceptance, and the 'falta de cabezas' was a total obsession with Olivares, applying not just to the military, but to the Councils, the *chancillerías*, and the *corregidores*. Besides, this complaint too was a very old one[7] and, given the international composition of Philip IV's general staff, it is difficult to see what contribution it makes to an understanding of Spain's military failure in the mid-17th century.[8] Not even with Condé in the team could the Spanish side avoid relegation.

The building up of the navy was among the first priorities of the new reign. 'Veo lo que importa que las cosas de la mar se refuercen y acrediten lo más que se pueda', was Philip IV's response to a *consulta* of the Council of War of 27 May 1621.[9] A naval force of thirty *navíos* and six *pataches* was ordered to be planned for the following year with its financial assignment guaranteed. Twelve *navíos* and half the *pataches* were to be royal ships, 'propios míos', and the rest provided under contracts with the provinces of Vizcaya, Guipúzcoa and the Cuatro Villas. In the early 1620s a long list of further contracts for the provision of squadrons and individual vessels under hire (with Judici, Martolosi, Marín, Oliste, Canovés, and with Galicia) and for the construction of galleons for the king's ownership (Arana) brought the number of major vessels in the five squadrons of the fleet up to some 38 or 40 *navíos* within two years, more than

---

[6] Domínguez Ortiz, 'Movilización', p.808 and note 22.

[7] Marcantonio Mula 23 Sept. 1559, E.Albèri, *Le relazioni degli ambasciatori veneti*, 15 vols. (Florence, 1839-63), Serie I, vol. 3, p. 399.

[8] Compare Aytona's largely favourable opinion of the commanders in the Netherlands in 1630, Conde de Clonard, *Historia orgánica de las armas de infantería y caballería españolas*, 16 vols. (Madrid, 1851-62), vol. 4, p. 398 note 1.

[9] AGS GA 3147.

IV

the Junta de Armadas thought were presently needed.[10] In 1623, at 1,080,000 ducats, the *consignación* for the Armada del Mar Océano was about fifty per cent more than in 1621,[11] and by 1625 the ministry was claiming that the total high seas fleet (excluding 20 Dunkirkers) numbered some 108 vessels.[12]

The reinforcement of the Atlantic fleets, however, also represented a reallocation of resources from the Mediterranean. In July 1621 the galleys of Spain were reorganized, cutting their number from 21 to 12, and the Mediterranean galley fleet steadily lost strength throughout the period, from some 75 galleys in 1619 to 42 in 1634, and 26 or so in 1649.[13] The galleys financed by Spain had cost 648,000 ducats in 1620; the average cost in the years 1632-38 was only 340,000 ducats.[14] By the end of Olivares's ministry Spain no longer dominated the waters of the western Mediterranean.[15]

Olivares's participation in a new Junta de Armadas which was formed in January 1622, meeting in his own apartments, must have been one of his earliest ministerial roles and is a mark of the centrality of naval reform in the Conde Duque's thinking. The impetus does not, however, seem to have been sustained. In the early 1630s the navy was again visibly in decline.[16] Naval funding in 1632-34 was down to just over 800,000 ducats. The Armada de la Guardia de las Indias had only a dozen galleons of its scheduled twenty in service, and in June 1635 there were only 19 fit ships in the Armada del Mar Océano, instead of the 30,000 tons the Junta de Armadas wanted.[17]

[10] AGS GA 3148, CJA [*consulta* of Junta de Armadas] 7 May 1623; AGS GA 889, CJA 10 Nov. 1623.

[11] ACC [*Actas de las Cortes de Castilla*], vol. 38, pp.27-8.

[12] *MC* 1, pp. 154, 244-6.

[13] M.Devèze, *L'Espagne de Philippe IV*, 2 vols. (Paris, 1970), 1, pp. 356-63.

[14] *ACC* vol. 55, pp. 441 ff.

[15] R.C.Anderson, 'The Thirty Years War in the Mediterranean', *Mariner's Mirror* 55 (1969):435-51, 56 (1970):41-57

[16] Corner 1631, N.Barozzi and G.Berchet, *Relazioni degli stati europei*, Serie I, *Spagna*, vol.1, p. 27.

[17] C.R.Phillips, *Six Galleons for the King of Spain. Imperial Defense in the Early Seventeenth Century* (Johns Hopkins U.P., Baltimore, 1986), pp. 198, 201

With the outbreak of war with France in 1635 another crash programme of shipbuilding and naval procurement had to be undertaken. By 1637 one million ducats had been added to the naval budget, some 150,000 extra were set aside for shipbuilding, and new contracts were made with the provinces and with private outfitters for the provision and maintenance of squadrons. By 1638 there were (it was claimed) upwards of 100 vessels in service in all maritime theatres.[18] The seventy, or so, sail that Oquendo led out of La Coruña in September 1639, the finest force seen since the 'Invencible', in the Conde Duque's estimation,[19] marked the climax - if not necessarily the end - of Spain's naval recovery.

Measures were also taken to increase the material resources for war and to promote the long-standing aim of making Spain self-sufficient in the munitions industries.

The most successful of these measures was the conclusion in August 1628 of a contract, originally made with the Liège iron-master, Jean Curtius, to set up a cast-iron cannon and shot foundry at Liérganes, near Santander. By 1640 over 72,000 quintals of material had been delivered in the shape of 1,171 guns and nearly 250,000 assorted pieces of shot. Two new furnaces were opened in 1637, giving the factory a capacity of some 15,000 quintals a year and making Spain self-sufficient in cast-iron artillery until the end of the 18th century.[20] In 1641 another shot foundry was set up at Corduente, near Molina de Aragón, to produce under contract some 2,000 quintals of shot a year.

In October 1621 the import of sulphur was prohibited in order to stimulate production at the royal mine in Hellín (Murcia),[21] and in 1627 the mine was rented out to a contractor to manufacture 2,000 quintals a year, three or four times more than was needed for military purposes.[22]

A more persistent problem was the supply of gunpowder. The royal mills in Cartagena and Málaga had the capacity to produce all the powder needed, but too often shortages of money and materials brought the works to a halt. An attempt

---

[18] *ACC*, vol. 55, pp. 441 ff.

[19] R.Estrada, *El Almirante Don Antonio de Oquendo* (Madrid, 1943), p. 148.

[20] J.Alcalá Zamora, *Historia de una empresa siderúrgica española: los altos hornos de Liérganes y La Cavada, 1622-1834* (Santander, 1974), p. 21.

[21] AGS GA 3147.

[22] AGS CMC 3ª [Contaduría Mayor de Cuentas, 3ª época] 2266 no.5, 2 May 1627.

6   SPANISH MILITARY AND NAVAL ORGANIZATION

was made first to top up supplies by contracting out regional monopoly rights for the sale of gunpowder to the public in return for the provision of given quantities to the Crown free of charge. Opposition in the cities and the Cortes forced the withdrawal of these monopolies (1624) and a new policy of centralizing production in private hands was gradually developed, initially through a contract with a middleman for saltpetre, and finally through a contract in 1639 giving the Genoese-born Antonio Graffior monopsony rights to all the saltpetre manufactured in Castile, with the title 'Administrador General de la Pólvora en Castilla'. The contract, initially to supply 41,000 quintals of powder in seven years, was still running in 1657.[23]

The Graffior contract was the outcome of a major reorganization of the munitions industries in Spain, undertaken in March 1633, on the recommendation of the 'Junta de Reformación del Aposento del Conde Duque sobre las consignaciones de la Artillería', endorsed by the Council of War, that all the royal munitions establishments should be put out to contract.[24] Even though Graffior's original target was not met, and powder and saltpetre still had to be imported, substantially more gunpowder was being manufactured in Spain in the 1640s than at any previous time on record.[25]

Manpower had been a problem of increasing intractability since the 1580s. By the 1620s the situation was acute. At the end of 1626 ten new companies arrived at Cadiz, Gibraltar and Seville with only 220 men. Two of the captains had been recruiting in Granada for a total of 27 months; they arrived with 57 men.[26]

The problem was demographic, economic and, of course, financial (inadequacy and irregularity of pay), but lack of discipline, the abuse of billeting rights and the terrorizing of the villages through which the companies passed were no lesser evils than the drain of manpower.

There was great pressure, therefore, to shift the burden of recruiting from Castile, by bringing in Walloons and Italians to man the fleets, and by raising

---

[23] AGS CMC 3a 115.

[24] AGS GA 1051, 12 Dec. 1632, and CCG 2 Mar. 1633.

[25] I.A.A.Thompson, *War and Government in Habsburg Spain, 1560-1620* (London, 1976), pp. 241, 251.

[26] AGS GA 927, CCG 10 Dec. 1626.

men in the peripheral provinces (Portugal, Galicia, Asturias, Aragon) to send overseas.[27]

Equally great was the desire to relieve the treasury of the cost of recruiting by shifting the financial and administrative responsibility onto the local authorities. The first measure was the proposal of October 1622 to replace the *millones* with a series of local commitments, by 'la común de cada pueblo', to maintain a force of 30,000 men.[28] The following year the Council of War urged the general reestablishment of the militia throughout Castile.[29] In 1626 the Union of Arms was proposed, and in 1631 the 'dotación de presidios', a scheme by which 18,000 men would be maintained jointly by Crown, cities, clergy, grandees and *títulos*, the Military Orders, and a variety of corporate bodies, the royal councils, the universities, the *consulados*, the Mesta, etc.[30] The first proposal and the Union of Arms failed, but the militia was successfully reestablished in April 1625 with the backing of the Cortes, and the 'dotación de presidios' was finally accepted in a modified form by the Cortes in 1634, continuing in operation at least into the mid 1640s.[31]

In the 1630s the emphasis moves away from long-term solutions to the immediate task of getting men and horses to the front. The measures are increasingly ad hoc, repetitive and peremptory: the formation of *coronelías* to be raised by the grandees (1631-2); the imposition on the aristocracy of the task of recruiting men on their own estates, and beyond; the traditional *llamamientos* to the cities and provinces to remit troops for the defence of the country, now extended for service outside;[32] the continuous raiding of the militias, deformed into a system of compulsory municipal levies, the men conscripted for the front by *repartimientos* and *quintos* and despatched with scandalous and self-stultifying violence, frecuently by *oidores* and *consejeros* sent out on commission; the

---

[27] AGS GA 900, CCG 30 Aug. and 8 Sept. 1624; AGS GA 912, CCG 14 Jun. 1625; AGS GA 913, CCG 3 Dec. 1625.

[28] A.González Palencia, *La Junta de Reformación* (Valladolid, 1932), pp. 404-7.

[29] AGS GA 889, 14 Jan. 1623.

[30] BL Add. [British Library, Additional Ms.] 9936 f.2; AGS GA 480, draft of 4 Aug. 1631.

[31] *Actas de las Juntas y Diputaciones del Principado de Asturias*, vol. 5 (Oviedo, 1955), p. 54.

[32] For an example, *Actas de las Juntas de Asturias*, vol.3 (Oviedo, 1954), pp. 196 ff.

demand for personal service or acceptable substitutes from the *hidalgos* and *caballeros*; the employment of entrepreneurs to provide men on a contract basis. By the mid 1630s the normal method of administrative recruiting by royal commission *(conducta)* that had prevailed hitherto had become rare.[33] The direct bond between the soldier-vassal and the king's service no longer prevailed. Now it was the intermediaries, the lords, the cities and their captains, the *sargentos mayores* of the militias, who served the king; the soldier was merely the passive instrument of that service, incapable of active participation in it or of sharing its honours and rewards. The recruiting system of the late 1630s signalled the collapse of the hoped-for re-militarization of Spain; it functioned in social terms not as an escalator but as a separator, increasing the gap in social-value between one estate and the other.

What all of Olivares's expedients had in common was that they sought to fix an obligation on intermediate authorities to guarantee men or money, either in the early reforming years by seeking to establish new relations of obligation, or in later years by the simple exploitation of existing obligations, the *lanzas* of the nobility, the personal service of the *caballero*, the common obligation to come to the defence of the country, the duty to attend the king's person in the field. The overt military intention was to ensure a constant supply of men and to settle their costs on local sources. The political intention was to conquer the Indies that lay within Spain itself. The 'dotación', the *coronelías*, the señorial levies, the *llamamientos* of the *caballeros* and *hidalgos*, were all devices for taxing the privileged, cloaking the socially unacceptable element of fiscal exaction in more acceptable, customary, military forms, and absorbing exempt individuals into non-exempt corporations.[34] Olivares's motives are clear enough from his observation that the Conde de Fuensalida should raise 3.000 men, 'porque la calidad es grande y está rico, y dicen que tiene mucho dinero de contado.'[35] Whatever their military value, as fiscal expedients, and at the level of direct contributions, they effected a real redistribution of the financial burden of the costs of the state.

---

[33] J.Contreras Gay, 'Aportación al estudio de los sistemas de reclutamiento militar en la España moderna', *Anuario de Historia Contemporánea* [Granada] 1981, p.20.

[34] R.C. [*Real Cédula]* 18 Feb.1633 to Marqués de Floresdávila, 'conforme al repartimiento que he mandado hazer, a tocado al mi Consejo de Guerra la paga de treinta soldados que monta 21.600 reales cada año en moneda de plata doble', RAH [Real Academia de Historia] K 16 f.60.

[35] *MC* 2, p. 124.

Despite the failure of the Union of Arms, the same intention directed towards regional privilege was also not without its successes. The Aragonese kingdoms, in particular, were drawn into the military system of the Monarchy to a remarkable degree. Seven infantry companies were recruited there in 1625, ten in 1630, fifteen in 1631, and in 1634 nearly 8.000 men were being raised in the Crown of Aragon for the armies in Germany and Italy. By 1634 it was Aragon that was being held up as an example to Castile.[36] After 1636 the complements of Catalans, Aragonese, Valencians and Guipuzcoans at the front were, if sometimes reluctantly sent, unprecedented.[37]

The Achievement

'Que mis armas tienen reputación, mis enemigos me estiman, mis aliados viven seguros'.[38] In 1627 Philip directed a report to the Council of Castile replete with self-congratulation and selective exaggeration of what had been achieved since 1621. Yet many of these early achievements were the culmination of projects undertaken in the last years of the previous reign. The programme of naval expansion had already begun in 1617 with the assignment of an extra 100,000 ducats for shipbuilding; the contracts with the Cantabrian provinces were all signed under Philip III in 1617 and 1618, and between 1618 and 1621 naval requirements rose from 600,000 to 900,000 ducats.[39]

The reform of the arms industries had also commenced under Philip III, and the establishment of the Liérganes foundry was the outcome of a privilege

---

[36] Felipe IV to Cortes, 2 Mar. 1634, '..gente que ha de passar a Italia y Alemania, para donde de sola la Corona de Aragon se levantan aora cerca de ocho mil Infantes, con que verais el exemplo que dan aquellos vasallos en estos aprietos, repartiendo los vezinos sin Cortes, siendo contra todos los fueros, solo por buena voluntad', AHN [Archivo Histórico Nacional, Madrid] Consejos leg. 52445.

[37] Guipúzcoa, for example, claimed in 1648 to have sent 200 men a year to the Catalan war at a cost of 14,000 ducats silver every time, and to have contributed 28,000 men since 1615, AHN Consejos leg. 4431 1648 n.86.

[38] MC 1, p. 246.

[39] AGS CJH [Consejo y Juntas de Hacienda] 401, Martín de Aroztegui 12 Jul. 1617; AGS GA 840, CCG 5 Dec.1619; AGS GA 853, CCG 2 Sept.1620; a 'Relación de los Navíos que Su Magd tiene al pressente', drawn up Sept.1620, AGS GA 853 with CCG 2 Sept.1620, projected a fleet of 36 vessels for 1621, with 14,089 tons and 6,609 men.

10 SPANISH MILITARY AND NAVAL ORGANIZATION

granted to Curtius in 1614.[40] In fact, much of the military and naval legislation leading up to the *Ordenanzas* of 1632 and 1633 was a confirmation and codification of acts of the previous reigns.[41]

The authentic achievements of the first phase of Philip IV's military reforms were limited. The militia was reestablished in Castile, thanks to the English threat in 1625, and was mobilized after the assault on Cadiz later that year; but the scheme to fund 30,000 soldiers by the localities had been rejected by the Cortes, and the Union of Arms had foundered in Catalonia, and been reduced to nothing more than an ill-performed money grant in Aragón and Valencia. The many contributions made by Catalonia, Aragon, Valencia, Guipúzcoa and other non-Castilian kingdoms in the 1630s and 1640s seem not to have been in any way obligations under the Union of Arms, which is not to my knowledge ever mentioned,[42] and I have yet to understand what the Union is supposed to have meant in Castile.[43]

By the early 1630s with the recruiting system unreformed, naval expansion halted, shortages of match-cord, saltpetre, sulphur and gunpowder,[44] complaints from the galleys of 'el miserable estado de necesidad en que se hallava,'[45] all the North African garrisons reported to be starving,[46] and only 7,000 men in the *presidios* instead of 18,000,[47] the achievements of the first ten years of the reign seemed far from spectacular.[48]

---

[40] AGS GA 876.

[41] For one instance, see Salas, *Matrícula de mar*, p.73 and chs. 7 and 8, on Philip III's naval ordinance of 1606 and the 'matrícula de mar'.

[42] BL Add. 13997 f.211, paper of José González 1642 'para prueba de la obligación que tiene el Reino de Aragón *según sus fueros* [my italics] de servir a S.M. con la gente necesaria para defensa de aquel Reino y reduzión del Principado de Cataluña.'

[43] *ACC* vol. 45, p. 249, proposal of Presidente 28 Jul. 1626.

[44] AGS Guerra Moderna 467, Sebastián de Arriola 8 Mar. 1633.

[45] AGS GA 1011, Alonso de Castilla 9 Sept. 1630.

[46] M.Hume, *The Court of Philip IV* (London, 1907), p. 242, Feb 1631.

[47] *MC* 2, p. 108.

[48] Corner 1635, Barozzi & Berchet, *Relazioni*, vol 2, p. 27.

The reality is not that Olivares's reform programme was wrecked by the storms of war after 1635, but that he was a failure as a military reformer during the calmer years, and a remarkable success as a military organizer during the crisis. The measures of the later 1630s are pragmatic, sometimes even desperate, responses to the pressure of events. They lacked any pretence of vision, but taken in a lump they worked. What was achieved in sheer quantitative terms was remarkable. In 1640 the Spanish 'military participation ratio' was probably at a record pre-modern high. 'Es de ponderar que ha más de un siglo que no se han visto tantos españoles juntos en campaña,' calculated Pellicer in June 1639, listing 133,000 in the various war zones[49] before either the Catalan or the Portuguese Revolts had taken place. There was a record number of over 17,000 Spaniards in the Army of Flanders, more Spaniards in Lombardy 'que jamás se ha visto',[50] and the royal army for Catalonia in 1642, with 30,000 infantry and 6,000 horse, was 'el mayor que se habrá visto en estos reinos'.[51] Yet where these figures were not at best ephemeral,[52] they were achieved only at horrendous cost. By the 1640s the recruiting system was an unmitigated disaster. 'The way it is at the moment,' reported the President of Castille in June 1644, 'it is a catalogue of difficulties, violence, injustices, and costs, with precious little return. What is needed is to seek measures of a different kind from those of the past, so that the kingdom can serve without the horrors that will be visited on it by more of the same, which is what is now being proposed.'[53]

---

[49] José Pellicer, *Avisos históricos* 28 Jun. 1639, in A. Valladares de Sotomayor, *Semanario erudito*, vols. 31 & 32 (Madrid 1790).

[50] *MHE* [*Memorial Histórico Español*] vol. 13, p. 252, 4 Sept. 1635.

[51] *MHE*, vol. 16, p. 343; F.M. de Melo, *Historia de los movimientos, separación y guerra de Cataluña en tiempo de Felipe IV*, 3 vols. (Madrid, 1879), I, 23.

[52] Marquis of Grana, 'il Regno, o'almeno quelle Provincie dell'Andalucia, pagano vinti mila huomini e non vi sono sei, restando tutto nell mani de'generali ed officiali del soldo,' 16 Jan. 1643, Vienna HHSA [Haus-hof und Staats Archiv] Sp. Korresp fasz 29 f.64.

[53] Presidente de Castilla, 14 Jun. 1644: 'la (forma) que hoy corre tiene mucho de dificultad, violencia, injusticia y gasto con poquísimo fruta, como porque es menester buscar medios de diferente especie que los pasados para que sirva el Reino sin el horror que le hacen los que hasta ahora se les han propuesto y repetido', *CODOIN* (*Colección de documentos inéditos para la historia de España*), vol. 95, pp. 169-70; paper of D. Luis de Haro, 2 May 1646, AHN Consejos leg 4429-30 1646 n.122

In much the same way the expansion of the number of ships available for service was impressive, but it was the least part of the problem. A squadron of ships could be built within a year or two. What was impossible was to provide the back-up and the skilled manpower, seamen, gunners and veteran 'soldados de mar'. The reports of Don Lope de Hoces after Guetaria and Don Francisco Feixó after the Downs are absolutely conclusive on that point.[54]

The importance of resource deficiencies is difficult to assess. Money, victuals and munitions are always inadequate, on all sides, and at all times. Philip II's administration had as much trouble getting fleets to sea before the autumn as Philip IV's. Richelieu knew that if the French fleet were destroyed it would take a decade to replace. 'Dice bien un discreto que en España no hay un real para estorbar de antemano que no suceda un daño, y hay millones enteros para gastarlos despues de haber sucedido el daño sin remedio.'[55] The complaint could have been made about anyone. No state could afford the premiums that had to be paid during the slack years in order to be assured of adequate cover when war came. 'No se puede negar que la guerra defensiva por mar es la Ruyna de qualquier estado'.[56] War, especially by sea, had to be made to work for its living, and that was most profitably and with least inhibition done privately. That was the great advantage the Dutch had, and the Dunkirkers, and it was the whole point of the Almirantazgos.

Mena's charge that Olivares 'de hambre ha muerto más vassallos a V.Mgd que en las guerras sus enemigos', and Grana's condemnation of the state in which the Conde Duque had left Spain's forces ('restando gl'esserciti qui in Spagna ancora non solo senza paga, ma anche con mancamento di pane & vino, artiglieria et ammonitione, con l'armada di mare incapace di uscire per alcuni mesi')[57] are more interesting as comments on the nature of the problem than on the failure of the solution. The ministers who succeeded Olivares made the same criticisms in 1643 as had been made in 1621; they professed the same principles, started

---

[54] *MHE* vol. 15, p. 44, 15 Sept. 1638; C.Fernández Duro, *Armada Española*, 9 vols. (Madrid, 1895-1903), vol. 4, pp. 227-35.

[55] *MHE* vol. 14, p. 443, 29 Jun. 1638.

[56] Colonel Semple to Olivares, 8 Jul. 1627, BNM [Biblioteca Nacional, Madrid] Ms. 2359 f.146.

[57] 8 Jun. 1643, Vienna HHSA Sp Korresp fasz 30 f.159.

out with the best intentions, and ended by continuing the very practices that they had begun by condemning.[58]

Spain's military failure was, of course, a failure of resources; but it was much more than that. The terms of armed conflict had turned against Spain in the 17th century. The factors in which Spanish forces had had the advantage in the 16th century - mass, obedience, endurance, prowess - were of less value than mobility, training, and expertise; war was more technical and more technological, the cavalry more important than the infantry, the galleon more important than the galley, the calculations of professionalism more pertinent than the spirit of the warrior. 'Para conquistar es preciso abordar. Para vencer cabe destruir.' (Oquendo) When Oquendo faced Tromp in September 1639 his weakness was not in numbers or size, but in handling, tactics and gunnery. He fought as the Armada had fought in 1588; Tromp fought as the English had. Oquendo wanted to fight *capitana* to *capitana*, as soldier to soldier; Tromp kept the fight at artillery range and, when he had overwhelming odds, sent in the fireships. The Spaniards felt disgusted and cheated ('guerra tan civil como la del incendio', Feixó, 15 November 1639). Such things have deep roots. Olivares undoubtedly knew that, but was, understandably, incapable of remedying it. As Braudel has pointed out, military supremacy is tied up with culture as well as with technology.

Internationalization

The king of Spain's wars were multi-national enterprises that Spain had never had the resources of manpower or expertise to be able to wage alone. The battle zones were cooperative spaces in which hegemony was mitigated. We might postulate, therefore, that the universalization of the front in the 1630s would tend to undermine the hegemony of Spain within the Monarchy, and the years of 'guerra viva' in the Peninsula to undermine the hegemony of Castile within Spain. Throughout the 1630s there was a steady de-Castilianization of the forces based in and remitted from Spain. By 1640 the armies in the Peninsula included Walloons, Burgundians, Germans, Italians, Mallorcans, Irish, even Angolan negroes, and only the minority might be Castilians. Pellicer's account of the Army of Aragon in August 1643 contains 4,000 Aragonese, 2,000 Valencians, 2,500 veterans from Rocroi, 4,000 Neapolitans, 1,500 Walloons, 1,000

---

[58] On the failure to solve the problem of recruiting, in particular, see D.Lope de los Ríos y Guzmán, 31 July 1663, Clonard, *Historia orgánica*, vol. 4, pp. 420-4.

14   SPANISH MILITARY AND NAVAL ORGANIZATION

Burgundians, and 2,000 Andalusians in a total of 24,000.[59] The armadas too were multi-national conglomerates, with squadrons, and their officers, from Dunkirk, Naples, Genoa, Ragusa, as well as English transports, and, of course, the Portuguese and Cantabrian squadrons. The galley fleets had never been predominantly Spanish, but not since the middle of the 16th century had the Spanish component been a smaller proportion. What went for the troops went a fortiori for the commanders, and not just on the battlefield. As generals, viceroys and councillors foreigners had a place in mid 17th-century Spain not paralleled since the reign of Charles V. In the Council of War between 1635 and 1643 one-third of the members were foreigners (mainly Italians and Portuguese), and, although the data are incomplete, nearly as many between 1644 and 1665.[60]

Olivares's ideal of a multi-national Monarchy was never nearer to being a reality than in the middle decades of the 17th century. This had not, I think, so much to do with Olivares's proclaimed policies - it is not for fourteen years that the Council of War had any significant number of non-Spaniards appointed to it - as with the pressing need for financial and military expertise, to reward political loyalty and to enhance the authority of military leaders. The internationalization of the government of Spain was the counterpart to the unprecedented contributions that the rest of the Monarchy was making, and was to make, to its survival.

For Castilians it was a colonization such as they had not experienced since 1517: 'la cossa más nueva que jamás se ha visto en estos Reinos, que es entrar en los Consejos de guerra y hacienda perssonas que no sean vassallos de la Real Corona de V.Mgd'.[61]   Were they to see it as internationalization or as de-Castilianization? Their response (at least that which is best recorded) was, as it was on the earlier occasion, a bitter, 'little Castilianist' resentment of the foreigner's political and military prominence in the government of Spain. 'Ya se vé el estado en que quedará la tierra sin naturales, y en poder de extranjeros y portugueses.'[62]   'Cómo ha de haber buenos sucesos, si quieren que en España

---

[59] Pellicer, *Avisos históricos*, 11 Aug. 1643.

[60] Calculations based on data kindly provided by Dr Patrick Williams.

[61] Andrés de Mena, 'Cargos contra el Conde Duque', *MC 2, pp.233-44*.

[62] *MHE* vol. 16, p. 313.

y Italia nos gobiernen los italianos? y estos los peores.'[63] 'En la guerra las Armas de VM en la maior parte gobernadas por estrangeros, los exercitos formadas de levas de naciones venales y mal seguras, los oficiales casi más que los soldados.'[64]

That prominence was only a symptom, of course, but a very visible and a very painful one. Castilians could not but have perceived that the balance of the Monarchy had been profoundly, and perhaps permanently, altered, and that perception, that displacement of Castile, must have had at least as much to do with the 'mentalidad peninsular de Westfalia', as Alcalá Zamora calls it, as the objective condition of the Monarchy itself.

Provincialization

Whatever the particular emphasis that has been placed on Olivares's concept of 'Unión', there has been no question but that its purpose was to unify. It may be, however, that the real implications of Olivares's policies in the sphere of military organization were just the opposite, and that the consequence of both military organization and military events under his guidance was not to advance the integration of the Monarchy, but to enhance provincialism and to create new institutional forms for the expression of provincial sentiment.

The Union of Arms would not in fact have produced an integrated army but an aggregate of separate, provincial forces, distinct in nationality, composed entirely of natives, with native officers, and with their finances in the hands of native paymasters.

Olivares could well have had in mind the example of the contracts signed with the Cantabrian provinces to serve with their own squadrons in the Armada del Mar Océano. This was certainly the direction that naval reorganization was intended to take, the royal *proposición* to the Cortes in 1623 envisaging 'que para la defensa de la mar se formen esquadras de navíos por provincias'. The squadrons, paid and fitted out by the provinces, were to sail under the province's name, be commanded by native generals, admirals and captains, manned by native seamen, winter in their own province, and, in the Galician case at least, serve provincial interests - 'para la guarda y defensa de la costa del Reyno de

---

[63] *MHE* vol.14, p. 314.

[64] Consejo de Castilla, Nov. 1654, BL Egerton 332 f.288.

16   SPANISH MILITARY AND NAVAL ORGANIZATION

Galicia'.[65] The overall effect, it was recognised, by shaking natives out into their own provincial squadrons, was to provincialize the entire Armada and to weaken the specifically royal component in the fleet. When the Crown tried to assert its own priorities by breaching the contracted conditions relating to appointments and operational procedures, the effect was simply to alienate the province from the royal service. That was the reaction of the *procurador* of Tuy in the Junta de Galicia, in January 1639: 'Seria mas conveniente pedir a su Magd fuese servido permitir que cesase dicha esquadra, porque asta oy no se a conseguido el intento para que la dicha esquadra se ha fabricado, que era para ebadir la obstilidad y inbasiones que los piratas acen en los Puertos de mar deste Reino, inpidiendo la pesqueria hen ellos y cautibando sus naturales, y principalmente Marineros, cossa que benia azer a dichos naturales de notable detrimento, y al serbicio de su Magd le serbia de impedimento, porque oi esperimentamos los mismos daños que entonces sin que tanto gasto como haçe el rreino con dicha esquadra le sirba de Remedio...y abiendose fabricado en su primero fundamento ssolo para que corriera sus costas, en ninguna dellas se a bisto asta oy la dicha esquadra, siquiera para que su bista sirbiera de consuelo a los naturales que tanto gastan en sustentarla y an gastado en su fabrica. Y ssolo sse a bisto en este Puerto de la coruña en donde biene ssolamente a Reforçarse, a llebar gente y ssacar los mantenimientos a la tierra, y a ocupar un ospital con los soldados que bienen enfermos y eridos, haçiendo muchos gastos...todo lo qual es aumentar males al rreino y no remediar ninguno.'[66]

On land, the most remarkable concession to particularism, in the interests of the war effort, was the authority given to the Catalans in 1637 to invade France 'por su cuenta', led by their own captains and annexing any gains 'para su corona'.[67]

Recruiting policy was leading in a similar direction, clear enough in the Crown of Aragon, but apparent to a degree also in Castile. Beginning in the late 1630s, the policy favoured increasingly in the following decades of transforming the militias into 'tercios provinciales', raised, officered, manned and reinforced by natives, with the 'tercio' taking its name, not from its *maestre de campo*, but from its place of origin, gave the component elements of the army a corporate permanence and a sense of association that was patrial rather than personal.

---

[65] AGS GA 900, CCG 12 Jul. 1624.

[66] M. Silva Ferreiro, *Galicia, Voto en Cortes* (Santiago de Compostela, 1925), p. 105.

[67] *MHE* vol. 14, p. 157, 20 Jul. 1637.

The very experience of war, especially of frontier provinces like Galicia, Extremadura and Andalusia, the demands on them for men and money, their unique suffering as war zones, heightened their feelings of exploitation and sharpened their sense of separateness.[68] This comes across most vividly in the detailed tally they kept of their services, usually presented to justify some alleviation of their burdens.[69] Army structure tended to reinforce this by taking on provincial forms, so that the war became a local war, locally financed and supplied. The most striking illustration of this symbiosis is the attempt by Leganés, as Captain General of the Army of Extremadura, to convoke an assembly of Extremaduran towns in 1645, followed, two years later, by another proposal, this time by Cáceres, to establish a Junta of the province.[70]

It was, significantly, as *provinces* that Galicia and Extremadura, by their contributions to the war effort, acquired their votes in the Cortes. But everywhere the intolerable burdens of war forced localities to think first of themselves and what was best for them and their regions, rather than of the generality, a process not, of course, stopping at provincial borders. The thought in Andalusia of breaking away from Castile altogether was the ultimate response, but there were worries about the loyalty of Extremadura and Galicia also.[71]

It may be, therefore, that one of the consequences of the war and the forms of military organization needed to sustain it, was a narrowing of mental horizons, not only the retreat of 'Spain' in the face of an Aragonese *neo-foralismo* in the second half of the century, but also a retreat of 'Castile', fragmented by its own internal particularisms. The abandonment of the Cortes of Castile was perhaps the clearest symptom of that fragmentation.

'Refeudalization'?

---

[68] 'Digo en suma que nuestra Extremadura está acabada', *MHE* vol. 16, p. 203, 25 Dec. 1641.

[69] Extremadura, BL Egerton 332 f.124; Guipúzcoa 1648, BL Add. 13,998 f.113; 'El Reyno de Galicia. Memorial y Relacion a S.Md. representando los largos y particulares servicios que ha hecho en cosas Militares de la guerra de Portugal', 24 Mar.1665, BL Egerton 346 ff.349-87v.

[70] I owe much of my information on Extremadura to the extremely informative and revealing PhD dissertation of Dr Lorraine G. White, 'War and government in a Castilian province: Extremadura 1640-1668', University of East Anglia, 1986.

[71] White, 'Extremadura 1640-1668', p. 367; Contarini 1641, Barozzi & Berchet, *Relazioni*, vol. 2, p. 104.

18   SPANISH MILITARY AND NAVAL ORGANIZATION

'En pleno siglo XVII había que hacer la guerra con huestes señoriales'.[72] Is it permissible to describe the developments in military organization that took place in the 1630s as a 'refeudalization' of war, and did war contribute to a more general 'refeudalization' of government and society in the 17th century?

Some definitions are called for. 1. 'Refeudalization' is not synonymous with 'seigneurial reaction'; the impetus can come from above as well as from below. 2. 'Refeudalization' will take forms specific to the nature of feudalism in any given society. In Castile it will take, predominantly, the forms of the *señorío*, rather than, say, the forms of the manor; it will be based on authority rather than on obligations, and may be corporate as well as aristocratic. 3. The concept 'refeudalization' applies to a general readjustment of social forces in the 17th century; but in specifically administrative terms it refers to a shift towards a form of government in which 'state' action is mediated through local agents whose authority derives from their own power in the locality, rather than exercised by agents whose local power derives from the authority of the 'state'.

The aspects of military organization particularly relevant here are: 1. the reassertion by the Crown of the personal and collective obligations of service and vassallage ('la obligación que le corre del servicio y vasallage que tengo en estos Reynos como Rey i señor natural'); 2. the employment of the local magnate in posts of military command; 3. the reliance on señorial administration, influence and resources for the raising of men.

Arguably, it was precisely a 'refeudalization' of war that Olivares was trying to bring about. He looked to revive the ideals of a society that ennobled its *bellatores*. He wanted a warrior aristocracy, creating in the *coronelías* of 1631-2 a form of military organization appropriate to the 17th century in which grandees and *títulos* would lead their followers personally onto the field in support of the king, in regiments that bore their names and carried their banners. He recalled the personal military services owed by *hidalgos* and *caballeros* in return for their privileges and was in principle hostile to their substitution or commutation. In his paper of 4 February 1634 he set out a complete blueprint for the employment of the great magnates in military commands in the areas of their greatest personal following, a blueprint which was in large part applied after 1636 with the appointment of Cardona, Santa Coloma, Los Vélez, Pobar in Catalonia, Medina Sidonia, Béjar, Alba on the Portuguese frontier, the Condestable and the Almirante in Old Castile and Cantabria, etc.

---

[72] Domínguez Ortiz, 'Movilización', p. 813.

None of these devices worked with any marked degree of success, largely because most of the nobility did not want to be 'refeudalized', at least not on Olivares's terms, nor did they directly alter the balance of military power between Crown and aristocracy. The aristocratic levies had no separate existence once they were absorbed into the royal army, and the independence of the magnate captains general was constrained by the supervision of royal staff-officers. From 1642 the marcher lords ceased to be appointed ex officio, as it were, to command the armies on their frontiers. Thereafter field commanders were chosen by the king without specific regard to their territorial affiliations.

However, if the control of military force was not refeudalized, a great deal of military organization was, the Condestable, for one, as Capitán General de España, exercising widespread authority in the north-east of Old Castile during the 1640s and 50s; and if the top ranks of the army were the king's, lower down the captains and lesser officials, sometimes even the *maestres de campo*, were local men, nominees, if not direct appointments, of the lords or cities. That largely seems to have been the case with both the Galician and the Extremaduran levies, as well as with the *tercios* raised by Madrid, for example.[73]

The reliance on the aristocracy to recruit men on their own estates and in the areas in which they had influence that Olivares had systematically developed after 1631, continued throughout the war, extending the administrative action of the noble concerned into areas of royal and ecclesiastical jurisdiction.[74] These duties were costly and burdensome, much disliked and frequently resisted - as no doubt feudal obligations had always been; but on the other side of the scales have to be placed the compensations and the concessions, the *ayudas de costa*, the

---

[73] *Regidor* D.Francisco de Luzón, *maestre de campo* ot Madrid's *tercio* of 20 companies, 1642.

[74] AM [Archivo Municipal] Soria, Libro de Acuerdos 11 no.2, f.134, 27 Jun.1644; 11 no.3 s.f., 7 Jul.1645; 12 f.182, 20 Jan. 1659; requests of Soria to Condestable 'para que aga merced a esta ciudad y tierra de quitarle alguna cantidad de soldados de los que se le an repartido para esta leva, atento sus necesidades y falta de jente y tener el agosto en las manos' (as 7 Jul.1645).

20 SPANISH MILITARY AND NAVAL ORGANIZATION

mercedes, the licences to break *mayorazgos*, the suspension of *pleitos*, particularly over *alcabalas*, the patronage, the extra exercise of local power.[75] We are dealing, in other words, with a balance of profit or loss on a transaction between Crown and aristocracy. The question is simply whether the *señor*'s position was strengthened or weakened by the military-administrative functions that were demanded of him, and to what extent his authority suffered from the encroachment of royal *corregidores* and *jueces de comisión* executing militia and 'presidio' levies in the *señorío*, and from his inability to protect his vassals from them.

The crucial issue is the balance of power within society, and that is a question less of the direct relationship between Crown and aristocracy than of the power that relationship gave the aristocracy over the other elements of the local community. The Crown's need for a cooperative, solvent and respected aristocracy to organize and finance its military levies gave it a powerful incentive to support a lord against his vassals, against his creditors, against the fisc, or indeed against its own justice.[76] As the Duke of Medina Celi insisted in 1655, 'El Rey es mas ynteressado en la authoridad de sus grandes que en la Zerimonia de sus juezes'.[77]

Developments in military organization were, of course, only one factor. Other war-related phenomena are also important, such as the multiplication of *señoríos*, the acquisition of fiscal rights, the purchase of royal offices by the *señor*, both in his own *lugares* and in the *realengo*, or, though less directly, the retreat of royal justice, and the revival of clientage in the cities as impoverished *regidores*

---

[75] For some examples, I.Atienza Hernández. '"Refeudalización" en Castilla durante el Siglo XVII: ¿Un tópico', *Anuario de Historia del Derecho Español* 56 (1986): 889-918, at p. 900 note 43; L.I.Alvarez de Toledo (Duquesa de Medina Sidonia), *Historia de una conjura* (Cadiz, 1985), p.118; Osuna's brother accused of 'insultos' whilst recruiting on Osuna estates, *CODOIN* 95, p.169; complaints of abuses by Oviedo in *repartimiento* and *paga* of levy, *Actas de las Juntas de Asturias* 3, p.220; use of the militia as an instrument of revenge by the *caballeros* of Córdoba after the disturbances there, 'para poder conseguir esta tiranía se han valido de estas milicias,' 11 Jul.1652, A.Domínguez Ortiz, *Alteraciones andaluzas* (Madrid, 1973), p.202; Junta de Galicia, 1676, bishops to intervene in local *repartimientos* 'para que se execute con igualdad y no sean oprimidos los pobres de los poderosos,' E.Fernández Villamil, *Juntas del Reino de Galicia*, 3 vols. (Madrid, 1962), vol. 3, p. 196 note 94.

[76] A.Domínguez Ortiz, *Política y hacienda de Felipe IV* (Madrid, 1960), pp.201-2, 56; R.Benítez Sánchez-Blanco, 'Expulsión de los mudéjares y reacción señorial en la serranía de Villaluenga', *Andalucía Moderna (Siglos XVI-XVII)*, 2 vols. (Córdoba, 1978), vol. 1, pp. 116-7; Atienza Hernández, '"Refeudalización"', p. 907.

[77] BL Egerton 347 f.170.

looked to service in aristocratic administrations.[78] It is, however, not without interest and relevance that the case for reviving the military contributions of the barons and the municipalities should have been so much favoured by none other than that arch- 'constitutionalist', Juan de Mariana.[79]

Privatization

The outstanding characteristic of the reign of Philip IV is the withdrawal of the state from the majority of administrative functions connected with military and naval organization. In the areas of procurement and naval administration the predominance of private over public administration is almost total.

Although the long-running argument over *administración* or *asiento* had still not been definitively resolved at the accession of Philip IV, the administrative practice of the reign was unequivocal. The provisioning of the armadas, the galleys and the African *presidios*, munitions procurement, shipbuilding and fleet organization, and the victualling of the armies for Catalonia and Portugal were effected almost exclusively by *asiento*. Olivares's own position was typical of that of the majority of counsellors, paying homage to the ideal of direct royal administration but at the same time actively promoting the reduction of direct governmental involvement: 'que no duda de que sería mejor hazerse las provisiones por administración que por asiento si el dinero se anticipa y los ministros hazen lo que deven en el exercicio de sus officios, pero que rezela que no todas vezes cumplen con esta obligación...y aunque como queda dicho sería lo mejor que corriese por los ministros todavia la experiencia ha mostrado que lo que combiene es que sea por asiento'.[80]

This was not, of course, the first reign to use *asientos*, but it was the first to be so totally committed to them. The direct administrative action of Crown officials was largely limited to the gaps between the breakdown of one contract and the commencement of the next, and to casual or to exceptional cases

---

[78] AM Salamanca, Actas 1673 f.134-5, 12 Jul.1673, *regidor* D.Joseph Martin wants city's support for his application for office with the Conde de Ayala, 'sus cortos medios, motivos de su pretension'; another *regidor*, D.Francisco de Barrientos y Solis, was *corregidor* of the Conde de Monterrey at the same time. In 1681 the Junta de Galicia claimed that now all the rents were owned by the Church, *títulos* and *grandes*, the ordinary nobility of Galicia, having been ruined in the royal service, Fernández Villamil, *Juntas de Galicia*, vol. 3, p. 13.

[79] *Del Rey y de la Institución Real*, ch.5 'Del Arte Militar'.

[80] AGS GA 889, CCG 2 Nov. 1623.

peculiarly favourable to *administración* (the Cartagena powder works, for example). What was more original, though again not without precedents in the late 16th century (Tomasso Fiesco, Juan Pascual), was a general policy of what might be called centralized privatization. The preferred procedure seems to have been to concentrate administrative and financial functions in the hands of a single, private or semi-private intermediary: Manuel Gómez de Acosta, 'Factor de las Provisiones de la Armada del Mar Océano, las Galeras de España, y la Armada del Estrecho'; Bartolomé Spínola, 'Factor General'; the Marqués del Monasterio, 'Tesorero y Proveedor General de los Presidios'; Antonio Graffior, 'Administrador General de la Pólvora en Castilla'; Martín Ladrón de Guevara, 'Factor General de Armadas', who had a contract in 1642 for 1,200.000 ducats to maintain the entire Ocean Fleet. All of these men were foreigners, Genoese and Portuguese, as were practically all the principal military contractors prior to the establishment of the Army of Extremadura. The policy may have been designed in order to facilitate control, or perhaps it was simply a reflection of a new balance of administrative power. One gets the impression that Olivares was a good deal happier working with the entrepreneur than with the bureaucrat, and a good deal more sympathetic toward him.[81]

Given the stated political preference for *administración* among most elements of government, the *asiento* was clearly a victory for administrative expediency. As an administrative practice, therefore, *asiento* must have seemed 'better', though such an evaluation was, and is, not an easy one, both advantages and disadvantages not always showing in the account books. What is more interesting, is what privatization implied for the functioning of the state as a system of government and what it reveals about Olivares's view of the nature of government authority.

It can be argued that what mattered was ultimate royal control, and that administrative devolution was by no means incompatible with the maintenance of such control, by means of inspection and audit in the case of the contractors, by the despatch of judges on commission and the royal appointment of officers and field-commissars in the case of the grandees and local authorities.

The defence of the *asiento* system and, indeed, of the competence and conscientiousness of the entire Spanish bureaucracy - and that would have elicited an interesting retort from the Conde Duque! - has recently been undertaken by

---

[81] Olivares in CCG 12 Dec.1622, 'que es justo que al asentista se le de satisfacion y se le pague lo que se le deviere, porque por las cartas que se an visto se juzga que no ha sido por culpa suya, sino de los tiempos forzosos que an corrido, el no aver dado las vituallas necesarias para sustento de la Armada,' AGS GA 876.

C.R.Phillips in a study of the shipbuilding contract taken with Martín de Arana in 1625.[82] This was the kind of contract with the least 'political' significance, but even so, what I find revealing about it is first, the number of failings and deviations from the specifications of the contract that the inspectorate had to condone - excessive tonnage, inadequate cables, light anchors, thin masts, shortage of sails, and one of the six ships so defective it had to be sold as 'not being appropriate for warfare';[83] and, second, how quickly the contractual relationship became litigious - disputes started within two months of beginning work.[84]

The relationship of order and obedience of *administración* was replaced in the *asiento* by reciprocal obligation and legal adjudication. In the light of Olivares's inveterate distrust of the bureaucracy of ministers and lesser officials and his repeated complaints about their lack of compliance with royal orders, one can detect throughout his administrative policy the search for a more precisely defined, and therefore more readily sanctionable, basis for 'obediencia' than could be imposed on the existing structure of military field-administration (semi-stipendiary, patrimonial, patrial, venal) with its service ideology of personal fidelity. 'Los españoles somos muy buenos debajo de rigurosa obediencia, mas en consentiéndonos somos los peores de todos.'[85] The common theme in the *asientos*, the 30,000 soldiers scheme, the reestablishment of the militia, the Union of Arms, the 'dotación de presidios', the commutation of the *lanzas* and, ultimately, the *jornada* of the king to the front is the determination to establish everywhere, either by explicit compact or by the reassertion of customary and traditional duties, an unambiguous obligation, not only of formal obedience ('obedecer') but also of compliance ('cumplir'), that was judicially enforceable. 'Conviene que el Consejo declare a V.M. lo que en justicia puede y debe mandar en la ocasión presente a todos sus vasallos sin excepción ninguna en todas partes, y como es caso en que ninguno puede excusarse ni dilatar el ir a servir a V.M. donde y como juzgare y fuere servido, y a la primera orden de los Consejos de Estado y Guerra de V.M., y las penas en que ipso facto sin apelación ni remisión incurra sin poder ser oído, porque el estado presente es tan

---

[82] *Six Galleons for the King of Spain* (1986).

[83] *Ibid.*, pp. 84-89, 189.

[84] *Ibid.*, pp. 55, 64, 66.

[85] *MC* 2, p. 76.

apretada que cualquiera breve dilación descaminará todo...'[86]   Even customary obligations, without ever being negated, were not weakened by being recast in the obligation of a formal accord.[87]

For Olivares 'obligation' seems to have been elevated from a principle into an instrument of government. The function of the state was simply to secure compliance with those obligations. Its role was essentially judicial, rather than executive, and its agents preponderantly judges, the arbiters of obligation and obedience; whence the perception of contemporaries that 'now letrados have become the grandees'.[88] Faced with massive administrative and organizational demands, Olivares retreated to a stolidly conservative conception of the role of government.

The demands of war first exposed, and then accentuated, the weaknesses in the apparatus of the state. The *corregidor*, on the one hand, and the long-established, though now greatly expanded, use of the councillor or *oidor* sent on mission as a sort of government trouble-shooter, were the twin pillars of royal government in the localities. Neither was without its limitations. The judges on mission functioned best in a judicial and transactional capacity as investigators and negotiators; they were too remote and occasional to be equally effective as administrators. The *corregidores*, on the other hand, were unreliable - 'Algunos tiene V.M. buenos, pero no muchos'.[89] Usually *regidores* of other cities themselves, they seemed often to be allies rather than managers of their *regidores*, as is suggested by the frequent requests of the cities that their terms of office be extended (very different from 1520). Instead of locking the *corregiduría* into the hierarchy of bureaucratic promotion, as the 'Gran Memorial' urged, the office tended to be used as a *merced* for *procuradores de Cortes*, and central control was seriously relaxed by the restoration to the *corregidores* in 1632 of the right to appoint their *tenientes*.

None of the existing instruments of local government was, therefore, entirely suitable for a permanent role in military organization. The judges on mission

---

[86] Olivares 4 Feb. 1634, *MC* 2, p. 115.

[87] *ACC* vol. 56, p. 52, RC 29 Jan.1639, confirming 'el acuerdo que el reyno hizo sobre los soldados para los presidios', 'aunque esto no depende de consentimiento sino de la obligacion que le corre nacida del servicio y vassalage que tengo en estos Reynos como Rey i señor natural.'

[88] C.Jago, 'The "Crisis of the Aristocracy" in Seventeenth-Century Castile', *Past and Present* 84 (1979): 60-90, at p.62.

[89] *MC* 1, p. 64, 25 Dec. 1624.

were remote and temporary, the *sargentos mayores* of the militias generally themselves members of the local ruling oligarchies and the subject of many complaints,[90] and the *justicias ordinarias* too tied up with local power groups, and if lawyers, professionally hostile to military jurisdiction and militia exemptions. Too often the levies of the lords were blocked by the local justices and by the competing demands of the municipal levies. The fragmentation of jurisdictions impeded military efficiency as much as it impeded justice. The consequences were spelled out by the Duque de San Germán in a paper probably written near the end of the reign: 'queriendo ocurrir su Magd a una promta defenssa para las levas ordinarias se encuentran con las dificultades que se experimentan, y si se quiere valer de las Justizias ordinarias suzeden menoscabos mui perjudiciales, o sea por la poca ynteligenzia, pasion o ynteres con que yncurren en el daño comun, sin que su Magd consiga el servizio que se neçesita, y si se embian ministros de authoridad y celosos, por no tener el conoçimiento de cada lugar no pueden conseguir lo que se desea con la brebedad que combiene.'[91]

The traditional judge on mission had been the only active solution Olivares had offered for this problem. Instead of new agencies to close the gap between centre and locality, the devolution of military-administrative functions upon local authorities and private entrepreneurs actually inhibited the development of a royal administration in the field, and in some cases dismantled elements of those agencies that already existed.[92] The increasing evidence for the sale of royal offices in military administration from the late 1630s is perhaps an indication of their functional marginalization.[93] There is no movement here towards the development of an 18th-century 'administrative absolutism'. It was left to ministers after Olivares to experiment (not always successfully) with executive measures (*superintendentes de milicias*, local militia treasuries, military

---

[90] Archivo Histórico Provincial Soria, Universidad de la Tierra, Caja 3467 f.27, Acuerdo 3 Sept.1638 to protest against the *sargento mayor* of Soria's milítia 'por los muchos excesos q a hecho en las ocasiones q se an ofrecido de sacar jente de las compañías de milicia, llebando muchas sumas y cuantidades de dineros por librar unos y poner otros, con general escandalo de toda la republica.'

[91] BL Egerton 332 f.132.

[92] Thompson, *War and Government*, p. 339 note 83.

[93] For some of these, F.Gil Ayuso (ed.), *Junta de Incorporaciones* (Madrid, 1934), no.966/23; A.Domínguez Ortiz, 'La venta de cargos y oficios públicos en Castilla y sus consecuencias económicas y sociales', *Anuario de Historia Económica y Social* 3 (1970): 105-37, at p. 133; AGS GA 3302, CCG 11 Jul.1650.

IV

governors) to remedy the disarticulation between central and local government. 'The advisability in these present times of combining political and military government is apparent, because of the obstacles which usually occur as a result of the conflict of jurisdictions,' was Philip IV's own assessment in 1644.[94]

Olivares (as, indeed, practically everybody else) identified the crux of the problem clearly enough: the gap between central command and local compliance, the failure of the *poderosos*, the *regidores*, the *corregidores* and other 'ministros inferiores' to put royal orders into effect - 'los enemigos de la Patria, los poderosos de los lugares y los perversos ministros de V.Md inferiores'. The inability to close this gap, the lack of a coherent policy to articulate central and local government, was the head and tail of Olivares's failure as a reforming minister. This seems to me the real lesson of military organization in this period.

---

[94] White, 'Extremadura 1640-1668', p. 348.

V

THE APPOINTMENT OF
THE DUKE OF MEDINA SIDONIA TO THE COMMAND
OF THE SPANISH ARMADA

THE death of the marquis of Santa Cruz (9 February 1588) left the Spanish Armada leaderless. On 14 February, for reasons that have never seemed remotely satisfactory, Philip II named Don Alonso Pérez de Guzman el Bueno, 7th duke of Medina Sidonia, to take his place. Medina Sidonia has been universally regarded rather like a rabbit pulled mystifyingly out of a hat by the king to the amazement of rabbit, spectators, and historians alike. Attempts to explain the appointment have been half-hearted and, until some recent revaluations of the duke's administrative abilities, have concentrated overwhelmingly on his character and social position. Portrayed as an amiable poltroon, loyal, unassuming, and characterless, utterly devoid of military experience but not too proud to be guided entirely by his expert advisers, he was just the man to do what he was told without questioning the instructions of the real admiral of the Armada in the Escorial, or cavilling at his subordination to the supreme commander of the invasion forces, the duke of Parma—issues which had already embittered relations between the king and the marquis of Santa Cruz. At the same time, personal jealousies among Santa Cruz's leading lieutenants, the refusal of the military to accept seamen on equal terms, and the presence in the Armada of a large number of titled and class-conscious gentlemen-adventurers all meant that the new commander had to be an outsider, a landsman, and a nobleman so illustrious that nobody need be ashamed to obey him or take precedence behind him. As the premier duke in Spain, Medina Sidonia's social qualifications were impeccable.[1] Some historians have pointed to the duke's religious devoutness as a further recommendation, others have wondered whether his promotion were not a sentimental memento of an extinct romance between Philip and the duke's mother-in-law.

Indeed, it may well have suited both Englishman and Spaniard to think of Medina Sidonia's appointment as a grotesque aberration. For the English, it epitomized Spanish hubris—that an amateur gentleman from the olive groves of Port St Mary (Drake's phrase, but it was not even Medina Sidonia's town)

---

[1] These views are to be found in all the major works on the Armada from Fernández Duro to Mattingly, and beyond. There is little point in cluttering the notes with bibliographical references most of which are already sufficiently well known, or which have no value except as expressions of attitudes. Bibliographical information may be found *via* Garrett Mattingly, *The Defeat of the Spanish Armada* (1959). I have used the Penguin edition (1962), from which subsequent references have been taken.

could match England's sea-dog professionals. It permitted an interpretation that, rejecting the contemporary faith in divine intervention, could both magnify the odds between the Spanish giant and little England and portray the result as the victory of the skills and spirit of a nation over a cynical reliance on money and material. For the Spaniard, the failure had to be a personal one. After all the successes of the sixteenth century, how could a Spaniard believe that God had been on Elizabeth's side?[2] Medina Sidonia was, from all points of view, the obvious scapegoat. It was either impolitic or unpatriotic to blame Philip II, the most Catholic and most Spanish of the Habsburgs. Anti-Philippists, on the other hand, accepted the unsuitability of Medina Sidonia as evidence of the king's imprudence, his 'lack of perspective or proportion', his preference for the mediocre lest his own mediocrity be exposed.[3] If, as is asserted, the same incomprehension and astonishment had been expressed at the time of the appointment, there might be nothing further to say.[4] In fact, this universal surprise is a fabrication. Contemporaries were not at all surprised, nor were they shocked. The command of the Armada was, after all, only the last of a long list of honours conferred on Medina Sidonia by the king: the temporary captaincy-general of the cavalry and infantry of Andalusia and the governorship of Milan in 1580, the Order of the Golden Fleece and the captaincy-general of the expedition against Larache in 1581.[5] As early as 1575, he had been thought of as a replacement for Don John of Austria as supreme commander at sea,[6] and in 1580 he had apparently been proposed by some as commander of the expedition against Portugal.[7] Two years later rumour had it that he was to be made 'general de la mar' (i.e. Mediterranean) and sent to capture Algiers[8]. In March 1586 he was being talked about by 'those who know' as the general of the Spaniards should the expedition against England take place.[9] The next year, after the relief of Cadiz, he was created captain general of Andalusia as a 'conspicuous proof' of the king's pleasure,[10] and in August, when he arrived at Court, it was a 'very general opinion that he will be made a member of the secret council and appointed to other posts'.[11] Naturally, when in February 1588 Medina

---

[2] Duque de Maura, *El designio de Felipe II* (Madrid, 1957), p. 278.

[3] E.g. R. Altamira, *Felipe II. Hombre de Estado* (Mexico, 1950), pp. 112–13; G. Marañón, *Antonio Pérez* (4th ed. Madrid, 1952), I, 45, 47; C. J. Cadoux, *Philip of Spain and the Netherlands* (1947), p. 114.

[4] J. A. Froude, *The Spanish story of the Armada* (1892), p. 22; David Loth, *Philip II of Spain* (1932), p. 251; R. B. Merriman, *The rise of the Spanish Empire*, (New York, 1934), IV, 528; Marañón, op. cit. I, 198 (repeated by P. Aguado Bleye, *Manual de historia de España* 9th ed. Madrid, 1964, II, 648); Thomas Woodrooffe, *The Enterprise of England* (1958), p. 221.

[5] For details of Medina Sidonia's career see Maura op. cit. and C. Fernández Duro, *La Armada Invencible* (Madrid, 1884), I, 219–36.

[6] See below, p. 209.

[7] Luis Fernández y Fernández de Retana, *España en tiempo de Felipe II (1556–1598)* (Madrid, 1958), II, 259.

[8] Biblioteca Nacional, Madrid, MS. 1761 fol. 101.

[9] C[alendar of] S[tate] P[apers] Venetian VIII, 148, 159.

[10] Ibid. p. 273.   [11] Ibid. p. 307.

Sidonia replaced Santa Cruz, neither Lippomano, the Venetian ambassador in Madrid, nor Stafford in Paris, nor Stephen Powle in Rome gave any indication of astonishment.[12] Lippomano, hearing the news of Santa Cruz's death on 13 February as he was completing his despatch, penned a hurried postscript, 'They say that the king will give the post of commander-in-chief to the Duke of Medina Sidonia, a prince of many parts, in spite of his never having been to sea.'[13] On the 19th, he wrote more consideredly, 'This nobleman is the first Grandee of Spain; he has excellent qualities, and is generally beloved. He is not only prudent and brave, but of a nature of extreme goodness and benignity. He will be followed by many nobles, and by all Andalusia. Only one might desire in him a wider experience of the sea, but all other possible appointments presented greater difficulties.'[14] Lippomano's assessment undoubtedly may have been influenced by the fact that he was 'under great obligations' to the duke,[15] but his predecessor, Vincenzo Gradenigo, who seems not to have known the duke personally, also reported that he was universally considered 'a diligent and prudent gentleman'.[16]

The disparity between the contemporary response and that of historians three centuries or more later stems I think from four sources: 1. a misinterpretation of the strategic methods and objectives of the Armada, or at least a serious oversimplification of its political purpose; 2. a large degree of ignorance of Medina Sidonia's career before 1588; 3. a naïve and uncritical acceptance of Medina Sidonia's famous letter of self-abnegation of 16 February;[17] 4. a tendency to read back the defeat of the Armada to the appointment of its commander by assuming that but for his personal defects the Armada would have been Invincible.

Possibly because Spaniards have generally found the subject distasteful, the English have monopolized Armada historiography and anglicized the Armada campaign. The objectives of the Armada have seemed self-evident—the invasion and conquest of England as an end in itself[18]—and the debates have concentrated mainly on the battle. Even Mattingly, for all his excellent treatment of diplomacy in Paris and Rome, makes no mention of the almost equally important negotiations in Constantinople, Morocco, and Scotland, nor of the crucial significance of Portugal in Spain's strategic thinking. The full Spanish story of the Armada has yet to be told and, although this is not

[12] Ibid. pp. 339, 340; C.S.P. Foreign XXI, 533, 569, 572.
[13] A better rendering than the translation in C.S.P. Venetian VIII, 339.
[14] C.S.P. Venetian VIII, 340.   [15] Ibid. p. 327.
[16] Ibid. p. 148. Parma also expressed his approval of the appointment (C.S.P. Spanish IV, 237), and Madrid's reply to Medina Sidonia, 20 Feb. 1588, claimed 'ha sido por extremo loada la eleçion...' (E. Herrera Oria, ed., La Armada Invencible, Archivo Histórico Español, II, Valladolid, 1929, p. 148).
[17] Even Mattingly accepts it at face value, op. cit. p. 222.
[18] One consequence of this has been the exaggerated importance given to the execution of Mary Queen of Scots as the essential precondition of the expedition. But the political objectives of the Armada did not depend on the deposition of Elizabeth.

V

the place to tell it, the qualities required of the new commander-in-chief can only be understood within the context of what the English Enterprise was intended to achieve and the particular problems that faced Philip II in February 1588.

II

The whole question of the appropriateness of Medina Sidonia's appointment has been confounded by this assumption that the sole objective of the Armada was the military conquest of England.[19] Invasion had to be on the cards, but it is arguable that success was not expected, had not always been intended, and certainly did not need to come in that way.[20] Contrast Medina Sidonia's meticulous sailing instructions with the almost complete absence of plans for the land campaign or for a political settlement in the event of victory. Philip's overriding objective was not to conquer England but to stop English interference in his affairs,[21] to compel Elizabeth to withdraw from the Nether-lands, from the Indies, and from support of the Portuguese pretender by making her concentrate her forces for her own protection, tie her fleet, or part of it, down to permanent coastguard service, and involve herself in heavy defence expenditures, or sue for peace.[22] For years every rumoured con-centration of Spanish shipping had caused panic in England, now it was

[19] M. Oppenheim, Introduction to Book I of Monson's Tracts, Navy Records Society, XXII (1902), 25, 'For Philip, then, the subjugation of England was always the objective.' G. J. Marcus, A Naval History of England (1961), I, 92, 'In order to arrive at a proper understanding of the course of the Armada campaign it is necessary to bear in mind that the true object of Spanish strategy in 1588 was the military conquest of England...'

[20] It is too often forgotten that the invasion of England was only one of many invasion plans (De Lamar Jensen notes 15 between January 1586 and July 1588, 'Franco-Spanish Diplomacy and the Armada', in From the Renaissance to the Counter-Reformation. Essays in Honor of Garrett Mattingly, ed. by Charles H. Carter, New York, 1965, p. 210) most of which concentrated on seizing a foothold in some peripheral area to establish a permanent diversion and possible stepping-stone from which to threaten England itself. (See Mendoza's cogent arguments in favour of supporting a rising from Scotland, well set out in J. R. Elder, Spanish Influences in Scottish History, Glasgow, 1920, pp. 134–6.) Ireland was considered the best prospect and the one that Philip himself seems to have preferred (C.S.P. Venetian VIII, 192), and as late as the autumn of 1587 it was Ireland where the first blow was to have been struck (Maura, op. cit. pp. 167, 169, 171; G. P. B. Naish, Documents illustrating the history of the Spanish Armada, The Naval Miscellany, IV, Navy Records Society, XCII, 1952, 8).

[21] Philip II certainly did not want England for himself and knew he could not possibly govern it personally (Naish, op. cit. p. 3). The candidacy of his daughter Isabella might have provided one solution, and undoubtedly the re-Catholicizing of England would have been very welcome, both on religious grounds and as a moral justification which could also win Papal support and funds and shame the Catholic French king into non-intervention. But faced with the much more immediate problems of heresy in the Netherlands and in France Philip had consistently resisted all pressures to start crusading in England. Now, as then, any attempt to annex England was obviously foolhardy. Militarily it was likely to open for Spain another ulcer like the one in the Netherlands; diplomatically no French king could ever accept it. The ideal policy was to loose upon England insurrection. If the Catholics deposed Elizabeth, all to the good; if they did not, with small injections of Spanish encourage-ment England would be neutralized by a prolonged civil war just as France had been. For Granvelle's lucid statement of this position see Martin Hume, 'The Evolution of the Spanish Armada', in The Year after the Armada (1896), pp. 187–8.

[22] C.S.P. Venetian VIII, 224.

V

necessary for Philip to prove that he was able to put an Armada to sea, that the threat was a real one.[23] For a man reputedly as afraid of war as a child was of fire, the ideal success would be diplomatic.[24] But was not the threat of war diplomacy also?—as the Venetian ambassador put it, 'vigorous preparations for war are the surest way to secure favourable terms of peace'.[25] With the Armada in the Channel, it was not impossible that the English Catholics would rise; that would be enough,[26] Elizabeth would have to treat seriously.[27] The *first* task of the Armada was to parade, to sail up the Channel and beat its chest before England's gates.[28] What mattered most was that it should look imposing, hence the inflation of its size by including as many ships as possible, however unserviceable, and exaggerating the number of troops by issuing false muster rolls, all duly printed and publicized by an official propaganda machine.[29]

Thus the real task for any new commander in February 1588 was to put the fleet to sea. The Armada had to sail in 1588, and it had to sail early. If it could not leave Lisbon before the English were ready, it might be bottled up again as Drake had bottled it up in 1587 and the junction with Parma in the Netherlands would never be possible.[30] To lose a third campaigning season would be intolerable. Too many opportunities had been wasted already,[31] and every delay enabled Elizabeth to strengthen her defences,[32] enlarge her navy, and strive for the breaking of the diplomatic vacuum without which an invasion of England dare not be risked. An English ambassador was in Constantinople urging on the Sultan a diversionary attack on the Spanish empire and, if the

[23] Ibid. p. 338; Herrera Oria, op. cit. p. 210.
[24] C.S.P. Foreign xx, 609; C.S.P. Venetian viii, 182, 224.
[25] C.S.P. Venetian viii, 172, 242, 238, 192.
[26] Ibid. pp. 309, 313.
[27] Neither side believed the other was sincere in its desire for peace. For English attitudes to the peace negotiations with Parma see Conyers Read, *Lord Burghley and Queen Elizabeth* (New York, 1960), pp. 396–407.
[28] Lippomano reported that it was thought likely that Drake, on Elizabeth's orders, would refuse battle, and Spain would then claim the honours and at the same time secure the safety of the fleet, her coasts, the Azores, and the Canaries. C.S.P. Venetian viii, 281.
[29] Fernández Duro, op. cit. i, 452, 473, 496; Mattingly, op. cit. pp. 264–5. The implications were fully spelled out by Philip in the sealed letter Medina Sidonia was to deliver to Parma, 'Si lo que Dios no permita, el suceso no fuese tan próspero que las armas lo puedan allanar, ni tan contrario que frente al enemigo de cuidado (lo cual, mediante Dios, no será) y se contrapesen las cosas de manera que se vea que no desconviene la paz, en este caso, procurando ayudaros de la reputación de la Armada y lo que más pudiéredes, advertid que fuera de las condiciones ordinarias...han de ser tres las principales en que se ha de poner la mira...', quoted in Carlos Ibáñez de Ibero, 'Algunas consideraciones sobre política naval de España y organización de sus Armadas en la segunda mitad del siglo XVI', *Anales de la Academia de ciencias morales y políticas* (Madrid, 1955), p. 332 n. 60.
[30] Herrera Oria, op. cit. p. 120; C.S.P. Venetian viii, 334.
[31] C.S.P. Venetian viii, 209, 338. Did these lost opportunities also include the million gold ducats the Pope had promised if the expedition was carried out in 1587?—see the terms of the agreement of 29 July 1587, printed as appendix 20 to A. O. Meyer, *England and the Catholic Church under Queen Elizabeth* (1967 edition).
[32] C.S.P. Spanish iv, 200 no. 209; C.S.P. Venetian viii, 329, 348. Nobody seemed to realize that delay might hurt Elizabeth also.

negotiations between the Persians and the Turks produced peace, he might yet be successful.[33] France for the moment was effectively neutralized by civil war, but the situation was inherently unstable, and who could say what turn the fortunes of any of the contenders would take in the next few months.[34] Neither Navarre, Henry III, nor the Guises could be expected to favour an unqualified Spanish victory. The king of Scotland, whose support had still not been despaired of, was unlikely to hold out much longer against English offers 'seeing that he is merely entertained with promises' by the Spaniard.[35]

Besides, every month the Armada delayed was costing Philip 700,000 ducats,[36] and the diversion of resources from Seville to Lisbon was disastrous for the Indies trade. Outgoing tonnage in 1587 was only 9 per cent of that of the previous year and was never to be as low again until 1650.[37] The consequences were to become obvious when the returns of 1588 came in. Over 10 million gold ducats had gone on preparations for the fleet in the first three quarters of 1587,[38] but all the time disease, corruption, and decay were eating away at the resources so painstakingly built up. To continue spending at that rate was out of the question. Yet to abandon the enterprise was equally unthinkable. Philip II had been goaded into a hatred of Elizabeth and a sense of personal outrage such as he had never shown in his life before.[39] Yet already his enemies were laughing at him[40]—that the monarch of half the world was at the mercy of a woman, the mistress of half an island![41] The king's very reputation was at stake. Even Drake had been surprised that nothing had been done in 1586;[42] and then 1587 had gone by. It could not be allowed to happen again. If it did the English would be encouraged and Spain would be exposed to the 'intolerable disgrace' of even more daring and more dangerous outrages on her shipping, on her ports, on her Indies.[43] The unheard-of sums

[33] C.S.P. Venetian VIII, 313 and Naish, op. cit. p. 8. On William Harborne's mission in Constantinople see Edwin Pears, 'The Spanish Armada and the Ottoman Porte', *English Historical Review*, VIII (1893), 439–66, and H. G. Rawlinson, 'The Embassy of William Harborne to Constantinople 1583–8', *Transactions of the Royal Historical Society*, 4th series, V (1922), 1–27; and on the attempt to involve Morocco in an anti-Spanish alliance M. Fernández Alvarez, *Felipe II, Isabel de Inglaterra y Marruecos* (Instituto de Estudios Africanos, Madrid, 1951).

[34] C.S.P. Venetian VIII, 334. French involvement in the Armada has been dealt with by De Lamar Jensen in 'Franco-Spanish Diplomacy and the Armada' and in *Diplomacy and Dogmatism. Bernardino de Mendoza and the French Catholic League* (Cambridge, Mass., 1964).

[35] C.S.P. Venetian VIII, 329. See also J. R. Elder, *Spanish Influences in Scottish history* and C.S.P. Spanish IV.

[36] According to the President of the Council of Finance, C.S.P. Venetian VIII, 336.

[37] H. and P. Chaunu, *Séville et l'Atlantique* (Paris 1959), VIII, 2, i, 754–60, 'La grande zone de silence de 1587 doit être considerée comme un des grands événements négatifs d'un siècle et demi d'histoire de l'Atlantique des Ibériques...' (p. 755).

[38] Again the President of the Council of Finance, C.S.P. Venetian VIII, 312.

[39] C.S.P. Venetian VIII, 182.

[40] For at least the last two years, the enterprise was being put increasingly in terms of 'dignity' and 'reputation' by the king's ministers, and regarded with increasing scepticism by his subjects, C.S.P. Venetian VIII, 144, 147, 189, 209, 218, 224, 272, 277.

[41] The expression was the Pope's, ibid. p. 345.   [42] Ibid. p. 210.

[43] Ibid. p. 329; Herrera Oria, op. cit. p. 120.

already expended could not now be thrown away merely to leave Spain with the even greater costs of a defensive war.[44] Nor would it be just the English who would be encouraged. Sixteenth-century statesmen, and Spaniards in particular, would have subscribed wholeheartedly to the domino theory. Defiance was contagious. The Spanish monarchy was held together by centripetal force. If she showed weakness anywhere, her position in Europe would collapse and her empire fall asunder.[45] Nowhere was the danger more serious than in Portugal. The loss of her independence was too recent, and annexation to Spain had also annexed her to an unwanted and disastrous war with England. The Portuguese felt that it was they who were bearing the brunt of the corsair attacks. It was their ships that were being captured and their commerce that was all but destroyed.[46] They were far better off, they said, under their own king, Dom Sebastian, than at present.[47] For two years they had been complaining. Now on top of the king's inaction, they had on their backs the apparently dead weight of this enormous Armada that was cornering their grain supplies and 'completing the ruin of the country'.[48] By 1588, they were 'at their wits' end'.[49] Every day revealed greater despair and discontent.[50] Plots were discovered.[51] With Elizabeth harbouring the Portuguese pretender and threatening to foster a revolution in his name, it was imperative that the Armada be lifted from their shoulders at the earliest possible moment, and that some show be made of meeting their grievances and protecting their interests. At the same time, complaints of an identical kind were coming in from the loyal provinces in the Netherlands.[52] In such circumstances, there was nothing to choose between delay and defeat. Whatever the outcome, Philip had to go on. The heretics must not be allowed to believe that it was God's will that they go unpunished. The obstacles that sprang up on every side were sent to try him for God's greater glory, maybe to punish him for his sins. If vengeance was to be the Lord's, he yet had an obligation to serve God in accordance with his conscience, if need be to sacrifice himself.[53] As far as the king was concerned, then,

---

[44] Herrera Oria, op. cit. pp. 35, 45.

[45] C.S.P. Venetian VIII, 190, 'the King cannot do less than punish the Queen, if he desires to preserve his reputation and his possessions'. And p. 272, 'these injuries inflicted by Drake will raise many considerations in the minds of other Princes, and also of the King's own subjects'.

[46] Ibid. pp. 144, 166, 331.

[47] Ibid. pp. 145, 295.

[48] Herrera Oria, op. cit. p. 102; C.S.P. Venetian VIII, 334.

[49] C.S.P. Venetian VIII, 329.

[50] C.S.P. Venetian VIII, 331.

[51] Ibid. p. 332. E. Armstrong, 'Venetian despatches on the Armada and its results', English Historical Review, XII (1897), 674 lists the plots reported by the Venetian ambassadors since 1581. Armstrong considers 'the ever-present danger of an English invasion in favour of Don Antonio was one of the chief causes of the Armada' (p. 673).

[52] Parma to Philip II, 31 Jan. 1588, 'This delay is causing the total ruin of the province of Flanders, and is hardly less disastrous to the rest', C.S.P. Spanish IV, 201.

[53] Philip II to Medina Sidonia, 1 July 1588, Herrera Oria, op. cit. pp. 210–12.

204

April was the deadline.[54] Six months before it had seemed to him a matter of such extreme urgency that he had even been prepared to risk sending the Armada to sea in the middle of winter.[55] Now, with every month that passed, the difficulties that had been foreseen were actually increasing.[56] By February, only an immediate and unhesitating efficiency could remedy the mischief caused by previous delays.[57] But it was precisely here that Santa Cruz, for all his experience and ability in naval command, had failed him. Deadline after deadline had not been met. If those peremptory and apparently insensate orders to attempt a winter crossing with whatever vessels were on hand had been intended to ensure that the fleet would at least be ready in time for the spring, they had not succeeded. The situation in Lisbon was chaotic.[58] What was needed now was an organizer, a top administrator, for the Armada by 1588 was overwhelmingly an administrative problem.[59]

A commander had to be appointed, of course, for all contingencies; yet the one quality that nobody seems to have thought of prime importance was ocean seamanship. Of the various persons proposed at one time or another for the command only one was a sailor with this kind of experience, and he had to propose himself.[60] One reason was probably that the difference between Mediterranean and Atlantic techniques did not seem so important. Sailing ships played a prominent, if auxiliary, part in Mediterranean warfare and transportation, and galleys themselves spent something like two-thirds of their travelling time under sail.[61] Men who had spent all their lives on the galleys were considered competent to supervise the construction of galleons,[62] and Santa Cruz's career had shown how easy it was to turn one's hand from one to the other with apparently equal success. In any case, 'driving' the Armada was

---

[54] It was thought favourable winds would be met only in April or August, but August was dangerous because with the onset of autumn could be expected high tides and north-easterly winds, C.S.P. Venetian VIII, 224.

[55] Herrera Oria, op. cit. p. 37 (14 Sept. 1587); Olivares to Philip II, 30 Nov. 1587, in J. A. Froude, *History of England* (1872 edition), XII, 322 n. 2. Mattingly, op. cit. p. 219, notes the change in Philip II from patience to urgency but does not explain it. The document in Naish, op. cit. p. 8 provides a good summary of some of 'the considerations which have led his Majesty to decide that success in this enterprise depends on the assembling of his forces with great speed and dissimulation; and on their speedy employment, to extirpate this evil thing at its roots' (14 Sept. 1587).

[56] C.S.P. Venetian VIII, 334.

[57] Ibid. p. 338: 'he believes that by rapid action it is still possible to remedy the mischief caused by previous delays' (13 Feb. 1588); Herrera Oria, op. cit. p. 151, Philip II to Medina Sidonia, 20 Feb. 1588, 'de lo que en Lisboa se ha de hazer vos teneys muy probada la intençion en la diligencia y cuydado y, pues nunca tanto fue menester lo uno y lo otro como agora...'.   [58] See Mattingly, op. cit. p. 223.

[59] J. Lynch, *Spain under the Habsburgs*, (Oxford, 1964) I, 321.

[60] Juan Martínez de Recalde.

[61] See E. Fasano-Guarini, 'Au XVIe siècle: comment naviguent les galères', *Annales E.S.C.* (1961), pp. 279–96.

[62] Don Juan de Cardona, who was sent to Santander in 1588 for this purpose, had from 1565 to 1585 been captain-general of the galleys of Sicily and Naples, B.M. Additional ms. 28,373 fol. 57; V. Fernández Asis, *Epistolario de Felipe II sobre asuntos de mar* (Madrid, 1943), nos. 811, 820–2.

not the captain-general's first job. If it were just a question of getting the ships from one place to another, he had assistants who could do that. In December 1587, when it was intended to send an advance fleet of 35 ships to carry 6,000 soldiers to Parma in the Netherlands and then return, Santa Cruz himself declared that it was not necessary for him to go in person for he would be of more service to the king in Lisbon, putting the rest of the Armada in order, 'which needs energy, experience, and conscientiousness'.[63] Once the main body of the Armada was ready, it too would just sail from *A* to *B*, hand over a large part of its soldiery to Parma and cover his crossing. From then on it would be up to Parma and the troops. A fighting commander would not be necessary; he might even be a disadvantage, jeopardizing the overall plan by unnecessary pugnacity.[64] All this is clear from Philip II's instructions;[65] but it is worth pointing out that these were not just a cover for Medina Sidonia's incapacity. Medina Sidonia's instructions were essentially the same as those drawn up for Santa Cruz the previous year.[66] This was a strategy made possible in the first place by the belief that the Armada was so powerful that Elizabeth dare not risk her navy and her kingdom on the hazard of a single battle.[67] In some quarters, this belief persisted to the end;[68] but, even if, as an increasing amount of evidence seemed to indicate, Elizabeth intended to make a stand at sea,[69] the experts were convinced that it was almost impossible to force an engagement between great sailing ships, especially on the open seas, if one of the combatants did not desire it.[70] The fighting that would take place, then, would take place on land. It was the soldiery that was the 'marrow' of the Armada,[71] and if there were fears about the lack of a suitable commander,

[63] Herrera Oria, op. cit. pp. 90, 93.

[64] This was exactly what was feared of Santa Cruz, who always advocated a direct attack on the English fleet.

[65] Printed in Fernández Duro, op. cit. II, 5–13, 'Esto del combatir se entiende, si de otra manera no se puede asegurar al Duque de Parma, mi sobrino, el tránsito para Inglaterra; que, pudiéndose sin pelear asegurar este paso al de Parma, por desviarse el enemigo, o de otra manera, será bien que hagáis el mismo efecto conservando las fuerzas enteras' (p. 10); and Medina Sidonia to Parma, 10 June 1588, the king 'has ordered me not to turn aside, and even if I am impeded, simply to clear the way and proceed to join hands with you...', quoted in Oppenheim's introduction to Book I of Monson's Tracts, p. 55. Oppenheim's view, which contradicts mine, ignores the passage from Medina Sidonia's instructions cited above; nor does he appreciate that the Spaniards thought the Armada could not be destroyed and, even if it could not destroy the English fleet, it could mask it while the troops crossed, and continue in being as a cover or a diversion.

[66] Herrera Oria, op. cit. p. 36. The same document is printed in an English translation in Naish, op. cit. pp. 7–11 and C.S.P. Spanish IV, 187, no. 193.

[67] C.S.P. Venetian VIII, 213, 281.

[68] Ibid. p. 336 (Don Alonso de Leyva, 6 Feb. 1588); C.S.P. Domestic 1581–90, p. 483 (Antone de Taso, ?18 May 1588); Herrera Oria, op. cit. p. 196 (Philip II, 21 May 1588); C.S.P. Spanish IV, 194, no. 203, 204, 215 (Don Bernardino de Mendoza, 16 Jan. and 7 Feb. 1588).

[69] C.S.P. Venetian VIII, 331, 351; C.S.P. Domestic 1581–90, p. 497; Herrera Oria, op. cit. p. 99. [70] C.S.P. Venetian VIII, 213.

[71] Philip II to Medina Sidonia, 1 July 1588, Herrera Oria, op. cit. p. 209. It was an opinion shared by the majority of Englishmen also, see Oppenheim, op. cit. p. 171 n. 10, and Conyers Read, op. cit. p. 411.

they were that there was nobody 'fitted to command so great an *army*' (my italics), fears expressed long before the death of Santa Cruz.[72] One writer would actually have disqualified the marquis from command because of his lack of experience on land.[73]

On the other hand, just to be a soldier was not enough. Sixteenth-century generals were not trained in staff-colleges. Rarely did they rise from the ranks. Generalship was a combination of flair and prudence, the willingness, the obligation to listen to expert advice and choose the best of the conflicting courses that were proposed. (Indeed, kingship itself worked on exactly the same principle.) Within Philip's own reign, had not Don John of Austria shown how much more important were birth and leadership than his one uneventful summer on the galleys before the Lepanto campaign? Besides, the invasion force already had its general, the duke of Parma. More than ever in 1588 had the captain-general of the Armada to be a man of great personal standing. The new appointment had to be made not only with a view to the immediacies of conflict but with a view to the eventuality of victory. Parma could not be in two places at once. If the invasion succeeded, somebody had to remain in England to represent the king while Parma returned to the Netherlands, or take over the government of the Netherlands while Parma stayed in England. The problem had been talked about before.[74] In 1588 it seemed (in Milan at any rate) that Medina Sidonia had been appointed expressly to take over in Flanders.[75]

III

What was required, then, was not an admiral, possibly not even a field-marshal, but a quartermaster-general, someone who could guarantee that the Armada would sail in 1588, or the whole thing might as well be written off. As an administrator there was nobody more suitable than Medina Sidonia, and a handful of authors have in fact disassociated themselves over the last decade from the general denial of any talents whatsoever to the duke. Nor indeed, was he a complete military ignoramus. He had led troops in 1580 to receive the submission of the Portuguese Algarve, and had been appointed, in 1581, to command a projected expedition against Larache, in North Africa. In neither event had generalship proved to be necessary, though in both cases he had had command of men and had gained valuable experience in the administration of war,[76] but in April 1587, when he rushed his forces to the defence of Cadiz, he met something like combat conditions and, however later historians have judged his intervention, there is no doubt that public rumour believed he had

[72] C.S.P. Venetian VIII, 191 (6 Aug. 1586).

[73] Memorial of Francisco de Estrada (c. 13 Apr. 1586), C. Riba y García, *Correspondencia privada de Felipe II con su secretario Mateo Vázquez 1567–91* (Madrid, 1959), I, 383.

[74] C.S.P. Venetian VIII, 191, 276.

[75] C.S.P. Foreign XXI, pt. I, p. 572 (opinion of the duke of Terranova, governor of Milan).

[76] The details are to be found in the previously cited works of Maura, Fernández Asis, and Fernández Duro, and in J. Suárez Inclán, *Guerra de anexión en Portugal durante el reinado de Don Felipe II* (Madrid, 1897), I, ch. 9.

been responsible for beating Drake off, and that the king was very impressed with his performance.[77] To the king he had proved himself a soldier, and this was thought likely to matter much more in 1588 than the fact that he had never fought at sea. But if he had never fought at sea, he knew all that was to be known about the fitting out and arming of ships, about the procurement of supplies and the raising of men. From at least as early as 1581 he had been largely responsible for the fitting out and provisioning of the ill-fated Straits of Magellan fleet and of the successive *flotas* of New Spain and *Tierra Firme*.[78] By the end of his life he was recognized as *the* expert on the Indies run.[79] From 1586, he was also taking an active and leading part in the preparations for the Armada itself, inspecting shipping, making decisions on which vessels would be serviceable and which not, ordering the necessary measures for making them seaworthy and fit for battle, and, making sure that they were fully manned.[80] At the same time, he was in charge of the recruiting of troops in Andalusia, appointing captains, designating recruiting areas, and issuing appropriate instructions to prevent the abuses and disturbances that so often accompanied military levies.[81] His formal appointment as captain-general of Andalusia, early in 1588, was no more than a recognition of the fact that he had been, in all but name, acting as a kind of unpaid viceroy in Andalusia since 1581.[82] By 1588 there is no doubt that Medina Sidonia was regarded as an expert in all branches of staff-work, logistics and procurement, both military and naval. He was being asked, and giving, advice on the best way to organize the raising of provisions, on contracting out the maintenance of the Portuguese fortresses in North Africa, on the upkeep and sufficiency of the garrison in Cadiz, on whether or not certain galleons were in a fit state to risk an Atlantic crossing, on diplomatic relations with the Barbary states and the need to control the North African coast, and on such vital strategic issues as the advisability of despatching a *flota* to New Spain in 1587, or the proper objective for the English expedition itself.[83] As well, and this is even more surprising, he was actually advising on the conduct of naval warfare, urging on Madrid the importance of having galleys with the Armada, comparing the sailing

[77] C.S.P. Venetian VIII, 272, 273, 307.

[78] Maura, op. cit. p. 88; Archivo General de Indias, Contratación legajo 5,014, Philip II to Casa de Contratación, 12 Aug. 1586.

[79] 'Discurso en que se condena al Govierno de los Reyes de las Españas Phelipes segundo y tercero el año de 1599', Haus-hof und Staats Archiv,Vienna, Spanien Varia fasz. 2 (1599), fol. 347v, 'El Duque de Medina Sidonia, siendo tan platico de las Indias que desde que tiene uso de raçon no entiende en San Lucar en otra cosa sino en despachar flotas, armadas y navios de aviso y que no ay alla Presidente ni oydor que no conozca ni sepa como procede y importando tanto las Indias y el conçierto de las flotas, que tan desconçertadas andan, y que no tenemos ninguno que sepa nada desta materia sino el Duque...'

[80] See the documents printed by Maura, Fernández Duro, and Fernández Asis.

[81] Maura, op. cit. pp. 149, 219, 237; C.S.P. Venetian VIII, 159; Fernández Duro, op. cit. I, 385.

[82] Maura, op. cit. p. 103.

[83] Maura, op. cit. pp. 147, 135, 151, 29, 167, 173, 169; Fernández Duro, op. cit. I, 345; A[rchivo] G[eneral de] S[imancas], Guerra Antigua legajo 81, fol. 91.

qualities of the fast English pirate ships, straight from dry-dock with new sails and no cargoes, and the heavily laden Indies fleets, in need of careening after eighteen months at sea and slowed down by torn and battered sails. As much as anybody else, he realized that the English tactic was to make use of their speed, gain the wind and, being able to dictate the range, lay off and batter the Spaniard with their great guns until the enemy was helpless.[84] The only answer was to make the Spanish Armada as large and powerful as possible and man it to the gunwales. Only by massive superiority in size and numbers to anything the English might assemble could it be made irresistible.[85] Maybe Medina Sidonia had no experience of the North Atlantic, but of that stretch of ocean between Sanlúcar and Larache he had 'very particular knowledge'.[86] In the days of quick and apparently successful commutation between Mediterranean and Atlantic, the distinction was probably too subtle for most Spaniards to consider important. At any rate, time and again the duke had proved to the king his ability and initiative, his 'cuidado y diligencia', in virtually every type of military activity,[87] and every time he came to Court it was thought that he was summoned to join the king's councils to add his advice on the great expedition that was in hand.[88]

If Medina Sidonia's professional abilities have been largely ignored, his other qualifications have been universally misunderstood. Medina Sidonia was perhaps the richest peer in Spain. This everybody has noted, but it has been considered merely as a biographical curiosity. He was also the first grandee in Castile, but the importance of this has been only to provide the Armada with a kind of constitutional monarch, an unguent for social susceptibilities. In fact, both wealth and status were military factors of the highest order.[89] This is best explained by looking at a much earlier and hitherto unknown episode in Medina Sidonia's career, which is important

---

[84] Maura, op. cit. pp. 172, 176.

[85] Ibid. pp. 169–71.   [86] Ibid. p. 126.

[87] Ibid. p. 218 and Fernández Duro, op. cit. I, 345—at the time of the raid on Cadiz, May 1587; Philip II to Medina Sidonia, 25 June 1587, thanking him for his successful recruiting efforts in Andalusia, 'y todo esto se debe atribuir á vuestro mucho cuidado y diligencia, por lo cual os doy muchas gracias', ibid. I, 368. As early as 1573, the Venetian ambassador reported that he was the only one of the Castilian nobility who had responded with any enthusiasm at the time of the Alpujarran revolt, E. Albèri, Le relazioni degli ambasciatori veneti (Florence, 1839, etc.), series I, VI, 397. Medina Sidonia's appointment to the governorship of Milan and captaincy-general of the army of Lombardy and Piedmont, a post as Granvelle described it, 'á la verdad importantísimo y de muy gran confianza, pues es adonde ordinariamente baten las cosas de la guerra' (C.O.D.O.I.N. XXIV, 522), was quite expressly a reward for the duke's outstanding services in the pacification of the Algarve and the surrender of Portugal's North African possessions in 1580 (see the commission of appointment, 18 May 1581, B.M. Additional Ms. 16,176 fols., 280–3), and an expression of 'la opinion que S.M. ha concebido de la persona de V.E. como quien muy bien conoce sus cualidades y lafeccion que como Principe valeroso tiene á las armas...' (C.O.D.O.I.N. XXIV, 551).

[88] C.S.P. Venetian VIII, 148, 307.

[89] Only Muro, in his life of the princess of Eboli (1877), has appreciated the military importance of the duchy of Medina Sidonia; reference in Fernández Duro, op. cit. I, 226.

in the light of future events because it was the first time that attention had been drawn to the duke as a candidate for high command. In 1574 the Crown decided to put the maintenance of the galley squadron of Spain out to contract. In August (probably), Medina Sidonia offered to take up the contract. The offer was examined in council and warmly recommended, for two reasons: 1. because he was willing to accept payment on the bullion fleets and not charge interest on any delays consequent upon their late arrival. This was considered of great advantage to the king's treasury; 2. because 'the duke, being the person he is, will keep (the galleys) in very good order, and sailing in them personally, he will be accompanied by many gentlemen of Andalusia'.[90] The objections came from the dukes of Alba and Medinaceli, in the Council of State, and these were entirely a matter of status (a nice twist on 1588). As galley commander, Medina Sidonia would have to be granted the precedence and privileges of his rank and this could easily entangle the chain of military command or prejudice agreements with future contractors. Nevertheless, Medinaceli thought the king might consider building up the duke to take over the galleys in the event of Don John of Austria's no longer being available at sea.[91] Later, Medina Sidonia began to modify the terms of his offer, demanding that all the generals of the different galley squadrons should be under his orders whenever Don John was not at sea, and the contract fell through.[92]

Already, then, Medina Sidonia was being considered for high military office. But the real attraction of his offer had been clearly expressed—he had money, and he had a following. Both were as vital in 1588 as they had been in 1574. Philip II had never had as much money available for his projects as in the 1580s, but by 1588, after twenty months of unprecedented spending, the financial situation was again critical.[93] Campaigns always cost their generals money.[94] What was the point now of appointing a captain-general who was as impoverished as his king? After all, in Portugal strong-arm tactics were politically inexpedient, and if there was no cash who would sell, especially when so many of the naval stores had to come from abroad in any case?[95] The king's credit was not to be trusted. Twice, three times he had renegued

---

[90] A.G.S. Guerra Antigua legajo 78, fol. 59; or as the duke put it himself, 'que se entienda alla quanto subiran de punto las galeras estando a mi cargo y quan hartas y bien proveidas andaran assi de bastimentos y municiones como de soldados y cavalleros deudos y criados mios para poder emprender qualquiera cosa...', Guerra Antigua leg. 175, fol. 14.

[91] A.G.S. Guerra Antigua leg. 78, fol. 97.

[92] A.G.S. Guerra Antigua leg. 80, fol. 145.

[93] Herrera Oria, op. cit. pp. 112, 124, 125, 136; Fernández Duro, op. cit. I, 519.

[94] The duke of Alba claimed to have spent over 80,000 ducats on the Portuguese campaign, Duquesa de Berwick y de Alba, *Documentos escogidos del archivo de la casa de Alba* (Madrid, 1891), p. 146; and the marquis of Santa Cruz more than 40,000 'assi en ospedar y regalar los cavalleros que venian a servir a V.Md. en ella como en dar de comer a mas de 150 soldados cada dia de los necessitados mas de 5 meses despues de llegados a esta cuidad...', A.G.S. Guerra Antigua leg. 109, fol. 334.

[95] Count of Fuentes to Philip II, Lisbon, 4 Feb. 1588, '...de la tierra no se puede haver sin pagarse luego', Herrera Oria, op. cit. p. 136.

V

on his bankers, and unpaid bills on the treasury were circulating at discounts of up to thirty per cent. A commander of conspicuous probity, whose credit was tied to the honour of the house of Guzman el Bueno and a rent roll of 150,000 ducats a year, was an opportunity not to be lightly discarded.[96] In the event, if he did nothing else, Medina Sidonia contributed nearly 8 million *maravedís* of his own money to the costs of the Armada.[97] But it was not only money of which the king was desperately short in 1588. The Armada was undermanned.[98] There was a lack of both soldiers and seamen, and this is where Medina Sidonia's title was at a premium. It was not primarily a question of blood, but of the duke's social, one might say 'feudal', position in Andalusia.[99] With the duke in command, his clients and relatives, and their clients and relatives, could be expected to go with him, as well as all those vassals of his who from hope of preferment or mere loyalty to their lord would be drawn to his side. As Lippomano put it, 'he will be followed by many nobles, and by all Andalusia';[100] and Andalusia mattered, it was the granary of the army, the centre of provisioning for the fleets, and the major recruiting area for soldiers.[101] Even in the most institutionalized monarchy of its day, the central government could never compete with the influence of the local magnate. Medina Sidonia's value, especially to facilitate the raising of troops, had been recognized explicitly in August 1587, when the king entrusted him with the raising of 400 soldiers in Andalusia, 'seeing that this could not be done by anybody but you with the same speed and assurance', for he knew better than the ministers in Madrid which areas still had something left to be tapped.[102] It is just this point that is underlined in the very letter in which Philip informed the duke of his appointment.

The last few days everyone has agreed that we should announce that the galleons are to sail to the Indies, so that the men, especially the sailors, sign on with greater

[96] F. Braudel, *La Méditerranée et le monde méditerranéen a l'époque de Philippe II* (2nd ed. Paris, 1966), II, 58.

[97] Michael Lewis, *The Spanish Armada* (Pan Books), p. 50, says nearly 9 million, but Martin Hume, on the basis of a reference in C.O.D.O.I.N. XIV, and the marquis del Saltillo, 'El Duque de Medina Sidonia y la jornada a Inglaterra en 1588', *Bol. de la Biblioteca de Menéndez Pelayo*, XVI, no. 1 (1934), p. 168, both agree on 7,827,358.

[98] Maura, op. cit. pp. 165, 219, 221; Fernández Duro, op. cit. I, 447, 453, 475, 477, 412, II, 135.

[99] As duke of Medina Sidonia and count of Niebla he was lord of Medina Sidonia, Vejer, Chiclana, Conil, Jimena, and Sanlúcar de Barrameda in the province of Cadiz, and of about half the present province of Huelva, quite apart from the influence he had in the lands of his close relative, the marquis of Ayamonte, A. Domínguez Ortiz, 'La conspiración del duque de Medina Sidonia y el marqués de Ayamonte', separate of *Archivo Hispalense*, 2nd epoch, no. 106 (1961), p. 2. [100] C.S.P. Venetian VIII, 340.

[101] Fernández Duro, op. cit. I, 425 (wine); Herrera Oria, op. cit. p. 304 (provisioning centre); Maura, op. cit. p. 237 (troops); A.G.S. Guerra Antigua leg. 499, Council of War, 10 Sept. 1597, Andalusia and Extremadura 'que ordinariamente han sido granero y posito para las provisiones de las Armadas'.

[102] Maura, op. cit. p. 237; Fernández Duro, op. cit. I, 412. See also Maura, op. cit. p. 125, 19 Nov. 1582, when the king refused Medina Sidonia permission to come to Madrid because the men and ships assembled for the expedition to Larache would disperse, 'siendo muy claro que lo uno y lo otro se entretiene principalmente con vuestra presencia y autoridad'.

alacrity. But now that you are to sail in the Armada, it could be that things will take a different turn. Knowing that they would be serving with you and under your command, both soldiers and sailors might prefer to join up for the Armada rather than for the Indies.

The king therefore left it up to Medina Sidonia to decide which course to follow and, although they stuck to the pretence that the Seville galleons were for the Indies, the point had been made.[103]

Two other features of Medina Sidonia's career must have provided additional, if less potent, recommendations. We have already noted the increasing hostility of the Portuguese to the expedition, but it was precisely at this moment, in early 1588, that the co-operation of the Portuguese was most essential if the Armada was to be provisioned and equipped in time.[104] Santa Cruz had been hated by the Portuguese.[105] Medina Sidonia was probably both known and liked by them. His wife was half Portuguese, his granddaughter was to be queen of Portugal. His grandfather, the sixth duke, had been on very good terms with the great Portuguese nobility; he had accompanied the Infanta Isabella from Badajoz to the Court of Charles V for her marriage in 1526 and, in 1543, went to Lisbon with the bishop of Cartagena to take her niece, Maria, to Salamanca to marry the future Philip II. The sumptuous reception she and her train were given as they passed through the duke's estates was something still memorable at the end of the eighteenth century.[106] In his turn, the grandson was called upon to perform what were to prove to be the last honours ever paid to Portugal's last real king, when, in June 1578, he entertained Dom Sebastian in splendid style at Cadiz for eight days before the young king and the gallants of his Court rushed off to their deaths at Alcazarquivir.[107] Medina Sidonia himself visited Lisbon in 1581 for his investment with the Collar of the Golden Fleece, and when he returned in 1588 he was welcomed by the duke of Braganza with a present of a pair of horses.[108] Santa Cruz had been associated with the destruction of Portugal; Medina Sidonia with her last moment of independence. If anyone could drag a bit of good-will and co-operation out of the Portuguese, it was he.[109]

But if the Armada was to sail from Portugal, it was to land in England. Nobody quite knew what was to happen when it did. Maybe the Catholics would rise. Maybe it would be necessary to impose some kind of temporary regency, or at any rate settle the succession by high-level negotiations with the English nobility. In any event, it could do no harm to have a commander who had contacts with England and who was known to be a great protector of the

[103] Herrera Oria, op. cit. p. 145.
[104] C.S.P. Venetian VIII, 312.
[105] Ibid. p. 144.
[106] Fernández y Fernández de Retana op. cit. I, 182–7; Maura, op. cit. p. 37.
[107] Maura, op. cit. p. 37.
[108] Saltillo, op. cit. p. 172.
[109] He apparently had previous successes to his credit, see Fernández Duro, op. cit. I, 353.

English merchant colony in Andalusia.[110] The duke had also been in touch, through intermediaries in Sanlúcar, with the earl of Leicester over the purchase of tin and copper for some artillery he needed for his estates, and he had actually received a letter from Elizabeth before the king decided that Medina Sidonia should break off the negotiations, 'because as they are such manifest heretics, he could not in good conscience reply'.[111] Nevertheless, six years later, he still had agents in England and secured a warrant from the queen permitting them to buy wheat for shipment to Spain.[112] That was probably the extent of Medina Sidonia's influence in England. It was not much, but it was better than nothing. The king knew about it, and it may have been yet another feather to place in the scales when the choice had to be made.

IV

What then lies behind Medina Sidonia's famous letter to Idiáquez pleading his complete incapacity for the task? It has been this more than anything else that has convinced historians of the duke's unsuitability, and it may be as well to underline its main points once again.[113] In essence there were four: (1) his health was too delicate for the sea; (2) he had no money; his house was 900,000 ducats in debt and he had 'not one *real* to spend on the expedition'; (3) he had, in his own words, 'no knowledge of the sea nor of war, for I have neither experienced it nor studied it' (*no lo he visto ni tratado*); (4) he would be taking command completely uninformed without knowing his officers, nor the purpose of the Armada, nor the intelligence there had been of English plans, ports, etc. Of (1) what can be said but that Medina Sidonia survived an ordeal that killed two hardened seamen like Recalde and Oquendo, and lived for another twenty-seven years into his late sixties? To (2) we shall return later. But the real substance of the letter lay either in modesty, which was Philip's view,[114] or in the validity of the last two points, accepted almost without exception by later writers. Yet they are utterly incompatible with what we already know of Medina Sidonia's career, incompatible with his activities between 1580 and 1588, incompatible with the advice he was never reluctant to give on both military and naval matters and which he continued to give in the selfsame letter in which he proclaimed his complete ignorance of such things, advice which, as we have seen, touched not only on the logistics but also on the actual conduct of sea warfare. How, moreover, could he claim to be ignorant of the state of the Armada and the objectives of the expedition when not two months before he had been at Court discussing the enterprise,

---

[110] The duke's family had granted Englishmen trading privileges in Sanlúcar de Barrameda for nearly 300 years, and he was himself continuing the policy, Gordon Connell-Smith, *Forerunners of Drake* (1954), pp. 8 and 82, and p. 213 below.

[111] A.G.S. Guerra Antigua, leg. 81, fols. 94, 97, 100 (Oct. to Dec. 1576).

[112] Great Britain, Historical Manuscripts Commission, Salisbury MSS. pt. 2, p. 535.

[113] The letter is printed in Fernández Duro, op. cit. I, 414–17, and Maura, op. cit. pp. 241–4, and in a shortened English version in C.S.P. Spanish IV, 207–8.

[114] Naish, op. cit. p. 12; Herrera Oria, op. cit. p. 150.

giving the Venetian ambassador information on the king's expenditures, and airing his opinions on the feasibility of the whole project?[115] And as to his not knowing the objectives of the Armada, this was not surprising when the previous November, as he himself had admitted, 'no express orders as to the operation to be carried out have been issued to the Marquis (of Santa Cruz) on account of the uncertainty whether the whole or a part of the fleet was going to put out'.[116] Who then expected Medina Sidonia to refuse? Lippomano certainly did not,[117] and Philip's ministers were having none of such excuses— 'nobody knows more about naval affairs than you'.[118] But it is not just modesty that explains the letter. Medina Sidonia wanted nothing to do with the expedition, and he hid his reasons from nobody. He thought the Armada was a mistake which had no hope of succeeding. Only a miracle could save it.[119] No more than Santa Cruz did he want to play into the hands of his enemies and throw away his reputation on a venture from which nothing could be expected but disaster. Even after his appointment, he continued to urge the king to call the whole thing off.[120]

The advice may well have been sound. It was also perfectly consistent with the duke's own interests. The growth and prosperity of Sanlúcar de Barrameda, and therefore the larger part of Medina Sidonia's income,[121] depended almost entirely on foreign trade, especially on trade with England, whose merchants had been encouraged by successive dukes to make Sanlúcar their headquarters in Andalusia by extensive grants of privileges.[122] Even during the war, Medina Sidonia was accused of conniving at illicit trade for his own profit.[123] How much more would a negotiated peace have suited him than these fruitless hostilities!

Whatever the outcome, it could not help costing the duke money, as in all probability it was intended to. The troops certainly took the substitution of a 'general of gold' for a 'general of iron' as a guarantee that they would get their pay,[124] and merchants who found letters of credit signed by the duke refused in Seville could legitimately come back and demand that he pay them. With justification, Medina Sidonia complained that nobody would accept his bills and that his credit was suffering.[125] All this he had foreseen. Indeed, he had experienced it before;[126] hence his promptness in disabusing Madrid of any extravagant hopes they might have had on that score.

[115] He was probably in Madrid from mid October to mid December 1587, Maura, op. cit. p. 238; C.S.P. Venetian VIII, 327, 319.
[116] C.S.P. Venetian VIII, 319.   [117] Ibid. p. 340.
[118] Herrera Oria, op. cit. p. 148.
[119] Ibid. p. 152; C.S.P. Venetian VIII, 319.
[120] Fernández Duro, op. cit. II, 135.
[121] In 1582 it was estimated that Sanlúcar was worth 80,000 ducats a year to him; A.G.S. Guerra Antigua leg. 109, fol. 428.
[122] Connell-Smith, op. cit. pp. 8, 81–2, 90.   [123] Braudel, op. cit. I, 575–6.
[124] Fernández Duro, op. cit. I, 225.   [125] Ibid. II, 190.
[126] In December 1583, he was still owed money he had spent succouring Ceuta and other African garrisons the previous January; Maura, op. cit. pp. 130, 140.

But there was a final reason for Medina Sidonia's reluctance. By 1588 he seems to have outgrown his earlier ambitions. His mother had brought him up in the hope that he would reject the life of the courtier led by his predecessor, remain on his estates improve his lands, and govern his vassals well.[127] After the galley contract offer fell through, he appears to have restricted his ambitions to Andalusia and to have avoided any appointment that would have taken him away from his estates. When, in October 1580, he heard that he was to be sent to Milan, he succeeded by a series of excuses and delays in putting off his departure until the appointment was revoked in January 1582.[128] Only the Secretary Zayas, his confidant, advised him that should the king summon him to Lisbon to join the Cardinal-Archduke he ought not to refuse, 'since it would be the same as being in your home; besides, Your Excellency owes the king a degree of love and respect that obliges you to do even the impossible'.[129] The same sense of obligation was to be called upon in 1588.[130]

But the motives for which Medina Sidonia wanted to remain in Andalusia were also reasons why the king should want to employ him elsewhere. Medina Sidonia was suspect. He had expanded his personal military forces in Sanlúcar by persuading foreign residents to enlist in return for certain tax exemptions,[131] he had attracted merchants by concessions made to the detriment of the king's finances and, so it was claimed, had for private motives thwarted measures for the defence of Andalusia by suborning the royal official in charge.[132] In February 1582, Dr Santillan of the Council of the Indies, the president of the *Casa de Contratación*, wrote to the king from Seville,

I write to advise Your Majesty that I am told the duke is making use of the authority he has from Your Majesty very much to his own advantage and to that of his vassals...It seems to me that he could serve Your Majesty in Milan, or elsewhere, as he is a man of ability, but in his own lands and in these to which he is neighbour and where he aims to be the most powerful man, there are serious disadvantages that do not arise with any other grandee of Spain not possessed of so many vassals, and those mainly in the ports and coastal villages which by rights ought all to be in the royal demesne.[133]

There is no evidence that Philip took this seriously. Nevertheless, the appointment of Medina Sidonia, first as governor of Milan and then as commander of the Armada, is perfectly consistent with the king's acknowledged policy of breaking the power of the great nobility by taking them from their estates and dissipating their financial resources in honorific but expensive offices abroad.

[127] Maura, op. cit. p. 12.
[128] Ibid. pp. 111–12, 117.
[129] Ibid. p. 115.
[130] Herrera Oria, op. cit. p. 148.
[131] Pedro Barbadillo Delgado, *Historia de la ciudad de San Lúcar de Barrameda* (Cadiz, 1942), p. 155.
[132] B.M. Add. MS. 28,366, fol. 205.
[133] A.G.S. Guerra Antigua leg. 109, fol. 428.

V

Who, then, could contend with Medina Sidonia's qualifications? At one time or another, a half dozen or so different alternatives had been proposed. Maybe each surpassed the duke in one particular talent, but none had so many. As the Venetian ambassador put it, 'all other possible appointments presented greater difficulties'.[134] Political objections ruled out the duke of Savoy and the Grand Duke of Tuscany.[135] The Prior Don Hernando de Toledo, and Don Alonso de Vargas were even less of sailors than Medina Sidonia. Don Alonso de Leyva was a soldier and a galley commander but not an ocean seaman either. The *Adelantado Mayor de Castilla* (Medina Sidonia's choice and his eventual successor in the 1596 and 1597 fleets) had experience of little else but Mediterranean galleys. Juan Martínez de Recalde (his own choice) was probably the nearest Spain could get to a sea-dog, but he had not the weight for the post and his honesty was not beyond question.[136] None could compete with Medina Sidonia's varied administrative experience, nor bring to the task either his money or his personal influence. These turned out not to be enough to bring the Armada success, but they were enough to enable it to put to sea in May 1588 in a condition that could hardly have been hoped for in February. This Philip was the first to recognize and to be grateful for, and others realized it too.[137] But in the narrow seas the Armada failed and contemporaries—some contemporaries, certainly not all—blamed Medina Sidonia, possibly, as Garrett Mattingly pointed out, because he was so willing to blame himself.[138] Later historians, believing the Armada to be invincible and with little to go on but the result and the unfortunate inclusion of some of Fray Juan de Victoria's defamatory libels in Fernández Duro's collection of documents,[139] took the fault back one step further, to the selection itself. This is not the place to attempt to justify Medina Sidonia's conduct at sea. It is enough to draw attention to Mattingly's full-scale vindication of the duke's generalship. It is not necessary to believe that he made no mistakes, only that the mistakes were legitimate ones that, in the circumstances, even Santa Cruz might have made. Nor did contemporaries rise in a unanimous chorus of condemnation. Some blamed Medina Sidonia, some Parma, some Diego Flores de Valdés; others blamed the fireships or, more acutely, the Dutch control of the shallows off

[134] C.S.P. Venetian VIII, 340.

[135] Ibid. p. 187 (Savoy), p. 290 (Tuscany).

[136] For these suggestions see Miguel de Oquendo to Philip II, 9 Feb. 1588, Herrera Oria, op. cit. p. 366; memorial of Francisco de Estrada, c. 13 Apr. 1586, Riba y Garcia, op. cit. p. 383; Medina Sidonia to Don Juan de Idiáquez, 16 Feb. 1588, Fernández Duro, op. cit. I, 416; Juan Martínez de Recalde to Philip II, 13 Feb. 1588, Herrera Oria, op. cit. p. 367; Fernández Asis, op. cit. no. 1159.

[137] Philip II to Medina Sidonia, 1 July 1588, and Oquendo to Philip II, Corunna, 15 July 1588, Herrera Oria, op. cit. pp. 213, 248.

[138] Garrett Mattingly, The *'Invincible' Armada and Elizabethan England*, Folger Booklets on Tudor and Stuart Civilization (Cornell University Press, 1963), p. 10.

[139] See Mattingly, *Defeat of the Spanish Armada*, p. 286.

Dunkirk. Medina Sidonia's chief informed critic, Don Pedro de Valdés, had been jaundiced by bad relations with the duke from the start.[140] On the other hand, the Florentine, Ubaldino, attributed to his foresight the Armada's impenetrable crescent formation.[141] Philip II, whatever foreign observers thought, never withdrew his confidence from the duke. Perhaps he knew more than most that the issue had always been in doubt, that in Spain the Armada had sailed amid fears and misgivings, and in Rome, Genoa, and Paris its failure had been regarded as all but certain.[142]

One will never really know why Philip II chose Medina Sidonia. He rarely committed that kind of information to paper. Yet in the light of what was needed and the evidence that was available, Medina Sidonia was the inevitable, maybe the only possible, choice. This is not to say that the standard explanations are invalid—though there is evidence to question the absoluteness of the duke's self-effacement and his willingness to be led by the nose[143]— they just do not go far enough. Medina Sidonia's appointment can no longer be regarded as Philip II's 'crowning blunder',[144] nor provide evidence for the king's ineptitude or for pseudo-psychological interpretations of his political behaviour. But it also becomes clear that, in a sense, Medina Sidonia's appointment was not a completely free choice at all. Centralized absolutist monarchy could operate effectively neither absolutely nor far from the centre. Spain's war effort in the Atlantic depended on the grain, the men, and the shipping of Andalusia, and nobody could mobilize the resources of Andalusia more effectively than Medina Sidonia. It is for this reason that the dukes of Medina Sidonia continued to play an ever-increasing role in the government of Andalusia until the conspiracy of 1641. The appointment of 1588 was one the earliest manifestations of this renewed and growing reliance on the private authority of the great nobility.

[140] C.S.P. Foreign XXI, pt. 4, p. 516.

[141] *Harleian Miscellany*, I, 124.

[142] Armstrong, op. cit. pp. 662, 667; C.S.P. Venetian VIII, 182, 191–2, 321, 338, 348, 354; Naish, op. cit. p. 4; Lawrence Stone, *An Elizabethan: Sir Horatio Palavicino* (Oxford, 1956), p. 22; C.S.P. Foreign XXI, pt. 1, p. 578.

[143] 'The Duke of Medina Sidonia has received no commission as yet, and one does not see how he can accept one, as his presence is incompatible with that of the Marquis of Santa Cruz, who wherever he may be, or wherever engaged, would always take rank as commander in chief in virtue of his earlier commission', C.S.P. Venetian VIII, 159 (1 May 1586); '...but if he goes into England, many say he will not acknowledge the Duke of Parma as his superior...', C.S.P. Foreign XXI, pt. 1, p. 572.

[144] Lewis, op. cit. p. 48.

VI

SPANISH ARMADA GUNS

'WHAT can be said but our sins was the cause that so much powder and shot spent, and so long time in fight, and, in comparison thereof, so little harm?' The relative unimportance of the gunner in the Armada battle that perplexed William Thomas in 1588, remains no less of a puzzle after 400 years. Between them, the English and the Spanish fleets carried well over 4,000 guns, yet by 6 August (NS), despite four days of prolonged artillery bombardment from both sides, the Spaniards had succeeded in parading along the whole coastline of southern England to anchor in Calais Road largely unscathed by enemy action, having in their turn inflicted but negligible damage on their adversary. Even in the day-long engagement off Gravelines on 8 August, the disorganized Spanish fleet lost, as far as we can tell from the confusing accounts of the action, no more than three or four ships, and the English hardly a mast. This contrast between the apparent might of the contending forces and the limited damage they were able to inflict on each other was not properly investigated until the late Professor Michael Lewis published a series of articles on Armada Guns in this journal in 1942–43.[1] Lewis completely overturned existing orthodoxy which portrayed the Spanish as contemptuous of the gunner and the Spanish Armada as lightly and inadequately armed, mainly with 9, 6 and 4 lb. shot, as Laughton, Corbett and the Spanish naval historian, Fernández Duro, had intimated at the end of the nineteenth century. Lewis, restricting his analysis to effective anti-ship guns throwing a 4 lb. shot or more, his 'countable' guns, concluded that, although the Spaniards were indeed much weaker than the English in long-range, light-shotted guns, they were, quite unexpectedly, a great deal more formidable in heavy-shotted, medium-range and medium-shotted, short-range guns. Concretely, although the English had more 'countable' guns than the Spanish by five to three, and three times as many longer-range, 'culverin' types, the Spaniards had three times as many 'cannon' types, seven and a half times as many 'perier' types, and two and a half times as many guns throwing a ball in excess of 9 lb. as the English. In other words, the two fleets were equipped precisely for their chosen tactical roles, the English to keep the action at long range, the Spanish to close, batter and board.

VI

Lewis's findings readily explained how it was that the English were able to score with their own guns while keeping out of range of the enemy, and why at extreme culverin-range so little damage would have been done. Yet, despite the meticulousness of his analysis, there is something not entirely satisfactory about this explanation. Had all the fighting been done at long range there would be no problem, but it was not. Repeatedly over the nine days of the battle, units of the two fleets came not merely within culverin range, but within musket range, within half-musket range, and finally within hailing range, even within pike range. On 31 July, Drake engaged Recalde in the *San Juan de Portugal* at about 300 yards, probably within point-blank perier range; on 2 August, Howard was caught off Portland Bill by Medina Sidonia and Bertendona and fought all morning at ranges down to half-musket shot; on 3rd, the *Gran Grifón* was bombarded from a similar close range, and the next day, off the Isle of Wight, fighting again took place at within musket range, and possibly down to 100 or 120 yards; off Gravelines on 8 August, admittedly with the Spaniard running short of ammunition, the fleets came to grips at arquebus range, then at hailing range, and in some cases even at boarding range.[2] If the Spaniards really had such a preponderance of heavy, battery pieces of the 'cannon' and 'perier' types as Lewis claimed, it was remarkable that at the close ranges at which these actions were fought they proved so incapable of inflicting any noticeable damage on the English. The possibility must exist that these assumptions about the nature of the Armada's fire-power are gross over-estimations, and so there is a clear need to re-examine the evidence on which Professor Lewis's conclusions were based.

It must be stated at the outset that Lewis's estimates are very much more satisfactory on the English side than on the Spanish. Although there is no surviving list of the English armament for 1588 itself, the figures he gives for the English are based on near-contemporary, official reports and proposals setting out the numbers and the types of the guns on the Queen's Ships almost immediately before and immediately after the Armada year. More evidence may come to light, but at the moment there are no reasonable grounds for rejecting the general picture of the English armament that Lewis paints, and, for the purpose of comparing the gun-strengths of the two fleets, I shall accept Lewis's figures as they stand.

For the Spanish fleet, however, Lewis had only fragmentary and indirect information. He did no original work in Spanish archives and relied entirely on material available in print. He had, in fact, detailed evidence for only eight of the 130 ships that put to sea in 1588; a report of the artillery and shot aboard the four Neapolitan galleasses and the two lesser Ragusans of the Levant Squadron, the *Santa Anunciada* and the *Santa Maria de Bisón*, that accompanied them on their arrival at Málaga from Naples, in July 1587; and the English inventories of the ordnance and munitions captured with the two capital ships disabled during the first day's actions, the *Nuestra Señora del Rosario*, flagship of the Andalusian Squadron, and the *San Salvador* of the Guipúzcoan Squadron. It was on the basis of this evidence that Lewis, with immense care and ingenuity, put together his reconstruction of the total armament of the entire Spanish Armada. The resultant Total Armada Gun-Strength was as follows:

'cannon' type[3]			
cannon	90		
demi-cannon	73		
		163	14·5%
'perier' type			
cannon-periers	326	326	29·0%
'culverin' type			
culverins	165		
demi-culverins	137		
sakers	144		
minions	189		
		635	56·5%
		1,124	

Lewis's reconstruction rested on two foundations; first, the enumeration and classification of the guns of the Fighting Galleons by extrapolating from the evidence of the *San Salvador;* second, an assessment of the weight of shot thrown by the typical gun in each class, based essentially on the theoretical figures given by contemporary writers on gunnery, with some corroboration teased painfully from the fragmentary and rather ambiguous material that was available on the Armada itself. It is now clear that neither foundation was sound. The *San Salvador* and the *Rosario*, which Lewis used as a control on his yardstick, both turn out to be most exceptionally heavily gunned.[4]

Fortunately, it is not necessary to undertake a specific refutation of Lewis's extremely intricate and speculative arguments in detail, for we now have direct evidence from the Spanish archives on more than three-quarters of all the guns on the fleet. The papers relating to the preparation and despatch of the Armada – still very unworked – are preserved in the Archivo General de Simancas. Among the well over thirty bundles of correspondence, there are a number of lists and reports prepared by the artillery officers, and in particular by the Captain General of the Artillery, Don Juan de Acuña Vela, detailing the guns existing in the fleet, or in parts of the fleet, at successive points in time. Four of these are of capital importance:

(1) a 'summary relation' of the 1,072 guns aboard the four galleasses and two *naves* from Naples, the five *naves* from Sicily, and the fifteen *naves* and twenty-eight *urcas* from Andalusia, remitted to Madrid by the Captain General of the Artillery from Lisbon, 26 September 1587, on the arrival of the ships in the Tagus to join the Armada.[5] Totals are given for each type of gun, not ship by ship, but grouped by squadrons, with a range of weights of shot for each type;

(2) a relation of the 123 bronze and iron guns on seven *naves* and four *pataches* of Miguel de Oquendo's Guipúzcoan Squadron, also in the Tagus, dated, Lisbon, 31 October 1587.[6] Details are given of all the guns carried on each ship, who owned them, and the weight of shot they fired;

(3) an inventory listing, first, the 295 pieces aboard the sixteen ships of the Squadron of Castile, ship by ship and gun by gun, with weight of shot thrown, and then, another 184 guns and all the munitions added to each ship in the other eight squadrons of the Armada since their arrival in Lisbon.[7] In the case of the added guns no information is given other than their type, the metal they were made of, and if they were newly cast in the Lisbon foundry. The inventory was compiled personally by the Captain General of the Artillery after the final preparations had been made for the Armada's departure, and dated, Lisbon, 14 May 1588;

(4) a list drawn up by the Captain General in 1591 of the artillery carried by four of the principal vessels of the Armada of 1588, as a guide to future policy.[8] The ships were the *San Juan* of the Squadron of Portugal, the vice-flagship of the fleet, described as 'the best-gunned ship in the Armada', the *Nuestra Señora del Rosario*, the Andalusian flagship captured by the English on 1 August 1588, the *Santa Ana*, the Guipúzcoan flagship, and the *San Cristóbal*, the flagship of the Castilian Squadron of Diego Flores de Valdés. In each case the guns are classified individually by type and by weight of shot. To these can be added an undated statement of the guns carried by the Grand-duke of Tuscany's great galleon, the *Florencia*, which sailed with the Squadron of Portugal in 1588.[9] Forty-seven iron guns are listed, five less than in 1588, and described, not consistently, but mostly by type and either by weight of metal or by weight of shot.

Taken together, these lists provide full and direct information on the armament of seventy-eight of the 127 ships and 1,770 of the 2,411 guns that appear in the final Lisbon inventory of 9 May 1588.[10]

These figures, however, suffer from three principal shortcomings: (1) they are incomplete; (2) the list of 26 September 1587, which provides sixty per cent of all our guns, does not itemize each individual piece but gives aggregate totals which, in many cases, cannot be broken down into self-contained categories, particularly in terms of weight of shot; (3) the information on the galleasses, the squadrons of Andalusia, Guipúzcoa, Vizcaya, the Levant and the *urcas* was drawn up at least seven months before the Armada set sail, and it is not impossible that substantial changes may have taken place both in the number and in the distribution of the guns.

The last difficulty is the least serious. The lists for the squadrons in question were drawn up at the time of their arrival in Lisbon in September and October 1587. During the earlier part of 1588 there are indications of 200 or 210 guns that could possibly have been added to the fleet from new castings in Lisbon, from wrecks, and from foreign ships in Spanish ports, and 184 of these are noted in the list of additions of 14 May. As the Armada already had all but twenty-one or twenty-two of the guns it was to sail with at the end of May by 10 April, the list of additions must be practically complete, and of the guns still missing sixteen were smallish iron pieces and probably not 'countable'.[11] In short, the guns listed in September and October 1587 plus the additions to 14 May 1588 correspond so closely with the grand total of 9 May as to make it extremely probable that the guns of 1587 were also the guns of 1588, perhaps with some minor redistribution from the *urcas* to the other squadrons[12] (Table 1). The only major discrepancy is in the Castilian Squadron, the inventory of whose guns dates not from 1587 but from only a fortnight before the fleet sailed. On 14 May, the squadron had 295 guns; yet on the 9th, it had 348 attributed to it. There is nothing in the documents to explain this difference, and the information on the flagship, drawn up in 1591, coincides much more nearly with the smaller number than with the 9 May figures, which are too uniform to be credible and which are probably best discounted.[13] The overall margin of error, therefore, though not entirely eliminated, can only be a narrow one.

TABLE 1: GUNS ON 53 SHIPS AND THE *URCAS* 1587–88

Squadron	ships	26 Sept.	31 Oct. 1587	14 May	9 May 1588
Castile	16			295	348[14]
'Andalusia'	15	354		+ 20	363
Guipúzcoa	11		123	+ 42	162
Levant	7	187		+ 7	207
Galleasses	4	204			200
Urcas	28	328		+ 85	384

The other difficulties pose greater problems. We lack information altogether on forty-nine ships: thirty of the thirty-six *pataches*, one, though one of the weakest, of the Guipúzcoan Squadron, three of the Levant Squadron, seven of the ten of the Vizcayan Squadron, and eight of the important Portuguese Squadron, the most powerful unit in the fleet and the one that was most involved in the actual fighting. In all some 641 guns remain to be accounted for. This deficiency can be reduced, first by discounting the twenty-seven *pataches* whose powder allowance was less than 100 lb. per gun and whose 105 guns were almost certainly small pieces of less than 4 lb. shot, as Michael Lewis correctly assumed, and therefore not 'countable' in the final analysis;[15] and second, by adding to the *San Juan* and the *Florencia* of the Portuguese Squadron, the armament of two other major Portuguese galleons, the *San Martín*, the flagship of the whole fleet, and the *Santiago*. These two galleons were among the ships that survived the Armada disaster and returned to Spain in September 1588. They both reappear in fleet lists of 1591 mounting nearly the same number of guns as in 1588, the *San Martín* forty-five (forty-eight in 1588), the *Santiago* twenty-six (twenty-four in 1588), with a broadside requiring a supply of gunpowder very close to what was actually carried in 1588, which, of course, included infantry needs also, the *San Martín* 122 quintals in 1591, 140 in 1588, the *Santiago* 42½ quintals in 1591, 46 in 1588.[16] I propose, therefore, to accept their 1591 gun-complements as a fair approximation of what they carried three years before.

With this addition, we have direct information on the guns of all the four galleasses, the complete squadrons of Andalusia and Castile, all but one of the squadron of Guipúzcoa, all the *urcas*, six of the thirty-six *pataches*, three of the ten ships of the Vizcayan Squadron, four of the Portuguese and seven of the Levantine. If we call these the 'Known Guns' of the Armada, we have 1,841, or 76 per cent of the total of 2,411 listed in the general muster of 9 May 1588.

Beyond this it is impossible to go, either towards making up the 465 guns missing after the pieces on the *pataches* have been discounted, or towards breaking down the large general categories in which many of the guns in the list of 26 September 1587 are expressed, except by extrapolation. Lewis did this by dividing the ships into classes – Fighting Galleons, perier-carrying auxiliaries, non perier-carrying auxiliaries. The considerable variation in the armament of the squadrons (Table 2), partly deriving from the origin of the ships, and the lack of any straightforward criteria for the classification of individual vessels that actually correspond to the facts of the lists, have led me to ignore this schema and to extrapolate along two lines: (1) extending the 'Known Guns' by number and

TABLE 2: ARMADA FIRE-POWER BY SQUADRONS
('Fighting-Ships' only; *all* guns)

Squadron	ships	broadside (in lbs)	broadside/ship	guns	average/gun
Castile	8	811	101·4	182	4·5
'Andalusia'	15	2,510	167·3 ⎫ 171·4	382	6·6 ⎫ 6·7
Guipúzcoa	4	747	186·8 ⎭	101	7·4 ⎭
Portugal	8	2,274	284·3	319	7·1
Levant	5	1,557	311·4	173	9·0
Galleasses	4	1,437	359·1	204	7·0
	44	9,336	212·2	1,361	6·9

TABLE 3: SPANISH ARMAMENT ('KNOWN' GUNS)

Shot in lb. / Type[17]	50-34	35-29	27-15	21-18	19-16	16	16-10	15	14-12	14-7	11-8	7½-5	4½-4	4-3	12-3	6-1	?	under 4	Total
cannon	19	8																	27
demi-cannon		28	7	9	16		1	1									2		64
cañoncetes									10	9							5		24
periers	1	2	3				31	10	46	56	7	3	31				14	54	258
culverins			1	9	3														13
demi-culverins									27	31	33	2					12		105
sakers										29	12	118	1				20		180
demi-sakers/ falconetes													38	24			14		76
iron											8				198	261	44	30	541
falcones/medios falconetes																		272	272
esmeriles/versos																		281	281
																			1,841

TABLE 4: TOTAL SPANISH ARMAMENT ('ADJUSTED')

Shot in lb. / Type	50-34	35-29	27-22	21-16	15	14-12	11-8	7½-5	4½-4	Total
cannon	23	8								31
demi-cannon			6	68	5	2				81
cañoncetes						13	11			24
periers	1	4		7	19	91	75	7	27	231
culverins			2	19						21
demi-culverins						71	77	3		151
sakers						8	44	170	2	224
minions									70	70
iron						23	26	108	107	264
	24	12	8	94	24	208	233	288	206	1,097
'non-countable'										1,297
										2,394

type to the Total, on a squadron by squadron basis; (2) allocating guns by weight of shot in accordance with the known proportion of each weight within each class in the fleet as a whole, giving 'Adjusted' figures for Total Guns. Where arbitrary allocations have had to be made, they have been made on the side of excess rather than under-estimation. How wide is the margin of error resulting from this procedure it is impossible to say. Perhaps the relatively high proportion of the Known to the Total justifies some degree of confidence in the results (Tables 3 & 4).

The first thing to note about the figures in Table 4 is that the number of 'countable' guns of 4 lb. and over (1,097) is almost the same as Michael Lewis's estimate (1,124). The distribution of guns by type is also remarkably close. The complicating factor is the category 'Iron Guns', a group which makes up 29·4 per cent of Known Guns but which is missing altogether from Lewis's analysis. The Iron Guns are a problem largely because, though carefully distinguished from the bronze guns and listed separately, the Spaniards made no consistent effort to classify them either by type or by weight of ball. They were clearly not given much attention, and all the evidence confirms their relative unimportance. There is certainly nothing to support the view that there was any considerable number of imported English culverins or other large iron pieces in the Spanish fleet.[18] The biggest of these Iron Guns threw a stone ball of 13 or 14 lb., but there were less than a handful of those; 198 fired shot of between 3 and 12 lb.; another 397 iron shot of 6 lb. or less, and only twelve are known to have taken a ball larger than 6 lb. Of the 119 that it is possible to classify definitely as 'countable' or 'non-countable', seventy-eight were in the latter category. In addition to the 541 unspecified Iron Guns and those in the *esmeril-verso* class, a further 118 were classified by type and are included within their types; they were, one *cañoncete*, eighteen periers, fourteen sakers, seventy-eight *falconetes*, four *medios falconetes*, three *falcones*. The typical Iron Gun was, therefore, probably a *falconete* of 1½–4 lb. shot, but, giving the benefit of the uncertainties to the heavier guns, the 'countable' Iron Guns, estimated at 264, should split into six *cañoncetes*, thirty-one periers, 125 sakers and 102 minions, and the overall classification, taking the Iron Guns into account, becomes:

	Spanish Armada	Lewis	English Fleet
'cannon' type	12·9%	14·5%	3·0%
'perier' type	23·9%	29·0%	2·4%
'culverin' type	63·2%	56·5%	94·6%

Our general estimate of the 'countable' guns of the Spanish Armada is therefore not all that different from Lewis's, 13 per cent fewer 'cannon', 20 per cent fewer 'periers', 9 per cent more 'culverins', and our overall conclusion with respect to range very much the same. In comparison with the English armament, the Spanish carried proportionately far more medium-range 'cannon' and short-range stone-throwers, but only two-fifths (45 per cent) as many long- and medium-range 'culverins'. The Spanish, therefore, with only 55 per cent of the long and medium-range guns carried by the English, would have been at a real disadvantage in any running sea-fight, as Lewis argued, and this disadvantage would have been even more marked at the longest culverin and demi-culverin ranges, for which the Spanish had, not the 302 guns that Lewis believed, but only 172, and the English 497, nearly three times as many (Table 5).

TABLE 5: ENGLISH FLEET AND SPANISH ARMADA BY TYPE AND RANGE OF GUN AND WEIGHT OF SHOT

	English Fleet	Spanish Armada	Lewis
Type			
cannon	1	31	90
demi-cannon	54	81	73
cañoncetes		30	
periers	43	262	326
culverins	153	21	165
demi-culverins	344	151	137
sakers	662	349	144
minions	715	172	189
	1,972	1,097	1,124
Range			
long:			
culverin	497	172	302
demi-culverin			
medium:			
cannon			
demi-cannon	717	491	307
cañoncete			
saker			
short:			
perier	758	434	515
minion			
Shot			
'Heavy' 29 lb.+	55	36	163
'Medium' 27–22	43	8	326
'Light' 21–15	153	118	165
14–8	344	441	137
7·5–4	1,377	494	333
Broadside (lb.)	14,677	11,000	19,369
Average weight of shot per gun	7·4	10·0	17·2
Average weight of shot per ship	85·3	86·6	156·2

An analysis of the Spanish armament by type and range alone would thus go a long way towards confirming the first of Lewis's two main conclusions. The second was that the Spaniard's huge numerical preponderance in the shorter-range 'cannon' and 'perier' classes should have given him the advantage in the kind of close fight, preparatory to boarding, that was the Armada's chosen tactics. However, if we turn from type and range to firepower, to an analysis of the guns in terms of the weight of shot thrown, the picture is very different. Lewis attributed a notional calibre to each type of gun: cannon 50 lb., demi-cannon 32 lb., perier 24 lb., culverin 17 lb., demi-culverin 9 lb., saker 5 lb., minion 4 lb. The schema was derived from the English material and from the classifications of contemporary writers and theorists, in particular Robert Norton's *The Gunner* (1628). On the Spanish side, the main support came from Santa Cruz's proposal of 1586, nearer fantasy than reality and never a very reliable source in artillery matters. The other evidence adduced by Lewis, the list of shot brought over from Naples by the galleasses in July 1587 and the 2,000 cannon, demi-cannon and culverin balls, averaging 33·6 lb. each, taken by the English from the *San Salvador* (enough for forty guns not just the dozen or so large pieces on board), clearly relates to the fleet as a whole, not to the guns of the vessels in question, and, therefore, cannot help establish what weight of shot was thrown by any particular gun, nor support Lewis's belief that the Spanish guns generally fired a heavier ball than their English equivalents.

Again, unless one is prepared to discount all the documentary evidence, it is not necessary to consider Lewis's arguments in detail. The Armada lists reveal not only a very wide range within each type, but also a much lower average than that adopted by Professor Lewis for all the guns in the heavy 'cannon' and 'perier' classes (Table 6). It was only within the 'culverin' class that the average of the Spanish guns was higher than the norms adopted by Lewis, a fact that worked to some degree against Spain's numerical inferiority in that class, without substantially altering it (37 per cent of English 'culverins' by number, 41·6 per cent by firepower).

TABLE 6: CALIBRE OF SPANISH GUNS
(in lbs.; 'Countable' guns only)

Type	Number	Maximum	Minimum	Mean	Lewis
cannon	27	50	30	38·4	50
demi-cannon	62	27	14	18·6	32
cañoncetes	19	14	9	11·1	—
periers	143	70	4	11·8	24
culverins	13	24	16	19·0	17
demi-culverins	93	14	7	10·9	9
sakers	160	12	4	6·5	5
demi-sakers	24	4	(3)	(3·5)	4
falconetes	246	4·5	(1·5)	(2·7)	

In the 'cannon' and 'perier' classes, on the other hand, the Spanish preponderance in numbers is reduced in terms of weight of shot from 258
to 170 per cent and from 609 to 299 per cent respectively.

A direct comparison of the number of English and Spanish guns by
weight of shot reveals even more clearly how this affected the firepower
of the two fleets (Table 7).

TABLE 7: ENGLISH AND SPANISH ARMADA GUNS BY WEIGHT OF SHOT

	Shot in lb.	English Guns	Spanish Guns	Lewis
'Heavy'	50–34	1	24	90
	35–29	54	12	73
'Medium'	27–22	43	8	326
'Light'	21–16	153	94	165
	15		24	
	14–12		208	
	11–8	344	233	137
	7·5–5	662	288	144
	4·5–4	715	206	189

In the 'heavy' and 'medium'-shotted range (the ship-battering guns of
24 lb. and over by Lewis's definition), the English had more than twice as
many guns as the Spanish, and even down to the 15 lb. level they had at
least half as many again as the Spanish. It was only in the 14–8 lb. range
that the Spanish were superior by five to four, with the result that in guns
of 8–9 lb. and upwards the two fleets were evenly matched, and at 12 lb.
and over the Spanish actually exceeded the English by nearly 50 per cent.
Below 8 lb. the English superiority reasserted itself by nearly three to one.

The contrast with Lewis's figures is startling, and it entirely reverses
the relative strengths of the two forces as described by him and accepted
by all historians for the last thirty years. Lewis put the full broadside of the
English fleet at 14,677 lb. ('countable' guns only), that of the Spanish at
19,369 lb. Now it is possible to calculate the total firepower of the Armada
in two ways; first, by a simple addition of the calibres of the guns, directly
where known, by estimation and average where not; second, on the basis
of the powder allowance for the fleet. The total amount of powder
carried was 5,175 quintals, of which 600 quintals was reserved for the
siege-train, another 630 quintals or thereabouts required for the arque-
busiers and musketeers,[19] and 60 quintals for the galleys. A series of
relations drawn up between 10 and 17 April 1588 sets out a total powder
requirement for the artillery of 3,715 quintals, together with the number
of stone-throwers and iron-throwers in each squadron.[20] Depending on the
coefficients used for iron shot (primed with two-thirds its weight of
powder) and for stone balls (primed at one-third), the full broadside for

the entire fleet works out at between 12,450 and 12,600 lbs. It could possibly be as high as 13,000 lb. if the total amount of powder for the naval artillery was as much as the 3,885 quintals suggested by the inventory of 9 May. This is perfectly consistent with a broadside for 'countable' guns alone of about 11,000 lb., which is the figure derived by the application of the first method of computation.

The total firepower of the 'countable' guns of the Armada is little more than half what Lewis estimated (56·8 per cent), and, instead of its being nearly one-third greater than that of the fleet mobilized by the English, it is almost exactly one-third less. The average shot thrown per gun is 10 lb. (compared with Lewis's 17·2 lb.) and the average broadside per ship 86·6 lb. (compared with Lewis's 156 lb.) Given the considerably smaller number of guns and ships on the Spanish side, the averages remain higher than on the English side (7·4 lb. per gun; 85·3 lb. per ship), but the differences are now marginal.

However, it is perhaps unrealistic to consider the problem solely in terms of the total fleets mobilized. It is clear both from their armament and from the accounts of the actions that not all ships were destined to play the same role in the battle. There was a hard-core of well-armed ships in each fleet which bore the brunt of the fighting, the thirty-four Queen's Ships on the English side, the Fighting Galleons and Galleasses on the Spanish, to use Lewis's nomenclature. Lewis selected thirty-three galleons, *naos* and *naves* on the basis of their apparent strength and their involvement in the fighting. Unfortunately for purposes of direct comparison, my lists do not enable me to follow Lewis's choices exactly nor to distinguish the armament of all the ships that one would ideally have placed in the Fighting Galleon category. I have thought it best, therefore, to regard all the fifteen ships that sailed from Andalusia in July 1587 and the five Levanters that accompanied them as Fighting Galleons, even though they include a number of relatively unimportant vessels which in other circumstances one would rather have omitted. To these have been added the eight principal galleons of the Portuguese Squadron (extrapolated from the four 'known' ships), the eight best galleons of Castile, and four of the seven ships of Guipúzcoa for which there is detailed information. The total of forty ships and four galleasses is rather higher than the thirty-seven in Lewis's Fighting Galleon and Galleass class, but it includes twenty-nine of Lewis's selection (and excludes four others as unimportant) and eighteen of the twenty-three ships mentioned in the various narratives as taking part in the battle.[21] Unfortunately, it also omits some important ships that undoubtedly were in the front line (the *Concepción de Zubelzu* and the *Maria Juan* of the Vizcayan Squadron, the *Regazona* and the *Trinidad Valencera* of the Levant Squadron).

This omission I have tried to counter-balance both by opting for a large number of Fighting Galleons and by including the guns added to the front-line ships which are not in my list because their main armament is not known. I have aimed, therefore, at a fighting force *at least* as strong as Lewis's Fighting Galleons and perhaps, on paper at any rate, rather stronger.

A direct comparison can now be made between the Queen's Ships and the Spanish Fighting Galleons and Galleasses, and between my assessment of the Spanish fighting component and Lewis's (Tables 8, 9, 10).

TABLE 8: ARMAMENT OF SPANISH FIGHTING GALLEONS AND GALLEASSES

Shot in lb. Type	50-34	35-29	27-15	21-18	19-16	16	16-10	15	14-12	14-7	11-8	7½-5	4½-4	4-3	12-3	6-1	?	under 4	Total
cannon	18	8																	26
demi-cannon		28	9	9	19			2	2										69
cañoncetes								8		9									17
periers	1	4	3				31	56	52	6	1	31				13		74	272
culverins			2	9	5														16
demi-culverins								38	29	49	2							2	120
sakers									29	19	105	2						3	158
demi-sakers/ *falconetes*												21	24						45
iron													198	4	22	20			244
falcones/medios falconetes																		220	220
esmeriles/versos																		174	174
																			1,361

TABLE 9: ARMAMENT OF SPANISH FIGHTING GALLEONS AND GALLEASSES ('ADJUSTED')

Shot in lb. Type	50-34	35-29	27-22	21-16	15	14-12	11-8	7½-5	4½-4	Total
cannon	18	8								26
demi-cannon			6	57	4	2				69
cañoncetes						8	9			17
periers	1	4		5		77	61	8	19	175
culverins			2	14						16
demi-culverins						51	66	3		120
sakers						5	34	117	2	158
minions									33	33
iron						23	11	50	39	123
	19	12	8	76	4	166	181	178	93	737

'non-countable' 624

1,361

TABLE 10: QUEEN'S SHIPS AND SPANISH FIGHTING
GALLEONS AND GALLEASSES BY TYPE AND RANGE OF
GUN AND WEIGHT OF SHOT

	Queen's Ships	Fighting Galleons	Lewis
Type			
cannon	1	26	90
demi-cannon	54	69	73
cañoncetes		23	
periers	38	206	196
culverins	130	16	165
demi-culverins	200	120	47
sakers	220	205	27
minions	40	72	132
	683	737	730
Range			
long	330	136	212
medium	275	323	190
short	78	278	328
Shot			
'Heavy' 29 lb.+	55	31	163
'Medium' 27–22	38	8	196
'Light' 21–15	130	80	165
14–8	200	347	47
7·5–4	260	271	159
Broadside (lb.)	7,960	8,000	14,626
Average weight of shot per gun	11·65	10·85	20·0
Average weight of shot per ship	234	182	395

The general characteristics of the two forces already revealed by Lewis
and by the figures for the Total Fleets are here confirmed: a Spanish predominance in 'cannon' types of two to one and in 'perier' types of over
five to one; an English superiority in 'culverin' types of nearly three to two
(rather less in each case than the proportions in the fleet as a whole).

However, the classification by 'type' alone is not particularly relevant.
What mattered was range and weight of shot, and in these areas the English
had the advantage all along the line, at long and long/medium ranges,
in 'heavy', 'heavy'/'medium', and 'heavy'/'medium'/top-'light' weights,
and this advantage, except at long/medium range where it was only four to
three, was always in the region of two to one. Combining range and firepower, the English superiority was overwhelming, eight to one at the full-
culverin weight-range, over two to one in 'heavy'-shotted, medium-range
pieces, seven to four in pieces of 'heavy'/'medium'/top-'light' shot and
medium range. Only in guns of all calibres above 7·5 lb. did the Spaniards
have a slight 9·7 per cent advantage, reflecting their overall superiority in all
'countable' guns. Despite that, however, the total firepower of the two

fighting components was virtually identical. By these criteria the contrast with what has been generally accepted about the relative strengths of the two forces is immense. The Spaniards had only 55 per cent of the total firepower Lewis attributed to them, one-tenth the number of full-culverins, and one-ninth the 'heavy' and 'medium'-shotted pieces firing 22 lb. or more.

TABLE 11: ENGLISH AND SPANISH ARMAMENT BY COMBINED RANGE AND WEIGHT OF SHOT

	English Fleet	Spanish Armada	Queen's Ships	Fighting Galleons
long range/top-'light' shot	153	21	130	16
medium range/'heavy' shot	55	31	55	26
medium range/'heavy' & 'medium' shot	55	39	55	34
medium range/'heavy' & 'medium' & top-'light' shot	208	131	185	109

The Spanish evidence, therefore, confirms Lewis in so far as he revealed the clear superiority of the English in the longer-range, 'culverin' type of gun. Indeed, it actually goes further than Lewis by eliminating the one serious weakness in his argument, which was that although the English were overwhelmingly preponderant in the 'culverin' class as a whole, he nevertheless gave the Spanish a substantial majority of the only guns that perhaps might have done some damage at long range, the 17 lb. full-culverins. What it does not do, however, is to support his view of the Spaniard's strength, that is in the medium- and short-range, heavy 'cannon' and 'perier' types. On the contrary, it now seems fairly certain that the Spanish were deficient not only at long range, but also in heavy-shotted, medium- and short-range armament as well.

Only in a very relative sense, then, can it be said that the Spaniards were 'going for weight', or that the Armada was specifically armed for any particular tactical purpose, and none of Lewis's conclusions as to the nature of Spanish gun policy prior to the Armada can be maintained without modification.[22]

The rehabilitation of the older 'light-shotted' view of Laughton *et al.* (in general terms, if not entirely in its details), also provides a much more complete explanation of the Spanish failure to dominate the battle, not only at the long ranges at which the English chose to fight, but also in the close combat into which the Spaniards hoped to draw their adversary, and why in the final, day-long engagement off Gravelines, it was not the English fleet but the Spanish that was shattered by the close bombardment of its enemy. This is not, of course, to say that the Spanish failed solely because they were outgunned by the heavy artillery of the English. Other factors, like the acute shortage of shot, perhaps the poor quality of their shot and powder, the inexpertness of their gunners, no doubt played a part. It might also be argued that, with 'heavy' and 'medium'-shotted guns making up only about 3 per cent of the total combined armament of the two fleets, neither side had enough ship-smashing potential to destroy the other or to win a victory that could decisively have altered the balance of naval power, even in the short-term, by firepower alone. If the English with ninety-eight heavy 'cannon' and 'periers' could not do it, it is hardly surprising that the Spanish with only forty-four were almost totally ineffective. What does seem certain is that the Spanish Armada was at such a decisive disadvantage in firepower, in both weight of shot and range, that it was probably incapable of winning the sea battle on whatever terms it was fought.[23]

Notes

1 Reprinted as *Armada Guns*, London 1961, which is the version I have used and will refer to.
2 Michael Lewis, *The Spanish Armada*, Pan edition, London 1966, p. 179, *Armada Guns*, p. 198; Garrett Mattingly, *The Defeat of the Spanish Armada*, Pelican, 1962, pp. 295, 314, 316, 320, 322, 347.
3 The breakdown of the 'cannon' types is from *The Spanish Armada*, p. 83.
4 Between them the *Rosario* and the *San Salvador* carried 4·8 per cent of the 'countable' guns of the Fighting Galleons and Galleasses, but 15·4 per cent of the cannon, 11·6 per cent of the demi-cannon, 12·5 per cent of the full culverins, and 11·8 per cent of all guns firing shot of 15 lb. and over. The *Rosario* had a 'countable' broadside of 285 lb. and the *San Salvador* 229–34 lb., compared with the average for the fighting ships of 182 lb.
5 A(rchivo) G(eneral de) S(imancas), G(uerra) A(ntigua), legajo 221, f. 39. The *naves* are nos 71, 74; 68–9, 72–3, 75; 14, 21–2, 43–52, 54, 62, in the list in N(avy) R(ecords) S(ociety), vol. II, pp. 376–81.
6 AGS GA 221, f. 41; *NRS* vol. II, pp. 376–81, nos 55–61.
7 AGS GA 221, ff. 147, 149–56.
8 AGS GA 347, no fol.
9 AGS GA 214, f. 80.
10 This excludes the twenty guns on the four galleys, but not the thirty on the *Santa Ana*, flagship of the Vizcayan Squadron, which also failed to reach the Channel, but which I have left in rather than distort the comparison with the total mobilized English fleet. The number of ships in the Armada is usually given as 130; however, 131 are named in the inventory of 9 May 1588, printed in full in E. Herrera Oria, *La Armada Invencible*, Madrid. 1930, pp. 384–405.
11 Squadron figures given in *relaciones* of 10, 16 and 17 April 1588 (AGS GA 221, ff. 127–9), together with the data on the Castilian Squadron on 14 May 1588, add up to a total of 2,389–90 guns, of which 1,471 were bronze and 918 iron; compared with 2,431, 1,497 bronze, 934 iron (with the twenty of the galleys to be deducted) in the list of 9 May. On 21 May, Acuña Vela confirmed that nothing of importance had been added since 7 May, AGS GA 223, f. 93.
12 There were twenty-eight *urcas* in the list of 26 September 1587, twenty-three on 9 May 1588.
13 The *capitana* of Castile was credited with thirty-six guns on 9 May 1588, thirty-one on 14 May 1588, and thirty-two in the 1591 list, the only significant difference between the last two being an additional *esmeril* in 1591.

14 The 348 of Castile excludes the thirty-six listed on 9 May 1588 on the Squadron's two *pataches*. Each gun is allowed only 6 oz. of powder per ball, and if included the total guns on the Armada would be 2,467 not 2,431. The detailed list of 14 May 1588 mentions no guns on the *pataches*, and I have followed this.

15 There were thirty-six *pataches* altogether. I am counting the three best armed, Nos. 99–101 in *NRS* vol. II, pp. 376–81.

16 AGS GA 347, no fol.

17 The description of gun types and qualities given by Lewis (*Armada Guns*, pp. 18–38) is broadly applicable to the Spanish armament also, with two exceptions: (1) *cañoncetes:* I use this expression to cover three types of small cannon that Lewis ignored, the *tercio cañon*, the *cuarto cañon* and the *cañoncete*. The *tercio cañon* was the largest piece, weighing *c.* 2,400 lb. and throwing an iron ball of 12–14 lb. The *cuartos cañones* and *cañoncetes* were about eighteen calibres long, weighed from 1,400 up to 1,800 or 1,900 lb., and fired iron shot of between 9 and 12 lb. With some doubts, I have counted the *cañoncetes* as medium-range pieces; (2) the Spanish did not use the term 'minion'. In Spanish classifications the guns next below sakers in size were *medios sacres* and *falconetes*, which fired a range of shot from 1½ to 4½ lb. The Spanish guns that I call 'minions' are the 'countable' members of the *medio sacre* and *falconete* classes.

18 *Pace* Lewis, *Armada Guns*, p. 137.

19 Extended from the 8,000 lb. (80 quintals) provided for the 2,458 infantry of the Squadron of Castile (12·7 per cent of the total of 19,295), AGS GA 221, f. 152.

20 AGS GA 221, ff. 127–9; figures for the Castilian Squadron, not in these *relaciones*, can be interpolated from AGS GA 221, f. 148.

21 My forty-four Fighting Galleons and Galleasses are *NRS* vol. II, pp. 376–81, nos 1–8, 14, 21–2, 27–30, 33, 35, 37, 39, 43–52, 54–8, 62, 68–9, 72–3, 75, 121–4.

22 Lewis, *Spanish Armada*, p. 82.

23 New evidence on the Armada and its armament is now being brought to the surface by the marine archaeologists. The findings are still fragmentary, but the guns and the shot discovered on the wrecks of the *Girona*, the *Gran Grifón*, the *Nuestra Señora de la Rosa* and the *Trinidad Valencera*, together with those salvaged from the Tobermory Galleon in the seventeenth century, are very much in line with what has emerged from the documentary sources. The only wreck for which a full comparison is possible is the *Rosa*. No guns have been found, but a quantity of iron shot of 50, 18, 9, 5 and 1 lb., and stone balls of 14 and 5 lb. The only denominations that do not correspond with the guns listed on 31 October 1587, and the additions to 14 May 1588, are the 5 lb. iron shot, for which the nearest piece is the demi-culverin of 7 or 12 lb., and the 50 lb shot. No full-cannon are listed on the *Rosa*, but as a number of vessels in the squadron were also carrying full-cannon or other heavy shot that does not fit their recorded guns (*San Salvador, Santa Barbara, San Buenaventura* – AGS GA 221, f. 41; *San Esteban* – AGS GA 221, f. 153), the likely explanation is that these were being carried in store. The full-cannon found on the *Trinidad Valencera* and the Tobermory Galleon (probably the *San Juan de Sicilia*) and the cannon-balls on the *Rosa* are all larger than the 40 lb.-calibre referred to in the documents, even in the technical descriptions of the very same 'Remigy' guns that have been salvaged. Otherwise, the lack of shot of between 18 and 48 lb. with the wrecks bears out my view of the lightness of Spanish demi-cannon and perier types. On this point I owe much to my conversations and correspondence with Colin Martin of the Institute of Maritime Archaeology, University of St Andrews, and his recent book *Full Fathom Five: Wrecks of the Spanish Armada*, Chatto & Windus, London 1975.

VII

Spanish Armada Gun Procurement and Policy

The engagements which took place between the Spanish and the English fleets in the Channel between 31 July and 8 August 1588 were the first great naval gun-battle in history. In that battle the armament, the gunnery and the sailing qualities of the two forces were the decisive elements. Those elements were not mere accidents, but expressions of the nature of the two states and societies that confronted each other. We now know just about as much as we are ever likely to know about the armament of the two fleets and the all-round advantage the English appear to have had at all levels of artillery and gunnery. If, however, we want to get behind the battle to a fuller understanding of the conflict as a conflict of systems (administrative, mental and technological) we need to know why the fleets were configured as they were and whether they could have been configured differently. This paper will try to show why the Spanish Armada was armed as it was, and to argue that the way it was armed was a reflection of the state that equipped it.

Historical opinion has differed over the nature of Spanish gun policy, and hence over the nature of Spanish objectives. Laughton, and following him, Mattingly, have argued that there was no sensible policy at all. Guns were got by hook or by crook without system or plan. Michael Lewis and Commander David Waters, on the other hand, argued for a more coherent gun strategy formulated, in the light of the experience of Drake's raid on Cadiz, in a deliberate attempt to bring Spanish armament into line with that of the English. It was a recognition of the fact that the key to the outcome of any engagement on the high seas would not be infantry, but gunnery. 'They appear, characteristically, to have gone in for big, long-range guns', Waters writes.[1] The result, he claims, was a doubling of

---

[1] D. W. Waters, 'The Elizabethan Navy and the Armada Campaign', *The Mariner's Mirror*, 35 (1949), 116.

long-range guns in the Spanish fleet between 1586 and 1588, so that by the time it sailed the Armada was even better equipped with full culverins than the English. More recently, Colin Martin has also argued that there was a coherent, if belated, gun policy, differentiating between the heavy artillery of the front-line, fighting ships and the defensive armament of the auxiliaries, and a last-minute redistribution of guns by Medina Sidonia to put that policy into effect.[2]

It is obvious, however, that there could be no coherent gun policy without determination in procurement, and until we can establish where, when and how the guns of the Armada were acquired we can say little meaningful about the reality or viability of any such gun policy.

The Guns of the Armada: Private and Royal

In fact, the great bulk of the ordnance carried on the Armada was not provided by the Crown, but was comprised of private guns which came with the ships. That itself was a function of the limitations of Spanish naval power and the lack in 1588 of a substantial, royal ocean fleet. Only thirty of the 131 vessels of the Armada were owned by the Crown, the rest were private vessels requisitioned or hired with their own guns already on board. Gun lists from mid-summer 1587 show that almost 90 per cent of the total of guns inventoried on the eve of the Armada's departure in May 1588 were in place nearly a year before.[3] The fifteen ships from Andalusia which served in the Andalusian, Guipuzcoan and Vizcayan squadrons in 1588 with 363 guns, were already carrying 357 guns on 21 June 1587. Seven other ships of Oquendo's Guipuzcoan squadron had 123 of their 162 guns on 31 October 1587. Twenty-six *urcas* and *pataches*, with 434 guns listed on 9 May 1588, had 355 guns on 18 July 1587. Five of the ships in the Levant squadron, with 220 guns in May 1588, had 199 guns when they arrived from Sicily in July 1587. Of the 1179 guns those vessels carried in May 1588, 1034 were already in existence by the end of October 1587. Of those 1034 at least 841 were ships' guns; only 123 are known to have been royal guns, probably added to the vessels after their enlistment in mid 1587.[4] Even of the front-line fighting units, three-quarters of the guns on the ships in the Levantine, Vizcayan, Guipuzcoan and Andalusian squadrons were private guns which came with the ships.

---

[2] See Colin Martin, 'The Spanish Armada Expedition, 1968–70', in *The Colston Papers*, vol. XXIII, ed. D. J. Blackman (London, 1973), pp. 453–7.

[3] The relevant gun lists are to be found in Archivo General de Simancas, Guerra Antigua [henceforth AGS GA], legajo 221, ff. 21 [21/6/1587], 2 [18/7/1587], 39 [26/9/1587], 41 [31/10/1587].

[4] AGS GA 199, f. 48, Acuña Vela, Lisbon, 18/7/1587, sending statement of 'todas las pieças de artilleria de bronce y hierro colado...que se han dado desde nueve de Mayo deste año hasta quinze deste mes de Julio despues que yo llegue aqui de los magazenes y Castillos de V. Md desta ciudad y su Ribera', noting 30 bronze and 75 iron guns.

Between the ships' guns and the royal guns there was an enormous difference of quality. The majority of the private guns were small pieces made of cast or wrought iron. Between 179 and 210 of 268 guns of the fifteen ships from Andalusia, and probably all, but certainly 83, of the 86 of the seven Oquendo ships were of iron. At least 71 of those 86 were 'non-countable', that is to say throwing shot of less than 4 lbs, and only one is known to have fired a ball greater than $4\frac{1}{2}$ lbs. All 326 guns on twenty-eight *urcas* in September 1587 were made of iron, and none threw a shot of more than 6 lbs. The Levanters were better gunned, the bulk of their guns being bronze (126 of 161), and more than half of them 'countable'.[5]

Iron guns, though numerous, were not thought much of. Though only about a quarter the cost of bronze pieces, iron lasted only six or seven years, tended to rust, burst easily and could not be recast as bronze could. Bronze guns were stronger, hence safer and capable of greater range. In the long run, therefore, iron was held to be nearly as costly as bronze and not as good. The official lists generally did not bother to distinguish iron guns by type, and often not even by calibre. The Andalusian ships, for example, were listed merely as having '182 piezas de hierro colado y de martillo de tres a doce libras de bala'.[6] The only concern was whether they threw iron or stone shot.

Royal guns, on the other hand, were predominantly of bronze. All 37 royal guns on Oquendo's ships, except for two iron *esmeriles*, and 83 of the 86 on the fifteen Andalusians, were bronze pieces. On the evidence of the Oquendo ships they were also likely to be bigger—18 of the 37 were 'countable', ten demi-culverins, two *cañoncetes*, six demi-cannon and two cannon, firing shot of 8 to 50 lbs.

Gun Procurement

The ordnance with which the Armada was equipped at the end of 1587, composed as it was overwhelmingly of small-shotted iron guns, provided for the defence of merchantmen and designed primarily to repel boarders and to provide that defence with as little loss of cargo capacity as possible, was clearly inadequate for the needs of the enterprise that lay ahead. The number, the size and the quality of the Armada's artillery were a major concern of all the fleet's commanders throughout the early months of 1588. 'The whole Armada is short of artillery', complained the marquis of Santa Cruz at the end of December.[7] Two months later it was the Captain-General of

---

[5] It is not possible to distinguish the guns of the fifteen ships of Andalusia by calibre; of the 354 guns 73 were 'countable', 81 'non-countable', 182 were listed merely as of between 3 and 12 lbs ball, and 22 as of 3 to 4 lbs ball: AGS GA 221, f. 39.

[6] AGS GA 221, f. 39.

[7] E. Herrera Oria, ed., 'La Armada Invencible', *Archivo Histórico Español*, vol. 2 (Valladolid, 1929), p. 97, Santa Cruz, 29/12/1587.

72

the Artillery, Don Juan de Acuña Vela, who drew attention to 'the need there is that this Armada be better equipped with artillery', and in March he was reporting again that 'many ships are signally short of artillery'.[8] All the main squadrons were inadequately armed. The Portuguese galleons were 80 guns short in December.[9] Recalde's artillery, even that of his flagship, was 'poca y chica'.[10] Oquendo's flagship was well-gunned, but his Guipuzcoan squadron as a whole was woefully under-equipped, still needing 125 guns at the beginning of March. As Don Alonso de Bazán wrote, 'There is so little artillery on this squadron that it is not being counted'.[11] The problem was as much the quality of the ordnance as its quantity. The Andalusian squadron had plenty of small, iron guns, but for ships of such size it was desperately short of 'hartillería gruesa'. Don Pedro de Valdés complained that he had only five big, bronze guns on nine ships, each of which was capable of carrying 15 or 20. He needed to replace his small pieces with at least 40 new guns just 'to be averagely equipped'.[12] The Levantine ships and the *urcas* also were in need of bronze guns.[13]

There was, therefore, in the three months before the Armada sailed an urgent need to find additional guns from every possible source. There were in fact three such sources. Most of the royal guns provided hitherto had probably come from stock, from the royal arsenal in Málaga, the Casa de Contratación in Seville, and the fortresses of the Lisbon estuary. Unfortunately, we have only limited evidence of the numbers or the types of guns chosen, but what evidence we have does not support the Lewis-Waters hypothesis. Statements of the guns in Seville and Lisbon that could be used on the fleet list seven demi-cannons, two *cañones pedreros*, eight sakers and nine demi-sakers,[14] and that profile is confirmed by what we know of the guns that were not taken. A complete statement of the holdings of all the Iberian forts and arsenals drawn up soon after the Armada in November 1588,[15] shows the Lisbon castles, the most obvious source of last-minute

---

[8] AGS GA 220, f. 224 (27/2/1588); AGS GA 222, f. 52, Acuña Vela, 5/3/1588, 'cierto no solamente las naves de Oquendo pero otras muchas estan faltissimas de Artilleria notablemente'.

[9] Herrera Oria, p. 97.

[10] AGS GA 220, f. 55, Juan Martínez de Recalde, Lisbon, 6/2/1588.

[11] AGS GA 219, f. 10; AGS GA 222, f. 52; AGS GA 221, f. 52, 'Relacion del Artilleria que a menester El armada questa a cargo de Oquendo', with letter of D. Alonso de Bazán, 5/3/1588, 'El artilleria que tiene esta escuadra es tan poca que por este Respeto no se pone aqui'; AGS GA 222, f. 60, Miguel de Oquendo, Lisbon, 19/3/1588, 'la cappitana tengo bien artillada y las demas estan faltosas'.

[12] AGS GA 222, f. 41, D. Pedro de Valdés, Lisbon, 5/3/1588.

[13] Herrera Oria, p. 135, Conde de Fuentes, Lisbon, 4/2/1588.

[14] AGS GA 221, f. 9, 'Relacion del artilleria que se podra sacar del Castillo desta Ciudad...para servir en el Armada', Lisbon, 6/5/1587; AGS GA 221, f. 33, 'Relacion de la Artilleria que paresce que truxo de la ciudad de Sevilla', 18/8/1587.

[15] AGS GA 365, 'Relacion general de la artilleria que ay en España', 17/11/1588.

additions from stock, to be still holding sixteen cannon, two *cañones cule-brinados* and six culverins, while the arsenals in Málaga and Cartagena were also holding seventeen full cannon. Even allowing for the needs of land defence, this suggests that the Spaniards were not taking the really big guns for the Armada, or at least that they had the resources to arm the fleet with far more of the big guns than they chose to employ.

The second source of last-minute additions was the compulsory pur-chase of guns from merchant ships in Spanish ports, or the confiscation of guns from ships taken in piracy. In February 1588 twelve guns from a con-demned English pirate were adjudicated to the king and given to Oquendo, and twelve guns were taken from a Scottish ship accused of piracy but ac-quitted by the auditor.[16] In March some sixty guns were compulsorily pur-chased from a score or so of German hulks.[17] In June the galleys captured two English ships off Bayona in Galicia with sixteen iron guns and twelve iron *pedernales*,[18] and other guns were taken from English ships trading in Andalusia and Portugal.[19] There is, however, no evidence whatsoever that the Spaniards had been buying up shiploads of English culverins, or that the Armada carried any iron guns of that type.[20]

The third source of guns was manufacture in the royal foundries. Ac-cording to the Venetian ambassador 200 guns were being cast in Lisbon in November 1587.[21] If his informant really was, as he claimed, close to the Marquis of Santa Cruz, he was probably being deliberately misled. The resources for casting new guns in Spain were in fact rather limited. Cannon-founding facilities existed in Málaga, Seville and Lisbon, but their capacity had never been sufficient for Spain's needs, and with the Armada projected to sail from September 1587 onwards, only Lisbon was a suitable site for new castings. Extra furnaces had to be set up in Lisbon, but their completion was delayed until August 1587 by inadequacies of funding.[22] At the end of November, thirty guns were being cast there, but work on them had halted for lack of money.[23] By January 1588 nearly 1200 quintals of artillery (forty guns) had been cast in the Lisbon foundries,[24] but progress was slow. There were shortages of materials, copper, wood (for wheels and carriages) and iron (for reinforcements and shot).[25] By January 1588,

[16] AGS GA 220, f. 12, 224.
[17] AGS GA 222, f. 21, 52, 63.
[18] AGS GA 224, f. 71.
[19] AGS GA 221, f. 21; J. Vanes, ed., 'Documents Illustrative of the Overseas Trade of Bristol in the Sixteenth Century', *Bristol Records Society*, XXXI, (1979), 141, 143.
[20] Michael Lewis, *The Spanish Armada* (London, 1960), p. 85.
[21] CSP Venetian, vol. 8, no. 603, p. 326.
[22] AGS GA 199, ff. 47, 52.
[23] Herrera Oria, p. 70.
[24] AGS GA 219, f. 65, Acuña Vela, 9/1/1588.
[25] AGS GA 219, f. 30; AGS GA 220, f. 7.

the price of iron was rising because corsair activity was inhibiting imports from Germany and even from Biscay, and there was only half the copper for all the guns that were required.[26] There were also shortages of skilled ironsmiths, foundrymen and polishers.[27] 'Because of the great shortage of craftsmen', the manufacture of guns in Lisbon took twice as long and cost two-thirds more than in Málaga.[28] Four guns had to be rejected because of faults in manufacturing,[29] and late in February an explosion during testing, caused by reloading too soon after firing and failing to clean out the barrel properly, killed two artillerymen and blew the arm off another.[30] That left only three foundrymen of any account. The Italian gun-founder, Bartolomé de Somorriva, was untrustworthy, his castings were unreliable and four more of his guns were rejected for being undermetalled and erratically bored.[31] Disagreements over terms with the master-founders, who were paid on a contract basis and claimed they were losing money because of the high prices in Lisbon, also slowed down work.[32] The staff of the Portuguese ordnance office offered to cast guns for Acuña Vela, but only after they had equipped their own ships, and in any case the guns they made did not suit the requirements of the Castilian artillery general.[33] As a result, by the end of February only sixty guns had been completed in a year[34] and, although a number of other guns may have been cast in Lisbon for the Portuguese squadron, only 62 new pieces were added to the Armada on the Spanish account between January and May 1588.[35] When on 14 May Acuña Vela remitted to Madrid a complete account of everything supplied to the Armada since his arrival in Lisbon, he listed 184 guns added since the original lists had been drawn up, reporting with satisfaction that 'eight days ago everything to be supplied was completed, and there is no need for anything else, nor indeed is there anything in the stores nor in the market, because everything that could be found has been provided'.[36]

Armada Gun Policy

Given the close correspondence between the guns listed on the ships in the summer of 1587 and the number carried by the Armada in May 1588,

---

[26] AGS GA 219, f. 27.
[27] AGS GA 219, ff. 35, 36.
[28] AGS GA 219, f. 30, Acuña Vela, 9/1/1588.
[29] AGS GA 220, f. 224, Acuña Vela, 27/2/1588.
[30] AGS GA 220, f. 15.
[31] AGS GA 220, ff. 14, 50, 224; AGS GA 222, f. 55; AGS GA 223, f. 90.
[32] AGS GA 220, f. 224; AGS GA 222, f. 25.
[33] AGS GA 220, ff. 22, 55, 56.
[34] AGS GA 220, f. 224, 27/2/1588.
[35] AGS GA 221, f. 147, 'Sumario general desta Relacion' ['de lo que lleva esta felice Armada de V. Mag...tocante al cargo del Capitan General de la Artilleria...'].
[36] AGS GA 223, f. 92.

the scope for any substantial change in gun policy consequential upon the presumed lessons of the actions off Cadiz at the end of April 1587 was very limited indeed, being restricted in practice to whatever could be effected by means of internal redistribution and to the selection of the 10 per cent or so of the guns that were added to the fleet between October 1587 and May 1588. A major redistribution of the ordnance aboard the fleet does seem to have been undertaken by the Duke of Medina Sidonia soon after his assumption of command. Since his arrival, he reported on 26 March, 'all the artillery has been moved around because it was impossible to use it in the way it had been deployed', and other adjustments had been made to the munitions stocks to lighten the burden of some ships and increase the load in others.[37] Unfortunately, not much can be inferred about the policy behind this redistribution beyond the desire to accommodate the weight of the ordnance to the size of the ship.

We are considerably better informed about the guns that were added to the ships of the fleet after their arrival in Lisbon. The account submitted by the Captain-General of the Artillery details 184 guns allocated by him to all the squadrons of the Armada, bar those of Castile, the Galleasses and the Galleys, prior to May 1588.[38]

Guns Added	Source		Squadron allocation[39]						
	old	new	u	p	P	V	A	G	L
cannon	8								8
demi-cannon	2	16	2		4	2	7	3	
cañoncetes	5	4	7		1			1	
cañones pedreros	1	25	1		4	4	2	13	2
demi-culverins	8	15	10			1		9	3
sakers	18		18						
falcones pedreros	11				4			4	3
falconetes	7		5					2	
falcones	5	2	3	4					
demi-sakers	14		14						
iron pieces	35		25					10	
versos/esmeriles	8								8
TOTALS	122	62	85	8	8	8	13	49	13

The question is whether it is possible from an analysis either of gun types or of squadron allocations to identify any coherent armaments policy. It is only the 62 new guns specially cast for the Armada in Lisbon which give

---

[37] C. Fernández Duro, *La Armada Invencible*, 2 vols (Madrid, 1884–85), I, 475, 486.

[38] AGS GA 221, ff. 147–56; the account does not include everything for the Portuguese squadron for which the Portuguese Purveyor, Luis Cesar, was responsible, AGS GA 223, f. 92.

[39] Squadron symbols: u=urcas, p=pataches, P=Portugal, V=Vizcaya, A=Andalusia, G=Guipúzcoa, L=Levant.

us any real indication of the kind of armament the Spaniards wanted. The guns got by confiscation were simply the guns the merchantmen happened to be carrying, and they were predominantly small, iron pieces of little real use. The artillery bought from the German hulks was described as 'mala y toda de fierro colado', which had to be taken nonetheless, because 'the great shortage there is makes it necessary to take whatever can be legitimately taken from their owners'.[40] Most of the larger 'old' guns were the royal battery and field train which had been brought from Málaga. The eight full cannon given to the Levant squadron, four demi-culverins given to the squadron of Guipúzcoa, and seventeen sakers and five *falconetes* put aboard the *urcas*, were equipped with carriages for both field and ship-board use and seem to have been reallocated to ships on logistical as much as tactical grounds. That was certainly true of the eight cannon, which were put aboard the ships of the Levant squadron solely because of their carrying capacity and the facilities they had for loading and unloading.[41]

Two things stand out from the way the guns were distributed among the squadrons. The first is that over half the guns were allocated to the *urcas* and *pataches*, auxiliary squadrons with no serious fighting role whose armament was essentially defensive in purpose. Another quarter was given to Oquendo's Guipuzcoan squadron. That was no doubt because the squadron was desperately under-gunned, and even after its allocation of 49 guns, remained some 75 pieces short. Yet nearly half the guns given to Oquendo were small and anti-personnel weapons, implying a secondary battle role for the squadron. The other thing which stands out is that the larger calibre guns seem to have been used, in the main, for the selective reinforcement of a small number of front-line ships. Excluding the battery cannon, 64 of the 76 larger calibre guns (demi-culverins and over) were given to fourteen ships, eight of them flagships. The *almiranta general*, the Portuguese galleon *San Juan*, got eight guns, four demi-cannon and four *cañones pedreros*, adding 120 lbs to her firepower; the *Nuestra Señora del Rosario*, the *capitana* of Andalusia, got six, four demi-cannon and two *pedreros*, adding 92 lbs of firepower; the *capitana* of Recalde's squadron also got six, four *pedreros* and two demi-cannon throwing 88 lbs of shot; Don Alonso de Leyva's *Rata Encoronada* and Oquendo's *San Salvador* each got five, four *cañones pedreros* and one demi-culverin, three demi-culverins and two *pedreros* with 50–60 lbs of shot. All these were guns of the new fabrication. That would seem to bear out Colin Martin's suggestion that there was, indeed, a rational distribution of guns in the Armada, the heavy artillery going to the front-line ships, the defensive weaponry to the second-liners.[42] However,

[40] AGS GA 222, f. 7, Medina Sidonia, 19/3/1588.
[41] AGS GA 219, f. 35, 23/1/1588.
[42] See note 2 above.

VII

such selectivity was by no means absolute. Eighteen sakers and a dozen larger guns (two demi-cannon, five *tercios cañones*, four demi-culverins, and a *pedrero*) went to eight secondary storeships of the squadron of *urcas*, and of the five ships which received all the 26 'countable' guns given to the Guipuzcoan squadron, two, the *Santa Bárbara* and the *Santa Marta*, the recipients of four *cañones pedreros*, one *tercio cañón*, and five demi-culverins, were clearly second-liners, and only one, the *San Salvador*, is recorded as having taken any active part in the fighting. It is clear from the evidence we have of successive additions to the armament of the Guipuzcoan squadron that the *San Salvador* was being deliberately built up into a powerfully-armed warship, but the logic behind the distribution of guns to the other ships of the squadron is not at all apparent.

Ships	Original		Added Oct 87		Added May 88		Total	
	guns	lbs	guns	lbs	guns	lbs	guns	lbs
San Salvador	14	35	7	170	5	65	26	270
N.S. de la Rosa	11	30	13	113	2	23	26	166
Santa Bárbara	14	13	2	1	12	85	28	99
San Esteban	10	40	2	22	7	104	19	166
Santa Marta	12	30	3	10	8	45	23	85

The impression one is getting is that the different role of front-line ships and lesser ships and auxiliaries in the fighting had not been fully worked out. It looks as if it was envisaged that every ship would be equally engaged in any action. There was no differential allocation of powder and shot, and every gun was apparently given a uniform allowance regardless of the vessel it was on. The Armada was not, therefore, munitioned for the convoy formation that was adopted in the Channel, and if, as so many of the participants insisted, the outcome of the campaign was determined by shortages of munitions among the front-line ships after Gravelines, that failure of tactical appreciation was to prove crucial.

It is clear from the correspondence, moreover, that no official gun-policy existed as such prior to the Armada. Preferences were essentially personal. Madrid had to authorise the work done in the cannon-foundries, but policy and distribution seem largely to have been determined by the generals themselves. Far from being the blind reactionary in artillery matters as he is sometimes portrayed, Santa Cruz's own concern seems to have been for range and mobility. His preferences were for relatively light-weight, medium-shotted guns with added length (presumably for range), like the generally despised, Manrique *cañoncetes*, which he had extended by $2\frac{1}{2}$ calibres to throw a 12 lb iron ball from a gun weighing no more than 18 quintals. Similarly, he wanted to modify the 12-pounder demi-culverins made by Gregorio Lefer of Augsburg in the 1540s, by reducing their metal from 44 to 34 quintals whilst maintaining a 33-calibre length.[43] Acuña Vela, on the other hand, disliked excessive length in naval guns and put his emphasis on shorter and more heavily-shotted pieces.[44] It looks, therefore, though the distinction was never expressed precisely in these terms, as if Santa Cruz stood for range and Acuña Vela for weight. In the event, the new castings of 1588 went for neither. The 62 new guns included no piece of more than 36 quintals, and no calibre greater than 16 lbs iron. Three quarters of the guns were 'cannon-type': sixteen demi-cannon with a 16 lb iron ball, four *cañoncetes* with a 12 lb iron ball, and 25 *pedreros* with a 14 lb stone ball. The rest were 'culverin-type': demi-culverins throwing iron shot of 7 and 12 lbs and two 3-pounder *falcones*. That profile confirms the evidence of the general artillery inventory of November 1588 that the Spaniards were not in fact going for heavy full cannon and long-range culverins after Cadiz, but were concentrating rather on shorter-bodied, medium-shotted pieces of short to medium range and intermediate weight. This lack of emphasis on range rather suggests that the Spaniards were not intending to make the running against the English fleet. With their armament they could hope for no more than to force the English to keep their distance. They were not even going for heavy 'ship-killing' guns. Even after Cadiz, Santa Cruz's orders for the new ordnance to be cast for the fleet were for nothing bigger than a 12-pounder.[45] It is true that Acuña Vela and others thought something heavier was needed for use at sea, and proposed the manufacture of a number of 20-pounder demi-cannon, 19 and 20 calibres in length, and weighing 35 or 36 quintals, as well as 40-pounder cannon, 10 feet long and 55 quintals in weight,[46] but in fact nothing larger than a 16-pounder demi-cannon seems to have been produced for the Armada. If there was to be a lesson in 1588, it was that both range and weight were needed.

The Lessons of 1588

The few retrospective comments that there are on the armament of the 1588 fleet confirm what has been said about the *ad hoc* nature of that armament and its selective and uneven distribution. The Armada was armed with whatever guns were available, and, apart from the flagships and a few other vessels, most of the fleet was very weakly gunned. 'The ships that sailed in this last Armada were armed according to the number and quality of the types and weights of the said guns ["según la calidad y cantidad del género y peso de las dichas pieças de artillería"; viz. in accordance with what guns there were], and the best gunned of them were the flagships and

---

[43] AGS GA 199, f. 51, Acuña Vela, 18/7/1587; AGS GA 365, Acuña Vela, Madrid, 29/1/1589, 'Sobre la fundicion de artilleria para mar'.
[44] AGS GA 199, ff. 51, 52.
[45] AGS GA 199, f. 52, Acuña Vela, 25/7/1587.
[46] *Ibid.*

other special ships, because many sailed with little artillery, and that poor, both in quality and in weight of shot thrown.'[47] The evidence that we have from official comment, from the analysis of new castings, and from the programmes for the fitting out of the post-Armada fleets shows how Spanish gun policy responded to the lessons of 1588.

The Spanish perception was that the English fleet had been much more *heavily* gunned than the Armada.[48] Their first concern, therefore, was not simply for lighter, longer-range guns, as Michael Lewis argued, but to equip the new Spanish fleet with the heaviest artillery possible ('la más gruessa que se pudiere'), that is to say with guns of at least 18–20 and up to 35 quintals.[49] But there was also a concern for range, and in particular to increase the number of demi-culverins and sakers.[50] It was this double concern for size and range that characterised Spanish post-Armada gun policy. The new guns Acuña Vela wanted cast in January 1589 were to be appropriate to the size of the ship 'and of a sort that can do damage from a distance because of their good range and from close range wreak notable destruction on the enemy fleet'. The majority of the guns should fire 'good-sized iron shot, and stone balls that can do more damage to the ships than the smaller iron equivalent'.[51] It is not true, therefore, that the *pedrero*

---

[47] AGS GA 347, unfoliated, undated *relación*: 'Las nabes que fueron en esta ultima armada se proveyeron de artilleria segun la calidad y cantidad del genero y peso de las dichas pieças de artilleria, y las que mas bien armadas yban dellas heran las capitanas y otras particulares, porque muchas yban con poca artilleria y rruin ansi en calidad della como en los calibos del peso de las pelotas'.

[48] AGS GA 280, f. 94, D. Alonso de Bazán, Ferrol, 3/1/1590: 'Desta [artilleria] ay tan poca y la que ay tan menuda que si V. Magd no se sirve de mandarlo remediar conforme la relacion que he embiado yra mal esta armada para buscar la del enemigo y pelear con ella, andando ella tam bien artillada como se sabe'; AGS GA 327, unfol., Bazán, Lisbon, Nov. 1591, 'se hiçiese mayores pieças porque la que trae el enemigo es gruessa'.

[49] AGS GA 280, f. 101, Bazán, Ferrol, 24/1/1590, 'y que la que se proveyere sea la mas gruessa que se pudiere'; f. 103, *Contador* Pedro López de Soto, Ferrol, 24/1/1590; f. 123, *relación*, 24/1/1590, 'y de la que les falta para estar medianamente artillados, advirtiendo que la mas de la que tienen es de 16 quintales avajo, y que la que se ha de proveer conviene que sea de 20 quintales hasta 35'.

[50] AGS GA 280, f. 256, Pedro de Yçaguirre Vergara, Pamplona, 20/1/1590, culverins or sakers 'serian de mas efecto para la mar (pues alcançaran mas que las pieças de batir)'; f. 123, López de Soto, Ferrol, 24/1/1590, 'los Navios que ay en este puerto estan tan faltos de Artilleria de alcançe que sino se refuerzca todos con 160 pieças por lo menos de 18 a 35 quintales, no podran salir a la Mar como conviene'; AGS GA 327, Bazán, Nov. 1591, 'y que la mayor parte sean de medias culebrinas, porque son pieças de mas alcançe'.

[51] AGS GA 365, unfol., Acuña Vela, Madrid, 29/1/1589: 'La Artilleria que se ha de fundir para la mar de nuevo pareze que haviendo de haver en una armada navios de gran porte, y mediano y menor, conviene que sea de manera que todos en su Razon lleven el artilleria competente a sus tamaños y portes, y de calidad que pueda offender de lexos, alcanzando bien, y de çerca pueda hazer en la armada contraria daño notable, y por esto aunque la mayor cantidad de piezas conviene que tiren pelota de hierro de buen tamaño y pelota de piedra que deshaga los navios con mayor daño que el que puede hazer la pelota de hierro por ser mas pequeña...'.

was rendered obsolete by the experience of 1588. The capacity to throw a large ship-smashing ball from a relatively light-weight piece was tactically and economically attractive, and Acuña Vela specifically recommended the casting of *pedreros*, though not the chamber-loading pieces which he said Santa Cruz had disliked and blamed for many accidents on board.[52] Despite this recommendation, there was a noticeable reduction in the amount of *pedreros* cast after the Armada. Some 40 per cent of the guns cast for 1588 were *cañones pedreros*; only 10 per cent of those cast thereafter. This does not, however, seem to have represented any definite change of policy in naval practice. Excluding the Portuguese squadron, in which the proportion of *pedreros* was extraordinarily high (45 per cent), less than 12 per cent of all the guns in the Armada had been *pedreros*, and that was very close to the figures proposed in post-Armada gun schedules.[53]

Nor have I come across any proposal for a reform of gun-mountings. It is true that English agents in Spain were reporting that the great ships were being rebuilt lower in the water, with larger gun-ports and with their ordnance placed very low, 'according to the manner of England', and that the guns transferred from the castle in San Sebastián were being put on low carriages for ship-board,[54] but they may have been referring to no more than the 'ruedas enterizas y bajas' which the Spaniards were making *before* the Armada.[55]

The post-Armada ideal, then, was for heavier and longer-range guns, though not the massive 55–60 quintal full cannon and full culverin which were too long and too heavy for use at sea. The preferred gun was the moderately heavy-shotted demi-cannon and the demi-culverin. In January 1590, for instance, two battery cannon of 35 and 37 lb shot were taken off the fleet and replaced by two demi-culverins or sakers, 'which will be more effective at sea since they have a longer range than the battery pieces'.[56] In March 1592, four 60-quintal cannons were recommended for transfer to Fuenterrabía, exchanging them for demi-culverins of 25–40 quintals.[57]

Immediately after the Armada, therefore, the Captain-General of the Artillery, Don Juan de Acuña Vela, recommended the casting of six new

---

[52] *Ibid.*

[53] See references in notes 59 and 60.

[54] R. B. Wernham, *List and Analysis of State Papers*, vol. I (Aug. 1589–June 1590), nos 612, 640.

[55] AGS GA 222, f. 53, Acuña Vela, 12/3/1588: 'Todos estos dias se entiende y se a entendido en aderezar y hazer caxas y ruedas por pieças de mar y de hazer ruedas gruesas enterizas y vaxas por piezas que en el Armada van de vatir para acomodallas en los Navios de manera que puedan ser de buen servicio'.

[56] AGS GA 280, f. 256.

[57] AGS GA 365, unfol., 'Relacion del Artilleria con que se podra armar los seis Galeones nuevos de Santander y Vilbao', Lisbon, 18/3/1592.

gun-types: demi-culverins of 7 and 12 lb shot, 28 and 27 calibres in length, weighing 24 and 40 quintals; demi-cannon of 16 and 20 lbs, 18 and 12 calibres long, 30 quintals in weight; *medios cañones pedreros* of 14 lbs, 12 calibres and 24 quintals; and *falconetes* of 33 calibres, 14 quintals and a 3-pound ball.[58] The essentials of this programme, however, had been laid down prior to the Armada battle on the basis of successful test castings and firings conducted in Lisbon under the supervision of the marquis of Santa Cruz and approved by the leading commanders (Leyva, Recalde, Oquendo, Valdés, and Medina Sidonia).[59] It represents the lessons of the Armada, therefore, only to the extent that Acuña Vela had modified the programme in the direction of a greater weight of shot for the *pedreros* and demi-cannon, dropping the lighter-shotted 12-lb *pedrero* and *cañoncete* cast in 1587–88 and adding the heavier 20-lb demi-cannon. The artillery construction programme which was carried out in 1590–92 largely followed these proposals of Acuña Vela, with the exception that the 20-pounder demi-cannon, twelve calibres in length and 30 quintals in weight, which he suggested only as a possibility for 'navíos mayores', was in fact cast in large numbers, and the 14-pounder *pedreros* he recommended were reduced to 12-pounders, weighing 22 quintals. His suggestion that some *falcones pedreros* throwing a 4-lb stone ball might be cast was also not acted upon. The records of the cannon-foundries in Lisbon and Málaga confirm this concentration on six gun types and the emphasis on heavier-shotted demi-cannon.[60] Between October 1590 and October 1592 the foundries cast 11,075½ quintals of ordnance, seventy 20-pounder demi-cannon, thirty-three 16-pounder demi-cannon, thirty 12-pounder *pedreros*, six 8-pounder *pedreros*, forty-one 3-pounder *falconetes*, two replacement *cañones de batir* of 40 lbs and 62 quintals, one 8-lb demi-culverin, two 5-lb sakers, and two small *falconetes* of 4 and 1½ lb ball. Forty per cent of the 347 new guns were demi-cannons and demi-cannon *pedreros*, 46 per cent demi-culverins, and 13 per cent minion types; 56 per cent threw a ball of 12 lbs or more. Compared with the 62 guns cast for the Armada in 1587–88, that represents a 90 per cent increase in the proportion of demi-culverins (24%), and

[58] AGS GA 347, Acuña Vela, 29/1/1589.

[59] *Ibid.*: 'y teniendo esta consideracion se hizo una fundacion de diferentes pieças en Lisboa para que llevase esta ultima armada, y salio açertada y approvada por el Marques de Santa Cruz, por Don Alonso de Leiva, Juan Martinez de Recalde, Miguel de Oquendo, Don Pedro de Valdes y ultimamente por el Duque de Medina Sidonia, y ansi todos quisieron llevar de ella en sus navios, como la llevaron'.

[60] AGS GA 365, unfol., *relación* of types and calibres of 219 guns cast in Casa Real of Málaga between 1590 and 15/10/1592; 'Relacion de las pieças de artilleria de la nueva fundicion que se an fundido en la ciudad de Malaga por mandado de V. Md', Málaga, 1/6/1591; 'Relacion del cobre y metal ligado que ha entrado en poder de los fundidores desde el 20 de octubre de 1590... hasta oy dia [17/10/1592] y de la artilleria que dello ha procedido'.

82

a 20 per cent increase in the percentage of 16-pounders and over. The same emphasis on 'culverin types' and heavier-shotted demi-cannon is found in two other post-Armada gun schedules, the recital of artillery chosen by the General Juan de Uribe for the best ships of the squadron he was fitting out in 1592, and the norm proposed for the arming of the new 1000-*tonelada* galleons being built for the crown.[61] No less than 62 per cent of Uribe's 'countable guns' were demi-culverins and sakers, and 25 per cent were the bigger 18- and 20-pounder demi-cannon.

	1588	1590–92	1000	Uribe
demi-cannon	33	34½	41½	25
demi-culverin/sakers	25	54	41¼	62
pedreros	41	11¼	17	13

A further aim can be discerned both in casting policy and in post-Armada gun schedules, and that is a desire for greater uniformity in the armament of ships of a similar size and a greater rationalisation of gun types. An ideal schedule for a galleon of 1100–1300 *toneladas*, based on the *San Juan*, the *almiranta* of the Portuguese squadron, reputed to be the best-gunned ship in the Armada, 'because its artillery was the most uniform in type and weight, being armed with guns made for the purpose', proposed a ratio of approximately 1 quintal of ordnance for each 1 or 1.2 *toneladas* of capacity.[62] Similarly the schedules for the new galleons of 1000 and 500 *toneladas* proposed a uniform complement of guns for each type of ship based on a similar ratio of between 1 and 1.2, a uniformity, in theory at least, much greater than on the royal galleons of the Castilian squadron in 1588. The new schedules also see a marked reduction of calibres within gun types. The Armada in 1588 carried 'countable guns' alone with at least twenty-eight different calibres of iron shot and seventeen of stone shot. The *San Juan* in 1588 had no less than nine different calibres of iron shot (20, 18, 16, 14, 12, 11, 10, 9, 1 lbs) and six of stone shot (14, 13, 12, 11, 10, 3 lbs), and the *capitana* of the Andalusian squadron, the *Nuestra Señora del Rosario*, had fifteen calibres of iron and two of stone. This multiplicity of calibres of ball must have made the provision of appropriate shot a logistical nightmare. The new proposals for galleons of the size of the *San Juan* reduced the number of different calibres to five of iron (16, 12, 7, 3, 1 lb) and three of stone (20, 12, 3 lbs), and the schedules for Uribe's *capitana* and *almiranta* had the same limited range of calibres on each ship, five of iron, two or three of stone. The new guns cast in 1590–92

---

[61] AGS GA 365, unfol., 'Relacion del Artilleria que el General Juan de Uribe a señalado para las quatro naves que se aprestan en Lixboa y dos en Ferrol', 1/4/1592; 'Relacion de los Navios de Armada que este año de 92 se podran armar de artilleria', 1/3/1592; 'Relacion del Artilleria con que se podra armar los seis Galeones nuevos de Santander y Vilbao', Lisbon, 18/3/1592.

[62] AGS GA 347, unfol., undated *relación*.

were essentially of only seven calibre types, five of iron and two of stone.

Conclusion

What conclusions can be drawn then from this examination of Spanish gun procurement and policy before and after the Armada? First of all, that there was no coherent gun policy at all before the Armada, or at least that what policy there was, was uncertain, and had only a marginal effect on the configuration of the fleet. New-made guns comprised only $2\frac{1}{2}$ per cent (or at the outside 5 per cent) of the Armada's artillery. The redistribution of existing guns was of greater importance, but apart from the rather general principle that big ships should have big guns and the concentration of firepower on the flagships and the ships commanded by the generals and the *maestres de campo*—a determination of tactics by status as much as anything else—it is not clear on what basis that redistribution was carried out.

The armament of the Armada in 1588 was primarily a function of the predominantly private ownership of its components, the immaturity of the royal navy as a fighting force in the Atlantic, and the largely pacific and defensive outlook of the Spanish merchantman, compared with the aggressive trading methods being adopted by an increasing number of English seamen in the 1580s. It is not without relevance that the most heavily and most uniformly armed squadron in the Armada, the Mediterranean galleasses, was the one with the longest tradition of naval warfare.

The armament of the Armada was also, however, a function of the lack of technological capacity and the administrative disunity of the Spanish monarchy. If only sixty medium-sized guns, probably weighing not more than 80 tons in all, could be manufactured in a year, that was as much because of a lack of technical skills, inadequate control over manufacturers and the manufacturing process, and failure of cooperation between Castilian and Portuguese administrations, as it was the fault of temporary shortages of funds or materials.

It could be argued therefore, that the patent weakness and unevenness of the Armada's armament, and the recognition that there was not much that could be done to remedy it, was a major element in determining the Armada's strategy in 1588, and hence its fate. The Armada, with only 138 guns of more than 25 lbs shot, was not armed to sink the English fleet but to keep it at long range, so minimising the destructive impact of its artillery superiority, and to prevent its closing for the kill by a massive preponderance in musketry and anti-personnel weaponry. The Armada was not a battle-fleet but an armed convoy. Its primary purpose was to transport soldiers to join the invasion forces of the Army of Flanders and to protect their crossing. Its strategy was defensive. It was a strategy of

84

mass. The huge numbers in the fleet, the size and strength of its ships, the impermeability of its 'crescent' formation, were all designed as a strategic counter to the anticipated tactics of the English. This strategy may have reflected Mediterranean galley traditions, a military rather than a naval ethos, or a 'territorial/central control ethic' negligent of the need for a home-based ordnance industry (Padfield);[63] it was undoubtedly the only realistic strategy for which the Armada was armed.

What lessons, then, were to be drawn from the disaster of 1588? The response to the failure of the Armada was not so much the reversal of pre-1588 gun strategies, but the definition and the more explicit formulation of already existing principles into a coherent policy, and the inception of a programme of ordnance construction in accordance with that policy. Whereas in 1588 guns had been procured on a hand to mouth basis, the artillery of the Armada determined largely by availability, in the two years or so after the Armada some 500 tons of ordnance were manufactured in the royal arsenals, purpose-built to a clear plan which concentrated on range, tactical firepower and uniformity. Not until after 1588 did Spain create a permanent, royal, high-seas fleet; only then could there be a coherent gun policy. The gun policy marked a new recognition of the importance of independent fleet action in naval warfare;[64] it was part of Spain's transformation into a major, ocean power.

---

[63] Peter Padfield, *Tide of Empires* (London, 1979), vol. I, p. 123.

[64] AGS GA 280, f. 94, Bazán, Ferrol, 3/1/1590, 'Desta [artilleria] ay tan poca y la que ay tan menuda que si V. Magd no se sirve de mandarlo remediar conforme la relacion que he embiado yra mal esta armada *para buscar la del enemigo y pelear con ella* [my italics] andando ella tam bien artillada como se sabe'; AGS GA 280, f. 201, Martín de Bertendona, Bilbao, 26/1/1590, 'la artilleria que abra menester esta nabe grande suplico a V. Md mande prebenyr pues no tiene ninguna de bronze y los enemigos de V. Md que en ella ponen su esperança y con ella azen sus efectos, y sino la llebamos tenemos notorio peligro'.

The Invincible Armada

WITH THE benefit of hindsight, the Enterprise of England seems to have been inevitable. One modern scholar has written, "The preparations for the Armada campaign may be said to date from the accession of Elizabeth to the Throne". From 1558, differences over religious, political, and colonial interests convinced many contemporary observers that a Spanish conquest of England was the only likely outcome. After Philip II's annexation of the Portuguese empire in 1580, rumours of an invasion of England, expectant, fearful, or merely curious, were everywhere, London, Paris, Lisbon, Madrid, Rome, Venice, Constantinople. The year 1580 was seen as confirming the King of Spain's thirst for hegemony in Europe and so strengthening his power, particularly his naval power, as to make that hegemony a real possibility. For modern historians, too, the conquest of Portugal has seemed to mark the beginning of a new, aggressive phase in Philip II's foreign policy, of which the Armada of 1588 was the logical culmination, a turn from the Mediterranean to the Atlantic made possible, diplomatically, by a truce with the Ottomans in 1578 and, financially, by a great increase in remittances of silver from the mines of Mexico and Peru.

The truth is rather different. The Armada was not a mature, long-planned, well thought out, strategic enterprise, but a hasty, rushed, and underprepared expedition with vacillating and uncertain objectives. The apparent continuity between 1580 and 1588 is false. The Enterprise of England marked not the culmination of long-prepared imperialist ambitions, but the end of what the French historian, Pierre Chaunu, has called "the military tranquility during the years 1582-1585". The proposal by the Marquis of Santa Cruz, the Captain-General of the Ocean Sea, in a letter of August 9, 1583, that his fleet, victorious over the Portuguese dissidents and their English supporters in the Azores, should be kept in being and sent against Elizabeth, was ignored. If the words of Philip II's reply seemed to leave the option open, his actions did not. The military apparatus that had conquered Portugal and the Azores was dismantled. The last 3,000 German and Italian troops in Lisbon were finally sent home in March 1584. A reform of the munitions industries, notably the reopening of the shot factory in Navarre that had been negotiated with an Italian entrepreneur on various occasions between 1578 and 1584, was suspended in 1585 and the matter not revived until July 1586. A contract for 10,000 cwt of Hungarian copper for gunfounding was negotiated some time before 1584, but only 4,000 of it was ordered to be taken up. The programme for the construction of 15,000 tons of shipping in Guipuzcoa and Vizcaya to serve as a kind of naval militia which had been first put forward in 1581, when the pacification of Portugal was still uncertain and it was feared that the French, the English, and the Dutch were planning attacks on Spain, was abandoned in October 1584 only a third completed. At the same time, the Crown was contemplating selling off the nine galleons that were being built for the Indies Guard to private buyers. It is clear that at the end of 1584 not only had Philip II no immediate plans for naval action in the Atlantic, but that he so little anticipated any such action that he was in the process of reversing a policy that had been intended to begin the creation of a permanent, Spanish high-seas fleet.

The policy decision to do something about the English problem was made only after Philip became aware of the Treaty of Nonsuch of August 1585 which committed Elizabeth to provide aid to Philip's rebellious subjects in the Netherlands, but not until the spring of 1586 was any administrative action taken to put the Enterprise in train. At the end of January, the King had asked Santa Cruz for his estimate of the forces that would be needed to send against England. Santa Cruz's plan reached the King at the end of March, and on April 21 a "Purveyor-General of the High-Board Fleets to be assembled in the Kingdom of Portugal on the account of the Crown of Castile" was appointed. On May 1, the secretaryship of war, vacant since early February, was split into two, with one office for land and the other for sea — a

move that had not been contemplated as late as November 1585 when the post had last been filled, and one that was clearly geared to the new administrative requirements of the war at sea.

These appointments, but perhaps first of all a Royal letter of April 4 to all the bishops of Castile asking for prayers throughout their dioceses for "the affairs of Christendom and good success for public matters", were the first real signs that the Enterprise of England was going to happen. Almost immediately, however, it was recognized that it was too late to do anything in 1586, and at the end of May, the Venetian Ambassador was reporting that everything was being suspended for a campaign the following April. Provisions began to be assembled after the harvest, a good one as it happened, and in September a special purveyor, Antonio de Guevara of the Council of Finance, was sent to Andalusia, where much of the wine and grain was to be procured. But by early December, it was decided that preparations were still insufficiently advanced for an April expedition, and the target date was shifted to August - April and August being thought the best months for the weather. Then Drake's activities cost Spain the summer, not so much because of his attack on Cadiz and the destruction of ships and stores there — the Spanish documents give that episode far less importance than English historians have done - as because Santa Cruz, with his squadron in Lisbon, was forced to put to sea from July 16 to the last week of September to protect the fleets returning with silver from America, "and on that alone to waste the greater and best part of the summer". By the time Santa Cruz returned, Philip II was desperate that the whole year not be lost, hoping to take advantage of what seemed like a brief Indian summer and fearing that over the winter Elizabeth would have time to strengthen her defences, negotiate foreign help, or organize a diversionary attack on the Indies.

Every day was wasting resources and costing Spain money and reputation, and the entire credibility of the operation was being put in doubt, not least because the delicate military and diplomatic balance that was temporarily neutralizing France and Turkey and on which the Enterprise depended, might well not survive into 1588. A succession of increasingly intemperate October and November deadlines was sent to Lisbon ordering Santa Cruz to sail immediately with whatever forces were ready and rather to leave ships behind than lose another day. But after their late-summer voyage, a number of the vessels needed careening, there were shortages of sailors and artillerymen, Miguel de Oquendo's squadron of seven ships from Guipuzcoa could not be put to sea for lack of cables, anchors, and sails. The troops were sickening and had to be put ashore to recover while their shipboard quarters were sanitized. Rain held up the transshipment of victuals, and a violent storm on November 16 damaged 17 fighting ships and 10 storeships, and another 15 days had to be spent on repairs. By November 9, Philip II was reconciled to the impossibility of any departure before the end of the month.

On November 30, Santa Cruz was ordered to put to sea within six to eight days with 48 fighting ships and the storeships, but on December 12 the Marquis estimated that he still needed 28 to 30 days before the fleet could sail. In another sudden change of plan, the King ordered the detachment of 35 ships to leave immediately to transport 6,000 picked troops to Flanders. What the object of this exercise was is not clear, whether to reinforce Parma for an independent invasion from the Netherlands, or simply to do *something*, to show that something could be done, regardless of the dangers of the season. In the event, information about the strength of the English fleet posed too many risks for any such limited exercise, and having failed to meet another series of winter deadlines in January, Santa Cruz died suddenly on February 9, 1588. It is difficult to know how far Santa Cruz was personally responsible for delaying the expedition over the winter, as many in Madrid suspected. He was cautious — perhaps excessively so considering the size of his force, probably justifiably so considering the dangers of a winter campaign — and he was unhappy with the strategic role he was to play, and it may be that his death was a disguised blessing for the Armada. The new commander, the Duke of Medina Sidonia, appointed on February 14, though not a sailor, was a capable and experienced naval administrator, and by no means the poltroon that for so long he has been portrayed. Within three months of his arrival, the Armada was at sea, and in much greater strength and in much better shape than it had been at Santa Cruz's death.

The Armada that sailed out of Lisbon water on May 30, 1588 was a very much more substantial force than it had been at the beginning of the year. Between January 4 and May 28, 7,920 soldiers and 2,622 sailors had been added, and since September 30, 1587 the number of ships had been increased by 35 and the tonnage by 18,758. In the last three months, the guns on board had been increased by up to 200, and munitions supplies by 2,000 cwt of powder and about 50,000 shot (20 per gun). Detained by contrary winds for two weeks off Cape St Vincent and hit by a gale off Finisterre on June 19-20, Medina Sidonia was forced to put into Corunna in Galicia to refit and reassemble, and when he left again on July 22 he had lost 10 ships, 600 seamen, and 1,500 soldiers. He nevertheless still had at his command incomparably the largest force ever seen in Atlantic waters. The last full muster of the fleet, dated Lisbon, May 28, 1588, gives it 141 vessels, 62,278 tons, 7,666 seamen, and 18,529 soldiers. The ships were divided into six front-line squadrons with a total of 63 or 64 fighting-ships, plus four great, oared galleasses from Naples, each carrying more than 600 men on board, and four light galleys. They were headed by the two élite squadrons of Royal galleons, apart from the galleasses and the galleys, the only specialist warships in the fleet, the flag-squadron of the Crown of Portugal with nine of the largest galleons, and the Castilian Squadron, under Diego Flores de Valdés, consisting of the nine galleons of the Indies Guard completed in 1584, and five privately owned ships. Almost all the other ships were privately owned. Two squadrons were composed of ships

from the northern province of Guipuzcoa, that under Miguel de Oquendo with nine ships and a hulk, and that under Juan Martinez de Recalde with 10. Though private vessels, many of these ships had been built with government subsidies as part of a long-standing programme for the encouragement of domestic shipbuilding in Spain. The 1,000-ton San Salvador in Oquendo's squadron, costing over 13,000 ducats, had been built with a loan from the Crown of 1,000 ducats, and its original owner received a bounty of 10,000 maravedis (c.27 ducats) a year for every 100 tons, as long as it remained in his possession.

To some extent, therefore, the Armada was a vindication of the efforts the Crown had made since the 1560s to build up a merchant marine in the Cantabrian provinces capable of serving when needed in the Royal service. The other two squadrons were the Andalusian, with 10 ships under Don Pedro de Valdés, so called because the ships had been requisitioned there in the spring of 1587 while preparing for a trading voyage to New Spain; and the Levant Squadron of Don Martin de Bertendona, composed of 11 ships, most of them very large, originating from different parts of the central Mediterranean, Ragusa (the present-day Dubrovnik), Venice, Naples, Sicily, and one a galleon belonging to the Grand Duke of Tuscany. They had all been requisitioned in Iberian ports, mostly in mid-1587, having arrived with grain and troops from Italy. In addition, there were the storeships, 23 hulks, mainly from the Baltic, and 11 small caravels, averaging 100 tons or so, a squadron of pinnaces, with their flagship and storeships (there were 32 of them in all, averaging less than 80 tons each), and 11 feluccas. The Armada was a spectacular and impressive sight, even to men such as the secretary of the navy, Andrés de Alva, who had spent his whole life at sea. Even so, it is worth pointing out that Medina Sidonia had fewer ships than the English were to assemble against him, only 25 per cent greater tonnage, and only one-third the men carried in the Christian fleet at the battle of Lepanto in 1571 against the Turks.

The despatch of the Armada has often been, and is now again in Spanish circles increasingly being, presented as a triumph of planning and organization, one of the wonders of the world of early-modern administration. Such an assessment, however, depends very much on how far the Armada of May 1588 conformed to the Armada that was planned two years before, and that we simply do not know. Although military preparations began in April 1586, it is by no means clear at this stage what it was precisely that Philip II was preparing.

There were, broadly speaking, three military options canvassed. One was a direct assault on England by sea from Spain. This was the approach advocated by Santa Cruz in his reply to the King's request for a plan of operations in January 1586. Another, favoured by Philip's governor in Flanders, the Duke of Parma, was a surprise invasion across the Channel by the army in the Low Countries, with the Armada from Spain following up to protect the rear and bring in reinforcements. The third was a diversionary landing in Ireland, Scotland, Lancashire, the Isle of Wight, or some

other peripheral area, to support or to incite a Catholic rising and compel Elizabeth to recall her forces for her own defence. Some combination of any of these was also possible, and as many as 15 different plans were floated in the 20 months or so before the Armada sailed. No firm decision on which strategy to employ seems to have been reached until the autumn of 1587, over a year after the military preparations had been put in train. Not until after the Spanish capture of the Belgian port of Sluys in August 1587 was the final plan, involving the despatch of the Armada to join up with Parma's forces in the Netherlands, reinforcing him with 6,000 soldiers from Spain, and covering the crossing of his troop-carriers, resolved upon. Even so, other options remained open. As late as December 1587, an independent assault direct from the Netherlands was still being contemplated and, according to one report, had the Armada been held up in July 1588 for another fortnight, it would have made not for England, but for Ireland.

It looks, therefore, as if for a year and a half, military preparations went ahead without any firm decision having been made about what the Armada's role would be and without relation to any fixed strategic objective. In the event, the strategy of the Armada was to be determined by the state of its preparations.

Cutting through the secrecy, the deliberate misinformation, the desire to keep all options open, and the sheer indecisiveness of Madrid, the evidence suggests that until the autumn of 1587 some sort of independent action was envisaged for the Armada, if not alone, at least as part of a larger strategy. The adoption of the 1588 plan, announced to Lisbon in an Instruction of September 14, 1587, has all the appearance of a sudden, if not precipitate, decision which radically altered existing expectations. It certainly came as an unwelcome shock to Santa Cruz, who was only just persuaded from resigning in protest against the merely passive role now attributed to his command in covering Parma's crossing and neutralizing the English fleet. That decision of Philip II's, fatally flawed as events were to prove, was the key moment in the history of the Enterprise, and it is worth considering why he took it. The reasons were clearly set out in the Instruction. "Not having been able to assemble this year everything called for in the estimates", and having lost the summer, the King had ordered his fleets in Andalusia and Lisbon to join up "in order that, as the forces of the two fleets were not as great as had been projected or were to be desired for the principal objective (*la empresa principal*), they should be employed this year to conquer Ireland, as had been discussed with the Marquis himself before he left, wintering there, and going ahead next year with new strength." The capture of Sluys, however, had opened up the prospect of a combined Hispano-Flemish operation that would eliminate the dangers of deferring the main attack over the winter. As the Instruction put it, "the forces that His Majesty has there and here, although neither by themselves sufficient, together, if we are capable of uniting them, will win the game".

The point is that after a year's preparations, Spain had simply not been able to mount *la empresa principal*. Why this should have been so cannot be understood without a closer look at the state of Spain's military forces and supply services at the moment when the Armada began to be organized.

In the middle of 1586, there was not a single branch of military organization that was adequate to the task. The preparations for the Armada took place against the background of a prolonged and serious run-down of the entire Spanish military machine. With the conquest of Portugal, Philip II had acquired a high-seas fleet of a dozen powerful galleons, but the nine galleons built for the Indies Guard and delivered in 1584 were nearly sold off, as we saw earlier, and the plan to increase Spain's naval strength by contracts with Basque outfitters was aborted. The galley fleets in the Mediterranean, about 150 vessels in 1576, had fallen to 88 by 1587. The 40 galleys of the Spanish squadron, based in Andalusia in 1580, had been dispersed and in November 1587 only 24 remained, and those were recognized to be very few and very ill in order - "fishing boats not galleys", Cardinal Granvelle had called them. It was also becoming increasingly difficult to recruit soldiers or sailors in Spain. The refusal of mariners to join the Royal service was a chronic problem, and in 1581 the King had had to attempt a form of conscription in the Cantabrian provinces to man the Indies fleets, without, however, much success. The persistent difficulty of raising soldiers voluntarily, on the other hand, was relatively new. Between 1571 and 1578 the average recruiting captain was raising 256 men; in the decade after 1580 the average slumped to 161, and even this was achieved only at the cost of inordinate expense to the Crown and intolerable suffering and humiliation to the villages through which the rapacious and licentious soldiery passed. Indeed, in the years after 1580, with the Crown unable to pay its soldiers and with the consequent breakdown of discipline, the entire recruiting system was falling apart. Serious attempts at reform and alternative methods of recruitment were beginning to be undertaken in 1586, precisely to meet the demands of war in the Atlantic, but by 1587-88 they were still largely untried.

A similar breakdown is apparent in the supply services. Again this was the result of a combination of insufficient funds and inadequate administrative control, brought to a head by the logistical demands of raising an army for Portugal and maintaining a substantial garrison there after 1580. Just as in recruiting, the 1580s were a period of constant complaint by the Cortes on behalf of peasants and artisans whose goods were requisitioned without payment and in excessive quantities by insensitive and unscrupulous purveyors. The problem of supply, particularly of grain and other agricultural produce, was made worse by the increasing difficulties of Castilian agriculture, reflected in a series of unreservedly bad harvests between 1580 and 1584, and by the reduction of imports from Northern Europe resulting from the Spanish embargo on English and Dutch shipping in May 1585, and the growing danger from piracy in Spanish waters.

It was the Spanish munitions indus-

tries which were in the worst position to meet these new demands. With the breakdown of the negotiations with the Prince of Salerno there was no cannon shot made at all in Spain. The Royal cannon foundry at Malaga had never been sufficient for Spain's needs, and the country's gunpowder manufacturing capacity, for reasons still not entirely clear, was on the decline. The only one of the war industries that was expanding in the 1580s was the small-arms industry in Guipuzcoa and Vizcaya, but this, like all the other munitions industries, was crippled by lack of money. The gunsmiths and pike-makers were owed 40,000 ducats in 1584, at least 31,000 in 1586, 48,000 in December 1587, 45,000 in May 1588. Repeatedly, the immediate cessation of production was threatened, and work did stop for a period in 1587. It was the same with gunpowder manufacturing. Between November 1580 and May 1587, there was not one grain of saltpetre worked at the saltpetre plant at Lérida (Catalonia) because there was no money to buy it. There was nothing unique about Lérida. An account of 1587 stated baldly, "in 1586 powder manufacturing ceased in all parts for lack of money". In November 1587, the casting of 30 guns was suspended and all ordnance work brought to a halt for lack of 10,000 ducats, and in 1588 the carpenters and iron-workers employed by the King in Lisbon stopped work because they had run out of materials. It was, therefore, against the background of an almost total collapse of the administrative and supply system that the decision to embark on the invasion of England was taken.

Coming when it did, the Armada and the means to equip it (with the exception of the 18 galleons of the Portuguese and Castilian squadrons) had to be created more or less from scratch and this, as it turned out, in something less than two years. The consequences of this were fundamental. Spain at sea was lacking in all the intensity factors necessary to fight the English on equal terms, and these were not things that could be produced in a summer — the nine galleons for the Indies Guard, for example, first ordered in February 1581, were not completed until April 1584, three years and three months later. The disadvantages of the Spaniards in ship construction, seamanship, and gunnery, and the realization that the English would seize the wind, lie off, and batter the Spanish fleet from long range, without allowing them to close sufficiently to board, meant that the strategy of the Armada had necessarily to be a strategy of mass. The Armada had to be as large as possible. It had to be too big to be defeated. It had to intimidate and overawe, even if its sheer mass actually meant that its effectiveness as a fighting force was even more impaired. Nothing better exemplifies this strategy of mass than Santa Cruz's fantastic blueprint of March 1586 asking for 510 ships of 110,000 tons, 46 galleys and galleasses, and 94,000 men, more than in the entire Christian force at Lepanto and twice the number that had conquered Portugal in 1580. This gargantuan armada was to conquer England on its own by a direct assault in overwhelming and irresistible force. It was a simple and uncomplicated plan. It was perhaps the only strategy that could

have succeeded, but it was a logistical impossibility. How seriously anybody took the plan we do not know. It is certain that nobody acted on it. By the end of 1586, it is clear from the financial allocations and procurement targets that we have that any scheme on that scale, if indeed it had ever been contemplated, had been abandoned. The inventories of the purveyors in Andalusia and Lisbon indicate that the numbers that were being catered for were barely one-quarter of those envisaged by Santa Cruz, and much smaller than all other proposals for the direct invasion of England were calling for. Already by that date it is clear that the Enterprise of England was not to be a purely Spanish enterprise. The allocation of funds shows that the strategic effort was to be divided between the Armada of Spain and the Army of Flanders. A special *junta* set up late in December 1586 was instructed to find 7 million ducats for the following year, one-third was to be for the Armada and two-thirds for Flanders.

From the summer of 1586 and throughout 1587 and 1588, there was a rush of reforms - the division of the secretariat of war, the expansion of the Council of War, the appointment of military governors in Galicia and Andalusia, the creation of a new office of *comisario general* to co-ordinate and supervise recruiting. New biscuit baking ovens were put up in Lisbon and Malaga. Surveys were begun to discover new mineral deposits; the privately owned sulphur mines at Hellin in Murcia were taken over by the Crown; the Lérida saltpetre plant was put to work again (May 1587); the cannon foundry in Lisbon was brought into production; negotiations were resumed to open the shot-works in Navarre, and the agreement with the Basque shipbuilders seems to have been taken up again at the beginning of 1587. But it was all too late. The first cannon balls, for example, were not cast in Navarre until the end of 1588 at the earliest, and, as with so much else that was used in the Armada, the shot had to be got from abroad. Fifteen thousand cwt of copper that the Council of War had wanted brought from Milan in May 1587 still had not arrived in Spain by September 1588, and although the Captain-General of the Artillery claimed that he could produce 4,000 cwt of gunpowder within six months, in April 1588, the Armada had less than half the powder it was thought to need and 550 cwt had to be bought from German merchants in Lisbon at more than double normal prices. To the last, the Armada remained critically short of munitions of all kinds. It was short also of biscuit and wine. The harvests of 1585 and 1586 were abundant; that of 1587 was expected to be equally good, and it may be that this favourable prospect helped with the decision to go ahead with the Enterprise. In fact, the harvest of 1587 failed to live up to expectations and this undoubtedly played a part in delaying the Armada in 1587 and contributed to the depletion of its reserves of biscuit and wine the following year.

In only one respect was the situation favourable for the Enterprise, and that was the financial. The trade difficulties that hindered the procurement of supplies meant that the Crown's Genoese bankers were looking for outlets for their capital and anxious to recover the debts and the specie export licences that had been suspended after the Crown "bankruptcy" of 1575. At the same time, increased taxes in Castile in the late 1570s, substantial revenues from sales of land and offices, and a doubling of bullion imports from the New World in the decade after 1578, bringing in 4 million ducats for the King in 1587 alone, provided the securities against which the financiers proved happy to lend. During 1586-88, the Crown was able to conclude a series of very large asientos on remarkably good terms, which left a considerable part of current revenues available for use.

The extraordinary cost estimated for the Armada for 1587 was a shade under 2 million ducats, 529,000 for the pay of the soldiers, 310,000 for the freightage of ships and seamen's wages, and more than 1,000,000 for provisions. The cost of artillery and munitions was accounted separately. In January 1587, Philip II appointed a small, select junta to raise 7 million ducats, "for the things which are in train and to be put in train this year"; 2-2½ million were to be for "costs of the naval expedition" and 4½-5 million for the recurrent and extraordinary requirements of Flanders. The junta met for the first time on the 31st, and at the end of a week had organized the funding of the million for the purveyors with two Spanish financiers, the Marquis of Auñón and Juan Ortega de la Torre, and was confident that cash and other assignations on revenues would meet the rest of the budget for the fleet. It had also arranged 2 million for Flanders, enough to last until May. On February 7, it was able to report, "as a result of all this, the Junta believes Your Majesty can rest greatly satisfied and content, and cease to worry that these funds will not be available when they are needed".

The Armada was, of course, to cost a good deal more than 2 million ducats. The figure bruited at the time, 900,000 ducats a month according to the President of Finance, was 10 million ducats, more than a year's revenue of Philip II, and something like seven years' of Elizabeth's. For the entire cost of the Enterprise between 1586 and 1588, including additional funding for the Netherlands, that figure might be possible. For the Armada alone, a nominal 4 million ducats is probably nearer the mark. From the roughly 70,000 a month budgeted in January 1587, the wages of ships and men had risen to 115,000 a year later, and to a peak of 166,600 in May 1588, 73,200 ducats for ships and seamen, 82,000 for the infantry, and 11,500 for the high command and staff officers. Provisions were costing another 100,000 a month. When it sailed, the Armada was costing Philip II £2,350 a day, four times as much as the English fleet was costing Elizabeth. From the financial point, it was as well that it left when it did, and it was fortunate that it did not all return. The financial provision of January 1587 could not last for ever. The bankers had been prepared to wait for repayment until the arrival of the silver fleets of 1587 and to take assignments on taxes due in 1588, but that meant that those revenues were now pledged. By the beginning of the year, the financial situation of the Armada was becoming serious. At the end of January, the soldiers, sailors, and

shipowners were owed 440,000 ducats, nearly four months' pay. Some of these debts were outstanding for years, and in the case of the men who did not return, were perhaps never paid. The widow of Captain Andrés Felipe, the owner of the Gran Grin, was owed 9,000 ducats in 1591, four-fifths of what her husband should have been paid for the 15½ months his ship was in the King's service, before ship, crew, and captain were all lost on August 28, 1588. The previous owner had foreclosed for the 8,000 ducats credit he had advanced for the purchase of the ship, and Felipe's widow had had to sell even the bed she slept in to pay him off. The bill for the Armada was picked up by a host of people like her, and by the population of Castile as a whole, whose representatives in the Cortes granted the King 8 million ducats to "wipe out the stain which this year has fallen on the Spanish nation".

The fact is that a strategy of mass posed insuperable problems for 16th century administrations. The greater the Armada, the more the ships and men, the more provisions and supplies that were needed, the longer the time it took to prepare and assemble; the longer it took to prepare and assemble the greater the wastage, the deterioration and the decay, and the more that was consumed merely to keep it in existence. There were soldiers being maintained on the Armada's account well over a year before it finally set sail. By November 1587, 1,400 of 5,000 who had already been embarked on their ships for six months had fallen sick. In the 11 months it was in Spain, between July 1587 and May 1588, the *tercio* of Naples (squadron) lost 25 per cent of its effectives. The same thing was happening with the troops in the Netherlands, but to an even greater degree. Provisions also began to be assembled in Andalusia and Extremadura after the harvest of 1586, and large quantities of biscuit were sent from Naples and Sicily. But with 43,000 tons of shipping already in being in September 1587 and never less than 16,000 mouths to feed, by May 1588, the Armada had already used in normal rations alone half as many victuals again as it was to carry with it out of Lisbon, in addition to all the wastage that we know to have occurred. Some of the food was already inedible by the beginning of 1588, and in June considerable quantities "in bad condition, stale, and rotten", had to be dumped into the sea. By July, the eight months' provisions that had been taken aboard in January had fallen to 60 days', as the Armada was delayed week after week fitting out the ships, increasing stocks of munitions, and awaiting the arrival of new recruits. Fresh victuals were taken on at Corunna, but even before it left Spain, the Armada was on short rations and sailed with biscuit for only 57 days. But it was all very haphazard. Some ships got back to Spain in September still quite well stocked; others were near exhaustion within a month. When, at the beginning of August, the English captured the Rosario, they found stinking fish, bread full of worms, leaky casks, and sour wine. By September, the biscuit that had been taken on in Lisbon only four months before was "in such a state that neither the pigs nor the dogs would eat it, even when it had been dunked in broth". In these circumstances, the

Armada from Spain could not possibly be an independent force. A rendezvous with Parma was essential if for no other reason than the need to restock with provisions and water in the Netherlands. When, after Gravelines, this hope of succour vanished and the Armada was reduced to its own resources, the men were living on one-third rations, 8 ounces of biscuit a day, $\frac{1}{2}$ litre of water, $\frac{1}{4}$ litre of wine, and the only way of saving them was to get back to Spain as soon as possible. That was three weeks after leaving Corunna.

There was a second reason why a direct invasion from Spain was out of the question. There were not enough soldiers available, either in Spain or in the Italian *tercios*, for such an undertaking, not only in numbers but also, and even more importantly, in quality. The soldiers were, as Philip II himself put it, "the marrow of the Armada and that which matters most for the execution of its purposes". Santa Cruz had wanted 55,000 soldiers, one for every two tons of shipping. Medina Sidonia thought the Armada should have at least one man for every ton so that troops could be landed without weakening the fleet. To have raised such numbers would have required the recruitment of 28,000 in Spain and Portugal, according to Santa Cruz's proposals. In light of the experience of the early 1580s that was a patent impossibility. The inability to recruit men was already holding up the despatch of the Indies' fleet in the summer of 1586, and it was apparently the lack of soldiers on board that prevented Santa Cruz from going out to intercept Drake off Lisbon and (Cascaes) in May.

Throughout 1587, the shortage of men continued. Even at the end of March 1588, the Armada was desperately undermanned, with perhaps only 9,000 or 10,000 soldiers in all. It was only the arrival of 3,000 men from Extremadura, the withdrawal of some troops from the garrison of Lisbon, and the late recruitment of 2,000 Portuguese in April and May that gave it a degree of numerical respectability — and even then there were only one-third of the men per ton that Medina Sidonia had thought essential the year before.

Moreover, all were agreed that the troops to be put ashore for any assault must be an élite of trained and hardened veterans, gente vieja. Santa Cruz had wanted 27,000 professional mercenaries from Germany and Italy, 11,000 experienced Spanish infantry from the tercios in Italy, the garrisons in Portugal and the Azores, and the Armada of the Indies Guard, and 17,000 new recruits from Spain and Portugal. The Armada in May 1588 had only 19,000 soldiers, and none of them Germans or Italians. Of these 19,000, 104 companies of the tercios of Pimentel from Sicily, Luzón from Naples, Toledo from Portugal, and Isla from the Indies galleons, with a total of 10,479 men, would seem to correspond to the 11,000 veteran Spanish troops that Santa Cruz had asked for, leaving the remaining 67 companies with something over 8,000 Spanish and Portuguese biso-ños, but a closer examination reveals that it is impossible to regard all these men as experienced veterans. Luzón's tercio of Naples, for example, is listed in the Lisbon muster as having 26 companies with 2,889 men. Yet we know that

when the tercio arrived in Spain in July 1587 it had only 10 companies with 1,864 men, and that by May 1588 there were only 1,396 of them left. In fact, a very substantial proportion of those four tercio is known to have been new troops raised in Spain during 1587 — at least 12 companies in Luzón's tercio, at least five in Pimentel's, at least four in Toledo's, and at least eight in Isla's. Pimentel himself declared that only 15 of the 32 companies of the tercio of Sicily were old soldiers, infanteria vieja. At an absolute minimum, some 2,500 of the 10,500 men who at first glance look like experienced, trained, veteran Spanish infantry turn out to be raw recruits, and the real figure could very well be double that. Moreover, even the "veterans", that is those not newly raised in 1587, were far from being battle-scarred warriors. At least four of the original 10 companies of the tercio of Naples had been initially raised in Castile no longer ago than 1584 (three in June 1585, one in March 1584) and a further five, at least, of the companies from the garrison in Portugal had been raised between 1584 and 1586. It is unlikely that any of them had ever fought. At the most conservative of estimates, no less than 60 per cent of the Armada's soldiers (11,000 of the 19,000), and maybe as many as 75 per cent of them, were raw recruits who had, in all probability, never been to sea, never fought, and knew no more about military manoeuvres, discipline, or the handling of their weapons than what they had picked up in a few months of training in their billets. Their inexpertness is all the more likely when one remembers that maybe half of these recruits were not volunteers, the *guzmanes* who had made the Spanish *tercios* famous throughout Europe, but conscripts levied by the lords and cities of Andalusia and Extremadura. This was the legacy of the collapse of voluntary recruiting after 1580. The Armada was the first time that Spaniards were conscripted for service overseas in this way. One can only guess at the morale and fitness of the men involved. The troops in Seville, levied for the fleet to flush Drake out of the Indies in 1586, were described as "poor, all raw recruits, from the scum of the people, raised by force and kept by force, prisoners in monasteries". The 400 Galicians sent by the Counts of Lemos and Monterrey to join the Armada were so old and decrepit, so underfed, and so ignorant of arms, that even their captains did not want them, and Medina Sidonia, rather than have them drop dead on board ship, sent them back home to their despairing wives and children. These were not men to conquer kingdoms.

It was apparent fairly soon, therefore, that there was no possibility of making Santa Cruz's ambitious project a reality. A comparison of the 1586 plan with the final Lisbon inventory of May 1588 reveals that on almost all counts the 1588 fleet was not only absolutely smaller (half the size in tonnage and capital ships, a third the size in manpower), but proportionately weaker as well. For every 100 tons, there were to have been 50 soldiers in 1586, there were 33 in 1588; in 1586, 15 sailors, in 1588, 13.9; for every man there were to have been 402 lbs of biscuit and 244 litres of wine in 1586, there were 357 lbs of biscuit and 217 litres of wine in 1588 — and that on the basis of

the May 1588 inventory which, with hardly any doubt at all, was a gross and fraudulent inflation of the provisions laden. Even in guns, the 1588 fleet failed to reach the standards of 1586 with, on the most favourable calculation, only one gun for every 23.8 tons, as against one for every 23.4 tons in 1586, and if one takes only the armed sailing ships into account, the 1586 figure rises to one for every 16.1 tons and the 1588 figure falls to one for every 26.2 tons. Only in cannon balls was the 1588 fleet at an advantage, and even that was negated by the failure to provide a proportionately greater supply of powder. Indeed, if one includes all the powder available in the fleet, there was only half as much per gun in 1588 as had been planned in 1586 (213 lbs and 406 lbs).

Philip II's realization that he was incapable of launching the empresa principal was the decisive moment in the long and uncertain evolution of the Enterprise of England. The dilemma was clear. The strategic requirements of a direct invasion made impossible demands on the supply system, and in turn the inadequacies of supply contributed to the adoption of a less demanding strategy, but one that was in other ways even more fundamentally unworkable. The course resolved upon in the Instruction of September 14, 1587 required that some means be provided by which Parma's soldiers in the Netherlands could be brought out across shallows dominated by the Dutch, which could not be navigated by the great galleons of the Armada. Having opted against Santa Cruz's plan for a direct invasion of England, this was the problem that had to be solved. That it was not solved might, tentatively, be associated with another and apparently unrelated change that took place between 1586 and 1588, the disappearance of the galleys. Santa Cruz had wanted 40 galleys. Only four sailed with the Armada in 1588 — not Portuguese galleys, as is often stated, but Spanish galleys based in Lisbon. The disappearance of the galleys has been seen as a modernization of the Armada, a conscious change of policy consequent upon the lessons of Drake's raid on Cadiz in April 1587, and a belated recognition of the new technology of naval warfare. It was nothing of the kind, and there is no substantive evidence whatever for such a belief. Even after Cadiz, Philip II believed that the galleys had demonstrated their effectiveness by checking the attacks of the English fleet on the Portuguese coast in May 1587, and everybody who had anything to do with the Armada in 1587 and 1588 wanted more galleys, not less, more than the four of 1588 — that is, eight or 12 at least. The galleys, they believed, had proved their ability to operate on the high seas in the Azores and in the Indies. They were invaluable not only in a calm, when they could manoeuvre independently or be used to tow the fighting galleons into position, but also in shallow waters, particularly for embarking and disembarking soldiers.

One can only speculate about whether the galleys could have been that last crucial link to cover Parma's egress and to bring the army and the Armada together. The four galleys that sailed with Medina Sidonia did not last a week. Would it have been different if there had

been eight, or 12, or 40? Could they, in any case, have held off the 25 Dutch cromsters standing off Dunkirk? Before and after, Spanish opinion certainly, and Dutch also, it would seem, did not doubt that the galleys were a match for the rebel coasters. Indeed, one of the last things the Marquis of Santa Cruz had said before his death was that had galleys been sent to Flanders the war would have been over long ago. Whatever lessons the Spaniards learned from Armada, it was not that the galleys should be abandoned, and in subsequent armadas in the 1590s there were far more galleys than in 1588. The absence of galleys in 1588, therefore, was not a policy decision, but a logistical one. With the run-down of the Mediterranean galley fleets, the renewed activity of the Algerian and Moroccan corsairs, and the breakdown of the truce with the Turks, it was impossible to release any more galleys for the Armada, and without the galleys whatever hope there was of making the new invasion plan work had gone.

With the rejection of Santa Cruz's plan and with the impossibility of uniting the Flanders army with the Lisbon galleons, there could be no landing in England. The only success the Armada could achieve was at sea. But the general procurement situation in which the Armada was prepared meant that it lacked many of the essential ingredients for success in battle, also. The restricted number of specialized warships in the Royal fleet forced Philip II to make up his Armada by the seizure and requisition of whatever Spanish and foreign merchantmen were to hand. Inevitably, many of those vessels were unsuitable for the tasks that faced them in northern waters and their masters unused to the disciplines of sailing in naval formation. On the evidence of the dimensions of 12 new warships built in Ragusa, Venice and Naples for the King of Spain's service in the early 1590s, the Mediterranean galleons were all deeper in the hold and even broader in the beam than almost all contemporary pundits, even Spanish ones, recommended. The unseaworthiness of such ships, suggested by the high mortality of the Levant Squadron in 1588, is confirmed by the dismissal of eight of the 12 new Ragusan galleons in 1596 because, in the opinion of the Council of War, "past campaigns had shown them to be ill-suited for those seas". Witnesses on both sides were unanimous that the English fleet was far superior to the Spanish in design, rigging and handling, and able no only to gain and keep the weather, but so manoeuvrable that they were capable of getting off two broadsides to the Spaniards' one.

No less important were the deficiencies of morale that were only to be expected in a force whose ships, sailors, and soldiers were largely conscripted from all corners of Europe. The Armada was a marine Babel. There were ships from Dubrovnik at one end, and from Danzig at the other; there was one, at least, from Scotland. There were Dalmations, Italians, Portuguese, Germans, Flemings, Frenchmen, Dutchmen, even Englishmen on board, whose commitment to the success of the Enterprise was by no means uniform. Ships captains, like Andrés Felipe, who had invested 20,000 ducats in his ship only two

months before it was requisitioned, in the expectation of making a handsome profit in the Americas, were unlikely to be the most enthusiastic of participants, or to want to expose their capital to avoidable risk. The *maestre de campo*, Don Francisco de Bobadilla, in one of the most revealing assessments of the action, asserted that, apart from some 20 ships which conducted themselves with honour, the rest of the fleet simply took flight whenever they saw the enemy attack. The collapse of morale was related also to the unhappy relations within the high command and between the seamen and the military. The admirals of the squadrons were all northerners from the Cantabrian coasts and all men of immense experience whose seamanship could not be faulted. Unfortunately, there was a good deal of discord among them and with the predominantly Castilian, military officers and their Andalusian commander-in-chief. Diego Flores de Valdés, deputed to be Medina Sidonia's chief naval aide, was clearly a difficult man, and Don Pedro de Valdés seems to have clashed with Medina Sidonia and his other colleagues early on, disagreeing about tactical dispositions and protesting that the Captain-General was disgracing him by insisting on vetting his disbursements. Don Pedro also complained bitterly about another problem in the Armada's command structure, the division of authority between the captain of the ship and the captain of the troops on board, and the disparagement of the sailor, and in particular of the sea captains of his squadron with years of experience in the Atlantic on the Americas run, by haughty and overbearing officers who knew nothing about ships or the sea. Valdés went so far as to claim that it was the demoralization of the sea captains that had been in part responsible for the dispersal of the fleet off Finisterre in July. It was perhaps no accident that one of the first disasters to strike the Armada was the crippling of the Andalusian flag-ship and the abandoning of Valdés to the English by his chief.

If the ships of the Armada were no match for the English, neither were their guns. An appreciation of the state of the munitions industries in Spain on the eve of the Armada, such as has been described above, must cast considerable doubt on the capacity of the Spaniards to have carried out the coherent, late change in gun policy that the naval historian, Professor Michael Lewis, attributed to them. Some guns were being cast by the Captain-General of the Artillery in the last months before the fleet sailed — the Venetian Ambassador spoke of 200 — but most of what was got was got haphazardly by purchase or by requisition from foreign ships in Iberian ports. The marine archaeologists have dug up not only obsolete but also ill-cast guns, not necessarily Spanish made.

Michael Lewis argued that the Spanish fleet was weaker than the English in long-range, light-shotted guns, but considerably stronger in heavy-shotted, medium-range guns and medium-shotted, short-range guns. According to Lewis, the average Spanish broadside, when it was within range, was nearly double that of the English fleet. There was the possibility, therefore, that in the right circumstances, the Spaniards could have done the English a great deal of damage. New documentary evidence from the Spanish archives now makes this seem very much less likely. Information on 1,841, or 76 per cent of the total guns in the Armada, itemizing gun types and weight of shot fired, reveals that not only was the Armada even worse off at long-range than Professor Lewis thought, with only 172 "countable" guns of 4 lb shot or more, compared with the English fleet's 497, but that even within the heavy and medium gun range the Armada was markedly weaker as well, with only 162 guns throwing shot of 15 lbs or more, as against 251 on the English side. Indeed, the Spanish firepower far from being double, was only about three-quarters of that of the English, as regards the total firepower of the two fleets and the average broadsides of their front-line fighting-ships. We have with these comparisons the beginnings, at last, of an explanation for the inability of the Spaniards to dominate the English even at those moments during the campaign when the opposing fleets were within arquebus, or even hailing range.

By August 8, there were other factors adding to this disadvantage — a shortage of powder and a shortage of shot. It had been pointed out before the Armada sailed that, even with the increases in the powder supply during April and May, it was carrying less than three times the amount that had been used in one day by a much smaller fleet in Santa Cruz's victory in the Azores. What may have compounded this deficiency was the notoriously poor quality of Spanish-made gunpowder (probably three-fifths of the total). A ship's pilot resident in Seville blamed the ignorance and the shoddy workmanship of the powder makers, who, he thought, ought to take an examination. The General of one of the Indies fleets in 1586 thought the gunpowder made in Spain "the worst in the world ... pure mud", that had to be double charged before it gave any response. If this was happening in the Armada, the effect on its gunnery and powder supplies must have been catastrophic. By the end of the day-long battle of Gravelines there was hardly a front line ship with any powder or shot left, and the galleon San Mateo was lost precisely because it was left without munitions and defenceless.

Don Francisco de Bobadilla's informed, yet little-known report, sent on August 20 to Philip II's minister of state, Don Juan de Idiáquez, is the best contemporary statement that I know of the deficiencies of the Armada as a fighting force. "You need to have been here to see and believe what has happened in order to recognize what a deception this great machine has been. You will now not find anyone who is not saying, 'I told you so', 'I predicted it', as always after the horse has bolted ... We found the enemy with a great advantage in ships, better than ours for battle, better designed, with better artillery, gunners, and sailors, and so rigged they could handle them and do with them what they wanted. The strength of our Armada was some 20 vessels, and they fought very well, better even than they needed, but the rest fled whenever they saw the enemy attack. Of that I will say nothing in my account to save the reputation of our nation. Furthermore, we brought so

few cannon-balls that I hardly had a fighting ship that had anything to fire. Thus, the San Mateo, having run out of powder and shot, was caught and destroyed, and if the enemy had attacked us one day more after we made to the north, the same would have happened to the rest of the ships."

The Armada then was sent off undermanned and under-equipped. It had neither the quantity nor the quality of the soldiers it needed to make a direct assault on England, and it had not the means of effecting a junction with the veterans of the Army of Flanders; it was encumbered by a hotchpotch of slow, crank, and unweatherly ships, many of them structurally unsuited to the northern seas; it was armed with guns that could give it an advantage neither at extreme nor at point-blank range, fired by powder that was in great part inefficient and unreliable, and that was not expected to last more than three days; and it was provisioned with moulding biscuit, souring wine, and putrescent fish which was becoming inedible almost before the ships left port and which, despite all the pious hopes and false relations, was in such short supply that within a month it had contributed materially to the decision to abandon the Enterprise and bring the Armada back to Spain. There was almost nothing in this catalogue of woes that had not been brought to the attention of Madrid and the Escorial over and over again in the months and the years before the disaster. By the time he reached Corunna, the commander of the Armada, the Duke of Medina Sidonia, was so disheartened by the sysiphean task of trying to improve

VIII

the condition of his fleet and by the inadequacy of the means at his disposal that he wanted, even at that late hour, to call the whole thing off.

What then was the point of sending the Armada to sea in such a condition? Had the decision been a purely military one, perhaps the answer would have been, none, but by July 1588 the Armada had long ceased to be solely a military venture. Maybe Englishmen have too readily assumed that the only thing that mattered about the Armada was whether it conquered England. Yet as far as Philip II was concerned, the invasion of England was only a means to an end, and, in the opinion of many of his advisers, not by far the most desirable of means. The basic aim of the Armada was not the conquest of England, but to shift the burden of war from Spain to England, to transform an immensely costly, passive and demoralizing, defensive war into an aggressive war in which the Spaniards would have the initiative and the English would have to pay the economic and psychological costs of eternal vigilance. Philip II's purpose was to put a stop to English interference in his affairs, to get Elizabeth out of the Netherlands, to make her abandon her support for the Portuguese pretender, and to drive the English pirates out of the Indies by compelling them to concentrate their forces at home for their own defence. To do this it was essential, not necessarily to conquer England, but to appear to be able to do so. The King of Spain had to show that he could put an Armada to sea. He had failed to do so in 1586, and even Drake was surprised. He had failed to do so in 1587, and Drake had sacked Cadiz. By 1588, men were beginning to laugh at

the King of Spain and his Armada. It had already cost millions of ducats and was costing a further 900,000 ducats a month. It was a massive burden on Portugal and Flanders. It was interfering with commerce and with the Indies trade. Further delay could only allow the English to strengthen their defences or again take pre-emptive action as they had done the year before, and increase the chances of a collapse of that delicately balanced diplomatic stalemate that was keeping the French and the Turks temporarily out of action at the critical moment. Further delay must finally destroy Parma's invading force and do who knows what harm to Philip II's cause in the Netherlands. If the Armada did not sail, the English would be completely unrestrained and Spain would be exposed to the "intolerable disgrace" of even more daring and more damaging outrages on its shipping, its ports, and its Indies. If Elizabeth went unpunished, what credibility would be left to the bubble reputation of Spanish power, either in Europe or in its empire. By July 1588, with half a dozen deadlines already passed, there could be no worse defeat than to leave the Armada rotting in port.

Besides, it was by no means certain that the Armada would have to fight at all. Ideally, it would not need to, and Medina Sidonia's orders were to avoid battle as long as his purposes were not thwarted. The very size and reputation of the huge fleet — its unheard-of numbers exaggerated by the flood of official propaganda broadsheets that flowed from the presses — the awe-inspiring sight of its towering ships, that would be enough. Elizabeth dare not risk her fleet and her kingdom against such a force.

She would have to make peace and the Armada would be vindicated. This curious mixture of fantasy and desperation is nowhere better manifested than in the admonition sent in reply to Medina Sidonia's defeatist letter from Corunna on June 24, 1588. The ships of the Armada, Medina Sidonia was told, despite all reverses, were still newer, larger, and stronger than the English, and their soldiers more numerous, more experienced, better trained, and disciplined. Reserves of victuals would be sent after the fleet from Lisbon and more could be taken on in Flanders. Parma's morale was high and his troops raring to go. With only six days of good weather it could be all but over. Furthermore, and this was the rub, "for our fleet to remain in Corunna is so far from strengthening our position (giving reputation to, literally) in any peace negotiation, should this be intended, that it would more likely give the enemy extra incentive for hostile action, thinking it a weakness ... Even if our purpose were solely to make peace, this could not be done on honourable terms without the fleet's going ahead and joining with the Duke of Parma, clearing from its path whatever might cross it". In short, "the shame of finding our fleet bottled up and ineffective" would merely be to "exchange offensive war for defensive, by which we would lose both advantage and reputation".

The Armada did not conquer England, it did not prevent English assaults on Spanish territory or English attacks on Spanish ships; it did not force England to abandon the Dutch or the dissidents in Portugal; but did it do any harm? Was Spain any worse off with the Armada a failure than if it had never

sailed at all? Financially, of course, it was — though we must not forget that one way or another there would have been massive defence costs. Santa Cruz, for example, in 1586, argued that it would cost in other ways four times as much if nothing were done. Materially, and in human terms, the losses were enormous. By November 19, only 7,486 men of 98 companies of infantry had returned; 60 per cent of those who had left on May 30 had not come back. The loss of ships is less exactly recorded, but half the total (63) is probably the upper estimate, one-third (44) probably the lower. Politically, there is obvious scope for argument about the effect of the Armada's failure on the fate of the Guises in France or the war in the Netherlands. Yet, in one way, the Armada succeeded. If the emphasis in this chapter has been on the structural and accidental inadequacies of the Spanish Armada, we should not forget that by contemporary lights it was a fearfully impressive looking force, and that despite everything, it reached its objective off Calais almost unscathed. That long-running fight up the Channel with its four battles, each one far exceeding what those who had been in both campaigns had experienced at Lepanto, did not destroy the reputation of Spanish naval power, it made it. Lord Howard of Effingham said it: "Some made but little account of the Spanish force by sea; but I do warrant you, all the world never saw such a force as theirs was". Within two years, Spain again had a fleet of 100 ships and 43,000 tons, and with the memory of that week in August 1588 behind them, no Englishman could feel confident that there would not be other Armadas and that the next one might not succeed.

IX

THE SPANISH ARMADA: NAVAL WARFARE BETWEEN
THE MEDITERRANEAN AND THE ATLANTIC

The 1588 Armada was a key event in the history of naval warfare and a decisive moment in the historic shift in the balance of power from the Mediterranean to the Atlantic. It was a clash between two military systems; a clash between a country that was placing itself in the van of new modes of Ocean warfare and a power whose naval forces had hitherto been concentrated mainly in the Mediterranean and which had operated in a very different framework of military imperatives. For Spain, therefore, the Armada marked a radical change in her military profile and presented her with serious logistical and administrative problems. Whether or not those problems were resolved, and the means adopted for their solution, had important implications not only for the configuration of the *Gran Armada* and the military outcome of the campaign, but also, by altering the balance of the Spanish military and political system, for the internal articulation of the Spanish Monarchy.

The first years of the reign of Philip II saw a spectacular expansion of Spanish naval power in the Mediterranean. Charles V never had more than about forty operational galleys in regular commission; between 1562 and 1574 Philip II tripled the Mediterranean fleet. In the peak years of the 1570s, around 1574, Philip II was maintaining a fleet of over 140 galleys in the Mediterranean (the equivalent of some 25,000 *toneladas* of shipping) with a supporting squadron of roundships (in 1572 consisting of 68 *naves* of 23,500 *toneladas*). This fleet carried in excess of 45,000 men (about 7,000 sailors, 25,000 rowers, 15,000 regular infantry — and many more for a major expedition), and mounted about 800–900 guns, firing 5,500–6,000 lbs of shot.[1]

The *Gran Armada*, in contrast — using the 'general muster' of 24 May 1588, not the unreliable printed inventory of 9 May — consisted of 66,000 tons of shipping, including four galleasses, four galleys and some ninety great ships, a total of 30,000 men (of whom 18,539 were soldiers, 7,666 seamen, and 2,088 oarsmen), 2,431 guns, firing about

13,000 lbs of shot, costing in all 256,588 ducats a month (282,247 *escudos*).[2] It was a force twenty times the size and cost of the only high-board squadron previously maintained by the Spanish crown in the Atlantic on a regular basis, the *Armada* of the Indies guard. In short, the Mediterranean fleet carried nearly 60% more men; the Armada had three times as many guns, two and a half times the firepower, 40% more tonnage, and consequently a greater quantity of stores (sails, cables and chandlery).

The Mediterranean war was a war of galleys, of more or less specialised warships, permanent instruments of the state, and in the 1570s mainly, though not always, state-owned; Atlantic war was a war of round-ships and galleons, mainly armed merchantmen, in great part privately owned and only temporary and occasional adjuncts of state power. Mediterranean war was a war of 'prowess',[3] though not without its skills, essentially a war of 'aristocratic dash',[4] like a seaborne cavalry charge. Atlantic war, though not without its valour, was a war of 'proficiency', of technical skill, of experience and expertise, a 'bourgeois' war.[5] Mediterranean warfare was labour intensive; Atlantic warfare was capital intensive. The Mediterranean war was a war of men, propelled by men and fought man to man; Atlantic war was a war of *matériel*, of sails and guns. Oarsmen made up about half the capital value of a galley, ordnance at least half the capital value of a galleon (c.10–12% of that of a galley). Only about one or two per cent of the running costs of a galley went on munitions, no more than a quarter of those of a galleon.[6] Mediterranean warfare was also relatively expensive. A galley cost as much to fit out and run as a 300-ton galleon nearly twice its size, carrying a similar number of soldiers and nearly four times its weight of ordnance.[7] It is worth noting, therefore, that the shift to the Atlantic coincided with, and reflected, the exhaustion of the traditional resources of Mediterranean warfare. It is perhaps no coincidence that the retreat from the Mediterranean took place at the moment when the demographic growth of the sixteenth century was faltering, and when the price differentials between foodstuffs and munitions most disfavoured the galley.[8]

Lacking most of the essential resources for naval power, Spain was in many ways ill-equipped for her maritime role. Practically everything needed for the galleys, except iron and timber, had to be imported: sails, oars, hemp and munitions from Naples and Milan; masts, spars, tar and pitch via Flanders; tin and lead from England; canvas and sailcloth from Brittany. And she was almost entirely dependent on Italian volunteers, especially Genoese, for seamen. Almost 90% of the material costs of a galley and over 30% of its running costs (excluding pay) were spent in Italy, Flanders and France.[9]

Philip II's Mediterranean power, therefore, had to be a 'Monarchial' enterprise, a cooperation between Spain and his other Mediterranean realms. Only fourteen of Philip II's seventy-eight galleys at Lepanto were Spanish and only 9,700 of his 24,800 infantry. Messina was the base, and Naples and Sicily the granaries and supply centres of the fleet. At Lepanto, Naples and Sicily contributed more than half the galleys, and more than one-third the costs.[10] In 1574, Naples supported fifty-three galleys and a *tercio* of infantry — the expansion of the Neapolitan and Sicilian squadrons being part of a deliberate royal policy 'so that correspondingly less of the extraordinary costs be provided by Spain'.[11]

But already by the mid 1570s the Spanish Monarchy was proving incapable of maintaining a naval force in the Mediterranean at the levels of the years of the Holy League. The spectacular expansion of the Mediterranean fleet, which was tripled in numbers within the twelve-year period 1562–74, had been achieved only by the exhaustion of resources and the sacrifice of standards. The new galleys were badly-built and ill-equipped, with inexperienced officers, chronic shortages of rowers and seamen, and high costs.[12] All this coincided with an acute financial crisis, which was to lead to the royal 'bankruptcy' of 1575. By 1574 three-quarters of the 420,000 ducats of the clerical *subsidio*, granted by the papacy in 1560 expressly to maintain sixty of the 100 galleys to which the king had committed himself, was being diverted to the war in the Netherlands.[13] By January 1575, thirty-one of the 146 galleys were unmanned and out of commission, and the forty-six galleys of the Spanish squadron needed 100,000 ducats spent on them to make them seaworthy.[14] In December 1576, after Philip II had recognised his inability to maintain a larger force, in view of the 'great expense' and 'considering how ill in order many of my galleys are and have been', the fleet was cut back to 102 galleys and committed to a purely defensive role, 'since it is not possible for my fleet to be numerous enough to be able to face the enemy'.[15]

The reduction of the fleet released perhaps half the scarce resources that had been tied up in the Mediterranean war and so might be seen to have facilitated the reappropriation of resources that the *Gran Armada* would require in 1588. The reality was not quite so easy. Mediterranean resources were not immediately transferable to other theatres, neither ships, seamen, nor soldiers were suitable, or available, for service in the Atlantic.[16]

Thus the run-down of the war in the Mediterranean meant less the release of resources than the displacement of the military burden from Italy to Spain. From 1578 the majority of the galleys, Italian no less than Spanish, were serving regularly in Spanish waters, with Spanish and Italian galleys regularly based in Puerto de Santa Maria, Sanlúcar, Cadiz and Gibraltar, and Andalucia was coming to displace Sicily as the centre for the provisioning of the galleys, with a new commissariat for victualling the *armadas* established in Seville in 1580 or 1581. Nonetheless, Andalucia was in many ways not a satisfactory alternative, not least because of the high level of prices prevalent there.[17]

Neither was the reduction of the Mediterranean fleet — ordered six months before news of the truce with the Turk reached Madrid — part of a planned restructuring of Spanish military force in preparation for a new set of strategic priorities, a conscious preparation for a decisive shift away from the Mediterranean to the Atlantic. The annexation of Portugal and the campaigns of 1582 and 1583 in the Azores had a great political impact internationally, but they were not the first steps in a new rearmament for an Atlantic military strategy. Santa Cruz's proposal in August 1583, after his victory in the Azores, that his fleet should be kept in being and sent against Elizabeth, was ignored. Instead, the military apparatus that had conquered Portugal and the Azores was dismantled. The last 3,000 German and Italian troops in Lisbon were finally sent home in March 1584. The programme for the construction of 15,000 tons of shipping in Guipuzcoa and Vizcaya to serve as a kind of naval militia, first put forward in 1581 when the pacification of Portugal was still uncertain and when it was believed that the French, the English and the Dutch were arming a great fleet to attack the King of Spain, was abandoned in October 1584 only a third completed. At the same time the crown was contemplating selling off the nine galleons that were being built for the Indies Guard to private owners. At the end of 1584 Philip II was actually in the process of reversing a policy that had been intended to begin the creation of a permanent, Spanish Royal high-seas fleet.[18]

Meanwhile, the reduction of the galley fleets continued. From their peak of about 146 in 1574, they had fallen to eighty-eight by 1587. Nor was anything done to reform munitions supply or to reverse the deterioration into which the arms industries were falling, despite the repeated admonitions of the captain general of the artillery. In 1584 a contract negotiated for the importation of 10,000 cwt of Hungarian copper for the casting of artillery was cut by 60%. The negotiations with the prince of Salerno — which had been going on sporadically since 1578 — to reopen the cannon-ball factory in Navarre, inoperative now for many years, were suspended in 1585 and the matter dropped until July 1586.[19]

The apparent continuity 1577–1580–1588 is, therefore, a false one. From the logistical point of view the 'enterprise of England' was not the culmination of a long-prepared military plan going back to the 1570s, but the abrupt reversal of a prolonged run-down of Spanish naval forces which had been temporarily interrupted, but not halted, by the campaigns of 1580–83. It was the end of what Chaunu calls, 'le calme militaire relatif des années 1582–1585'.[20]

The shift from Mediterranean to Atlantic brought, in round terms, an immediate doubling of military demand for men and *matériel*, but even more important, a logistical shift from areas of relative Spanish strength (men, morale, discipline) to areas of Spanish weakness, ships, guns, and technology (seamen, gunners, gun-founders).[21] Spanish round-ships played only a small part in the Mediterranean wars. Of the 33,000 *toneladas* projected for the attack on Algiers in 1573 no more than 4,000 were to come from Spain. Of the thirty-nine great ships assembled for the Portuguese campaign in 1580 not one was Spanish.[22] By around 1580, with shortages of masts, spars, planking and pitch, a decline of shipping, and little activity in the shipyards, men like the great advocate for a strong Spanish naval presence in the Atlantic, the *contador* Alonso Gutiérrez, were despairing of the possibility of assembling a native-built fleet.[23]

One of the reasons why it was thought so difficult was the problem of manning a Spanish fleet with sailors, pilots or gunners. Various schemes to conscript seamen or, failing that, to induce them to sign on voluntarily by offering them pay in advance, and a substantial bonus, proved largely ineffective, as did efforts to enlist and train gunners.[24] Spain was also chronically short of artillery for such a fleet. Not only was she dependent on imported copper and tin, but the cannon-founding facilities of Malaga and Seville were insufficient for the demands of naval warfare in the 1570s. In order to arm the forty-nine extra galleys fitted out in 1572, not even Spain's share of the prize-guns taken at Lepanto sufficed, and Philip had to try to borrow artillery from the petty states of Italy (Savoy, Genoa, Florence, Ferrara, Malta) and to negotiate the purchase of iron guns from England, via the earl of Leicester.[25]

However, it was the Spanish munitions industries which were in the worst position to meet the huge increase in demand. With the breakdown of the negotiations with the prince of Salerno there was no cannon-shot made at all in Spain, and the country's gunpowder manufacturing capacity was actually less in 1587 than it had been in 1580 (from a daily output of twenty cwt in 1580 to twelve cwt in 1587).[26] The only one of the war industries that was expanding in the 1580s was the small-arms industry in Guipuzcoa and Vizcaya, but this, like all the other munitions industries, was crippled by lack of money. When the captain general of the artillery took up his post in Lisbon in 1587 to start equipping the fleet, he reported major deficiencies in everything, right across the board:

> I have drawn Your Majesty's attention to the great shortage there is of all kinds of artillery, both for land and for sea. I have to say the same for gunpowder, matchcord, lead, iron, steel, rope, equipment and machinery, so Your Majesty can see to the great need that there is. It is apparent that for each of these items time is required, and there are problems which cannot be sorted out except by continuing the procurement of everything and making every effort to assemble large quantities in all provinces, especially of saltpetre and facilities for milling gunpowder, since everywhere there is such great need, and in all parts no less shortage of cast-iron shot for the guns.[27]

All these failings are well known, but what is important to note is that what was lacking was precisely the qualities required for the new warfare. As Leonardo Donà had noted in 1570, good ships were in short supply because those employed in Atlantic waters were small 'and so not suitable for the actions that are envisioned'; while those engaged on the Indies run, though large, were undergunned and short of seamen.[28] But in addition to these long-standing inadequacies, there were new ones arising. It seems that it was precisely at this moment that the apparently inexhaustible supply of volunteers for the *tercios* was beginning to run dry. In the early 1580s it was becoming increasingly difficult to recruit soldiers, a development perhaps connected with the levelling off of population growth and an upturn in the levels of real wages. Between 1571 and 1578 the average recruiting captain was raising 256 men; in the decade after 1580 (1580–91) the average slumped to 161, and even this was achieved only with inordinate expense to the crown and intolerable suffering to the villages through which the unpaid and undisciplined soldiery passed. In the years after 1580, the complaints of the *cortes* bear witness to the breakdown of the entire recruiting system.[29]

A similar breakdown is apparent in the supply services. Just as in recruiting, the 1580s were a period of constant complaint by the *cortes* about the extortions of the purveyors.[30] The problem of supply, particularly of grain and other agricultural produce, was made worse by the increasing difficulties of Castilian agriculture, exacerbated by a series of bad harvests between 1580 and 1584, the reduction of imports from northern Europe resulting from the Spanish embargo on English and Dutch shipping from May 1585, and the growing danger from piracy in Spanish waters.

It was, therefore, against the background of an almost total collapse of the administrative and supply system that the decision to embark on the invasion of England was taken. The Armada had to be created from scratch out of a logistical vacuum at the moment of a general crisis of procurement.

The first requirement was a system of military administration geared to the needs of large-scale ocean warfare. There was neither a permanent naval commissariat nor an established naval base on the Atlantic seaboard adequate for the needs of 1588. The council of war was expanded, its secretariat doubled with a separate office of naval administration under the ex-purveyor of the galleys. Andrés de Alva. The military governorship of Galicia was revived, a new governorship created in the Canaries, and the duke of Medina Sidonia appointed captain general of Andalucia. In April 1586, Francisco Duarte, factor of the Casa de Contratacíon of Seville, was made purveyor general of the high-board fleets maintained at Castilian expense in Portugal, and in October the councillor of finance, Antonio de Guevara, was appointed purveyor general in Andalucia.[31]

The lack of an established naval base on the Atlantic beyond Cadiz raised the problem of finding a site that would reconcile both the 'operative' (or strategic) and 'logistical' functions of a base. As long as war was in the north and provisions in the south, the problem remained intractable, and it remained unresolved thirty years later. Some consideration seems to have been given to fitting out the Armada on the more strategically placed Cantabrian coast (as in 1574), but the scale of the Armada's requirements and the importance of Lisbon's commercial nexus and its ordnance facilities determined the choice.[32] The logistical factor prevailed, therefore, but both for political and administrative reasons Lisbon was in other respects unsatisfactory. The limited jurisdiction of the Castilian commissariat meant that it was not possible to employ the arbitrary measures used in Castile and local purchases had to be made in cash; conflicts with the Portuguese commissariat, Portuguese hostility to Castilians, especially to the soldiers, even confusion between Castilian and Portuguese weights and measures, restricted control, impeded effectiveness, increased opportunities for fraud and deceit, and contributed a great deal to the provisioning failure in 1588.

In Castile the Armada preparations generated a stream of reforms during the summer of 1586 and throughout 1587 and 1588, intended to remedy the most glaring defects of the system of military organisation. New biscuit baking ovens were put up in Lisbon and Malaga. Measures were proposed to find 'a way to organise provisioning without so many complaints against the purveyors and their officials', schemes to get the lords and cities of Andalucia to contract to provide fixed quantities of their harvests, for example, or to get the town councils to do the buying of the grain and act as guarantors of payment, or to establish official grain quotas in accordance with the capacity of each village.[33]

A major reform of the recruiting system was undertaken. New regulations for recruiting captains were issued in 1584. A commissary general with judicial authority to coordinate billeting and supervise recruiting was appointed in 1587, and a second the following year, dividing their jurisdiction between Castile and Andalucia. A preliminary listing was made of veteran soldiers living in retirement, and initial investigations set up with a view to the establishment of a national militia. Of most significance, however, were a proposal in October 1586 to get the cities to take responsibility for raising soldiers, and a series of agreements with the lords and cities of Andalucia to raise quotas of men from their estates in order to avoid the problems caused by royal recruiting captains — both measures of a decentralizing nature analogous to those proposed for the provisioning of grain.[34] Although some thirty companies were recruited in 1587 by royal captains, a similar number of the companies serving in 1588 were levies of Andalucian, Extremaduran and Castilian cities and of lords like the count of Benavente, and the dukes of Bejar, Feria and Alburquerque.[35]

There were reforms also in munitions procurement. Surveys were begun to discover new mineral deposits; the Lérida saltpetre plant was put to work again (May 1587); the cannon foundries in Lisbon were expanded and brought into production; negotiations were resumed to open the shot-works in Navarre, and to take over for the crown the privately owned sulphur mines at Hellín in Murcia; and the agreement with the Basque shipbuilders, in suspension since 1584, seems to have been taken up again at the beginning of 1587.[36]

A plethora of reforms then, but to what extent was it possible to remedy in two years chronic inadequacies in the military–administrative structure? Was the very existence of the *Gran Armada* the vindication of Philip II's bureaucratic system, as some have claimed — if not a military victory, an administrative triumph?

There were assembled in the estuary of the Tagus on the eve of departure some 130 vessels — not counting the 10 caravels. Of these, nine galleons and two *pataches* of the royal squadron of Portugal (annexed to the crown in 1580), the same number of galleons and *pataches* of the squadron of Castile, and a further four galeasses and four galleys belonged to the king, and the remaining 100 or so *naves*, *urcas* and *pataches*, freighted or requisitioned for the occasion, were privately owned.[37] The make-up of the Armada suggests that there had been some late improvements in Spain's shipbuilding capacity, up to twenty-nine or thirty of the forty-five best private vessels in the fighting-squadrons were of Spanish origin, a good number of them built in accordance with agreements made with the royal superintendent, Cristóbal de Barros.[38] After the disaster, in October 1588, when the reconstruction of the royal fleet was being undertaken, it was claimed that no less than forty galleons of up to 500 *toneladas* could be built on the coast between San Sebastian and San Vicente de la Barquera within a year.[39] An exaggeration no doubt, but a much more optimistic comment than would have been possible only a few years before. The negative side, however, was that this quantitative success in 1588 was achieved only by creaming off the big ships from the Indies route. The result was a severe tonnage-crisis in the American trade. Tonnage sailing outward in 1587 was only 11.9% of the average of 1583–86, the lowest figure until 1650.[40]

There were ships enough in 1588, therefore, but the problem of manning them remained unsolved. There was still an acute shortage of seamen. One of the reasons for diverting the ships of the Indies *flotas* was to incorporate their sailors into the Armada, which even as late as the end of March 1588 was incapable of putting to sea 'because of the very great shortage there is of sailors'.[41] When it sailed at the end of May, it carried only 10.9 seamen per 100 *toneladas*, only two-thirds of the norm established for the navy in the seventeenth century, and it would not have got those without the press ganging of foreign mariners in Spanish ports.[42] Some of the problems of ship-handling that arose during the voyage no doubt had something to do with the shortage of seamen and the inequality of their distribution among the ships and the squadrons, some of which had three times more mariners pro rata to tonnage than others.[43] In all this there were serious operational dangers. Foreign pilots and sailors deserted at the first opportunity, and significantly the squadron which suffered the heaviest losses, the Levantine, was the one with the lowest ratio of seamen.

Something similar could be said of the shortage of gunners. Years later, the duke of Medina Sidonia was to say that to rely on German and Flemish gunners was to hold a lighted bomb in one's hand — he had in mind, perhaps, the tragic fate of the *San Salvador*.[44] Lacking too was the capacity to equip the ships with adequate artillery. There can be no doubt that the Armada was woefully undergunned. 'The whole Armada is short of guns', wrote the marquis of Santa Cruz.[45] Although new furnaces were set up in Lisbon, there were neither sufficient master founders, polishers, adjusters and ironsmiths, nor the materials (copper, iron, timber) and money. At the end of February 1588, the captain general of the artillery declared that in the year he had been in Lisbon he had been unable to cast more than sixty guns, about 180 cwt, 'since they are things which, even with a surplus of money, cannot be had nor made without a long lead-time'.[46] The new-cast pieces comprised a mere 2½% of the guns carried in the Armada, totally insufficient to remedy the shortage of artillery on the private vessels, three-quarters of whose guns were their original 'ship-guns', overwhelmingly small, cast-iron pieces, of little but defensive value.[47]

On the other hand, if we are to believe the inventory of 9 May 1588, the targets for munitions appear to have been met. However, there is reason to doubt the veracity of that inventory. The victualling account was certainly fraudulent, and the uniformity and exactness of the munitions listings simply do not accord with the data that we have from other and subsequent accounts. The squadron of Castile, for example, on 14 May, had more than enough powder for the sixty shot per gun with which it was credited in the inventory of 9 May, but each gun had no more than twenty-five shot. Here again, there was no uniformity from squadron to squadron. In mid-April, although the galleasses and the Andalucian squadron were well-munitioned, the Levant squadron was 383 cwt of gunpowder short, and the hulks had none at all.[48]

The attempts to reform munitions production had come too late. The first cannon-balls from the new shot-foundry at Eugui, in Navarre, did not come on stream until the end of 1588, at the earliest, and the bulk of the shot for the Armada came from abroad. Fifteen-thousand cwt of copper from Milan, requested by the council of war in May 1587, still had not arrived in Spain in September 1588, and the agreement over the Hellín sulphur mine was not concluded until 1589. Although the captain general of the artillery claimed he could produce 4,000 cwt of gunpowder within six months, Medina Sidonia found the Armada at the end of May 1588 with no more than 3,000 cwt, less than half it was thought to need, and 550 cwt had to be bought from German merchants in Lisbon at more than double the normal price.[49]

Yet, however well or ill the Armada was stocked, equipping it had left the defences of the peninsula dangerously denuded of munitions of all sorts. In September there were no more than 100 balls of shot and 15-20 cwt of powder in La Coruña, and the other arsenals and fortresses of Spain were 23,000 cwt of gunpowder short.[50]

The Armada was also weak in infantry. It was the lack of soldiers that had prevented Santa Cruz going out to intercept Drake off Lisbon in May 1587, and even at the end of March 1588 there were barely 10,000 soldiers on board.[51] It was only the arrival of 3,000 men from Extremadura, the withdrawal of troops from the Lisbon garrisons, and the last minute recruitment of 2,000 Portuguese in April and May which gave the Armada a degree of numerical respectability. It put to sea on 30 May with thirty-one soldiers for every 100 *toneladas* of shipping, more than the norm for the 1624 Armada, but less than the (perhaps unrealistic) figures projected by Santa Cruz in March 1586, or by Medina Sidonia in March 1587.[52]

However, what is in doubt is not so much the number as the quality of the troops involved. All were agreed the troops to be put ashore for invasion must be a trained and experienced elite of 'gente vieja'. Santa Cruz had wanted 27,000 mercenaries from Germany and Italy, and 11,000 veteran Spanish infantry from the *tercios* in Italy, the garrisons of Portugal and the Azores, and the Armada of the Indies Guard. In May 1588 the *Gran Armada* had less than 19,000 soldiers, none of them Germans or Italians, and at least twenty-nine of the 104 companies of the *tercios* of Pimentel from Sicily, Luzón from Naples, Toledo from Portugal, and Isla from the Indies galleons, were new companies raised in Spain in 1587. A minimum of 60%, and possibly as many as 75% of the infantry on the *Gran Armada* were raw recruits, many of them not even volunteers, but conscripts levied by the lords and cities of

Andalucia and Extremadura. The *Gran Armada* was the first time that Spaniards were conscripted for service overseas. This was the legacy of the collapse of the voluntary recruiting system after 1580.

Given that contemporary experts believed that it took three times as long to train a soldier for service at sea, one can only guess at the fitness, morale and military capacity of such men. Despite some satisfaction in court circles with both the number and the quality of the soldiers aboard,[53] the duke of Medina Sidonia was a good deal less impressed: 'the men are not as well-trained as they should be, nor are the officers'.[54] The 400 Galicians sent by the counts of Lemos and Monterrey were described by Medina Sidonia as

so useless they cannot serve even as pioneers. Besides, they are all married, with numerous children, and most of them old and infirm . . . Even their own captains have not wanted to accept them, because apart from dying and taking up space on the ships, they are no good for anything, for none of them knows what an arquebus is, nor any sort of weapon. They have let themselves become like dead men, and some have not eaten for two days. In view of this I have dismissed them all, and they have gone back to their homes.[55]

The victualling requirements for the Armada called for twice the amount of wheat normally procured by the Castilian military commissariat in Andalucia in an ordinary year, a quantity itself considerably increased since 1580, and three times the amount of wine, in addition to all the provisions brought from Sicily, Naples and other parts of Castile. These demands were all the more difficult to meet because the 1587 harvest was poor and the very existence of the Armada and the fear of embargo or English interception inhibited grain shipments from the Baltic.

Ultimately, however, the failure was not one of procurement, though success in this respect was achieved only at the expense of Andalucia, Galicia and Portugal, and the victualling of the Indies fleets, but of the erosion of supplies by delay, wastage and fraud. Consuming nearly 15,000 quintals of biscuit and 1,500 pipes of wine a month, by the time it sailed the Armada had already consumed in normal rations half as much again as it took with it, in addition to the massive wastage caused by conditions of shipboard storage and by the processes of loading and unloading. In January 1588 bread and biscuit was being embarked for eight months; in April the Armada had five months supply; and it sailed at the end of May with enough for four months. The optimistic reports of the ministers, however, had been based on statements from the purveyors and quartermasters which were either fraudulent or incompetent.[56] On 14 June, only two weeks after sailing from Lisbon, Medina Sidonia was writing, 'I carry a great shortage of victuals', and some ships put in to La Coruña on 19 June without water.[57] The fleet restocked in La Coruña, but when the English captured the *Rosario* on 1 August, they found stinking fish, bread full of worms, leaky casks and sour wine. When the Armada sailed out of La Coruña on 22 July, it was carrying biscuit for only fifty-seven days, and less than three weeks later Medina Sidonia was forced to cut rations by two-thirds simply in order to enable the men to get back to Spain. After the disaster, on 28 September 1588, the council of state, complaining of 'the malice and corruption that there was in the provisioning', concluded 'the principal reason for the decision to return was the shortage of victuals'.[58]

It looks then as if it was the incompleteness of the solutions to the logistical problems raised by the demands of the Atlantic that determined the configuration of the Armada, and hence its strategy and fate.

The salient characteristic of the *Gran Armada* was its heterogeneity, a heterogeneity in ownership, manning, armament, and loyalties. Such heterogeneity was by no means unique but it was a characteristic that was of greater disadvantage for the effective conduct of a strategic offensive, in which unity of action and uniformity of purpose are of the essence, than it was for defence, as the English themselves found in the 'counter-Armada' of 1589. But in contrast with the situation in the English fleet in July 1588, many, if not most of the shipowners — like Andrés Felipe, the captain of the *Gran Grin*, who had invested 20,000 ducats in his ship in the expectation of doubling his money on the Indies run only two months before he was embargoed[59] — the empressed German, Dutch, Flemish and Portuguese sailors, and the conscripted soldiers on the Armada simply did not want to be there. As the *maestre de campo general*, the chief military staff officer, Don Francisco de Bobadilla, observed in a letter from the flagship to the king's confidant, Don Juan de Idiáquez, on 20 August 1588: 'The strength of our Armada was twenty or so vessels, and those fought very well, even better than was needed, but most of the rest fled whenever they saw the enemy attack'.[60]

The need to employ whatever ships were available regardless of sailing and handling qualities, the insufficiency of mariners and artillerymen, the inability to arm the fleet on a rational basis or with adequate firepower, meant the Armada lacked all the intensity factors needed to bring the English to battle or to destroy their fleet if it encountered it. The *Gran Armada* was not equipped for an offensive role *at sea*; its tactical imperative had, therefore, to be one of defence. The Armada had to be 'invincible', and that meant reliance on the one factor in which Spain was preponderant, size. The strategy of the fleet had to be a 'Mediterranean' strategy, the strategy of Lepanto in which a vast arc of over 200 vessels blasted its way through the enemy front, a strategy of mass. All the Spanish planners were of one voice in insisting that 'His Majesty's Armada must not be restricted, but the biggest and most powerful that it can be'.[61] The Armada had to be too big to be defeated, its ships too large and powerful, even if 'less nimble and less seaworthy', its soldiers too numerous, as much for the defensive firepower of their arquebuses and muskets as for boarding and landing, as they proved at Gravelines.

But a strategy of mass posed insuperable problems for sixteenth-century administrations. The greater the Armada, the more the ships and men, the more provisions and supplies that were needed, the longer the time it took to prepare and assemble; the longer it took to prepare and assemble the greater the wastage, the deterioration and the decay, and the more that was consumed merely to keep it in existence. There were soldiers being maintained on the Armada's account well over a year before it finally set sail. In the eleven months it was in Spain, between July 1587 and May 1588, the *tercio* of Naples lost 25% of its effectives, and the same thing was happening in the Netherlands to an even greater degree.[62] Similarly, provisions had begun to be assembled after the harvest of 1586. By May 1588, as we have seen, the Armada had already used in normal rations alone half as many victuals again as it was to carry with it out of Lisbon, in addition to all the wastage that we know to have occurred. The inadequacy of the administrative infra-structure − in Galicia there were not even storehouses for sorting the shot − simply accelerated the logistical instability inherent in all great sixteenth-century expeditions.

These problems of logistics and manpower made it impossible for the Spanish fleet to act as an independent force. So much was admitted by Philip II in the instruction of 14 September 1587, ordering a late change of strategy: 'the strength of the two fleets not being as great as was estimated to be desirable for the principal enterprise . . . not having been able to assemble this year everything projected in the plans'.[63] It was the impossibility of assembling a force large enough for direct action against England which made the fatal plan for a junction with Parma unavoidable, if for no other reason than the need to restock the Armada with water, provisions and munitions in the Netherlands.

Without enough 'gente vieja' or veterans, it was impossible to mount an invasion directly; without more powerful artillery it was impossible to destroy the enemy's fleet; without munitions it was impossible to resist their attacks; without victuals it was impossible to maintain the Armada as a fighting force at sea: 'from that (shortage of victuals) has followed not only the loss of so much treasure and the uncountable revenue Your Majesty has spent on this Armada, all fruitlessly, but the loss of the Armada itself, the men on it, and as a result everything else that we see'.[64]

Conclusion

The most fundamental problems faced in the creation of the Armada were consequences of the incomplete transition from Mediterranean to Atlantic modes of warfare. The Armada was the first stage in that transition; it was, in that sense, too early — administratively and culturally premature. The persistence of a 'Mediterranean mentality' can be seen, for instance, not only in the tactical dispositions adopted and in the 'cavalry' attitudes of men such as Don Alonso de Leiva, but, even more damagingly, in the status conflicts between sailors and soldiers, which, reinforced by social conflicts between gentlemen and commoners, and national conflicts between Castilians-Andalucians, on the one hand, and Basques-Cantabrians, on the other, must have had a shattering effect on morale. Don Pedro de Valdés, admiral of the Andalucian squadron, complained of the subordination of his sea-captains and ships' masters, men with years of experience on the Indies run, to 'men who have never been on the open sea nor understand its ways. For that they are held in disdain and have little desire to serve. This was not the least reason why the Armada was dispersed in the recent storm which scattered it' near La Coruña.[65] The Guipuzcoans, on their return, blamed the soldiers for causing many of the losses on the Irish coast by their violence towards the crews and by preventing the pilots and sailors from navigating freely.[66]

It was, of course, the failure of the Armada which then made necessary the regularisation and institutionalisation of Atlantic warfare in the years after 1588 with the establishment of a permanent *Armada del Mar Océano*, and that permanence in turn actualised the wider implications of the shift from the Mediterranean to the Atlantic.

The first implication was a long-term shift in the balance of military power. The Mediterranean system of warfare involved the control of an enclosed maritime space by the symbiotic operation of galley fleets and coastal fortifications.[67] It was a state war of permanent fleets and fortress outposts, maintained by the treasury and manned by the employment of state power — in Spain's case by the condemnation of criminals, prisoners of war and heretics to galley service by the royal courts. The Atlantic system of warfare was an ocean war on the 'open sea', a war not of control but of disruption, a 'little war' involving the raiding and defending of 'moving' targets (coasts, trade, routes), a war of sporadic and irregular action by part-time forces, sustained by independent capitalist activity and manned through market mechanisms by men with marketable skills. In this kind of war state power was not cost effective (not at least until there was a greater differentiation between warship and merchant ship) and the great monarchy had no military advantage over the small.[68] In the Atlantic all the more grandiose expeditions were spectacular failures, to a greater or lesser degree, for reasons not dissimilar to those which influenced the outcome in 1588 and because of the disassociation between sea and land.

The internal dimension of that shift was a shift from public to private in the organisation of war. Vicens Vives has drawn attention to the connection between the development of the state and the institutional-isation of war in the Mediterranean in the 1530s.[69] With war in the Atlantic and with the Atlantic war invading the Mediterranean from the 1580s that process was being reversed. The expansion of the Mediterranean war had involved an expansion of the role of the 'public sector' in military organisation. In 1560 the squadron of Naples comprised six royal galleys and ten private; in 1574 it had forty-nine royal and only four private. Only twenty-nine of the 146 galleys Philip II was maintaining in 1574 were privately owned, serving under contract. The heavy war galley, with in excess of 170 oarsmen, was not economically viable either as a merchant vessel or as a pirate unless it was 'salaried', and it was not mannable except with the help of the state.[70] The cut back in the galley fleets in 1576 was also, therefore, a cut back of the 'public sector' — that was explicit in the instruction of 27 December 1576. The economics of the round-ship, on the other hand, the little structural differentiation between the *nave* and the galleon, the relationship of crew space to cargo, the inability of the state to compete for free labour, favoured the private sector. The shift from galley to round-ship, therefore, was also a shift in the balance between the 'public' and 'private' share in war. If at Lepanto 80% of the galleys were the king's, in the fleet at Terceira in 1583 only three of thirty-six capital round-ships were the king's (excepting the two galeasses and twelve galleys), and in 1588 only thirty of the 130 vessels and less than one-third of the front-line ships. Philip II's creation of a large, permanent ocean fleet in the 1590s was an attempt to translate into the Atlantic the predominance of the 'public sector' in the Mediterranean. As such it did not succeed — the royal galleons never exceeded one-third of the ships in the expeditionary fleets of 1596 and 1597.

The logistics of the high seas fleets also promoted a more general movement of privatisation as the state was unable to employ its coercive power to import *matériel* for naval warfare from outside its jurisdiction, or to counteract the exhaustion of local resources and technical skill shortages. The maintenance and supplying of fleets by contracts with private entrepreneurs and the reforms in the system of grain procurement and recruiting, referred to above, were the administrative dimension of this public-private shift.

At the same time, however, the greatly increased demand for the fleets — the Armada in 1597 required 7,000 cwt of powder and 8,000 cwt of hemp,[71] four times more than the total requirement of the galleys of Spain and Portugal and the Armadas de Indias — by increasing Spain's negative foreign trade balance and exposing Spain's naval forces to the risk of an interruption of supplies from overseas, promoted more state intervention in the strategic sectors of the economy, mining, munitions, manufactures and shipbuilding, and an extension of controls over the arms industries. Royal shot and armour factories were set up, the output of gunpowder in the royal powder mills doubled and the treasury budget for domestic arms and munitions expenditure tripled between the early 1580s and 1600.[72]

In economic and fiscal terms the shift from Mediterranean to Atlantic meant also a shift, in both benefits and burdens, from east to west. The beneficiaries of war in the Mediterranean were the Catalans, the Neapolitans, the Sicilians and the Genoese. It was there that the galleys were built and where the greater part of the two and a half million ducats a year that the war in the Mediterranean was costing was spent. The beneficiaries of war in the Atlantic were rather the sea-board provinces on the western and northern peripheries. The more than

40,000 *toneladas* of shipping built in the Basque yards between 1588 and 1599 cost in excess of one million ducats, to which has to be added annual payments for freightage and wages for officers and mariners which, in 1590, amounted to some 250,000 ducats. A rough estimate would put some 20% of gross income in the Basque country in those years as coming direct from the royal treasury. Galicia, which had remained on the margins of military spending during the 1560s and 1570s, was another beneficiary of the 1590s, recovering in wages and purchases for the fleet perhaps half of what it paid in taxes. Even Andalucia, ravaged by naval purveyors and their commissaries, may have recovered as much as a third of its enormous tax burden by way of military spending in the province. All this, both before and after 1580, but even more so thereafter, meant a huge payments transfer from the Castiles to the peripheries — Portugal, Aragon, Cantabria, Vizcaya, Navarre — the greater part of them contributing little, or nothing, to disposable royal revenues.

The shift from Mediterranean to Atlantic is also a shift in the balance of the Monarquía Hispánica. The shift to the Atlantic led to the progressive hispanisation of war. In 1580 all the large sailing ships employed in the conquest of Portugal came from the Levant; in 1583 at Terceira, half the ships were of Mediterranean origin; in 1588, only one in eight of the major vessels were.[73] At Lepanto only 40% of Philip II's troops were Spaniards; in the *Gran Armada*, Spaniards comprised 90%, and the rest were Portuguese.

The war in the Mediterranean had been an instrument for the integration of the Spanish Monarchy and for the maintenance of Spanish dominance in Italy. As Don García de Toledo explained in November 1571, only one month after Lepanto, the importance of the victory lay in 'demonstrating to friends and enemies that when there is true union with His Majesty there must needs be very great success in everything'.[74] In the Mediterranean, Castile, Aragon and Italy were interdependent. In 1574 thirty-eight of the galleys maintained by Castile were in Italian waters, and Castile between 1571 and 1576 was sending on average 800,000 ducats a year to Italy. By the early 1580s the current was reversed; the galleys of Naples and Sicily were serving in Spain and both Naples and Sicily were contributing men and money to the Armada.[75]

The point is not that this represented a greater burden than in the 1570s — by the early 1580s Naples's expenditure on the galleys was only half that in 1574 and fiscal pressure in the 1590s was less severe than it had been in the 1570s[76] — but that it now represented an expatriation of *servicios*, whilst Italy was left to sustain the cost of its own defence largely unaided. During the 1560s and 1570s the Mediterranean kingdoms got the protection of Spain and the economic benefits of military spending in return for political subordination to Madrid; after 1580 they had not only to protect themselves, they had also to protect Spain.

One is getting the sense, in the last years of the century, of a distancing of the Mediterranean kingdoms from the Monarchy. Reglà has contrasted the participation of the Catalans in 1571 and their absence in 1588, and Koenigsberger has noted the reluctance of Sicilians in 1589 to contribute to 'causes not their own'.[77] Whereas the threat to the Spanish Mediterranean from the Sicilian channel seems to have had a cohesive function, the threat from the Straits of Gibraltar seems to have been disjunctive. The Atlanticisation of war in the 1580s changed the framework of association between Castile and Spain and between Spain and the Mediterranean kingdoms, and that in turn contributed to the acute Castilian sense of isolation which is the leitmotiv of the history of the 'Monarquía' in the seventeenth century.

NOTES

1. There were, for example, 24,800 soldiers paid by the King of Spain on the galleys at the battle of Lepanto in 1571.
2. AGS GA 221 f. 158 'Relación sumaria del estado de la Real Armada', referring to the 'French-style muster' of 24 May, sent to the king with a letter dated 28 May 1588; AGS GA 223 f. 99 Francisco Duarte to the King, Lisbon 30 May referring to the 'general' muster of 24 May. See Casado Soto below for a discussion of tonnages.
3. M. D. Feld, 'Middle-class society and the rise of military professionalism: the Dutch Army 1589–1609' in *The structure of violence. Armed forces as social systems* (Beverly Hills/London, 1977) pp. 169–203 at p. 169.
4. P. W. Bamford, *Fighting ships and prisons. The Mediterranean galleys of France in the age of Louis XIV* (Minneapolis, 1973) p. 24.
5. See Feld, note 3.
6. Slaves on the galleys were valued at 700 *reales* in the 1570s, and *forzados* at 330 *reales*; a gun cost c.176 *reales* per cwt. A galley had (at that time) a

crew of 164 oarsmen, and carried about 100 cwt of cannon. An account of 1570 (AGS E 453 'Relación de lo que vale una galera ordinaria') put the total cost of a galley at 142,830 *reales*, including 63,370 for the crew. According to a document of 1591, the ideal armament for a galleon of 1,300 *toneladas*, valued at 32,500 ducats, would cost 18,656 ducats, AGS GA 347 s.f.

7. Fully armed with crew and artillery, a galley cost 13,000 ducats; that would have fitted out and gunned a ship of about 317 *toneladas*; in 1624, on the 65 ducat per *tonelada* estimate of the secretary of the Navy, Martín de Aroztegui, the running-costs of a galley were the same as those of a 300-*tonelada* light-galleon, AGS GA 899 s.f., 18 Nov. 1624.

8. J. F. Guilmartin, Jr., *Gunpowder and galleys. Changing technology and Mediterranean warfare at sea in the sixteenth century* (Cambridge, 1974) pp. 222–5. Whilst the price of biscuit increased fourfold between 1523 and 1587, the price of gunpowder only doubled, and that of bronze guns between 1544 and 1587 rose by one-third, A. Carrasco, 'Apuntes para la historia de la fundición de artillería de bronce en España', *Memorial de Artillería*, XV (1887) p. 182.

9. I. Bauer Landauer, *La marina española en el siglo xvi* (Madrid, 1921) pp. 453–8.

10. G. Parker and I. A. A. Thompson, 'The Battle of Lepanto 1571. The costs of victory', *MM*, LXIV (1978) pp. 13–21.

11. AGS E 448 Philip to Don Juan de Austria, 26 Jan. 1572.

12. AGS E 453 'Relacion que Marcelo Doria dio al Sr Don Juan sobre el dar Su Md las Galeras por asiento', n.d.

13. I. Cloulas, 'Le "subsidio de las galeras" contribution du clergé espagnol à la guerre navale contre les Infidèles de 1563 à 1574', *Mélanges de la Casa de Velázquez*, III (1967) pp. 289–326, p. 319 and Table 1; AGS GA 78 f. 58.

14. AGS E 453 'Lo que ha parecido en consejo', 22 Jan 1575; AGS GA 80 f. 129.

15. BPU Geneva, Coll. Favre t. 28 ff. 83–7, 97–101v (courtesy of Professor Geoffrey Parker).

16. J. Alcalá-Zamora, *España, Flanders y el Mar del Norte (1618–1639)* (Barcelona, 1975) p. 81; Italians, noted Tomé Cano, 'are not high sea sailors', *Arte para fabricar y aparejar naos* (1611, edn E. Marcos Dorta, La Laguna, 1964) p. 50; Guilmartin, *Gunpowder and Galleys*, pp. 64–6 on the different requirements of Mediterranean and Atlantic seamanship; and Philip II's comment to Medina Sidonia on the Ragusan ships, 'I can see very well that, as you say, the Levant ships are less nimble and more weatherly for these waters than the ones we build here', Herrera Oria, *Armada* p. 217.

17. Codoin II p. 173, J. A. Doria argued (12 May 1594) that Spanish galleys

should be sent to Italy every other year for refit, 'because there they could be provided with better and cheaper things than here'.

18. Thompson, *War*, pp. 190–1.
19. Thompson, *War*, p. 252.
20. VIII/ii/1 p. 701.
21. But cf. Rodríguez-Salgado on navigation and cartography, below pp. 142–3 and Casado Soto on shipbuilding, below pp. 107–9 (edd.).
22. J. Suárez Inclán, *Guerra de anexión en Portugal durante el reinado de don Felipe II* (2 vols., Madrid, 1897–8) II p. 363.
23. BNM mss 1749 ff. 361–70, Gutiérrez's memorandum 23 Oct 1577 where he stated that it would be impossible to raise a fleet in Spain 'as navigation and the use of the sea have declined in our coasts', and because of the difficulties getting seamen, ships, etc.; port of Bilbao to Philip II complaining that 'it has no ships or sailors', T. Guiard y Larrauri, *La industria naval vizcaína* (Bilbao, 1917) p. 69; AGS GA 91 f. 74, Francisco Duarte, 24 Nov 1579: 'I detect such little enthusiasm and spirit among the people who could exercise these tasks that I doubt if it will be possible to carry out what we intend in a long time . . . and they assure me that in Vizcaya and Guipuzcoa no more than four or five ships are being built', despite a bounty of two ducats per *tonelada* over 300 *toneladas*. On the shortage of masts, spars, planking and pitch in Cantabria, Cristóbal de Eraso, 17 Nov 1577, AGS GA 82 f. 215; Cristóbal de Barros, 15 Feb 1581, MNM Navarrete XXII, doc. 76, f. 292v, and Juan Martínez de Recalde, 25 May 1581, MNM Navarrete XII, doc. 76 ff. 297v–99v.
24. A form of maritime conscription was instituted in Vizcaya and Guipuzcoa in 1581 to man the Indies fleets, but it was not successful. In 1583 in order to raise seamen in Guipuzcoa recruits were offered three ducats a month, four months in advance, plus three ducats bonus 'so that they may come and serve more willingly', Guiard, *Industria naval vizcaina*, p. 306; AGS GA 214, 'Recuerdo de García de Arce', 1587; AGS GA 199 f. 49, Juan de Acuña Vela, captain general of the artillery, 24 July 1587: 'no one seeks to become a gunner anywhere, and many of those who are offered such posts refuse them and do not want them, and so there are many vacant positions everywhere, which, unless we give them to people who are no good, cannot be filled'.
25. Leonardo Donato's report of 1573 on the lack of artillery in Spain, E. Alberi *Relazioni degli ambasciatori Veneti al senato durante il secolo decimosesto* (15 vols, Florence, 1839–63) serie 1, vol. VI p. 399; AGS E 448 R.C. to Don Juan of Austria, 30 Nov 1572; AGS GA 82 f. 163 negotiations for the purchase of 200 iron guns from England 1577.
26. Thompson, *War* p. 241.
27. AGS GA 199 f. 49 to the king, 24 July 1587.
28. 15 Nov 1570, M. Brunetti and E. Vitale, *La corrispondenza da Madrid*

dell'ambasciatore Leonardo Donà (1570-73) (Venice-Rome, n.d.) vol. I
no. 56 p. 144.

29. Thompson, War pp. 104-5, 112-15.

30. Ibid., pp. 211-17.

31. I. A. A. Thompson, 'The Armada and administrative reform: the Spanish
council of war in the reign of Philip II', English Historical Review, LXXXII
(1967) pp. 698-725.

32. M. Bustamente Callejo, 'Consejos del capitán laredano Don Lope de Ocina
y de la Obra al rey Felipe II para la conquista de Inglaterra', Altamira I
(1952) pp. 75-82, at p. 77.

33. Thompson, War pp. 218-20.

34. Ibid., pp. 115-16, 123-4.

35. Herrera Oria, Armada p. 4; AGS GA 199 f. 83; GA 221 ff. 6, 17, 18, 19;
GA 223 ff. 79, 230.

36. AGS GA 1299 'Relacion sobre lo que toca a la fabrica de las naos que se
hazen en Vizcaya', and the Junta de Galeras, 25 Sept 1584 with the king's
decision, 11 Oct 1584; AGS GA 233 f. 155 cuenta of the paymaster of
Avellaneda's asiento, Hernando de Aguirre, 20 April 1588: 20,000 ducats
paid to seven outfitters for construction of eight ships, totalling 5,175
toneladas.

37. AGS GA 221 f. 158, 28 May 1588.

38. See Casado Soto below pp. 99-101, 111, 113.

39. AGS GA 347 Orduño de Zamudio, 3 Oct 1588.

40. Chaunu VIII/ii/1. p. 754.

41. FD I p. 475 Medina Sidonia, 26 March.

42. For the 1624 norms, AGS GA 899 Martín de Aróztegui, 18 Nov 1624; on
the shortage of mariners, Rodríguez-Salgado below pp. 144-8.

43. AGS GA 221 f. 158, 28 May 1588: 6,766 mariners for 62,278 toneladas
(excluding galeasses, galleys, zabras and pataches), only 2/3 of the 16/100
norm of 1624. The Portuguese squadron had a ratio of 1,134 men for
7,373 tons (=15.4); the Castilian 1,216/8,144 (=14.9); Biscay squadron
810/6,562 (= 12.3); Andalucian 775/8,402 (= 9.2); Guipuzcoan
644/6,937 (= 9.3); Levantine 837/9,537 (= 8.8). A few individual
examples will serve to emphasise the differences in manning within each
squadron: in the Levantine squadron the Rata had 10.2, and the Regazona
6.4; in the Guipuzcoan squadron the Santa María had 11.5, and the Santa
Cruz 5.3; in the Biscay squadron, the Santa María de Montemayor had
6.4, and the María Juan 15; the Portuguese galleons averaged 16, the
Florencia had 9.

44. P. Pierson, Commander of the Armada (New Haven & London, 1989)
p. 222.

45. Herrera Oria, Armada p. 97, 29 Dec 1587; individual captains also
complained about the inadequacy of ordnance, e.g. AGS GA 222 f. 60

92

Oquendo, 19 March 1588 declared it to be deficient; GA 220 f. 55, Recalde, 6 Feb 1588 said it was too little and too small; GA 222 f. 7 Valdés, 19 March 1588 that it was too small.

46. AGS GA 220 f. 224, 27 Feb 1588; and AGS GA 199 ff. 47, 52, 15 July 1587.

47. Only 46% of the Armada's guns were 'countable' in Michael Lewis's terms (= 4lb shot), and only 6.8% threw a ball of 15 lbs or over (162, cf. 251 English); I. A. A. Thompson, 'Spanish Armada gun procurement and policy', in *God's obvious design*, ed. P. Gallagher and D. G. Cruickshank (London, 1990) pp. 69–84 at p. 70.

48. On 14 May 1588 the Castilian squadron with 295 guns had 566 quintals of powder; even deducting 80 quintals for the infantry, it had 77 quintals more than it needed for its guns at 60 shot per gun; but it only had 25.3 balls per gun (7,474 balls, including stone and fancy shot), AGS GA 221 ff. 148, 152. On 17 April 1588 the other squadrons (excluding that of Portugal), with 1,750 guns, were short by 21,700 iron and 2,340 stone balls and by 1,268 quintals of powder — but distribution was uneven: the galeasses and Andalucian squadron were more or less supplied up to scratch; the Levant squadron was 38,363 lbs of powder short; the hulks had none, and needed 43,575 lbs, AGS GA 221 f. 143 (9 May 1588), f. 127 (10 April 1588), f. 129 (17 April 1588).

49. FD I pp. 482, 527 (23 April 1588), 195 *reales* per quintal; contractors in Granada were supplying it for 84 *reales*.

50. Herrera Oria, *Armada* p. 283, Governor Cerralbo 12 Sept 1588; AGS GA 365 'Relacion general de la artilleria que ay en España', 17 Nov 1588; fortresses and arsenals needed 23,423 quintals of powder, which was 70% of requirement, 7,731½ quintals of lead (66.5% of requirement), 7,757 quintals of match (63%), 774 guns (60%), but 545 or 77% of naval gun types (demi-cannon, demi-culverin, sakers, *pedreros*) and 23,968 shot (10.75%). On the bad quality of Spanish gunpowder, AGS GA 191 Alonso Moreno, pilot of Seville, 13 Nov 1586; GA 302 'Relacion tocante a la polvora' of 1589; *ACC* XI p. 518 petition 12, of 1588.

51. FD I p. 475.

52. In the 1624 fleet there were 26 soldiers per 100 *toneladas*; Santa Cruz wanted a ratio of 50 men to 100 *toneladas*, Medina Sidonia wanted 100 per 100 (5 March 1587), Maura, p. 169. In 1588 the soldiers averaged 31 per 100 *toneladas* (20,181 men — 873 on the galeasses for 62,278 *toneladas*). The soldiers for the campaign have been the subject of two recent monographs in the Naval Institute's *Gran Armada* series: M. Gracia Rivas, *Los tercios de la Gran Armada (1587–1588)* (vol. VI, Madrid, 1989) deals with the men on the fleet; H. O'Donnell y Duque de Estrada, *La fuerza de desembarco de la Gran Armada contra Inglaterra (1588)* (vol. V, Madrid, 1989) with the forces in the Netherlands under Parma.

53. FD II p. 100, 21 May 1588; and Herrera Oria, *Armada*, p. 210, 1 July 1588; *ibid.* p. 249 Andrés de Alva, 19 July 1588; also AGS GA 225 f. 68.
54. FD II p. 137, letter of 24 June 1588.
55. FD II p. 204, letter of 19 July 1588. Most of the veteran troops were with the duke of Parma in the Netherlands.
56. Andrés de Alva, La Coruña, 19 July 1588, thought there was bread and wine for four months and other things for two or more, 'it honestly has enough victuals which are absolutely essential, that is bread and wine' — Herrera Oria, *Armada* p. 250; Bernavé de Pedroso, La Coruña, 6 July 1588 said: 'I do not think that it will be short of water, and what they have taken is good quality', he thought they had sufficient supplies for four and a half months, AGS GA 225 f. 58; FD II p. 152 letter 5 July 1588.
57. FD II pp. 118, 119 letters of 14 and 19 June 1588.
58. Marquis of Almazán in the council of state meeting. With some exaggeration for effect he went on, 'when the fleet left Lisbon on 30 May we were informed that it had provisions for six months, and that is what those in charge of victualling and provisioning wrote; on 24 June when it took shelter in La Coruña the wastage and fraud in victualling was discovered, and after taking on new provisions, it was said and confirmed that it was now better provided than before, with more than six month's provisions, and now we have seen that in the twenty-seven days it sailed — for that is the length of time that elapsed between 23 July when it left La Coruña to 20 August when the duke of Medina Sidonia wrote to say he had cut down rations so that they would have enough to last for a month — the shortage of victuals was evident'. AGS E 1945.
59. AGS GA 343, petition of Doña Ana de Avila, 26 June 1591.
60. F. Pérez Mínguez, *Don Juan de Idiáquez, embajador y consejero de Felipe II* (San Sebastián, 1934) p. 237 note 256.
61. Don Juan de Idiáquez, 28 Feb 1587 in Maura, p. 167.
62. The *tercio* of Naples, listed with 2,889 men in twenty-six companies at the Lisbon muster, had 1,864 in ten companies in July 1587, 1,803 at the end of August, and 1,396 in May 1588, FD I p. 387, AGS GA 221 f. 37; there were a total of 11,389 soldiers on 2 December 1587, and 1,053 fewer on 8 January 1588. See Gracia Rivas below pp. 204–5 for an explanation of some of these losses.
63. Herrera Oria, *Armada* p. 34.
64. AGS E 1945 council of state, 28 Sept 1588.
65. AGS GA 225 f. 55, 15 July 1588; Rodríguez-Salgado below p. 146 for a further discussion of this letter.
66. FD II pp. 469–76; Rodríguez-Salgado below pp. 154–5.
67. Guilmartin, *Gunpowder and galleys*, ch. 3.
68. AGS E 165 f. 229 Alonso Gutiérrez, 9 June 1587.
69. J. Vicens Vives, 'The administrative structure of the state in the sixteenth

and seventeenth centuries' in H. J. Cohn (ed.), *Government in Reformation Europe 1520–1560* (London, 1971) pp. 58–87.

70. The king provided the galley contractors with a number of *forzados* specified in the contract, usually fifteen a year.

71. AGS GA 482 Santa Gadea writing from Ferrol, 27 Feb 1597.

72. Thompson, *War* pp. 242–8.

73. 26 Feb 1580, 'there are thirty-nine large Levantine ships and not a single one from these realms', Suárez Inclán, *Guerra de anexión en Portugal* II p. 363; in 1583 about half the Terceira fleet was of Mediterranean origin (17 vessels out of 36, 11,000 out of 20,000 *toneladas*), *CSPVen* VIII no. 148 p. 60, in 1588 only one in eight of the larger ships.

74. Codoin III p. 30.

75. Codoin II p. 173, J. A. Doria, 12 May 1594: 'the galleys of Spain used not only to come to Italy but to stay there for years on end'. The *cortes* were wont to complain that the coasts of Spain were unguarded because all the galleys were in Italy, *ACC* II p. 428 (1566); now Sicilian and Neapolitan galleys were serving in Spain (11 of the 16 Sicilian galleys in 1588, 12 of the Neapolitan in 1596), and both Naples and Sicily contributed with men and money to the *Gran Armada* (e.g. the *tercio de Sicilia* and six vessels from the Levant were charged to Sicilian revenues, FD I p. 308; Viceroy Alva de Liste claimed Sicily spent 533,000 *scudi* in 1588, H. G. Koenigsberger, *The government of Sicily under Philip II of Spain* (London, 1951) p. 132.

76. A. Calabria, *State finance in the kingdom of Naples in the age of Philip II* (Ann Arbor, 1978) ch. 5.

77. J. Reglà, *Felip II i Catalunya* (Barcelona, 1956) p. 205; Koenigsberger, *Government of Sicily* p. 56.

X

PHILIP II: WHAT IF HE HAD WON?

On 27 August 1588, with Europe ringing with reports of a great Spanish victory in the Channel, the Venetian Senate voted 186 to 1, with 1 abstention, to send their official congratulations to the King of Spain. The reports were exaggerated and the felicitations premature, but the Senate was wise to show such enthusiasm. The conquest of England could have left Philip II the arbiter of Christendom and made an end of the European Reformation.

Without English support the Protestant rebels in the Low Countries would have had to submit to the Catholic King, and, defeated in the Netherlands, Protestantism could not have survived in France, nor in Geneva, against whom Papal designs had already been laid, nor in Scotland, where, for the havering, young James VI, faced with Catholic threats from both north and south of the border, Edinburgh too would have been worth a mass. Even the remoter Sweden, Denmark and the petty states of Germany would have found it difficult to withstand the insistence of Pope Sixtus V that the whole of Christendom be brought back into obedience to a resurgent, Counter-Reformation Rome.

For historians of the age of liberalism and empire, like Macaulay, Green, and Froude, this prospect was too horrible to contemplate. The Nineteenth Century would not have existed. Instead of the Empire, constitutional monarchy, parliamentary democracy, religious toleration, and freedom of thought and expression, we should have had the Spain of Philip II universalized. Instead of the Protestant Ethic, the Scientific Revolution, industrial progress and intellectual advance, the bigotry of despots and the rigid dogmatism of the Inquisition would have condemned us to moral and material degeneration. One had only to compare, as Macaulay did, the fruits of Catholicism and Protestantism since the Reformation: "The loveliest and most fertile provinces of Europe, under her (Papal) rule, have been sunk in poverty, in political servitude, and in intellectual torpor, while Protestant countries, more proverbial for sterility and barbarism, have been turned by skill and industry into gardens, and can boast of a long list of heroes and statesmen, philosophers and poets."[1] Mr Albert Close, the author

---

[1] J.W.Burrow, *A Liberal Descent. Victorian Historians and the English Past* (Cambridge U.P., 1981), pp.244-52, on Macaulay, Green, and Froude, for whom 1588 was the most fateful year in English and European history: "the defeat of the Armada saved the Reformation and thus determined the fate of Europe as a place where life and energy were possible."

X

of *The Great Harlot on the Seven Hills* and *The Hand of God and Satan in Modern History*, in a brief volume written for the Protestant Truth Society in 1913, could only conclude, "Had Philip succeeded in his enterprise, it is appalling to think what at this hour would have been the condition of the world."[2]

What credence should we give to this apocalyptic vision of the Armada as the life and death struggle of the cosmic forces of good and evil? Was the defeat of the Armada really the hinge of history? What would have happened if Philip II had won?

With the Duke of Parma and his 17,000 veterans of the Army of Flanders ashore on the Margate coast, the callow militias that opposed him dispersed, the Queen killed or captured, and London fallen, there is no reason why a Habsburg regime should not have been successfully established. The most optimistic voices in Rome and Madrid expected half of England to rise in support of the Armada. That the English Catholics did not do so in 1588 and professed undying loyalty to queen and country thereafter should not lead us to assume that they would have behaved in the same way had the invasion succeeded. In fact, a full-scale Catholic rising could not have taken place in 1588, and would not have been necessary. The leading Catholic suspects in the counties had been disarmed, interned, or put into "protective custody" in the homes of reliable local families. Until the outcome was clear, only the most reckless of either persuasion would have shown their hands, but with Parma victorious protective custody would have become a Trojan horse for the subversion of the custodians. The peerage was divided, and a powerful group of Catholic lords, led by the earls of Arundel, Northumberland and Worcester, might well have been joined by others regarded as neutrals, moderates, or atheists. Neither the Council nor the Court would necessarily have remained firm. Philip II had pensioners in both and was not without hope that even Sir Walter Raleigh might enter his service.[3] Nor might the common people have reacted entirely unfavourably. The burdens of the war and a simple nostalgia for the rituals of the Old Religion and times when "all

---

[2] Albert Close, *The Defeat of the Spanish Armada* (Protestant Truth Society, London, n.d.), p.47. In the section, "North and South America Contrasted after 400 Years", he writes: "After 400 years of fruit-bearing what do we see? South America, after having been peopled by Roman Catholic Spain and other Papal countries, and under the baneful yoke of Rome for 400 years, is to-day, with the exception of those states which have thrown off the yoke of the priest, little better than the heathen nations of the Far East. North America, on the other hand, which has been peopled mainly by the Protestant nations of Europe, has, under the blessing of a dominating Protestant faith, developed during the same period into one of the most powerful, prosperous, progressive, philanthropic, enlightened, and happy countries in the world. The one has been blessed, the other blighted and cursed, like Papal Ireland is today."

[3] *Calendar of State Papers, Spain* IV (1587-1603), pp. 2, 24 (8 Jan. and 18 Feb.1587).

things were cheap", might have induced "a multitude of vulgar people", as Lord Burghley feared, to look with indifference, if not relief, on the change of regime in Westminster. One villager of Ash, in Kent, proclaimed that "the Spaniards were better than the people of this land, and therefore he...had rather that they were here than the rich men of this country." A Sussex clerk declared, "he thought yt best that yf the Spaniards should come yt ware best to yield to them."[4]

With the starving and disease-ridden English fleet, destitute of powder and shot, unable to face up to Medina Sidonia's Armada, reformed in Calais Road and restocked with provisions and munitions from Flanders, or to prevent the despatch of reinforcements from Spain; and with London, "the centre and heart of the kingdom", in Parma's hands, the most Protestant corner of England under the heel of a foreign army, and the most resolute of the gentry and nobility dead on the field, it is difficult to see where any coherent resistance could have come from, or for how long it could have been sustained.

What sort of regime would the Habsburgs have then established in England? Amazingly there seems to have been no official programme for the pacification of the country after its conquest. Elizabeth was to have been deposed, Philip's right to the throne through the Lancastrian line and the will of Mary Queen of Scots vindicated, the succession passed to his elder daughter, the Infanta Isabella, and Catholicism restored, but the details were left to be worked out on the ground. The best indication we have of how the Spaniards would have proceeded comes from a Proclamation printed in 1597 for distribution on the occasion of a later invasion attempt.[5] Philip's intention, had the 1597 programme been followed, was as far as possible to leave existing organs of local government and justice intact and to make every effort to secure the collaboration of incumbent officials with the new regime. Only inveterate heretics and notorious persecutors of Catholics were to be purged, and they were to be replaced by men selected by the communities themselves. Cooperation would be bought not only by the grant of personal honours and rewards but by the promise to confirm the cities, towns, universities and corporations in their ancient privileges and freedoms and to honour and enhance them with new favours and graces. There was to be no hispanization of government in England. The Spaniards clearly intended to appeal not only to those of the Old Religion but also to a broad spectrum of conservative forces disaffected towards the Tudor state. Far from wanting to establish an autocratic regime, all the signs are that

[4] A.J.Loomie, *The Spanish Elizabethans* (London, 1963), p.7; Peter Clark, *English Provincial Society from the Reformation to the Revolution. Religion, Politics and Society in Kent, 1500-1640* (Hassocks, 1977), pp.249-50.

[5] A.J.Loomie, "Philip II's Armada Proclamation of 1597", *Recusant History* XII (1974), 216-25.

X

Philip II would have appeared as an ally of provincialist sentiment in the North, in Ireland and in Wales, and as the restorer of the ancient magnate families threatened by the Tudor monarchy. It is likely too that Parliament would have played as important a part in the new regime as it had in Mary's reign. Packed with new bishops and peers in the Lords, and with compliant burgesses and knights of the shire in the Commons, Parliament would have been summoned to declare the succession upon the Infanta Isabella, and then to revoke the existing religious legislation.

A Habsburg regime in England is likely, therefore, to have turned away from the absolutist tendencies of Tudor government and to have set up some sort of "Aragonese" constitutionalism similar to that which Philip II had accepted eight years before when he had annexed the Kingdom of Portugal to his dominions. Indeed, a proclamation drafted to accompany a projected invasion in 1603 spoke of "returning the political governance and the municipal laws to the form of Magna Carta and as it once was in the happy times that Catholic kings governed."[6] Such a form of "aristocratic constitutionalism" would have reversed the trend of class development. 1588 would not then have been a crucial moment in the history of the political consciousness of the bourgeoisie, as some have argued,[7] and the English Revolution, if it had happened at all, would have been merely the restoration of a national monarchy, in the person of King Charles I of Scotland, a monarchy, as in the simultaneous revolt against Spanish domination in Portugal, more absolute than that which it replaced.

The conciliatory nature of the political settlement might well have eased the way for the reformation of religion. This would, of course, not have been the first time that Catholicism had been restored in England, and the record of what had happened in Mary's reign is worth keeping in view. The Marian Restoration had, in fact, gone remarkably smoothly. The ecclesiastical hierarchy had been replaced, many of the clergy purged, Catholic divines appointed to the universities, the mass restored and England received back into the bosom of Rome with scarcely any resistance. Wisely dropping any threat of the restitution of monastic properties, the government met little opposition from either country or parliament on purely religious grounds. Undoubtedly, much was different in 1588. Elizabeth had been on the throne thirty years, Protestantism was much better organized and more firmly rooted, and a quarter-century of anti-Romish and anti-Spanish propaganda had associated the Catholic cause inextricably with the hated and bloodthirsty foreigner. But Catholicism too was a much younger and more vigorous, intellectual and spiritual force than it had been in the 1550s. Around a hard-core of some 5,000 recusants, heavily concentrated in Yorkshire,

---

[6] Loomie, "Philip II's Armada Proclamation", p.220.

[7] A.L.Morton, *A People's History of England* (London, 1938), pp.201-03.

Lancashire, and the North, but by no means absent elsewhere, some contemporaries thought that two out of three Englishmen, though outwardly conforming, were Catholic at heart. Moreover, as the Pilgrimage of Grace of 1536 and the Northern Rebellion of 1569 had shown, Catholicism was a vehicle that could carry a variety of secular causes, social hostility to noble upstarts, risen in the service of the state, the defence of the local community against the encroachment of London and central government; and a multitude of popular discontents.

The new dispensation would have made Cardinal Allen Archbishop of Canterbury and papal legate, and possibly Thomas Metham Archbishop of York,[8] but, with only about 300 seminary priests and some 200 of the older clergy in England, there would have been a crippling shortage of priests to serve the 10,000 or so parishes, even with the return of English ecclesiastics from overseas. It is here, and in the hierarchy and the universities that the influx of Spanish and Italian divines would have been most notable. This would have made the re-Catholicization of the country a long and alien process, and it is unlikely that there could have been a sufficiently extensive apparatus of religious supervision and repression to have eliminated Protestantism. Even in Spain, the penetration of the Inquisition was only skin-deep, and there is no evidence of any plan to set up a formal Inquisition in England. Protestant recusants would no doubt have survived in the same way Catholics had, under similar penalties and disabilities, and would have done exactly what other non-conformists had done in the 17th century, set themselves up as free men in America, as unmolested by the Spaniards as masters as they were by the Spaniards as enemies. As long as Spain's dominion lasted, there might not have been a British Empire, but there might well have been a British North America.

With the succession settled on the Spanish Infanta, and Isabella still young enough to conceive, a marriage now to her cousin and future husband, the Archduke Albert, could not only have secured the dynasty but also, when in due course they were ceded the government of Flanders, have united England and the Netherlands under a single ruler, as the marriage of Mary and Philip would have done had there been issue. A natural alliance, in many ways, it would have realised Charles V's great strategic conception of a Habsburg Atlantic Empire, altered the balance of power in Europe, and set up a solid buffer against French and German aggression which could have prevented some of the worst tragedies in Europe's history.

It would also have given the English merchant community a real interest in the new regime. For many the direct trade to Spain had much more to offer than the risks of piracy and freebooting, and it had only been Philip II's trade embargo in 1585 which had turned them from petitioners for peace to advocates

---

[8] Archivo General de Simancas, Estado, legajo 950, folio 22.

of war. Now they had the prospect of the renewal of the historic Anglo-Burgundian *magnus intercursus* and direct participation in the lucrative American trade monopoly via Seville, Cadiz and San Lucar. The 1597 Proclamation, proffering great commercial benefits for both kingdoms, suggests that Philip II might even have been prepared to offer the English special trading rights. English merchants would then have been directed into trade through Spain, and the English economy would have developed as an integral part of Europe, and not into the closed, colonial, trading system, with a separate circuitry, which for too long enabled Britain to treat Europe as a largely irrelevant offshore continent.

The English seaman too might have found a role in the Spanish system. Just as English and Irish contingents were hired to fight in the Peninsula and the Low Countries in the wars of the 17th century, so too squadrons of English warships, complementing the fighting qualities of the other regional flotillas, would have made the united, Spanish navy the mistress of the seas.

It is just possible, then, that 1588 might have ushered in the new millennium, the body of Christ reunited under the Church Universal and a Pax Hispanica devoted, in the words of Philip II's 1597 Proclamation, to "establishing peace and concord with the rest of the states and princes of Europe". Much more realistically, the ideal of perpetual peace would have been as remote after the Armada as it had been before it. None of the princes of Europe, not least a Pope who compared himself to Philip II as a fly to an elephant, could have tolerated such an aggrandizement of Spanish power. A great anti-Habsburg Holy League, promoted by Rome and pitting France, Scotland, the United Provinces, the states of Italy and Germany, Denmark, Sweden and the Ottoman Porte against Spain and her half-hearted, Austrian cousins, would have brought what was, in all essentials, the Thirty Years War forward to the 1590s, leaving the map of Europe at its end much as it was to be after the Peace of Westphalia. After 1648 the history of Europe is back on course. In this revised version only one chapter has had to be rewritten.

There still remains, however, much the most likely scenario, that the conquest would not have been completed. There were many on the Spanish side, including Parma himself, who feared they were in for a long and bloody struggle, "for the English never yield; and although they be put to flight and broken, they always return, thirsting for revenge, to renew the attack, so long as they have a breath of life."[9] Sustained resistance to a regime seen even by Catholics as foreign and illegitimate, especially if Elizabeth remained at large, or if James VI, relying on French backing, chose to cross the border in furtherance of his own claim, would surely have convinced Spain that enough had already been achieved to secure the principal purposes of the expedition without

---

[9] Quoted by J.S.Corbett, *Drake and the Tudor Navy* (London, 1898), vol.2, p.162.

stretching scarce resources further and risking another gaping wound like that in the Netherlands. An English withdrawal from the Low Countries, the checking of piracy, toleration for Catholics, a financial indemnity and the surrender of some strategically placed cautionary towns could have provided the terms of a satisfactory settlement from Philip II's point of view. Elizabeth might then have died with "Dover" engraved upon her heart, or the Isle of Wight been still a duty-free, Spanish base, overrun by Barbary apes.

Speculation apart, one thing is certain. "1588" would now have a very different meaning in England's history: no longer, in Garrett Mattingly's words, "a heroic apologue of the defence of freedom against tyranny, an eternal myth of the victory of the weak over the strong, of the triumph of David over Goliath";[10] no longer the evident proof of a nation "miraculously preserved" of God for a providential mission in the world; the Invincible Armada would have been, on one contemporary tally, the fifteenth time that the English had been defeated by an invading force. "There has hardly been a nation that has attacked them, that has not vanquished and mastered them", contended a Spanish homily of 1588.[11] Instead of "Gloriana", "the monstrous regiment" would have chalked up another disaster - Mathilda, Mary, Elizabeth. Not "the skonce and forte of all Europe" (Francis Bacon), England would have been more like a western Poland. What then of Stanley Baldwin's Englishman, "made for a time of crisis, and for a time of emergency"? Without her faith in the navy and the "moat defensive", England must have faced Louis XIV, Napoleon, Wilhelm II, and the Luftwaffe with rather less confidence in her ultimate destiny. Not so easily would she have been able to despise her continental neighbours for needing so often to be saved, nor those neighbours find it so difficult to forgive her for so often saving them. The smoke of the guns that defeated the Armada was like the Channel fog that isolated the Continent. Had England been conquered, she must have become more European; she would not, on that account, have been any less English.

---

[10] Garrett Mattingly, *The Defeat of the Spanish Armada* (Harmondsworth, 1962), p.418.

[11] Pedro de Ribadeneyra, *Historias de la Contrarreforma* (Biblioteca de Autores Cristianos, Madrid, 1945), p.1346.

XI

A Map of Crime in Sixteenth-Century Spain

SPANISH *arbitristas*, from the middle of the sixteenth century onwards, attacked repeatedly the hordes of bandits and idle vagrants, estimated by one writer at 150,000, whom they saw both as a parasitic drain on the nation's resources and as a symptom of an economy lacking in opportunity and hampered by unfavourable social attitudes.[1] Yet, in spite of the continuing belief in its relevance as a factor in the country's economic decline, with the exception of the work that has been done on *bandolerismo* in Catalonia,[2] virtually nothing is known about crime and vagabondage in Habsburg Spain. Attention has been drawn to the subject largely on account of its connexion with the picaresque novel, while historians have interested themselves in justice rather than in delinquency. What little is known comes either from the novel or from the statute book. Yet an analysis of the incidence and distribution of crime has obvious and important implications for the more general social and economic picture. At one level, it offers the chance of reimposing an overall pattern on an age tantalizingly deficient in global figures and so permits some assessment of the relative condition of different parts of the country on the basis of a homogeneous set of data, as previous attempts exploiting figures for population, taxation, and emigration have done;[3] at another, it might inject some precision into the characterization of Spain as an "otiose and vicious republic" (González de Cellorigo), and provide a measure of reality against which to relate the preoccupation of writers of the Golden Age with idleness and delinquency as the all-pervading evils of their day.

I

Unfortunately, there are no state-wide records of criminality as such in sixteenth-century Spain. Split into a thousand jurisdictions, the administration of justice was much too fragmentary for scholars to be able to piece together the records, even had they thought about it. Much could be done at a regional level by patient research in the archives of the royal *chancillerías* and *audiencias*, but a total study of crime is, I think, impossible. Nevertheless, the question is of sufficient importance to warrant some effort and to permit some approximation, even if in the final account we are left with a margin of error that in other circumstances might be unacceptable.

Perhaps the only statistical sources capable of providing nation-wide figures

---

[1] See, for example, the treatise of the *contador* Luis de Ortiz (1558), printed in Manuel Fernández Alvarez, *Economía, sociedad y corona* (*Ensayos históricos sobre el siglo XVI*) (Madrid, 1963), p. 387.

[2] See the bibliography in *Historia social y económica de España y América*, ed. J. Vicens Vives, III (Barcelona, 1957), 584 (subsequently referred to as *Historia social y económica*). I have unfortunately not had access to Joan Reglà, *El bandolerisme català*. I. *La historia* (Barcelona, 1962).

[3] Javier Ruiz Almansa, 'La población de España en el siglo XVI', *Revista Internacional de Sociología*, III (1943), 115–36; Alvaro Castillo, 'Population et "richesse" en Castille durant la seconde moitié du XVIe siècle', *Annales E.S.C.*, xx (1965), 719–33; V. Aubrey Neasham, 'Spain's Emigrants to the New World, 1492–1592', *Hispanic American Historical Review*, xix (1939), 147–60.

have hitherto proved too elusive for their potential value to have been recognized.[1] These are the lists of *forzados*, "men forced by the King, going to serve in the galleys", as Sancho Panza described them. " 'What! Men forced?' asked Don Quixote, 'Is it possible that the King uses force on anyone?' 'I don't say that,' answered Sancho, 'but they are men condemned for their crimes to serve the King in the galleys, and they go perforce.' "[2]

Galley service had been prescribed as a punishment for serious criminals at least as far back as the reign of the Catholic Kings. A decree of 1502 committed to the galleys only those "deserving capital penalties",[3] but, as the galley fleets grew and the difficulty of manning the benches increased, galley service came to be extended to an increasing number of crimes. As the result of a series of laws in 1530, 1552, and 1566, condemnation to the galleys became the mandatory sentence for thieves, cut-throats, accessories, receivers, and anyone who harboured criminals or resisted the justices, while the normal penalties for assault and other forms of violent crime could be commuted for galley service wherever appropriate.[4] Not all on the galleys were criminals of this type. As early as 1539, gypsies aged between twenty and fifty were being sent to the galleys for six years, "being males without employment or living without a master", and, in 1552, the penalty for vagabondage was increased to include four years on the galleys for a first offence, eight years for a second, and life for a third. For the purposes of the law, vagabonds were defined as including "gypsies and foreign tinkers whom the laws and pragmatics of these kingdoms have ordered to be deported, and the healthy mendicant poor who ... beg and wander as vagabonds..."[5] Vagabonds and gypsies almost certainly formed an increasingly large proportion, probably even a majority, of galley oars from the middle of Philip II's reign when there was growing pressure for stricter enforcement of the laws against them.[6] By the middle of Philip II's reign, heretics, blasphemers, bigamists, inhabitants of Granada who were found taking artificial baths and thereby demonstrated their relapse into Mohammedanism, and various other people who fell foul of the Inquisition could also be sent to the galleys; so, for example, could commoners who used, possessed, made, or sold gambling dice, or false witnesses in civil cases who were liable to punishment by having their teeth torn out.[7] Few *forzados*, however, could have been condemned for "white-collar" offences. Contemporaries thought, if Cervantes' picture can be generalized, that most of them

[1] A nation-wide inquiry was conducted in 1573 when *corregidores* throughout Castile were asked to submit an account of all criminals in gaol awaiting transportation to the galleys, but the replies, though providing valuable information on judicial processes and unique details of individual crimes, do not extend to the kingdoms of Aragon and are incomplete even for Castile.—A[rchivo] G[eneral de] S[imancas] Diversos de Castilla, legajos 28, 29. See Alfonso María Guilarte, *El régimen señorial en el siglo XVI* (Madrid, 1962), p. 132, n. 32. I am grateful to Mr N. G. Parker for assistance on this point.
[2] *Don Quixote*, trans. J. M. Cohen (Penguin, 1950), p. 171.
[3] Archivo Municipal de Sevilla, Sección Ia, carpeta 5/41, R.C. Madrid, 14 Nov. 1502.
[4] Pedro Aguado Bleye, *Manual de historia de España* (9th edn, Madrid, 1964), II, 936. *Recopilación de las Leyes destos Reynos hecha por mandado ... del Rey D. Philippe segundo ...* (Alcalá de Henares, 1598), pt II, bk 8, title XI, laws 5–10, fos. 192, 192v, title XXII, law 7, fo. 223v.
[5] *Recopilación*, pt II, bk 8, title XI, laws 13, 6, 11, fos. 192, 193, 193v.
[6] An anonymous memorandum of 31 Jan. 1589 speaks of "las leyes destos Reinos que hablan en el castigo de los bagabundos que es de donde se probeen la mayor parte de los galeotes".—A.G.S. Guerra Antigua, leg. 264, fo. 2.
[7] Felix Sevilla y Solanas, *Historia penitenciaria española (La galera)* (Segovia, 1917), pp. 30–2. *Recopilación*, pt I, bk 5, title I, law 7, fo. 311; pt II, bk 8, title XXVI, law 15, fo. 233.

were criminals of a conventional kind. Of the six that Don Quixote interviewed one was a young lecher and one an ancient whoremonger, and neither need have been where he was had he been able to afford to bribe his way out. The remainder were thieves of varying degrees of ambition, or were described as thieves by their guards.[1] Eight of the dozen men awaiting confirmation of their sentences in the prisons of Mondéjar and Sanlúcar de Barrameda, in 1573, had been convicted for murder, larceny, or assault, two were gypsies, one a vagrant, and the offence of the twelfth was unspecified.[2]

Galley service cannot, however, be directly equated with crime. There is no way of knowing for what reason any particular set of oarsmen was condemned to the galleys, or how great was the criminal substructure from which each individual who did not succeed in escaping arrest or conviction sprang. It can only be hoped that the galleys contained a reasonable cross-section of the distribution of criminals throughout Spain. The sentencing of men to the galleys was general to all the provinces of Spain, and applied to all jurisdictions royal or seignorial.[3] The galleys, therefore, probably contained the great majority of serious offenders convicted in Spain, for commutation to galley service was the likely punishment for even the most heinous of crimes. Many offences were, of course, too venal to deserve a sentence that frequently amounted to "civil death",[4] but with the great expansion of the Mediterranean fleets in the 1560's and the heavy losses incurred as a result of enemy action between 1559 and 1571, and of exposure and malnutrition during years of continuous royal penury, there was a constant shortage of galley oars.[5] Consequently, considerable pressure was put on justices not to be self-indulgent in their charity and to send off as many men as possible to the galleys with all conceivable haste, even if this meant that the condemned man's right of appeal was restricted.[6]

---

[1] *Don Quixote*, pp. 172-7.   [2] Guilarte, op. cit. app. 34, p. 455; app. 35, p. 456.

[3] In the kingdoms of Aragon galley service was also prescribed as a punishment for healthy mendicants.—Manuel Colmeiro, *Historia de la economía política en España* (new edn, Madrid, 1965), II, 603.

[4] *Don Quixote*, p. 176. In fact, by 1653, life sentences to the galleys had been fixed at ten years.—Sevilla, op. cit. p. 33. The plight of the galley-oar has never been better summed up than by Dr Alcalá in *El donado hablador*, "La vida de galeote es propia vida de infierno; no hay diferencia de una a otra sino que la una es temporal y la otra es eterna"—quoted in C. Fernández Duro, *Disquisiciones náuticas* (Madrid, 1876-81), bk 2: 'La mar descrita por los mareados', disq. octava: 'La vida de la galera', p. 113, n. 14. Gregorio Marañón, 'La vida en las galeras en tiempo de Felipe II', in *Vida e historia* (Colección Austral, Madrid, 1958), explains why in scarifying detail.

[5] Gian Andrea Doria to Philip II, Genoa, 28 Oct. 1582.—A.G.S. Estado, leg. 454.

[6] Anonymous memorandum (Madrid, 31 Jan. 1589): "El Rey nuestro señor tiene la necessidad que vuestra merced sabe de galeotes, y de buena boya son muy pocos los que se pueden haver, y por esto andan las galeras tan mal atrippoladas y proveidas como a todos es notorio ... pues de solo los que van condenados a ellas se ha de haçer; y esto agora, de pocos años a esta parte, anda corto y coxo porque los del Consejo que vissitan las carceles los sabados son en grande manera piadossos y sueltan asaz assi a los condenados a ellas como los que estan pressos para condenarse ... y el remedio seria facil, mandando que, por agora hasta que se mande otra cosa, en las vissitas se abstengan de meter la mano en visitar ni tratar de los que estubieren presos por bagabundos ni de los que estubieren condenados al servicio de galeras."—A.G.S. Guerra Antigua, leg. 264, fo. 2. The report of a "Junta sobre lo que toca a los galeotes", of the same year, made similar points and recommended, "Que las causas de los que fueren condenados a galeras por ladrones y vagamundos se acaben y feneçcan abiendo dos sentencias conformes en la dicha condemnacion de Galeras, una de la Justicia ordinaria o de comision y otra de los alcaldes y juezes de los Consejos y audiencias a donde fuere en grado de apelacion, y que no se puede suplicar de la segunda sentencia siendo confirmatoria de la primera..."—A.G.S. Consejo y Juntas de Hacienda, leg. 173, with a note of 7 March 1589. (Abbreviations have been extended.) The only indications I have as to the portion of criminals sentenced to the galleys comes from Henry Kamen, *The Spanish*

II

Convicted criminals were sent by their local justices to the central prisons of the appropriate judicial area (Soria, Toledo, Seville, etc.). When there were a dozen of them, they were chained together and manacled, "strung by the neck like beads on a great iron chain",[1] and marched, under guard, across country until they reached the galleys.[2] Oarsmen were taken on at all the Mediterranean ports of call between Cartagena and Seville, particularly at Malaga, Gibraltar, and the Puerto de Santa María. A general register of all *forzados* was kept at the Superintendency General of the Galleys in Cartagena,[3] but separate lists for each galley were also drawn up and revised every four months, apparently for the benefit of the commissariat. It is these lists that provide the material for the present analysis. The oarsmen were divided into four categories: volunteers (*buenas boyas acordados*), criminals who had completed their sentences (*forzados buenas boyas* or *buenas boyas de galera*), criminals still serving their sentences either at the oar or occasionally as unpaid soldiers or deck hands, and lastly slaves. Each man's name was recorded and also, apart from a few omissions, his place of origin, the name of his father, where appropriate certain personal information (Negroes, mulattoes, slaves, *moriscos*, gypsies, brand-marks, and deafness were all noted), and sometimes the nature of his employment. There is no obvious reason why the information given in the lists should not be taken at face value. Much of it must have been compiled from the transcripts of the sentences sent with the condemned men by their original justices, and so should have been generally reliable.[4]

If continuous galley records existed they could provide the basis for a study of long-term trends in regional crime patterns in Spain until galley service was abolished in 1748. Unfortunately they do not. The *Generales de Asiento*, that still survived in Cartagena fifty years ago, seem to be fragmentary and not to extend back farther than the seventeenth century.[5] Complete series of the separate muster lists may lie hidden at Simancas or elsewhere, but until now only a handful have come to light. The following is an analysis of muster lists found for 19 of the 26 galleys of Spain in service in the Mediterranean in 1586 and for 22 of the 24 serving in 1589.[6] A further eight Spanish galleys formed a separate squadron stationed in the Tagus near Lisbon, but about these we have no information. Because the lists contain details of men transferred to and from other galleys, and because five of the missing galleys of 1586 are included in the lists for 1589, we have in all data sufficient for about 45 of the 66 galleys. As, with a

---

Inquisition (1965), p. 182. Between 1575 and 1610 the Inquisition of Toledo punished 1,233 persons, of whom 91 were sentenced to galley service. (The punished presumably included women.)

[1] *Don Quixote*, p. 171.

[2] Soria, for example, was the central prison for the bishoprics of Calahorra, Osma, Siguenza, and Pamplona, the archdiocese of Burgos, and the kingdom of Navarre.—J. Castillo de Bovadilla, *Política para corregidores y señores de vasallos* (Barcelona, 1624), bk v, ch. 6, para. 24, p. 788.

[3] Sevilla, op. cit. p. 57.   [4] Ibid. p. 43.   [5] Ibid. *passim*.

[6] A.G.S. Contaduría Mayor de Cuentas, IIa época, legs. 1225, 1232; 1586, galleys *Brava, Forteza, Leona, Luna, Lupiana, Marquesa, Palma, Patrona de España, Peregrina, Porfiada, Quimera, Sagitaria, San Augustín, San Francisco, Serafina, Serena, Ventura, Vitoria, Vigilancia*; 1589, galleys *Fé, Florida, Forteza, Fortuna, Granada, Leona, Lupiana, Palma, Patrona de España, Peregrina, Quimera, Sagitaria, San Francisco, San Telmo, Santa Ana, Santa Barbara, Santa Catalina, Santa Olalla, Serena, Soberana, Vitoria*, and the galliot *Santa Isabel*.

very few exceptions, the minimum sentence was two years,[1] the lists include all the criminals serving on these galleys in the four years from 1586 to 1589, apart from a few dozen sentenced in 1587 and 1588 who died before 1 January 1589. By giving each man a separate slip it has been possible to avoid duplication. The nationalities of the *forzados* and *forzados buenas boyas* who remain are as follows:

Spain	4,955		Italy	67
Mallorca	41		France	268
Minorca	2		Burgundy	15
Ibiza	3		Netherlands	49
Sardinia	8		England	295
Corsica	2		Ireland	4
North Africa	28		Germany	25
Canaries	21		Hungary	3
New Spain	37		Greece	3
Peru	4		Others	6
Portugal	159		Unlocated	458
Azores	8			
Portuguese Indies	2			6,463

If the same proportions prevailed among the oarsmen of unknown provenance and throughout the missing galleys, we can claim to have placed two-thirds of all Spaniards on the benches between 1586 and 1589.[2] The size of the sample is large enough to warrant some confidence and the spread of years wide enough to offset the accidents of aberrant local conditions —maybe as many as 10 per cent of the men had been on the galleys since 1580; one man was released in 1589 after twenty years. The use of material of this kind is fraught with difficulties. Often there is more than one place of the same name or the capriciousness of sixteenth-century orthography makes it impossible to locate the place at all; others have changed their names or just disappeared in the course of the centuries. The fact that it has been possible to check data on up to six different lists has helped resolve many ambiguities. Complete contradictions have been gratifyingly few and for practical purposes can be discounted. One important element of uncertainty arises from the lack of a constant expression of provenance in the records. Two-thirds of the *forzados* are described as *naturales* or natives of a particular place; a bare half-dozen are called *vecinos* or residents; the rest are simply described as *de* or from a given town. A slightly larger relative proportion of *naturales* does seem to have come from the more transient populations of the cities than from rural areas, and the terms may well

[1] Sevilla, op. cit. p. 33. Of the 399 occasions on which the length of the sentence was recorded (always in connexion with the completion of a sentence), only three were of less than two years. There were 234 of either four or six years, and the average sentence was just under six years.

[2] There were, no doubt, some Spaniards on the Italian galleys, but probably no more than one or two hundred at the outside. There is nothing surprising about the large number of "foreign" oarsmen. Many were natives of other possessions of the king of Spain. The majority of the Englishmen were probably prisoners of war or contrabandists—203 of them had been captured in the "Counter-Armada" of 1589. Many of the Frenchmen, especially Gascons, must have been immigrants in Aragon and Catalonia, and the others were possibly some of the thousands of foreigners come in trade or pilgrimage, who stayed to beg or steal.—Fernández de Navarrete, 'Toda la inmundicia de Europa ha venido a España'; see C. Viñas Mey, *El problema de la tierra en la España de los siglos XVI–XVII* (Madrid, 1941), p. 169, and Colmeiro, op. cit. p. 609. The 41 men from America (New Spain and Peru), more than from the entire kingdom of Navarre, are a sharp reminder that movement between Europe and the New World did not flow only in one direction.

not have been used with strict consistency. It is clear that the lists were not compiled with any great rigour; but the indications are that the place of origin was intended to be the place of birth. This was the recommended practice with regard to the lists of Spanish troops in the Netherlands and internal evidence suggests that the same applied to the galleys. Firstly, there are some hundreds of examples of duplicated entries in which de and natural are interchanged; only one in which the same man appears both as natural and vecino. Secondly, of 306 morisco oarsmen whose origins are known 126 came from the kingdom of Granada; yet by the 1580's all but a small percentage of moriscos had been expelled from Granada and dispersed throughout the rest of Spain. Of the 272,000 moriscos expelled from Spain between 1609 and 1614 only 2,000 came from Granada.[1] The number of Granadan moriscos on the galleys is so disproportionate that "Granadan" here can only mean the province of their birth. In the same way, there are no "Frenchmen from Catalonia", although many of the Frenchmen on the galleys must have been resident in Catalonia where maybe 20 per cent of the adult male population was French in origin and, so it was claimed, was 90 per cent of the banditry.[2] What we have, then, is not a direct statement of the areas in which crime was committed but, what is even more valuable, an indication of the types of environment in which criminals and vagabonds were being bred. If for simplicity's sake the terms "crime" and "crime-rate" are used throughout this article, it is in this sense that they should be understood.

III

For sixteenth-century commentators crime was primarily a social phenomenon. Paupers, vagrants, rogues, and felons were commonly seen as associated or even indistinguishable categories; one led to another,[3] "poverty and roguery were cut from the same quarry."[4] Spanish writers, claiming to surpass the world in delinquency as in all else, marked the "picarization" of precisely those sectors of society most affected by the economic impoverishment of Spain, decayed gentlemen, peasants driven from the land, unemployed labourers, ruined craftsmen, unpaid soldiers, indigent students.[5] They noted also the temporary effects of famine and plague on the breakdown of law and order,[6] and the more permanent and more ominous association of vagrancy and brigandage with racial discrimination and political discontent.[7] The other evidence now available on historical crime has tended to substantiate these impressions. In the Mediterranean

[1] H. Lapeyre, Géographie de l'Espagne morisque (Paris, 1959), p. 205.
[2] J. Nadal and E. Giralt, La population catalane de 1553 à 1717 (Paris, 1960), pp. 62, 91.
[3] As the authorities in Catalonia put it, "Bien sabéis que soportar vagabundos en el país es criar ladrones en él", quoted in Historia social y económica, III, 143; or the viceroy of Catalonia, in 1566, "vemos todos los días por experiencia que los vagabundos y pícaros que vagan por el territorio jugando y haciendo el gallofo se vuelven ladrones y bandoleros y salteadores de caminos...", ibid. p. 27.
[4] La pícara Justina, quoted in José Deleito y Piñuela, La mala vida en la España de Felipe IV (Madrid, 1959), p. 128.
[5] Marcelin Defourneaux, La vie quotidienne en Espagne au siècle d'or (Paris, 1964), p. 250.
[6] Nadal and Giralt, op. cit. p. 26.
[7] Ibid. p. 195. Groups of intransigent moriscos resisted the expulsion order by forming themselves into bands of brigands; J. Vicens Vives, Historia económica de España (Barcelona, 1964), p. 312, on the political associations of banditry in Catalonia. See also E. M. Leonard, The Early History of English Poor Relief (2nd edn 1965), pp. 80–1, on the connexions between vagrancy and the rebellion in the north of England, 1569–72.

region, banditry seems to have been closely associated with barren mountain areas, frequently straddling state frontiers, where both natural and jurisdictional barriers impeded the execution of justice.[1] The apparent increase of brigandage throughout the whole area at the end of the sixteenth century may have been connected, Braudel has suggested, with the generalization of hunger, with the general crisis of subsistence of the 1590's.[2] In Latin America, also, vagabondage and delinquency were associated with social disruption, with the psychological and economic crises of the Conquest. They were phenomena of the frontier, the frontier of war, the frontier between the mountain and the plain, between good land and bad. They were also phenomena of irregularity, often found in areas of extensive pastoralism, where transhumance created a type unattached to the soil, mobile and fugitive, or among occasional labourers, equally unstable and unattached.[3] In Spain, where there is other evidence of delinquency or the conditions for delinquency available, there is such a sufficient concordance between this and the distribution of *forzados* as to give a considerable circumstantial validity to a more general association. One particular example may suffice. M. Bennassar has shown how much more heavily poverty weighed on the social structure of Valladolid than on the commercial centre of Medina del Campo less than 30 miles away. Not only were there considerably more paupers in Valladolid, they were much more concentrated. While the highest proportion of paupers in a single suburb of Medina was 15·3 per cent, Valladolid had four parishes with more than one-fifth of their populations impoverished, and in one case the proportion was nearly twice as high. Medina del Campo, as Bennassar puts it, did not have "ces groupements massifs et dangereux de misérables, foyers d'épidémies brutales, sources de vols, de rixes, de crimes, d'effrois nocturnes";[4] nor was it so well represented on the galleys. Valladolid, with a population in 1591 three times that of Medina, had nearly five and a half times as many *forzados*. The picture of crime in Madrid and the other great cities that emerges from the evidence of the galleys fits equally well into what is already known from literary and other sources. There is, then, a not unreasonable warrant for postulating crime statistics as a socio-economic pointer, provided that no great precision is expected of them. Crime is best considered an indicator of instability and tension; whether this has economic or psychological roots, or whether crime is the expression of political, racial, or other group hostilities cannot be determined in general terms but only in the context of each particular case. Within the limitations already pointed out, an analysis of the men condemned to serve a term on the galleys may thus provide a new approach to an understanding of Spanish prosperity and social stability, at a regional level, at what appears to be a pivotal stage in Spain's economic and demographic fortunes.

[1] Fernand Braudel, *La Méditerranée et le monde méditerranéen à l'époque de Philippe II* (Paris, 1949), pp. 649 ff.
[2] Ibid. p. 658.
[3] Norman F. Martin, *Los vagabundos en la Nueva España, siglo XVI* (Mexico, 1957), pp. 17, 36, 103, 120, 135; Mario Gongora, 'Vagabondage et société pastorale en Amérique latine (spécialement au Chili Central)', *Annales E.S.C.* xxi (1966), 159–77; J.-P. Berthe, 'Conjoncture et société. Le banditisme en Nouvelle Espagne', *Annales E.S.C.* xx (1965), 1256–8.
[4] Bartolomé Bennassar, 'Medina del Campo. Un exemple des structures urbaines de l'Espagne au XVIe siècle', *Revue d'Histoire Economique et Sociale*, xxxix (1961), 481–3.

IV

Table 1 sets out the "overall" rate of crime on the galleys on the basis of modern provincial divisions, with the exceptions that Galicia, the three Basque provinces (here called Biscay), Granada, Aragon, Valencia, and Catalonia have been retained as regional units because so many of the criminals were described simply as natives of one region or the other. Modern provincial divisions have been used both to facilitate the location of place-names and because they are geographically more meaningful, save that for the latter reason the Condado de Treviño, an outlying part of the province of Burgos, has been treated as part of Biscay.

Table 1. *Overall Distribution of* Forzados

Province	(a) Population in vecinos	(b) Forzados	(a/b)	Rank
Cadiz	20,021	333	60	1
Seville	61,435	641	96	2
Granada	71,904	559	129	3
Cordoba	48,554	264	184	4
Murcia	18,320	89	206	5
Jaen	56,656	265	214	6
Albacete	17,574	45	391	12
Ciudad Real	36,552	93	393	13
Huelva	22,989	53	434	15
Badajoz	63,895	128	499	18
Cuenca	62,376	108	578	22
The South	480,276	2,578	186	
Valencia	85,000	365	233	7
Aragon	58,000	161	360	10
Catalonia	70,000	141	496	17
Aragon	213,000	667	319	
Valladolid	48,498	162	299	8
Galicia	125,708	320	393	13
Logroño	25,217	56	450	16
Biscay	40,000	70	571	20
Palencia	36,799	64	575	21
Zamora	41,237	71	581	23
Oviedo	39,411	62	636	24
Santander	27,035	42	644	25
Burgos	52,234	65	804	27
Navarre	30,833	38	811	28
Leon	57,652	71	812	29
The North	524,624	1,021	514	
Madrid	53,932	153	352	9
Toledo	77,303	202	383	11
Segovia	30,571	60	510	19
Salamanca	48,341	75	645	26
Avila	39,972	49	816	30
Caceres	61,176	72	850	31
Guadalajara	50,894	52	979	32
Soria	25,792	26	992	33
The Centre	387,981	689	563	
Total	1,605,881	4,955	324	

It was necessary to adjust the population figures for 1591, printed by González,[1] to fit present-day boundaries, and although this involved a good deal of approximation the results are probably only marginally inaccurate. No reliable population figures for the same date exist either for the Aragonese kingdoms or the Basque provinces and Navarre. Domínguez Ortiz's estimates for 1600 have generally been accepted, with some slight scaling down to compensate for probable growth after 1591 where necessary.[2] For Aragon, however, González's figure for 1603 has been preferred as more consistent with the likely population of the kingdom on the eve of the expulsion of the *moriscos*.[3] The populations of Aragon and Catalonia have been further reduced to take into account the large number of French residents there who would appear on the muster lists only as natives of France. The French in Catalonia may have amounted to between 10 and 20 per cent of the total male population at this time, and those in Aragon would appear to be no less.[4] A reduction of the population by approximately 13 per cent is therefore a slightly conservative compromise. All populations are given in *vecinos* or households. Contemporaries and a majority of subsequent writers have generally allowed five persons per *vecino*, and although this is probably about 10 per cent too high, this is the coefficient that has been used whenever *vecinos* have been translated into persons, or vice versa.

The overall distribution is considerably distorted by the disproportionate amount of delinquency in the great urban agglomerations. In virtually all the larger centres, the rate of crime was at least double the national average. 37·2 per cent of the oarsmen came from the 13·2 per cent of the population that lived in the 49 cities of 2,000 *vecinos* and over (Table 2).[5] More than two-fifths of the *forzados* from the provinces of Cordoba, Toledo, Madrid, Segovia, and Valladolid came from the capital cities alone. An attempt has been made to give a fairer indication of the spread of crime by excluding the larger urban centres whose social and economic structures set them apart from the surrounding countryside and where crime and the law most proliferated and were most organized.

Table 2. *Urban Distribution of* Forzados

City	Province	(a) Population in vecinos	(b) Forzados	(a/b)
Osuna	Seville	2,460	63	39
Utrera	Seville	2,687	55	49
Cordoba	Cordoba	6,257	122	51
Malaga	Granada	3,357	57	59
Ecija	Seville	5,078	77	66
Ronda	Granada	2,097	32	66
Jerez de la Frontera	Cadiz	6,816	96	71
Granada	Granada	13,757	183	75

[1] Tomás González, *Censo de población de las provincias y partidos de la corona de Castilla en el siglo XVI* (Madrid, 1829).

[2] Antonio Domínguez Ortiz, *La sociedad española en el siglo XVII* (Madrid, 1963), pt I, ch. 3.

[3] Ibid. p. 103. It was estimated that the population of Aragon had increased by a quarter between 1495 and 1603.—González, op. cit. p. 137.

[4] Nadal and Giralt, op. cit. pp. 62, 162.

[5] These percentages are worked out on an estimated total of 5,400, which includes the Spaniards among the *forzados* of unlocated provenance who can all be assumed to be countrymen.

City	Province	(a) Population in vecinos	(b) Forzados	(a/b)
Antequera	Granada	4,041	51	79
Moron de la Frontera	Seville	2,086	26	80
Seville	Seville	18,000	216	83
Madrid	Madrid	7,500	83	90
Alcala de Henares	Madrid	2,545	26	98
Murcia	Murcia	3,370	34	99
Ciudad Rodrigo	Salamanca	2,009	20	100
Valladolid	Valladolid	8,112	76	107
Baeza	Jaen	5,172	47	110
Valencia	Valencia	12,327	110	112
Marchena	Seville	2,170	19	114
Játiva	Valencia	2,380	20	119
Toledo	Toledo	10,933	91	120
Badajoz	Badajoz	2,805	23	122
Jaen	Jaen	5,595	42	133
Ubeda	Jaen	4,672	34	137
Alcazar de San Juan	Ciudad Real	2,057	15	137
Burgos	Burgos	2,665	19	140
Andujar	Jaen	2,900	20	145
Zaragoza	Aragon	5,000	34	147
Avila	Avila	2,826	19	149
Segovia	Segovia	5,548	37	150
Salamanca	Salamanca	4,953	32	155
Talavera de la Reina	Toledo	2,035	13	157
Ocaña	Toledo	3,150	20	158
Cuenca	Cuenca	3,095	19	163
Lucena*	Cordoba	4,481	27	166
Medina de Rioseco	Valladolid	2,006	12	167
Orihuela	Valencia	2,520	14	180
Arjona	Jaen	2,116	11	192
Medina del Campo	Valladolid	2,760	14	197
Lorca	Murcia	2,232	11	203
Alcala la Real*	Jaen	2,457	12	205
Ciudad Real	Ciudad Real	2,049	8	256
Barcelona	Catalonia	6,400	24	267
Estepa*	Seville	2,420	9	269
Palencia	Palencia	3,063	11	278
Toro	Zamora	2,314	8	289
Martos	Jaen	2,183	7	312
Villaviciosa	Oviedo	2,507	6	418
Aracena*	Huelva	2,583	2	1,292

* Population includes other settlements not represented in *Forzado* column.

Seville and no doubt other cities had their guilds and fraternities of thieves just as Valladolid, Granada, Seville, Zaragoza, and Madrid had their *chancillerías*, *audiencias*, and *alcaldes de corte*.[1] A line has been drawn at populations of more than 10,000 (2,000 *vecinos*). This is the lowest limit that can be employed with any accuracy on the basis of González's figures, and it has the merit of involving 23 of the 33 criminal provinces. Table 3 represents what can be called the rural crime-rate.

[1] Defourneaux, op. cit. p. 256.

Table 3. *Rural Distribution of* Forzados

Province	(a) Population in vecinos	(b) Forzados	(a/b)	Rank
Cadiz	13,205	237	56	1
Seville	26,534	176	151	2
Granada	48,652	236	206	3
Murcia	12,718	44	289	4
Cordoba	37,816	115	329	6
Jaen	31,561	92	343	7
Albacete	17,574	45	391	8
Huelva	20,406	51	400	10
Ciudad Real	32,446	70	464	13
Badajoz	61,090	105	582	16
Cuenca	59,281	89	666	22
The South	361,283	1,260	287	
Valencia	67,773	221	307	5
Aragon	53,000	127	417	11
Catalonia	63,600	117	544	14
Aragon	184,373	465	397	
Galicia	125,708	320	393	9
Logroño	25,217	56	450	12
Biscay	40,000	70	571	15
Valladolid	35,620	60	594	17
Zamora	38,923	63	618	18
Palencia	33,736	53	637	19
Santander	27,035	42	644	20
Oviedo	36,904	56	659	21
Navarre	30,833	38	811	24
Leon	57,652	71	812	25
Burgos	49,569	46	1,078	30
The North	501,197	875	573	
Toledo	61,185	78	784	23
Caceres	61,176	72	850	26
Guadalajara	50,894	52	979	27
Soria	25,792	26	992	28
Madrid	43,887	44	997	29
Segovia	25,023	23	1,088	31
Avila	37,146	30	1,238	32
Salamanca	41,379	23	1,799	33
The Centre	346,482	348	996	
Total	1,393,335	2,948	473	

From a comparison of Maps 1 and 2 a complex but intelligible pattern of crime emerges. Spain can be broken down into three well-defined areas: in the south, the ancient kingdoms of Seville, Granada, Cordoba, Jaen, and Murcia, together with the modern provinces of Badajoz, Ciudad Real, and Cuenca; in the north, the rest of Extremadura and New Castile, Old Castile, Leon, Galicia, and the Cantabrian provinces; in the east, the tripartite kingdom of Aragon. These divisions are all administrative. The boundary between north and south falls, as far as provincial divisions will show, along the line of the Tagus—the Tagus, the line of demarcation between the slow Reconquest of assimilation in

DISTRIBUTION OF FORZADOS

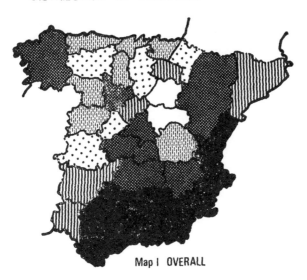

Map I OVERALL

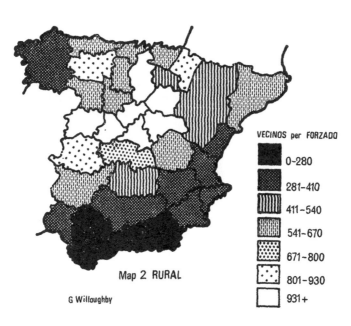

Map 2 RURAL

G Willoughby

VECINOS per FORZADO

0~280

281~410

411~540

541~670

671~800

801~930

931+

the north and the more abrupt Reconquest of recolonization in the south that still showed up clearly in the demographic patterns of late sixteenth-century Castile;[1] but, more important, the frontier between the jurisdictions of the *chancillerías* of Granada and Valladolid. The kingdoms of Aragon were, of course, independent judicial and administrative areas. The point is the obvious one. Convictions reflect both criminality and justice, but in what proportions it is impossible to say. For this reason, the three areas should be treated independently and comparisons across their boundaries drawn only with caution.

The South. There can be no doubt that the galleys grossly overstate the general crime-rate in Andalusia and Murcia relative to the rest of the country. Presumably, justices in the areas closest to the base ports were more alive to the needs of the galleys than in the more protected inland communities. The costs of transportation were also less and fewer *forzados* died on the way.[2] The south can be considered the catchment area of the base ports, their impact declining in a regular regression towards the interior of the country. Nonetheless, the excessively high number of condemned men, from Andalusia particularly, is neither entirely divorced from social reality nor at variance with the extensive literary evidence.[3] An enormous preponderance of landless labourers, extending as far north as Ciudad Real, made Andalusian society as mobile as any in Spain. Seville was a boom-town. Its population had more than doubled in the space of half a century, and from everywhere men flocked to share the wealth of the Indies or to await their turn on the overladen merchant ships of the Atlantic convoys. Seville pullulated with foreigners, with disaffected *moriscos*, vagrants, ruffians, thieves, and the whole picturesque underworld of the picaresque that threaded its way from all over Spain into the chosen quarters of the great cities of the south, the seafront at Sanlúcar, the *Percheles* at Malaga, the *Rondilla* at Granada, the *Potro* at Cordoba, the *Compas* at Seville.[4] Here, stimulated by the juxtaposition of fabulous wealth and massive poverty, and aided by the corruption and maladministration of justice and the anonymity and flux of the most populous city in Spain, crime flourished.[5] The author of the *Floresta Española* wrote, quite correctly, that there were more men from Seville serving on the galleys of Spain than from any other place.[6] Seville, in an exaggerated way, epitomized conditions throughout Andalusia. With some exceptions, such as Cordoba, the only city in Andalusia to have declined in population in the sixteenth century and the capital with by far the highest crime-rate of all the 18 great cities of Spain, Granada, devastated by the rebellion and expulsion of the *moriscos* and the ruin of its important silk

---

[1] Noel Salomon, *La campagne de Nouvelle Castille à la fin du XVIe siècle d'après les Relaciones topográficas* (Paris, 1964), p. 22.

[2] It cost the Crown about 50 *reales* for every day that a chain of *galeotes* was on the road.—Castillo de Bovadilla, op. cit. bk v, ch. 6, para. 24, p. 788. In France, chains might lose up to a quarter of their men before they reached the galleys.—Paul Walden Bamford, 'The Procurement of Oarsmen for French Galleys, 1660–1748', *American Historical Review*, LXV (1960), 44–5.

[3] See Francisco Rodríguez Marín's introduction to Cervantes' *Rinconete y Cortadillo* (critical edition, Seville, 1905).

[4] *Don Quixote*, p. 41. Antonio Domínguez Ortiz, *Orto y ocaso de Sevilla* (Seville, 1946), p. 70. "Informe de los Jurados de Sevilla a Felipe IV", 30 Dec. 1621, "En esta Ciudad ay muchos vagamundos que se recojen en ella de todo el Reyno, delincuentes y de mal vivir." On Cordoba's position as "Aduana de desengaños" on the highway between Madrid and Seville see Deleito y Piñuela, op. cit. p. 184.

[5] Domínguez Ortiz, *Orto y Ocaso de Sevilla*, pp. 68 ff; Rodríguez Marín, p. 69.

[6] Domínguez Ortiz, *Orto y Ocaso de Sevilla*, p. 67.

industry in the 1560's;[1] and Cadiz, where it was claimed taxation had destroyed trade and halved population in the ten years prior to 1584,[2] the south as a whole, benefiting from the increased demand for wine and oil for the Indies, seems to have remained fairly buoyant. On the evidence of the *millones*' assessment of 1593 the south was easily the most prosperous area in Castile.[3] The evidence of the galleys would suggest that little of this prosperity percolated down to the mass of the labouring class who bore the brunt of the widespread distress caused in Andalusia and southern Extremadura[4] by the tax collector, the recruiting captain, and the officers of purveyance.

Aragon. The relatively high rate of crime in the kingdoms of Aragon is also perfectly consistent with known facts. Catalan banditry was a sufficiently serious social and political problem already to have received considerable attention from historians,[5] and many of the factors giving rise to banditry in the principality were equally effective in Aragon, the fastnesses of the Pyrenean frontier, the large-scale immigration from France and the contacts with the Huguenots of Languedoc, the opportunities offered by the bullion trains on their way to Genoa, and the general pressure of population on a static economy. More striking is the disparity between the three provinces. It is Catalonia that has the great reputation for lawlessness, yet Catalonia that is least represented and apparently considerably less delinquent than the "northern" province of Galicia, or even Logroño. The figures must surely reflect the differences in the effectiveness and penetration of royal government in the three parts of the Crown of Aragon. As far as Valencia, and to some extent Aragon, is concerned, the pattern of crime seems to be unaffected by the frontiers of national liberties. Valencia might well be treated as part of the southern coastal bloc. Although there is evidence of a spread of lawlessness in the kingdom in the last quarter of the century,[6] this does not seem to be accounted for by any intrinsic weakness in Valencian society— the large *morisco* population would appear in fact to have been under-represented.[7] What is clearly important is its propinquity to the galley ports and the fact that Valencia was considered "more amenable in its privileges".[8] In Catalonia, on the other hand, the viceroys were never able to eradicate banditry, and this was largely because they were never able to secure the full co-operation of the local nobility in permitting the entry of the forces of justice into all the fragmented private jurisdictions of the principality.[9] Even when a criminal was apprehended,

[1] K. Garrad, 'La industria sedera granadina en el siglo XVI y su conexión con el levantamiento de las Alpujarras (1568–1571)', *Miscelánea de Estudios Arabes y Hebráicos*, v (1956), 73–104.

[2] Memorandum of the city of Cadiz, with an accompanying letter of the marquis of Santa Cruz, 15 March 1584.—A.G.S. Guerra Antigua, leg. 172, fo. 152.

[3] Castillo, op. cit. p. 732.

[4] By the 1580's, Seville was the main centre in Spain for the provisioning of the galleys, the North African garrisons, the Indies fleets, and the Atlantic galleons. From Seville purveyors and commissaries radiated outwards sweeping up local supplies, and preparing the way for the passage of troops from Italy and Germany into Portugal.

[5] See p. 244, n. 2, above, to which can be added the remarks in J. H. Elliott, *The Revolt of the Catalans* (Cambridge, 1963).

[6] Braudel, op. cit. p. 659.   [7] See p. 263 below.

[8] See Olivares's famous memorandum to Philip IV, where he remarks that the Valencians have been hitherto considered "los mas moles en sus fueros".—B.M. Egerton MS 347, fo. 283v.

[9] *Historia social y económica*, III, 150. Of jurisdictions in Catalonia, 71 per cent were outside royal control.—Elliott, op. cit. p. 98.

the temper and the privileges of the Catalans often combined to thwart what was regarded as a hostile and alien law.[1] Judicial autonomy was one of the most cherished marks of political integrity. Consequently criminals not infrequently found themselves the pretext for an outburst of patriotic indignation, and the bandits who turned on their pursuers with cries of "visca la terra" and "death to traitors" clearly saw themselves, in one role, as an activist vanguard of the Catalan cause.[2] Much of the lawlessness in the kingdoms of Aragon was inspired as well as abetted by a kind of national anomie. The high figures for Aragon itself are particularly interesting. The problem of civil order there, though recognized, has been overshadowed by the attention given to Catalonia; yet the situation of the peasant in Aragon was worse than in Catalonia and provoked various unconcerted risings of vassals against their lords as well as a virtual civil war in 1585 between the Old Christians of the mountain areas and the landlord-backed *moriscos* of the lowland estates.[3] The fact that the hostility of the peasantry was directed in the first instance against the nobility rather than against the government, as it was in Catalonia,[4] was an important reason why the extensive lawlessness of Aragon on the eve of the revolution of 1591 did not have more serious political consequences. Nevertheless, the high rate of crime in the Crown of Aragon may well have had much to do with Madrid's suspicions of the eastern provinces and its unwillingness to trust any of the Aragonese with arms for their own defence;[5] it may even have influenced its decision to end abruptly one of the most persistent threats to its authority by expelling the *moriscos* from Aragon and Valencia.

It is only within the Crown of Castile from the Tagus northwards, but excluding Navarre which had an independent judicial system based on Pamplona, that peculiarities of situation and administration cease to be of major importance and the number of *forzados* on the galleys is less equivocally a reflexion of criminality as such. This area again breaks down naturally into two parts: a northern band, running along the Atlantic coast from Portugal to Navarre and extending as far inland as Zamora, Valladolid, and Logroño, with an overall crime-rate of one *forzado* to 502 *vecinos* and a rural rate of one to 562; and a central block of eight Old and New Castilian provinces with an overall rate of one to 563 and a rural rate of one to 996.

The North.[6] Crime has been associated almost axiomatically with poverty and deteriorating living conditions. The density of crime in the north-west of Spain bears out the evidence of the tax returns that these were the poorest provinces in Castile. The distribution of the *servicios* of the Cortes shows the lowest *per capita*

---

[1] A Catalan paymaster, sentenced as a result of a judicial investigation at the end of 1578, six years later had still succeeded in avoiding punishment by appealing to *fuero* and enlisting the support of other natives, among whom may have been included the judges and prosecutor of the *Audiencia* of Barcelona. Secretary Delgado to the count of Chinchón, 13 Dec. 1584, A.G.S. Guerra Antigua, leg. 172, fo. 163.

[2] Elliott, op. cit. p. 147; Vicens Vives, op. cit. p. 312.   [3] *Historia social y económica*, III, 131, 222.

[4] Ibid. p. 132.

[5] A.G.S. Guerra Antigua, leg. 81, fo. 169, Delgado to Philip II, 4 Jan. 1576, on Valencia; Guerra Antigua, leg. 712, *consulta* of the Council of War, 3 June 1609, on Aragon.

[6] The argument of this section would have had a sounder and more subtle basis had it been written after the publication of Bartolomé Bennassar, *Valladolid au siècle d'or: une ville de Castille et sa campagne au XVIe siècle* (Paris/The Hague, 1967).

assessments in Santander, Oviedo, Galicia, and Leon,[1] and when, in 1593, the *millones* were reassessed to take into account changes in wealth and population, the six lowest *per capita* contributions were paid in order by the fiscal areas Leon–Oviedo, Zamora–Galicia, Burgos–Santander, Valladolid, Soria–Logroño, and Palencia. Alvaro Castillo's division of Castile into an impoverished northern band and a rather more prosperous centre seems to be equally valid as a portrayal of crime.[2] Poverty, however, does not explain everything. Leon and Burgos are obvious anomalies. Leon, partially cut off by its mountains, is an island of that stability and conservative resignation characteristic of an area of extreme but unchanging poverty. The situation in Burgos is better possibly because the real decline in Burgos's wool trade had come some twenty-five years before. There are indications that it was able to maintain the level of its exports to Italy, at least for a full generation after 1561,[3] and it may well be that the precipitous decline of its rural population is not properly discernible until the very end of the century.[4] Galicia, Oviedo, and Santander were not only the poorest provinces in Castile; they were also, together with Biscay, provinces with an exceptionally large proportion of *hidalgos*. On the one hand poverty, on the other a refusal to recognize any betters; these were two of the most characteristic qualities of the *pícaro*.[5] In Galicia, the strikingly high incidence of crime is a counterpart of the strong and constant emigration that typified the province during the second half of the sixteenth century, and confirms the picture of drastic overpopulation described by Ruiz Almansa.[6] By the 1580's, the poverty and misery of Galicia were recognized facts.[7] In 1593, Galicia–Zamora dropped in its *per capita* tax assessment ranking from a clear third-from-bottom to within a *maravedí* of last place, suffering an apparent decline of prosperity more than five times as great as that of any other province.[8] Oviedo shared the poverty and many of the qualities of the north-west corner.[9] Both Asturians and Galicians were prominent in the resettling of Granada and among the flotsam that daily added to the population of Madrid;[10] but it may be that the representation on the galleys of Oviedo, Santander, and Biscay is also a pointer to the state of the shipping industry on the Cantabrian coast. This would suggest a less optimistic view than that sometimes proposed,[11] and would support various contemporary opinions

[1] Salomon, op. cit. p. 234, n. 1.   [2] Castillo, op. cit.
[3] Manuel Basas Fernández, *El Consulado de Burgos en el siglo XVI* (Madrid, 1963); see the tables on pp. 261–4.
[4] *Corregidor* of Burgos to Council of Castile, Dec. 1616, "faḻta de diez años a esta parte mas de la mitad de las labranças que avia y lo propio de gente, por lo qual no se labra la mayor parte de la tierra que ay". —B.M. Egerton MS 356, fo. 44.
[5] Ricardo del Arco, in this context, talks of the "sentido de dignidad superior, nativo en el español de raza".—'La ínfima levadura social en las obras de Cervantes', *Estudios de Historia Social de España*, II (Madrid, 1952), 211. See also the same author's 'La crítica social en Cervantes', ibid. p. 320.
[6] Javier Ruiz Almansa, *La población de Galicia (1500–1945)* (Madrid, 1948).
[7] *Actas de las Cortes de Castilla* (Madrid, 1861 etc.), x, 56, debate of 29 April 1588, "por ser aquella tierra tan pobre y miserable como se sabe, y estar muy cansada y gastada por el alojamiento de los soldados que por ella han andado y andan..."
[8] Castillo, op. cit. p. 731.   [9] Domínguez Ortiz, *La sociedad española*, p. 62.
[10] Ibid. p. 133, n. 13; *Historia social y económica*, III, 220; Viñas Mey, op. cit. p. 129, n. 11.
[11] Abbott Payson Usher, 'Spanish Ships and Shipping in the Sixteenth and Seventeenth Centuries', in *Facts and Factors in Economic History (Articles by former students of E. F. Gay)* (Cambridge, Mass., 1932), p. 193, thinks the latter part of the sixteenth century was a period of relative prosperity for the northern industry. J. Carrera Pujal, *Historia de la economía española*, II (Barcelona, 1943–4), 118, argues along similar lines.

that by the 1570's shipbuilding in the north was already in decline.[1] The Dutch war, which disrupted Spanish maritime activity in the north Atlantic, also had its effects on the interior. The figures for Valladolid, and, to some extent, for Palencia, may well reflect the social consequences of the collapse of the commercial network centred on Medina del Campo with the rupture of the Medina–Antwerp axis and the "bankruptcy" of 1575, and those for Zamora and Logroño provide an early indication of the troubles that by 1600 had resulted in a marked diminution of their rural populations.[2]

The Centre. Crime in the eight central provinces was dominated by the four great cities, Toledo, Madrid, Salamanca, and Segovia, which together supplied rather more than a third of the *forzados*. Madrid, with all the attractions of the capital, a burgeoning population, and the opportunities offered by the ostentation and extravagance of courtiers and grandees, drew to it all the importuners, the adventurers, and the dissolute of Spain, and had a rate of crime unsurpassed by any of the great cities outside the southern area. Throughout the last three-quarters of the Habsburg era, Madrid had a reputation and a record unparalleled for violence, dishonesty, and licentiousness.[3] Salamanca had its university, Toledo its "Taverns", and Segovia its *pelaires*,[4] but the latter were also important textile centres with a numerous working class.[5] There is no doubt that by the 1580's the economy of Toledo was disintegrating. In 1578, the city petitioned for the remission of its share of the *alcabalas* on the grounds that "because of the present poverty and barrenness of the land, this city and the district around it are so ruined and hard-pressed that tradesmen and farmers cannot pay their assessments or even keep up their homes, and so they are going to live in places where they are not so burdened..."[6] Segovia's crime-rate, 25 per cent lower than Toledo's, seems to bear out the relatively more prosperous state of the Segovian cloth industry indicated in the Cortes of 1583, 1588, and 1592.[7] But outside the cities, the central area emerges as uniformly placid and well adjusted, containing seven of the eight provinces with the lowest rural crime-rate, as well as the four with the lowest overall rate.

V

It would be unwise, considering the uncertainties of our figures and the imprecision of galley-crime as a concept, to try to do much more at a provincial level than provide support for trends already evident. At a national level, where the margin of error is greater, some more general observations might be appropriate.

[1] Duro, op. cit. bk v, p. 20; Usher, op. cit. p. 193; Francisco Duarte, *factor* of the *Casa de Contratación* of Seville, to Philip II, Seville, 24 Nov. 1579.—A.G.S. Guerra Antigua, leg. 91, fo. 74.

[2] Domínguez Ortiz, *La sociedad española* ..., p. 118.

[3] Anonymous memorandum, 31 Jan. 1589, "la corte esta llena de bagabundos y ladrones y cada dia se cometen hurtos".—A.G.S. Guerra Antigua, leg. 264, fo. 2. Hopton wrote of Madrid, around 1633, that there were "more idle men to be spared than in half Spain".—Martin Hume, *The Court of Philip IV. Spain in Decadence* (1907), p. 266. See also Deleito y Piñuela, op. cit. pp. 93, 182, 203–15.

[4] A type of *pícaro*, ibid. p. 183.

[5] There were said to be over 30,000 cloth workers in Segovia at one time in the sixteenth century —*Historia social y económica*, III, 172.

[6] Petition of the city of Toledo, 7 June 1578.—A.G.S. Consejo y Juntas de Hacienda, leg. 125. But Domínguez Ortiz, *La sociedad española* ..., p. 138, thinks Toledo's misfortunes were only just beginning in 1591.

[7] José Larraz, *La época del mercantilismo en Castilla, 1500–1700* (Madrid, 1963), p. 43.

In absolute terms, the number of *forzados* condemned every year, half of whom probably died in their chains, and the consequent loss of population to the galleys was negligible, something in the region of 1,000 men a year, or one for every 1,600 of the adult male population.[1] This, together with the constant difficulty faced by the government in finding enough oars to man the galleys, suggests that vagabondage was not the widespread problem that the *arbitristas* imagined. The incidence of these convictions, however, was not uniform and in certain cases it can be considered a minor, but measurable, factor in population drain. Of the eight men who had left the town of Valdepeñas (Ciudad Real) in the years before 1582, one was a *forzado* on the galleys, one was in the Indies, two were in Italy, two others were at the wars, and two had just gone away.[2] It would be interesting to know how general such a pattern was. In Seville, Cadiz, Granada, and in several Andalusian cities, where something like one man in every 500 must have been taken off to the galleys every year, crime may have been almost as important a source of population drain as emigration to the Indies or recruitment in the army. It is not impossible that crime, emigration, and military service were, in some sense, alternatives. Emigration to the Indies, for example, was often seen by contemporaries as a flux of volatile humours unassimilable into the body politic, as an escape for the lawless, and an opportunity for the unsatisfied to make their fortunes in the New World in ways that the Old did not allow.[3] In certain provinces (Caceres, Guadalajara, Burgos, Salamanca, Avila, Badajoz), emigration has something of the role of a safety-valve; in others (notably Murcia, Valencia, Aragon, Catalonia, Galicia, Logroño) an insignificant rate of emigration finds its counterpart in a high level of criminality (see Table 4). The endemic banditry and widespread delinquency of the kingdoms of Aragon can, from this point of view, be seen as a natural corollary of Madrid's reluctance to open the Indies to non-Castilians.[4]

Table 4. *Crime and Emigration**

Province	Emigration rate	Emigration rank	Overall crime rank (*from Table 1*)
Seville	183	1	2
Badajoz	447	2	18
Cadiz	715	3	1
Caceres	784	4	31
Toledo	869	5	11
Huelva	1,210	6	15
Ciudad Real	1,218	7	13
Biscay	1,250	8	20

[1] One can estimate that a fifth of the crew was replaced each year. Contractors were allowed to write off a *forzado* after five years, at a rate of eight ducats a year.—A.G.S. Estado, leg. 460 (Libro 42), fo. 16*v*. In 1589, each galley took on an average of 35 new men during the year and lost 15 by death. For 34 galleys, this gives a total of 1,190, one-sixth of whom would have been foreigners.

[2] A.G.S. Consejo y Juntas de Hacienda, leg. 135.

[3] G. Escolano, *Historia de Valencia* (1610), "como por lo común apetece aquella carrera gente borrascosa o desvalida al olor del oro, antes nos sirve de purga para limpiarnos, y de lo que sirve la sangría, si bien a vuelta de ellas se van algunas gotas de sangre buena", quoted in Domínguez Ortiz, *La sociedad española . . .*, p. 90.

[4] The restriction, in fact, was only properly effective if a complaint was laid by an interested party; see R. Konetzke, 'La legislación sobre inmigración de extranjeros en América durante el reinado de Carlos V', in *Charles-Quint et son temps* (Paris, 1958), p. 97.

Province	Emigration rate	Emigration rank	Overall crime rank (from Table 1)
Guadalajara	1,272	9	32
Jaen	1,574	10	6
Valladolid	1,732	11	8
Salamanca	1,859	12	26
Burgos	1,866	13	27
Madrid	1,997	14	9
Granada	2,179	15	3
Segovia	2,184	16	19
Santander	2,253	17	25
Avila	2,498	18	30
Cordoba	2,554	19	4
Palencia	3,067	20	21
Zamora	3,172	21	23
Leon	3,603	22	29
Albacete	4,394	23	12
Cuenca	4,798	24	22
Catalonia	5,000	25	17
Soria	5,158	26	33
Oviedo	5,630	27	24
Logroño	6,304	28	16
Aragon	11,091	29	10
Galicia	13,968	30	13
Navarre	15,417	31	28
Valencia	21,250	32	7
Murcia	—	33	5

* Table based on 1,144 Spaniards registered as emigrants between 1575 and 1586. Data from V. Aubrey Neasham, 'Spain's Emigrants to the New World, 1492–1592', *Hispanic American Historical Review*, XIX (1939), 147–60. Lists of registered emigrants do not of course tell the whole story. For a discussion of the inadequacy of the registers see Juan Friede, 'Algunas observaciones sobre la realidad de la emigración española a América en la primera mitad del siglo XVI', *Revista de Indias* (1952), pp. 467–96.

Over half the *forzados* came from the southern area that contained one-third of the population of Spain. The south, among its other peculiarities, was also, on the basis of the unsatisfactory evidence at present available, the most heterodox in religion. It seems to be in the southern part of Spain that the Jews were least effectively assimilated, and in Andalusia that the Inquisition in its early years found most of its victims.[1] It was Granada, until 1570, that contained the largest and most obdurate group of crypto-Mohammedan *moriscos*. The galleys, in so far as they were themselves one of the punishments open to the Inquisition, naturally reflect deviant behaviour in religion as in all else. But was there a more subtle relationship between crime and religion than this? In some countries the underprivileged could give vent to their feelings by destroying images; in Spain it was best to make use of them. Poverty or malice certainly drove many to trade on religious sentiment and superstition by selling their prayers, faking miracles, or simulating infirmities. Inevitably, they brought charity into disrepute and "turned religion into a laughing stock",[2] or themselves "lived like gentiles, without confessing, or communicating, or hearing mass".[3] Poverty that had weakened the sincerity of their own faith in its turn helped to weaken the faith of others,

[1] H. Lapeyre, 'La dernière croisade', in *L'Espagne au temps de Philippe II* (Paris, 1965), p. 138.
[2] Arco, 'La infima levadura social', op. cit. p. 232, quoting from *El Licenciado Vidriera*.
[3] Ibid. p. 233, quoting Cristóbal Pérez de Herrera's *Amparo de pobres*.

and as fraud in religion looked like both crime and heresy, the literate faithful were not slow to brand the performers of quasi-religious puppet shows and fake *pordioseros* as "vagrant, worthless, and useless people; wine sponges and bread weevils".[1] Crime and irreligion were often different sides of the same coin.

A disproportionate number of *forzados* certainly came from among the 60,000 *morisco* families in Spain. The *morisco* population, less than 4 per cent of the total, provided 6·8 per cent of *forzados* (367), and this is undoubtedly a minimum figure. This was almost entirely because of the exceedingly high rate of crime among Granadan *moriscos* (one to 95 *vecinos* on the basis of Lapeyre's estimate of Granadan *moriscos*,[2] or three times the national average). As very few of the Alpujarran rebels could still have been alive on the galleys nearly twenty years later, this figure must reflect the failure of Castile to assimilate successfully the 60,000 Granadans expelled from their homes after the revolt. It bears out to the hilt Braudel's statement that the expulsion merely transferred the *morisco* problem from Granada to Castile, and goes a long way towards explaining the recurrent fears that overtook the Council of State for the next forty years.[3] The predominantly rural, landlord-protected *moriscos* of Valencia, on the other hand, although amounting to 33 per cent of the population in 1609, provided less than 27 per cent of Valencia's criminals (and only 32 per cent even adding in a proportion of the unlocated *moriscos*); and the relative proportions in Aragon were very similar.

What the *moriscos* were in southern Spain, the gypsies were in Castile—a minority sub-culture, suspect partly in religion, partly in honesty, partly in their way of life, hated largely for being different.[4] There were 158 gypsies on the galleys in 1586–9, or 2·9 per cent of the total. Whereas 80 per cent of located *moriscos* had come from Granada, Valencia, and Aragon, and 15 per cent from the rest of Castile, 75 per cent of gypsies came from Castile and only 18 per cent from Granada, Valencia, and Aragon.

	Moriscos	%	Gypsies	%
Granada	126	41·2	11	8·7
Valencia	98	32·0	7	5·6
Aragon	23	7·5	5	4·0
Murcia–Albacete	9	2·9	7	5·6
Andalusia	25	8·2	39	31·0
Extremadura, Castile, Leon	22	7·2	56	44·4
Catalonia and Navarre	3	1·0	1	0·8
	306		126	
Unplaced	61		32	

A full analysis of the jurisdictional distribution of crime might make it possible to test the conflicting claims of contemporaries—who, generally speaking, were convinced that life in areas of private jurisdiction offered better terms than under the Crown and who complained that the royal domain was being denuded by

---

[1] Ibid. p. 232, quoting from *El coloquio de los perros*.

[2] Lapeyre, *Géographie*, p. 130. If a proportion of the unlocated *moriscos* is added, the rate rises to one to 79.

[3] Braudel, op. cit. p. 589; Lapeyre, *Géographie*, pp. 123–4, 126, 130.

[4] See Arco, 'La ínfima levadura social', pp. 246–57, on Cervantes's attitude to gypsies.

a steady stream of migrants moving into the protection of seigniorial jurisdictions to escape the unrelieved demands of every royal commissary, recruiting captain, and tax collector[1]—and many modern writers who see evidence rather of a general desire to remain within the jurisdiction of the Crown.[2] Unfortunately, sufficient geographical studies of lordship do not exist. It has been possible to analyse the jurisdictional incidence of crime only within the 569 settlements of New Castile that Noël Salomon has described in *La campagne de Nouvelle Castille*.[3] The survey is confined to one contiguous and fairly homogeneous area composed largely of the present provinces of Madrid, Guadalajara, Cuenca, Ciudad Real, and Toledo, and no general conclusions valid for other parts of the monarchy can be drawn from it; but as an area containing one-tenth of the total population of the kingdom of Castile it has considerable value in its own right.

	Towns	(a) Population in vecinos	Pop. %	(b) Forzados	F. %	(a/b)
Royal	178	34,111	24·8	62	25·8	550
Ecclesiastical	68	13,927	10·1	22	9·2	633
Military orders	96	42,546	30·9	99	41·3	430
Lords	227	46,828	34·1	57	23·8	822
	569	137,412		240		

Royal towns had a crime-rate 51 per cent higher than that of seigniorial towns and marginally higher (5 per cent) than that of all other towns combined. However, the sentencing of criminals to the galleys in areas of seigniorial jurisdiction was probably inhibited by the reluctance of the lords to pay the cost of transporting them from their localities to the prisons of the royal *chancillerías*,[4] and by the inability of the ordinary justices of the Crown to enter private jurisdictions.[5] The results are therefore not entirely conclusive, but they do give some support to the unfavourable comparison between royal and seigniorial towns. The high crime-rate in towns of the Military Orders is interesting in tending to substantiate the complaints of Luis de Ortiz, in 1558, that the new owners of estates of the Orders being sold by the king were turning the land over to pasture and bringing about considerable depopulation.[6]

As writers and novelists pointed out three and a half centuries ago, crime in Castile was overwhelmingly urban. Nowhere outside the southern coast does the rural crime-rate come near to approaching the level of all but two of the 49 cities. A man born in a town of 10,000 people or more was four times more likely to end up on the galleys than a countryman.[7] Information available on the occupations of 223 of the Spanish *forzados* also indicates that crime was very markedly

1 See the complaints of Toledo, 7 June 1578—A.G.S. Consejo y Juntas de Hacienda, leg. 125; Cadiz, about 15 March 1584—A.G.S. Guerra Antigua, leg. 172, fo. 152; and Tripiana (Burgos), 1585—Guerra Antigua, leg. 173, fo. 45.
2 *Historia social y económica*, III, 70; Salomon, op. cit. p. 212.   3 Ibid.; see the tables on p. 204.
4 Guilarte, op. cit. p. 133.
5 See Luis del Marmol Carvajal, *Historia del rebelión y castigo de los moriscos del reino de Granada*, Biblioteca de Autores Españoles, XXI (Madrid, 1946), 160. I owe this reference to Prof. K. Garrad.
6 Alvarez, op. cit. p. 450.
7 The 49 towns of 2,000 *vecinos* and more had a total population of 212,446 and 2,007 *forzados*—a rate of one to 106 *vecinos*. The remaining 1,393,335 *vecinos* had 3,393 of the 5,400 Spanish *forzados*—a rate of one to 411.

a factor of urbanization. At a time when some 80 per cent or more of the population must have been peasant, no more than between one-third and two-fifths of these *forzados* were directly employed in agriculture. On the other hand, criminals were a much more prosaic group than the novelists portrayed. At least three-quarters of them were tradesmen, artisans, or peasants. The typical *pícaro*-prone classes of literature—students, poets, actors, soldiers, barbers, innkeepers, muleteers, cooks, lackeys, public porters, etc.[1]—made up only 6 or 7 per cent of the sample (Table 5). There were also on the galleys 10 dons or sons of dons, 8 graduates or sons of doctors and graduates, 1 son of a captain, and 17 friars. As personal titles were unlikely to have been omitted, this probably represents virtually all men of this kind on the galleys at this time.

Table 5. *The Occupational Structure of Crime*

Artisans and small tradesmen						
lime-burner	2		gunpowder-maker	1	b/f [6]	
stone-cutter	3		glazier	1		
mason	6		potter	1		
brick-maker	1		jar-maker	1		
tile-maker	2		gilt-decorator	1		
carpenter	4		butcher	1		
Building trades	—	18	pastrycook	2		
			Miscellaneous	—	14	
wool-carder	4		Total artisans and small tradesmen	—		98
weaver	6					
cloth-weaver	1		Agricultural workers			
cloth-shearer	1		husbandman	50		
velvet-weaver	4		market-gardener	8		
satin-weaver	1		chicken-dealer	1		
silk-drawer	1		shepherd	4		
silk-spinner	1			—		63
silk-thrower	1		Unskilled			
linen-scutcher	1		labourer	29		
dyer	2		public porter	1		
Textile industry	—	23	charcoal-burner	1		
			water-seller	1		
draper	2			—		32
tailor	14		Services			
doublet-maker	4		cook	1		
hosier	3		coachman	2		
shoemaker	9		groom	1		
sandal-maker	2			—		4
Clothing trades	—	34	Others			
			muleteer	3		
smith	4		fisherman	3		
pin-maker	1		sailor	5		
bell-founder	1		soldier	3		
sword-maker	2		innkeeper	1		
shovel-maker	1		miller	2		
Metal trades	—	9	barber	2		
			bookseller	1		
chandler	1		cleric	1		
cordwainer	1		clerk	3		
candle-maker	1		notary	1		
soap-maker	2		fencing master	1		
wheelwright	1			—		26
	c/f [6]		Total			223

[1] Arco, 'La crítica social en Cervantes', op. cit. pp. 314, 316–18.

Of the rural environments, established pastoral areas were not normally breeding grounds of crime. Leon and Soria were both among the least delinquent of provinces. If a generalization is possible, it is that crime is most prominent where man has lost the security of a stable and personal relationship with the soil, in Galicia where everybody had so little land that by most it was best abandoned, or in Andalusia where very few had any land at all. Guadalajara, where the landless or almost landless labourer was never numerous, had one of the lowest crime-rates in Spain. Those seventeenth-century reformers who urged the fostering of the smallholder may well have had such considerations in mind.[1]

VI

In general terms, the pattern of crime distribution confirms a picture of Spanish social and economic development suggested by other sources. Within the kingdom of Castile the areas of highest instability are to be found in the extreme north and the extreme south. It is a pattern consistent with a view of Old Castile as an area in decline, its commercial network disrupted, its arable land contracting, its population falling, maybe as a result of substantial migration to the south, and with a view of Andalusia as the melting-pot into which too much was being poured. It was Andalusia that was probably the goal of many of those who drifted down from the more northerly parts of Spain, but it was a parasitical rather than a productive influx—one has only to remember the difficulty with which Granada was being resettled to be aware of that. The immigrants came not to Granada but to Seville, the "Castilian Babylon",[2] the clearing-house for the Indies, the waiting-room for all the unfulfilled hopes of the hopeless. This was the "via picaresca" along which a Diego de Carriazo would travel, from Burgos to Madrid to Toledo to Seville, the capital, and maybe to Zahara, the Mecca of the picaresque world.[3] In contrast, the centre of Castile was nearing an equilibrium. Population was still rising, but rising with the diminishing momentum of an impetus that was no longer vital.[4] It was an ageing but not yet a disintegrating society. The galleys do not show the high rate of delinquency among the country-born population that could be expected if the crime-prone, doss-house areas of the larger towns were being flooded by displaced and disorientated peasants. The low incidence of crime outside the great cities bears witness to the continuing vitality of peasant agriculture in New Castile,[5] and warns against a too early generalization of the economic and social collapse of Spain north of the Douro. What rural emigration there was must have been a gentle process which the cities were, by and large, able to accommodate. It was the pause before the great demographic collapse of the following century.

A final point may be noted. The centrifugality of crime is yet another striking confirmation of the fundamental dualism of Spanish history, the bitter dialogue between Castile and the outlying provinces of the monarchy. In the two generations after 1589 the peripheries were in an almost constant ferment. It was successively Aragon, Valencia, Biscay, Catalonia, and Andalusia that were seen to pose the most serious threats to the authority of Madrid and the integrity of the

[1] *Historia social y económica*, III, 274.
[2] Luis Vélez de Guevara, *Más para el Rey que la sangre*, reference in Deleito y Piñuela, op. cit. p. 192.
[3] Defourneaux, op. cit. p. 261.   [4] Salomon, op. cit. p. 48.   [5] Ibid. pp. 135, 184.

monarchy. Castile remained passive, earning for itself a reputation among political commentators for unswerving loyalty and obedience.[1] What disturbances there were in Castile were urban phenomena associated particularly with the great delinquent cities, Madrid, Toledo, Valladolid.[2] The dichotomy between the endemic lawlessness of the cities and the law-abidingness of the countryside may help to explain both the recurring role of the cities in political opposition and the failure of that opposition ever to attract the widespread support necessary to make it effective. We do not know how persistent was the pattern of lawlessness that prevailed in 1586–9, but it may well be that the varying responses to governmental pressure in the seventeenth century are only to be fully understood within the context of the more permanent attitudes of society as a whole towards the bonds of law and order that held together the Spanish state. In a very approximate sense, then, the structure of crime under Philip II can be seen as a sociological paradigm of political revolution under Philip IV. It reflects a pattern of tensions that has continued to be one of the main determinants of Spanish history.

These observations are hardly more than an indication of possibilities. Further research must certainly modify provincial details as well as fill in the long-term trends, but, until more is known about regional patterns of land tenure and exploitation, family structure, social customs and standards of living, population movements and opportunities off the land in service and industry, about the class structure of urban areas, the concentration of poverty, the effectiveness of victualling policies and social-welfare organizations, or about the growth of deprivation consciousness and popular attitudes towards life and property, ease and toil, ostentation and indigence, and particularly the strength of the restraints, both moral and physical, of the law and of the Church, there can be little hope of adequately integrating delinquency into the full complexity of the social and economic order. Nevertheless, one can only regret that the quantitative study of historical crime, so central to an understanding of the cohesion and stability of past society, has been so long neglected. The recent indications that the beginnings of this work are at last being undertaken[3] are a welcome recognition of its relevance to an age preoccupied, no less than the sixteenth century, with a problem of delinquency that it can neither understand nor control.

The Flinders University of South Australia

---

[1] For example, the mid-seventeenth-century "Stato della Monarchia de Spagna sotto il governo del Confessore della Regina. Dialogo fra Don Giuseppe Villalpando e Don Alonso de Salamanca".—B.M. Add. MS 8703, fos. 28–42, especially fo. 41v.

[2] For example, 'Cartas de Jesuitas', *Memorial Histórico Español* (Madrid, 1861), XIII, 81; XIV, 431, 458.

[3] In addition to references already made in this article, see F. Billacois, 'Pour une enquête sur la criminalité dans la France d'Ancient Régime', *Annales E.S.C.* XXII (1967), 340–7; Yves-Marie Bercé, 'Aspects de la criminalité au XVIIe siècle', *Revue Historique*, CCXXXIX (1968), 33–42, and the titles noted there.

XII

THE CONCEJO ABIERTO OF ALFARO IN 1602
The struggle for local democracy in seventeenth-century Castile

A fundamental change in the organization of municipal government took place in Castile in the middle of the fourteenth century when Alfonso XI suppressed the *concejos* (town councils) in a number of the most important Castilian cities and replaced them with corporations composed of officers appointed by the Crown for life (*regimientos perpetuos*). As a result the government of the great municipalities became increasingly oligarchic and irresponsible, and the old medieval representative forms increasingly attenuated. With the sale of *regimientos* under the Habsburgs, the annually elected *concejos* disappeared from the majority of small towns and villages as well. Nevertheless, the ancient democracy of the general assembly (*concejo abierto*) of all citizens assembled at the sound of the bell was never suppressed, and *concejos abiertos* met from time to time even in the sixteenth and seventeenth centuries.[1] Historians have generally regarded these as serving rather to provide popular ratification and support for the actions of their local ruling groups in times of difficulty than to act as a form of opposition or as a restraint on their rulers.[2] That this often was not the case and that a kind of local democracy, if occasional rather than regular, still remained alive in the seventeenth century is demonstrated by the *concejo abierto* which took place in the town of Alfaro in June 1602. By chance, because the corporation of *regidores* (*ayuntamiento*) appealed against

---

[1] There is information concerning other *concejos abiertos* in the district in Pedro Gutiérrez y Achútegui, 'Historia de la Muy Noble, Antigua y Leal Ciudad de Calahorra', *Berceo* XII (1957), p.473 (1616), XIII (1958), p.82 (1645); see also Pedro Sanz Abad, *Historia de Aranda de Duero* (Aranda, 1975), p.226 (1650).

[2] For example, Bartolomé Bennassar, *Recherches sur les grandes épidémies dans le nord de l'Espagne à la fin du XVIe siècle* (Paris, 1969), pp.25, 59.

the decision of the citizen body to the Royal Council in Valladolid, a virtually complete account of the way a *concejo abierto* was conducted has been preserved in the documents of the Archivo General de Simancas. Besides being the most fully documented example of which I am aware, the issue with which it was concerned was also one of crucial importance for the history of the political and economic government of the Castilian towns, namely whether or not to continue with the regime of the *regimiento perpetuo*.[3]

One of the fiscal devices most commonly employed by Charles V and Philip II was the sale of newly created municipal offices and the transformation of annually-elected councils into permanent corporations of transmissible offices (*renunciables*) which were bought from the king and then in turn resold by the purchasers, or passed on to relatives and heirs by renunciation (*renunciación*). At the same time, the right to suppress these newly-created corporations and to restore the previous council in its traditional form was also sold. When these sales began on a general basis in 1543, Alfaro, which with some 5,000 inhabitants was the second largest town in the ancient province of Soria,[4] still retained its council of annually-elected councillors. In that year the old council was suppressed, and seven permanent councillorships were created and put up for sale; another was sold in 1549 for 250 ducats,[5] and further offices were created in subsequent years. By 1581 Alfaro had some twelve

---

[3] A[rchivo] G[eneral de] S[imancas], Cámara de Castilla, Serie XII: Oficios, legajo 1 (Agreda), 'Diligencias echas por cedula Real por Marcos de Horobio teniente de Coregidor de la villa de Agreda sobre el consumo de los Regimientos y otros oficios de la Villa de Alfaro. Año IUdcii. Escrivano Juan Frayle de la Cal', and on the envelope, 'La villa de Alfaro ssobre el consumo de rreg [torn] de aquella V^a S° Peñarrieta en 30 de Julio de 1602 Al Licen^do Morales autos'; sewn bundle of 76 folios.

[4] I have no information for 1543. In 1591 the population of Alfaro was 1,207 *vecinos*, some 6,000 people, after half a century of growth. Only Soria, with 1,279 *vecinos*, had a larger population in 1591.

[5] AGS Consejo y Juntas de Hacienda, leg. 25 (antiguo 38), f.153, 'Copia del memorial que fué con la consulta sobre los oficios que se an de acrescentar (1549). Los oficios que paresce que se podran acrescentar en otros pueblos principales del rreyno donde heran añales que se hizieron de por vida'.
AGS Consejo y Juntas de Hacienda, leg. 23 (antiguo 35), f.226, 'relación de las veinticuatrías, regimientos y juraderías que no se han vendido en el Reino hasta 14 de mayo 1567 de los que Su Majestad ha mandado acrescentar en el'.

3   THE CONCEJO ABIERTO OF ALFARO IN 1602

offices of *regidor* in existence. Then, as a result of a new general increase (*crecimiento general*) proposed in 1581, eight more *regimientos* were put up for sale in the last sixteen years of the century. In 1584, four were sold for 500 ducats each, and another at a lower price to replace an office which had fallen vacant; another was sold in 1595, and two more in 1600, all three for 600 ducats a piece.[6] In 1602 the *ayuntamiento* of Alfaro consisted of the royal justice, the *alcalde mayor* Don Baltasar de Medrano; the hereditary municipal standard-bearer (*alférez mayor perpetuo*), Valerio Saez, who had bought his office around 1575 for 700 ducats from Don Pedro de Salazar; the treasurer (*depositario general*) whose name I do not know — the office was usually granted for two lives; eighteen transmissible offices of *regidor* for life (*regidor de por vida renunciable*), held by Don Diego de Frías, Gómez de Frías, Don Francisco and Don Ambrosio Pérez de Baraíz, Pedro and Gerónimo de los Rios, Francisco Valdero de Puelles, Pedro de Grávalos, Gerónimo de Ablitas Moreda, Martín and Juan del Pueyo, Alonso Pérez de Araciel, Don Fernando Ezquerra, Melchor, García and Pedro Vallés, Ximén Ximénez Valdés, and Baltasar Saenz de Ezcari. In addition, there were twelve annually elected *diputados* with a voice and a vote in the town council, six nobles (*hidalgos*) and six commoners (*labradores*), who were appointed by the six wards (*cuadrillas*) of the town. What the role of the *diputados* was in the *ayuntamiento* it is impossible to discern either from the depositions of the witnesses or from the report of the judge commissioned to carry out the *concejo abierto*. This total silence suggests that they contributed little to the defence of the general interest, and in the new regime proposed by the citizen body they were to be abolished along with the permanent councillors.

The *concejo abierto* of Alfaro began with a royal authorization (*cédula*) issued on 7 April 1602 by Cristóbal de Ipeñarrieta, the secretary of the Council of Finance, at the request of Miguel López, *vecino* (householder) and *procurador síndico general* of Alfaro (a sort

---

[6] AGS Dirección General del Tesoro, Inventario 24, leg. 322, under 'Logroño y otros lugares': *regimientos* sold in 1584 to Rodrigo de Moreda, Diego Ruiz de Frías, Pedro de Grávalos, Diego López de Caras (?), and the *Licenciado* Martín de Moreda, in 1595 to Hernando Ezquerra, in 1600 to Don Francisco and Don Ambrosio Pérez de Baraíz; the clerkship of the *ayuntamiento* was also sold in 1584 to Hernando Ezquerra for 135,000 *maravedís*.

of public ombudsman), "in the name of all the other *vecinos*", and directed to the royal governor (*corregidor*) of nearby Agreda. The *procurador síndico* had requested the king to order the abolition of the offices of the *alférez*, *depositario* and *regidores*, and to make them once again elective and annual, in order to put a stop to the abuses being committed by the *regidores*. "With the power they have, because their offices are perpetual, the *regidores* consume the grain, vines, pastures and other grazing with their animals, and strip the woods, without any opposition. They sell their bad wines, whilst other citizens of the town are not allowed to market their much better quality wine, until the *regidores* have sold all theirs. They irrigate their own properties illegally, and commit many other misdeeds against the said citizens. As a result the poor of the town suffer greatly and the town's communal properties (*propios*) are defrauded." In return for this favour the townsmen were prepared to offer the king whatever sum would be just.

Nothing is known of the origins of this petition. However, a very similar case in Huete, a few years before, gives a clue as to what is likely to have happened.[7] A number of townsmen (110 in Huete), perhaps first assembling in secret and for their own private ends, issued their power of attorney to the *procurador síndico* and committed themselves mutually to bear their share of any costs occasioned by their suit. A petition drawn up in those terms was then seen in the Council of Finance, which was the body responsible for the sale, or suppression (*consumo*) of new offices, and whose recommendation sufficed to put in train the lawful assembling of the whole body of the town in an open meeting.

The *cédula* of 7 April 1602 ordered the *corregidor* of Agreda, or his lieutenant, to go to Alfaro and organize the assembling of all the townsmen and residents who wanted to come to the *concejo abierto*. The meeting was to be called on a holiday, at the sound of the town's bells, in order to ascertain the will of the people concerning the *consumo*. The current *regidores* and their relatives, servants and friends were to be excluded from the meeting. Once the *consumo*

---

[7] AGS Consejo y Juntas de Hacienda, leg. 254 (antiguo 359), no fol: petition of the city of Huete in the Council of Finance, remitted by the President, the marquis of Poza, 2 Aug. 1596; and petition of the *procurador síndico* and *vecinos* of Huete, 16 Sept. 1596.

5   THE CONCEJO ABIERTO OF ALFARO IN 1602

had been approved by the individual votes of those present, the judge was to see that the townsmen issued full powers before the end of the meeting mortgaging the *bienes propios* and revenues of the town to the payment of the cost of the *consumo*. However, the decision of the *concejo abierto* was not in itself conclusive. The judge was also to inform himself independently of the true facts, and the remedy that was best in the common interest. He was also to enquire into the resources available to the town to pay compensation to the *regidores* and for the 'service' offered to the king, and how the sums required could be raised. All of this he was to report to the Crown.

On 22 June, the *procurador síndico*, López, presented the royal *cédula* to the *corregidor* of Agreda, the Licenciado Maldonado, and demanded his compliance. The *corregidor* thereupon deputed Marcos de Horobio, *regidor perpetuo* and *depositario general* of Agreda, his lieutenant, to go in his stead to Alfaro to carry out the royal commission. The next day, Horobio appointed as his bailiff the constable (*alguacil*) of Agreda, Francisco de Tormes, and as his notary the public notary and clerk of the council of Agreda, Juan Frayle de la Cal, men who could be thought to be impartial and above suspicion.

Horobio and his officers arrived in Alfaro the same day. There he presented his commission to the *alcalde mayor*, Medrano, and asked for his full support and assistance in carrying it out. The next morning he began his task with the publication of three decrees. First of all he ordered a proclamation that all the townsmen should go to the church of San Miguel de Arriba at one in the afternoon in order to confer on the matters specified in the royal *cédula*; then he ordered that neither the *regidores*, nor their relatives, servants or friends should attend the meeting, on pain of a fine of 50,000 *maravedís*, expulsion from the assembly and loss of their right to vote; and finally, he ordered that no one should try to persuade any other townsman either to go to or to abstain from going to the meeting, or from saying freely what he thought was best for the service of God, the king and the "pro y bien de la república". He threatened any potential instigator of trouble or disturbance with a similar fine and condign punishment.

During the course of the morning, these proclamations were read at the beat of the drum by the town-crier, Domingo Franco, who was accompanied by the notary of the commission, recording officially everything that was done. They went first to the main square, and then to a street where a number of streets met in a small square, and then to a place near some houses called the Indian's, and then to another place called the Plonponilla district, and after that to the districts called the Plazuela de Garcia Vallés, the Puerta Santistebán, the Puebla, and the Puerta Tudela ward; everywhere there were many people around.

Despite the judge's prohibition, a certain amount of politicking did take place in the town. Small groups congregated in the squares discussing the matter and debating in particular the problem of how they were to pay the costs of what was proposed, or asking each other if they were going to go to the meeting that afternoon. It also seems that there were some attempts on the part of the *regidores* to influence the outcome of the vote by spreading misinformation hostile to the *consumo*. The *procurador síndico* wasted no time in laying complaints before the judge against certain individuals. In particular he accused one Pedro Marín (or Martín) of "violently and against the tenor of the royal *cédula* and the public proclamation, going about telling the townsmen that they should not vote to abolish the *regimientos* because if they did so they would have to pay for them, and of saying other evil and dishonest things." Juan de Acereda, Francisco Ximénez, Miguel de Rada and García Vallés de la Parra all testified that while they were in the town square that morning with a group of other townsmen discussing how the buying out of the *regimientos* could be financed, Pedro Marín had said to them that if the rentable properties of the town were insufficient, those who voted in favour of the abolition of the *regimientos* would have to bear the cost themselves. García Vallés and Francisco Ximénez had replied that it was not true, and "that as long as they had not given their written authority (*poder*) they were not obligated." In consequence of this information, and perhaps rather "to avoid trouble and disorder and anything that might ensue thereafter" than because Pedro Marín had exceeded the normal bounds of politicking, the judge ordered him arrested and put in the town gaol. The bailiff Tormes carried out the order and deposited him in the custody of the gaoler, Melchor de Soria.

But Pedro Marín was not the only one whom the *procurador síndico* had to silence before opposition to the *consumo* grew too strong. Another witness, Juan Nabarro, deposed to the judge "that being in the church of San Miguel, where many of the men of the town were gathering to see whether the *regimientos* were to be suppressed or not, Francisco García de la Cantosa arrived and said that everyone should watch what he did, because if today they abolished the *regimientos* the place would go to hell and would be ruined for ever without remedy, as it would cost over twenty thousand ducats, and the town had nothing to pay it with, and that would cause great disturbance." Yet another witness, Juan Gadea, said that, "that same day, while he was going along a street, he met another resident of the town, Roque de Munilla, and said to him, 'Señor, let's go to the meeting, and get rid of the *regimientos.*' Roque de Munilla replied that they should stay away from it, because if they abolished them the charge would be put on the subsidy (*servicio*), and that was all."

As it was now near the time for the meeting, the judge did not arrest anyone else but, fearing that "some townsmen might give cause for a breach of the peace or a disturbance, because of the differences of view and opinion," sought to organize a procedure for speaking and voting, "which would not give rise to rowing, shouting, or disputes, but would leave everyone free to express his opinion and to discuss whether or not the *regimientos* and other offices should be suppressed, and if they were to be abolished what measures should be applied to pay for them so that least harm was done to the town, without their turning to any other business or crossing words with each other." An edict to that effect, setting a fine for its breach of 20,000 *maravedís* for the Crown, to be enforced with full rigour, was published by Horobio, and the town crier was sent to the church of San Miguel de Arriba to ring the great bell to summon all the townsmen to the *concejo abierto.* The bell having rung for a good while, 274 persons gathered at the church.[8] That was rather less than one-quarter of the 1,207 heads of families listed in the town in the 1591 census. It was a rather small proportion, far smaller than the 900 townsmen present in a similar *concejo abierto* held in

---

[8] In his report the judge wrote of up to 290 people in the meeting, but there are only 274 names listed in the notarized account.

Logroño in 1595, for example,[9] and difficult to explain except on account of the rapidity with which Horobio had proceeded,[10] or on the assumption that many people kept away for fear of finding themselves obliged to contribute to the costs of the *consumo*.

With the townsmen assembled, the notary stood on a bench and in a loud voice, so that everybody could hear, read out the royal *cédula*. The judge then having ordered that they should discuss and confer together, in the words of the notarial record "the question whether or not it was best to consume the said *regimientos* was considered by all the people present in the said *concejo abierto*, and after discussing it, each then gave his opinion and voted on it in the following manner." The first vote was that of Don Pedro de Salazar, and it was his which was the dominant voice in the decision reached in the meeting. He insisted that it was in the service both of God and the king that the twenty existing offices and the twelve *diputados* should be abolished, "because, as there are so many in the town council, there is much disagreement amongst them and they form factions, and they do not govern as they should and as their office requires. Furthermore, the said *regidores* who have sheep and cattle graze them by use of force on protected pastures, both those set aside for the butchers and those for the plough oxen, and on vineyards, gardens and irrigated lands, regardless of the will of the owners. They also sell their poor quality wines and prevent other townsmen who have better wine from selling theirs. The same *regidores*, through their servants and other persons sent on their orders, are destroying the oak woods by felling and cutting down the trees throughout the year, and the other townsmen are prevented from collecting the brushwood. When water is needed for irrigation within the town's boundaries, the *regidores* impose heavy penalties for its regulation, but then irrigate their own properties, diverting the water from those who by rights should have it. Moreover, some of the said

---

[9] There were 933 *vecinos* in Logroño in 1591; of the 900 present at the meeting, 881 voted for the abolition of the *regimientos perpetuos*, and 19 against, Archivo Municpal de Logroño, Libro de Actas 8, *ayuntamiento* of 7 Aug. 1596.

[10] That there was insufficient publicity is suggested by the testimony of Francisco Ximénez, a witness presented by the *procurador síndico* against Pedro Marín, who said, "he knows there has been some proclamation, but he does not know what the words were that were spoken."

regidores, to the detriment of the royal revenues, collusively appoint themselves and others who are not nobles (*hidalgos*) but commoners (*labradores*) to noble offices ('officios de yjosdalgo'). When they are subjected to judicial investigation (*residencia*), all their costs and fines are paid out of the town's properties and the grain deposit. In the fish shops, they have all the best sardines and fish and eels set aside for themselves, all topped and tailed. If any of their animals die they have them sent to be sold in the butchers, so that the poor get bad meat, but the meat they themselves are given has to be the best in the butcher's and all boned. If day-labourers do not want to work on their estates they threaten them with higher tax assessments, salt quotas and soldiers billeted on them, and many times have carried that threat out, for which reason, out of fear the labourers drop their own work to go to work for the *regidores*. It was resolved by His Majesty that the offal from the butchers was to be distributed among the poor and that the *regidores* were not to take it for themselves and their servants, they nonetheless do so. All of which is to the greatest detriment of the town and its people, and as the justices are on friendly terms with the *regidores*, it is not possible to remedy it and it is the cause of enormous harm. Thus the said offices should be consumed and abolished."

Nearly two-hundred of the townsmen present followed Don Pedro in his view without further ado, "because", as Juan de Arieta said, "it is the truth." Others who had personal experience of how the town had been governed confirmed what Salazar had asserted. Miguel de Lobera, who had been public notary for thirty years and for many years *diputado* on the town council, said, "he knows the abolition to be useful and beneficial to the good service of God and His Majesty." Martín Romero was of the opinion "that they should be abolished, and that all the pastures should be rented out, because yesterday he went to sell a good wine and they knocked a *maravedí* off the price of every measure (*azumbre*), and as the duty *regidor* for the week was also selling his own, he was not allowed to sell." Juan Garcés de los Fayos said, "they should be abolished for the reasons given by Don Pedro, and because when he was *regidor del campo*, a water channel was cut and the cost apportioned, but none of the *regidores* wanted to pay." Dr Caballero de Abendaño, canon of the collegiate church of the town, added to the reasons adduced by Don Pedro de Salazar, "that although the *regimiento* of the town was ordered by the courts to participate corporately in both public and votive processions, as is the custom, none of them does so, but the *alcaldes mayores* watch from their windows, or remain in the *plazas*, causing much comment and scandal, and the *alcalde mayor* holds court while the processions are going on." The parish priest, Jorge Vallés, in a lengthy vote, repeated the most important points made by Salazar about the consumption by the *regidores'* sheep and cattle of the common meadows and pastures, and even of the wheat and fruit-trees in private enclosures, their abuse of irrigation, the appointment of "personas llanas labradores" (common husbandmen), relatives, servants and clients of theirs, to *hidalgo* offices, and the threats to impose soldiers or onerous offices by which they bent the supervisors of pastures, the collectors of strays, and simple farmers and husbandmen to their wills. Others needed fewer words: "they should be abolished thirty-times over" (Francisco de Frías); "they should be abolished sixty-times over" (Nicolás Pérez); "they should have been abolished twenty years ago" (Juan Polo); Juan Garrido, Juan de Lacarra and others thought it was now time to throw out the *regidores* "on account of the great disorder there is in this town" (Miguel Gil Quartero), "because of the great damage they do" (Juan de Cascajares), "for the souls of the *regidores*" (Pedro Ximénez del Portillo), "for the good of the *regidores'* souls" (Gandioso Ximénez), "because they lord it over the place" (Miguel Sánchez), "because they are absolute rulers" (Domingo Serrano), "because one king and one law are enough" (Martín de Oyz). The public condemnation of the government of the town was all but total. No less than 268 of the votes given agreed with the abolition of the *regimientos*. Apart from one who said, somewhat Delphically, that they should be abolished "if God will be best served, and if not, not" (Esteban de Altamira), in the end only four voices spoke out against the abolition. Juan de Guaras Villalba and Alonso de Pérez opposed it because it would interrupt the lawsuit the *regidores* were conducting against some of the neighbouring towns, and Juan Ximénez and another Alonso de Pérez "because it makes more sense to pay off the town's debts and the obligations (*censos*) it owes to Don Diego de Castejón than to spend money on the *regimientos*." One has to remember, however, that the most active supporters of the *regidores* had been excluded from the meeting.

11   THE CONCEJO ABIERTO OF ALFARO IN 1602

It is clear that what gave most cause for concern was the question of where the necessary money was to come from, and it was on this question that the opposition to abolition concentrated. No concrete figure had been discussed in the meeting, but everybody was aware that the total value of the offices for which the *regidores* would have to be compensated came to 10 or 11,000 ducats, and that the general rule was that the king was paid three times that for the favour of revoking the offices and restoring the elective *concejo*. Agreement was finally to be reached with the Royal Treasury on a price of 14,480 ducats, bringing the total that Alfaro had to pay out to 25,000 ducats.

The supporters of the *regidores* tried to weaken popular support for abolition by highlighting the financial difficulties and claiming that the burden would fall exclusively on those who had voted for the measure, and not on those who were opposed to it. The next day, the 25th of June, Pedro Marín, who as we have seen had been excluded from the *concejo abierto*, went before the judge, "on my own behalf and in the name of all those who want to adhere to my position", to contradict judicially that the *regimientos* be consumed at the cost of the town or its properties. He declared that the town's revenues were mortgaged for more than 13,000 ducats, on which interest of nearly 650 ducats a year was being paid to Don Diego de Castejón, resident of Agreda, quite apart from the costs of lawsuits and the subsidy (*servicio ordinario y extraordinario*), also paid from communal revenues. As a result the revenues were so encumbered that more than sixty claims to nobility (*pleitos de hidalguía*) which the council was challenging in the courts were suspended for lack of money with which to pursue them. If they sold the pastures to pay for abolition, Marín said, "the townsmen would be deprived of their livelihoods and the husbandmen and the needy would be completely ruined"; with the distress of agriculture, even the church would be brought to "total perdition and ruin", because there was no trade in Alfaro other than farming. He also opposed putting taxes on food because it would be at the expense of the needy and the labouring poor who made up the greater part, if not almost the entirety, of the population. If the *regimientos* were to be consumed, the cost, he insisted, should be borne only by those who had given their proxies, and not met from communal revenues.

The steward (*mayordomo*) of the town's revenues, Martín Ruiz, in a sworn statement before the judge, in which he asserted his disinterest and dispassion and lack of any family connection with any of the *regidores*, also believed that the communal properties could not bear such a cost. A further twenty-seven of the men who had voted in favour of abolishing the *regimientos* in the open meeting also opposed any additional charge on or mortgaging of the revenues. Nevertheless, the meeting by the agreement of 268 of those present ended by issuing full powers to seven proctors (Don Pedro de Salazar, Gerónimo Vallés, Juan de Frías, Juan Nabarro, García Ximénez, Hernando de Alfaro and Miguel López) to go to treat with the king and his councils in Valladolid over the abolition and "to serve His Majesty with whatever sum they should think right." They were given a free hand to borrow whatever was necessary by mortgaging the town's properties, and to ask for authority to levy taxes or to rent out communal lands to cover the interest and repay the capital of the loan.

The financial situation of the town faced with this new obligation was the principal consideration in the royal decision, and once the meeting was concluded the judge began his own private inquiry, both to assure himself that the popular will was really in the public good and to find out what form of government should replace that of the permanent *regidores*, and how the service to the king and the compensation for the *regidores* was to be paid. The judge began immediately on 25 June by calling for a transcript of the municipal accounts for the two preceding years. On the 25th, 26th and 27th he listened to the sworn evidence of thirteen of the town's most trustworthy and best informed residents, namely, the acting steward of the town's properties, Martín Ruiz; an ex-steward, Pascual de Briones; the public notary, Diego Rodríguez; the canon of the church of Alfaro, Francisco Acereda; another cleric, Francisco Malimbres; two of the *regidores* of the countryside (*regidores del campo*), Hernando de Alfaro and Miguel de Rada; the canon Lope de Frías; the prebendary of the collegiate church (*magistral*), the Licenciado Martínez; Juan Aznar, a familiar of the Inquisition; Vicente Vallés; the Licenciado Francisco Garcés de los Fayos; and Juan Garcés de los Fayos. The last seven were all related or connected more or less closely with one or more of the existing *regidores*. Of these thirteen, only one, the steward Martín Ruiz, denounced by the *procurador síndico* for being "on the side of the *regidores*", did not agree that the *regimientos* should be suppressed. The others, including the seven relatives of the *regidores*, all believed it was essential for the good government of the town and the welfare of the poor that the permanent *regidores* should be deprived of the power they had to oppress and lord it over the poor people of the town, and that the town council should be reduced to only eight or twelve annual offices, half commoners, half nobles, picked by lot from a list of candidates chosen either by the wards, or by an electoral college, or by the investigating judge. The fiscal measures they proposed to finance the abolition with the least harm to the poor were: 1) a series of taxes on meat, fish and eel, whale oil (hitherto exempt from the royal *Millones* tax), and wood from the Yerga hills; 2) the renting out of the right to graze during the winter all the vineyards, orchards and privately-owned fields not enclosed for pasture, as well as the Tranbarria area, and to fence off parts of the woods. They estimated that these measures would produce some 2,000 ducats a year on top of the 3,200 ducats of existing revenues which were already earmarked in their entirety for other expenses.

On the basis of the near unanimous view of these witnesses, as well as everything else he had seen and heard, Horobio was fully convinced of the justice of the representation made by the *procurador síndico* in the town's name, and that it was right that the permanent offices should be suppressed. On his return to Agreda on the 9th July, he drew up his official recommendation to the king in which he endorsed everything of substance in the proposals put forward by Don Pedro de Salazar and the twelve others.

Faced with the imminent threat of losing their offices, the *regidores* split. Some freely threw in their lot with the popular party, and four days after the 24th of June meeting, the *ayuntamiento* with eight of the *regidores* present made an agruement with the proctors of the town to accept the decision of the meeting and to associate themselves with the petition to the king that he order the offices consumed. It may be, however, that this was no more than a tactical retreat. Once the judge had left, a group of nine *regidores*, including six of those who had voted for the agreement of 28th June, returned to the fight and issued powers to Don Fernando Ezquerra to go to Valladolid to oppose the abolition in the royal courts (12 July 1602). All in vain. The 14,800 ducats offered by the meeting was enough to achieve a favourable outcome for the town. The annually elected town council was restored on the basis of the financial measures proposed and with the solemn promise of the king that never again at any time would he create and sell more *regimientos* in Alfaro. That promise was to last less than thirty years.

The events in Alfaro in June and July 1602 reveal not only a confrontation between the populace and their *regidores*, but also a political and social division at the very heart of the *ayuntamiento*. There are grounds for believing that the split within the *regimiento* over the restoration of an annual council was a reflection and a continuation of the "many disputes", "conflicts", "factions" and "lack of accord" among the *regidores* to which the witnesses had referred, discords which, in the words of Juan Aznar, himself a relative of some of the *regidores*, were both bitter and had a clear social dimension: "as there are so many of them and with such different views and backgrounds (*estados*), there are often conflicts among them which lead to tumults." If this internal division is matched with the guiding elements behind the popular party, it is possible to suggest a social explanation of the politics of the town that though speculative is conformable with the existing evidence.

It is clear from his role in the *concejo abierto* that the dominant figure in the party opposed to the *regidores* was Don Pedro de Salazar, and that that party included among its leading members the other proctors deputed by the meeting to get the abolition that had been agreed on put into effect, namely, Juan de Frías Salazar, Gerónimo Vallés, Diego Alonso Barrionuevo, García Ximénez, Juan Nabarro, Hernando de Alfaro, Diego Alonso de Cornago (a relative of García Alonso de Cornago, *diputado* of the nobility), Antonio de Beamonte, the widower García Vallés, and Rodrigo Ortiz de Bobadilla. We have only a few clues as to what the motives of this group might have been. First of all, the group contains at least two ex-*regidores* currently out of power, Don Pedro de Salazar, permanent *alférez mayor* until he sold his office to Valerio Sanz somewhere around 1575, and Antonio de Beamonte, a relative without doubt of the Diego de Beamonte whose *regimiento* escheated to the Crown and was resold to Don Fernando Ezquerra in 1595. There is the possibility then that we are dealing with two families now no longer capable of maintaining themselves at the head of a society, control over which was falling into the hands of those who were able to find enough money to buy their place in government. Second, there are in the group of proctors two Vallés, members of a numerous Alfaro family which at the time had four representatives in the *ayuntamiento*, three of whom (Pedro, García and Melchor Vallés) in a petition of 26th June came out openly in favour of the abolition which had been voted by the meeting two days before. It is worth noting here that all the *regimientos* of the Vallés date from before 1584, and that none of the offices sold after that date went either to the Vallés or to any other of the most established families of the town. It is true that Diego Ruiz de Frías bought an office in 1584 and that there was a connection betwen the Frías and the Salazar, but there are two *regidores* called Frías in 1602 and I am not sure that we are dealing with one family or with two separate branches. Moreover, it seems that one of the Frías *regidores* also leant towards the popular party. Don Diego de Frías, although he did not associate himself with the petition of the Vallés, did not join the nine *regidores* who on 12th July appealed to Valladolid against the decision of the *concejo abierto*, and his brother, the canon Lope de Frías, with the two Garcés de los Fayos, also relatives of Don Diego, testified unambiguously in favour of restoring the elective council. Apart from the Vallés, the Frías and the Sáez, it is apparent that the *regidores*, especially the more recent of them, although from Alfaro, did not belong to the town in the fullest sense. Among the participants in the open meeting there was not one Los Rios, not one Pérez de Araciel, nor any Valdero, Puelles, Moreda, Ablitas, Grávalos, Ezquerra, or Baraíz, and only one Pueyo. Account must be had of the fact that the family, relatives and friends of the *regidores*, as well as the *regidores* themselves, were formally excluded from the meeting by royal decree; nevertheless, there were present at the meeting five Vallés, eight Sáez, or Sáenz, and four Frías, including the brother of the *regidor* Don Diego de Frías, who said he was a relative of other *regidores* as well. It is impossible not to believe, therefore, that the absence from the meeting of any family of eleven of the twenty *regidores*, and it needs to be stressed of seven of the eight who had bought their offices since 1584,[11] is not a reflection of their position in the town itself.

It seems, therefore, that the *concejo abierto* was the instrument of the reaction of the old families of Alfaro who used to dominate the town against the erosion of their predominance in the town council, an erosion caused both by their own abdication and by the creation of new offices bought by new men and new families. Together with this, there also seems to have been a social reaction of a somewhat complex and ambivalent nature against the new *regidores*, a reaction both by the old *hidalgos* on the one side, and by the non-noble population on the other. The *hidalgo* reaction can be seen in the complaints of Don Pedro de Salazar against the devices adopted by the *regidores* to insinuate themselves and their relatives and friends into the ranks of the nobility, a complaint implicit also in the testimony of the canon Lope de Frías ("they appoint their friends, dependants and clients to offices of honour and profit"). The plebeian reaction is expressed in the demand that the new council be composed half of officers elected by the nobility and half by the "goodfellow commoners" ("los buenos hombres pecheros"). Seen in this light, the suppression of the *regimientos* is to be interpreted as a protest against the obscuring of social origins implicit in the lack of formal class distinctions among the permanent *regidores*. What seems to have been happening was a double process by which the *regimientos* were being bought by rich commoners, hoping to further their advance into the noble estate, but also by genuine nobles, with the result that the social balance within the old council was being upset. It is worth noting that the last three offices sold in 1595 and 1600 were all held by Dons, of only four Dons in the council in 1602. However, until we have more information about the social and economic status of the *regidores*, all this can be no more than hypothesis.

Nevertheless, the *concejo abierto* of Alfaro has an importance which is not limited to the history of one town. What was happening in Alfaro was in its way typical of the whole Rioja region. The

---

[11] Namely, Grávalos, López de Caras, the two Moredas, Ezquerra, the two Pérez de Baraíz; and of those prior to 1584, two Los Ríos, Valdero de Puelles, and two del Pueyo. Pérez de Araciel, however, was descended from an Alfaro family ennobled in 1350.

17   THE CONCEJO ABIERTO OF ALFARO IN 1602

suppression of the permanent *regimientos* which took place in Alfaro in 1602, took place also in Logroño in 1596 and in Calahorra in 1603, and in all these towns the perpetual *regimientos* were again restored around 1630. This can be explained in part by the fact that the old system of annually elected councils survived in all the cities and important towns of the region well into the sixteenth century, and in some of them (Logroño, Santo Domingo, Calahorra) it was only in the 1580s that *regimientos* held for life were reestablished. At the end of the sixteenth century, therefore, there was still a living memory of elective councils which survived as an alternative polity against which to measure the abuses that were so visible in the existing municipal administration ("all of which would cease if the said *regimientos* were abolished and made annual again as they were before", Lope de Frías).

It is true that the crucial importance of the regulation of irrigation in the region, about which Alfaro was conducting lawsuits with various neighbouring towns (Cintruénigo, Arguedas, Valtierra), made the abuse of their powers over the economy of the town by the permanent *regidores* peculiarly burdensome. However, the complaints of the townsmen against the manipulation of the local economy by the *regidores* can be found repeated throughout Castile wherever the offices of *regidores* had been sold and the annual councils transformed into perpetual *regimientos*. The vote of the people of Alfaro can, therefore, serve as an example of a much more general reaction and a clear illustration of the disastrous consequences for the populace, especially in small and middling towns, of the policy pursued by the king and his councils in their interminable search for money that suppressed the democratic machinery of local government and sold the government of the towns to the powerful and self-interested. Moreover, the *concejo abierto* of Alfaro shows unequivocally what the purchase of a permanent *regimiento* could be worth. The purchasers did not pay 600 ducats (225,000 *maravedís*) in order to draw their salary of 500 *maravedís*, nor, I think, for the honour of calling themselves *regidores* of Alfaro. What they were buying was a share in the administration and judicial control of the town, and with that a free hand in the exploitation of the municipal economy. That freedom was rooted in their permanence in office and in their patronage over the forest and pasture guards, the damage adjustors, and the assessors of council charges, in their control over the use and distribution of municipal revenues, and frequently in their collusive friendship with the justice. That was something demonstrable in the case of the *alcalde* Medrano, not only because that is what the witnesses affirmed, but also because of Medrano's refusal to grant travel costs and expenses from municipal funds to the proctors appointed by the *concejo abierto* to go to Valladolid to negotiate the abolition with the king (6 July 1602). As a result the *regidores* enjoyed almost total immunity in the abuse of their power over the economic life of the town, abuses like the breach of irrigation regulations, or allowing their animals to graze the ox pastures and private olive groves and vineyards, or their monopolizing of the sale of wines, their cutting down of woodlands, their avoiding contributing to common expenses for such purposes as fountains, paving, roads, stock recapture, their defrauding of the public granary by diverting a great part of the capital borrowed at interest for the purchase of grain to their own use, or their terrorizing of the labourers and the poor to work for them on their own estates. "As there are so many *regidores* and they are so powerful and permanently in office, and have such influence with the justice, they are very much lords in the town...and hold the men of this town and the poor in thrall." Deprived of irrigation, unable to get adequate compensation for the damage done by the sheep and cattle of the *regidores*, and with their own working animals diminished by the loss of common pastures, the townsmen's holdings were falling into such decay that much of the land about was left unsown.

What all this meant to the townspeople can be inferred from the fact that the residents of Alfaro took upon themselves the payment of no less than 25,000 ducats to free themselves from their rulers. That meant a burden nearly eight times greater than the annual income of the town council, or, at an average of 230 *reales* per family, the equivalent of about 100 days of labour of an ordinary workman. For the interest and the repayment of the capital of the debt, Alfaro undertook to raise in taxes, and by the sale and renting of its properties, around 2,000 ducats a year; that sum was perhaps as much as, or little less than, the total amount the town, though

19   THE CONCEJO ABIERTO OF ALFARO IN 1602

exempt from the *alcabala*, normally paid in taxes to the royal treasury.[12] The fact that such a possibility still existed in 1602 should make us think again about the picture of a Castile crushed under the insupportable weight of the royal fisc. But neither can we ignore the fact that the ransoming of its self-government meant a very serious worsening of the financial situation of the town, and that with the sale and renting out of its meadows and communal properties that same ransom contributed as much to the erosion of common rights and usages as the evil it was intended to remedy. As a result, only twenty-seven years later, in 1629, in order to help pay a donative of 40,000 ducats to the king, Alfaro had to give its consent once again to the sale of the twenty offices with a voice and vote in the council that had been abolished in 1602.[13]

The *concejo abierto* of 1602 therefore restored to Alfaro, although only temporarily, a kind of democracy in the election of town councillors and in the formal guarantee of representation for the non-noble orders as well as for the nobility. The important thing, however, is that it shows the people of the town acting successfully and in a constitutional manner against the interests and the wishes of their governors. That such a thing was possible should be regarded as one of the most important factors contributing to the absence in Castile, by and large, of the revolts and popular disturbances which were characteristic of much of seventeenth-century European society. In Castile it was still possible for the people to take action against their governors, even though they could not do so independently. At every stage the support of the king was essential. The general meeting could not have assembled without royal authorization, or without the supervision of a royal commissioner; nor could it deal with anything except one single predetermined issue; nor could it carry out its decisions without a royal order. Once the political unity of the municipal "república" had been fractured by the creation and

---

[12] I have no direct information about Alfaro, but the taxes paid by Logroño, also an exempt city, were estimated in 1594 at 2,000 ducats a year, Biblioteca Nacional, Madrid, Ms.1749, f.351v. On the exemptions of Alfaro, see Modesto Ulloa, *La hacienda real de Castilla en el reinado de Felipe II* (Madrid, 1977), p.471, and Faustino Gil Ayuso, *Junta de Incorporaciones* (Madrid, 1934), no.389.

[13] Archivo Histórico Nacional, Consejos leg. 4429-30, año 1644, no.90, *consulta* of the Consejo de la Cámara, 17 Oct. 1644.

sale of permanent *regimientos*, the absolute monarch reappeared as the sole saviour of the people from local tyranny. Unfortunately, as with everything in the Spain of the Habsburgs, there was no salvation without a price, and that price was a very high one indeed.

DOCUMENTS

N° 1

'Al Corregidor de la Villa de Agreda o su Theniente q vaya a la Villa de Alfaro y haga juntar a concejo avierto sobre si converna consumir los officios perpetuos que ay en ella.

El Rey. Mi corregidor de la Villa de agreda o Vro lugar theniente en el dho officio. Por parte de Miguel Lopez vezino y procurador sindico general de la Villa de Alfaro en nombre de todos los demas vezinos della se me ha hecho Relacion que en ella ay veinte Regidores un Alferez y un depossitario y doçe diputados los quales con la mano q tienen por ser los officios de los dichos Regidores Perpetuos se comian con sus ganados los panes viñas y dehessas y otros sottos y talavan los montes sin Resistencia y vendian sus malos vinos haviendo entre los Vzos de la dicha Villa otros mucho mejores y no queriendo consentir los vendiesen hasta ser acavados los suyos y regando sus heredades contra Derecho y haziendo otros malos tratamientos a los dhos vezinos con lo qual los pobres de la dicha Villa eran muy vejados y molestados y los propios del concejo desfraudados = Supplicandome que para Remedio de ello mandase consumir los dhos officios de Regidores alferez y Depossitario y fuesen Añales ofreciendo me servir Por esta mrd con lo que fuesse justo. y visto en mi consejo de hazienda He tenido por vien de dar la presente por lo qual os mando que luego que con ella fueredes Requerido vays a la dha Villa de Alfaro con bara alta de mi justicia y hagais juntar a concejo avierto en dia de fiesta a campana tañida a todos los vezinos y moradores que en el se quisieren hallar presentes y estando juntos les hareys leer esta mi cedula y tratareys y confirireys con ellos cerca de lo sussodicho y si todos tienen por vien y consienten que los dhos officios se consuman, o ay alguno que lo contradiga y quien y como y por que caussa resciviendo de cada uno de por si sus voctos en el qual dho concejo no consintireys q entren los dhos Regidores alferez ni depossitario ni sus parientes criados ni allegados y los que quisieren dar poder para hazer el dho consumo y obligar los vienes propios y Rentas de la dha Villa por el prescio dello hagan antes de salir del dicho concejo, y hecho lo susso dicho ayais informacion averigueis y sepais que officios del concejo son los que al presente ay en la dha Villa y que utilidad o daño se siguira de consumirse, y proveyendose lo que asi se pide quantos officios de Regidores converna que aya añales para el buen Govierno de ella. Y otrosi averiguareys q bien propios y rentas tiene la dha Villa y que deudas y censsos estan sobre ellos cargados y haviendo effecto el consumo de los dichos officios donde se podra sacar asi lo que se ha de pagar a los dichos Regidores y demas dueños dellos como a mi por el dicho consumo y que Arbitrios se le puedan conceder para ello de que resultase menos daño y perjuicio, y de todo lo demas q sobre ello os parezca hazer la dicha ynformacion lo hagais y firmada de vro nombre signada çerrada y sellada en manera q haga fee con vro parecer de lo que en ello se deva hazer lo entregareis al dicho sindico para que lo traiga al dho mi consejo de hazienda a manos de mi infra escripto secretario para q visto en el se provea lo que convenga. fha en Valladolid a siete de Abril de Mill y seisçientos y dos años.

Yo El rey

Por mando del Rey nro Señor
Christoval de Ipeñarrieta'. (cinco rúbricas)

N° 2

Parecer de Don Pedro de Salazar en el concejo abierto de 24 de junio de 1602.

'El dho Don P° de Salazar dixo questa villa tan solamente tiene asta mill y docientos *vos* sin tener aldea ni otros lugares de jur^{on} y en ella ay veynte rregidores perpetuos y en los dos dellos estan yncorporados el off° de alferez mayor y depositario g^{ol} y doze diputados que todos estos tienen boz y boto y entran en el Ayuntamiento desta dha villa con la Just^a della y con un procurador sindico, y que conbiene al serbicio de dios y de su mag^d que los dhas oficios de rregidores alferez y depositario general y off^{os} de diputados se consuman, porque de ser tantos los que ansi entran en el dho Ayuntamiento entre ellos ay muchas discordias y se azen parzialidades y no se aze en el gobierno lo que deben y estan obligados en sus off^{os} y porque los dhos Regidores que an tenido y tienen ganados lanios y mayores con ellos se comen las yerbas bedadas asi de las dehesas de las carnizerias como de las dehesas boyales, viñas, huertas y rregadio por fuerza y contra la boluntad de los dueños, y tanbien benden sus malos binos y no los dexan bender a los otros vezinos teniendo los mejores, y de una sierra y monte que tiene de leña denzinar y rrobledad los dhos rregidores por sus criados y otras personas que ynbian los destruyen talan cortandolos pies de dho monte en todo el año y a los demas v^{os} se les denieigan el traher de las rramas de los dhos pies y que quando ay nezesidad de agua para rregar los terminos desta dha villa los dhos regidores la pone por orden con grandes penas y luego los dhos rregidores Riegan sus heredades quitando las aguas a quien de dr° les biene y perteneze, y tambien algunos de los dhos rregidores contra el Patrimonio Real se nonbran y azen nonbrar en off^{os} de yjosdalgo no siendo yjosdalgo y nonbran y azen nonbrar a otros en el dho off° de yjosdalgo siendo labradores porque disimulen con ellos y quando se les toma Residencia todas las costas y condenaciones lo pagan de los propios

y del posito y en las tiendas de pescados azen tirar y apartar para si las
mejores sardinas y pescados y congrios y les azen que se los den qui-
tadas las cabezas y colas de los congrios y demas pescados, y si se les
muere algun ganado lo azen pesar en las carnicerias y azen que todo lo
malo lo coman la gente pobre, y tambien azen que la carne les den sin
grueso y lo mejor en las carnizerias y si los jornaleros no quieren yr a
sus aciendas los amenazan de echar libros de preserias, rrepartimientos
de sal y que los echaran soldados y lo an executado y echo ansi muchas
bezes, y ansi por ello y de miedo dexan sus aciendas para yr para los dhos
Regidores, y estando por ex^a de Su Magd que los menudos de la carne
de la carnizeria sean y se rrepartan para los pobres y que no los puedan
llebar los dhos Regidores por si y por sus criados se los lleban para si,
todo lo qual es en grandisimo daño desta dha villa y vezinos della porque
las Just^{as} como tienen amystad de hordinario con los dhos Regidores es
ynposible el poder lo rremediar, y ansi es en grandisimo daño y conbiene
se rresuman y consuman los dhos oficios de rregidores diputados alferez
y depositario general, y que tan solamente ayan ocho regidores añales,
quatro de yjosdalgo y quatro labradores y el procurador sindico, con los
quales esta dha V^a y sus vezinos sera mejor gobernada, y se quitaran
todos los ynconbenientes dhos, y para el consumo de los dhos off^{os}
se podra tomar la cantidad que montare los dhos off^{os} de rregimientos
alferez y depositario general sobre los propios desta villa para que con
brebedad aya efecto el dho consumo, y para lo que ubiere de aber Su
magd porque les conzeda pribilegio para que Xamas se tornen a bender
los dhos rregimientos alferez y depositario general se podra echar en sisas
de carnes y en arrendamientos de yerbas y sacarse de deudas que se deben
a esta dha villa, y de lo que sobrare de la rrenta de los propios y
ganancia del posito y de la ganancia de las carnizerias que a abido durante an estado por administracion en esta dha villa, y pagado Su magd
de las dhas sisas que pasen adelante asta que los propios se desenpe-
ñen de lo que se cargaren y adeudaren para el dho consumo de los dhos
rregimientos alferazgo y depositario general asta que los dhos propios
enteramente queden en el ser que estan de presente, y para azer las
diligencias ante Su Magd y ante quien conbenga y obligar los propios y
rrentas y tomar sobre ellos todo el dinero que nezesario fuere conforme
a la zedula de Su Magd nonbraba por procuradores y daba poder a si
mismo y a Ger^{mo} Balles, Ju^o de Frias Salazar, Di^o Al^o Barrionuebo, y Mgl
Lopez procurador sindico, y a todos y de por si e ynsolidum y con poder
de sostituyr uno o mas procuradores y los rebocar y poner otros de nuebo
y que aya y llebe de salario de los propios e rrentas desta villa el que
fuere a azer las dhas diligencias doze rreales, y esto es su boto y parecer,
y lo firmo de su nonbre'.

N° 3

'Ynformacion.

En la villa de Agra (sic) a veynte y cinco dias del mes de Junio de mill y seiscientos y dos años, su md del dho Marcos de Horobio teniente de corregidor en la villa de Agᵃ. y juez de comision susodho para azer ynformacion sobre lo tocante a la dha rrᵃˡ zedula mᵈᵒ parezer ante si el canonigo Lope de Frias canonigo de la yglesia desta dha villa de Alfaro, el qual parescio y del fue rrecibido juramento en forma de drᵒ puesta la mano en el pecho ynberbos sazerdotes por las hordenes de San Pᵒ y San Pablo e despues de aber jurado e siendo preguntado al tenor de la dha rreal zedula dixo que sabe que en esta villa de Alfaro ay un alferez y un depositario gl y asta diez y siete o diez y ocho rregidores perpetuos los quales los usan y exerzen en el tpo questan en esta vᵃ y ansimismo sabe y tiene por muy cierto que de consumirse los dhos rregimientos alferazgo y depositario sera de mucha utilidad y probecho a esta Vᵃ y mucho serbicio a dios y a su magd por queste tᵒ de quarenta aᵒˢ a esta parte tiene mucha notᵃ de las cosas desta villa por aber sido su padre Regidor y al presente ser lo Don Diᵒ de Frias su hermano y otros que son sus deudos y por que la conserbacion desta villa pende de la conserbacion de los terminos y aguas y dehesas por ser todo ello acienda de grangerias, y en espᵃˡ en las aguas por que lo principal del trⁿᵒ desta villa es de Regadio y tiene costunbre todos los vᵒˢ que las heredades se rrieguen por su horden y como los Regidores son tantos y tan poderosos y perpetuos y tienen tanta mano con la Justᵃ que riegan muchos dellos sus heredades contra la horden dada y sin guardar la horden debida y a esta causa resulta muncho daño a los pobres desta Vᵃ porque se les pierden sus heredades y frutos por no podello regar, y porque ansimismo se comen con sus ganados las dehesas boyales donde se an de conserbar los ganados mayores de labranza de donde suzede perderse muchos ganados de labor y los labradores benir en mucha diminucion por esta falta, pendiendo el prinzipal sustento y grangeria desta villa y vᵒˢ della de la labranza, y ansi por falta de ganado y de pastos se queda mucha parte del terⁿᵒ por senbrar = Y ansimismo se comen con sus ganados las biñas y olibares y pᵃˢ questan bedadas y no son pastos comunes en grande daño y perjuicio de los vᵒˢ y por ser Regidores y nonbrar ellos las guardas y administradores no los osan prendar ni les executan las penas como debrian ansi en esto como en los Riegos de arriba = y ansimismo los apreciadores de los frutos que se comen en las heredades como son nonbrados por ellos segun es puᶜᵒ y notorio si saben que deben los daños a los Regidores no osan a preciar los dhos daños por temor de los dhos Regidores y que ansimismo es puᶜᵒ y notorio en esta villa que en el tpo que los dhos rregidores o sus parientes amigos o allegados tienen algunos binos que bender aunque sean peores que los que tengan otros vᵒˢ no los quieren dar licenᵃ para que los vendan asta que se ayan bendido los susodhos y de los dhos sus deudos amigos o allegados y que ansi mismo a oydo dezir por publico y notᵒ que si algunos vᵒˢ piden Justᵃ de los agrabios que azen los Regidores o se quejan dellos los nonbran los dhos Regidores en offᵒˢ trabajosos y de mucha costa de donde les biene mucho perjuicio y daño y que los offᵒˢ onrrosos y de probecho los probeyen a sus amigos criados y allegados quitandolos a los que los merezen y son mas conbenientes para la rrepublica y ansimismo a oydo y entendido por publico y notᵒ que los criados de los dhos Regidores talan mucho

25

los montes sancandola leña de quazo y cortandola por pie contra las
hordenanzas de la dha villa de donde rresulta grande daño por ser esta
tierra muy falta de leña y por que lo que ansi se corta no buelbe a nazer
por no guardarse, por las quales rrazones los dhos rregidores tienen a los vᵐ
desta Vᵃ y pobres oprimidos, todo lo qual zesaria si los dhos rregimientos se rresumiesen y fuesen añales como lo herán antiguamente, y que al
parezer deste tº por las dhas rrazones seria de mucho serbizio a dios nro
Sᵒʳ y a su magd y grade bien desta rrepublica que los dhos rregimientos
sean añales y que para questa Vᵃ estubiese bien gobernada le pareze
conbendria que en cada un año se nonbrasen doze rregidores en esta
manera que en sus quadrillas que tiene esta villa e cada quadrilla se
nonbrasen quatro rregidores dos del estado de los yjosdalgos y dos del
comun y que de aquellos saliese por suertes los dos, uno del un estado y el
otro del otro, y desta suerte lo llebasen las dhas seis quadrillas sin aber
diputados ni otra cosa que tubiesen boto mas de tan solamente los dhos
rregidores y el procurador gl que se quedase como al presente se esta
elegido en cada un año como asta aqui se a echo y que los propios
y rrentas questa vᵃ tiene este tº tiene notᵃ dellos en espⁱ de la cañada
que rrenta en cada un año setecientas y cinquenta anegas de trigo poco
mas o menos y ansimismo los sotos questan a la horrilla de hebro que
son muchos y de mucho valor y el trᵒ de tanbarria y los sequerales y el
rramalete bermejo y el soto que dizen los abades y la deheseria y la
cantara que todos son de mucho valor y con su poco mas o menos entiende que los dhos propios rrentan en cada un año un quento de mrs
con los demas aprovechamientos que la dha villa tiene, y que esta villa
tiene sobre estos propios asta treze mill dusº tomados a zenso con facultad rreal, a rrazon de a veynte y que tanbien sobre la dha cañada de
la rrenta della se paga en cada un año el servicio hordinario y estrahordinario que se carga y rreparte a esta villa, y que para la paga del dho
consumo siendo su magd serbido para lo ques la paga de los dhos
offᵒˢ se an de tomar a zenso sobre los propios desta villa y dellos pagar
el rredito asta en tanto que los arbitrios que se tomen se bengan a quitar y rredimir = y que para la cantidad con que se ubiere de serbir
a su magd por la md que yziere a esta villa y prebilegio que se le a de
dar para que no se puedan bolber a vender en ningun tpo los dhos
offᵒˢ de rregidores y depositario y alferez se podra sacar de cargar quatro
mrs en cada libra de carne que se bendiere e la carnyzeria el carnero
y en la carne de barato dos y en las tiendas de azeyte de ballena dos
msº en cada libra y en los pescados y congrio otros dos msº en cada libra, y ansi mismo que se arriendan en cada un año las yerbas de todas
las biñas y guertas y eredades que no sean zerradas y el trᵒ de tranbarria para que se pueda pastar desde Todos santos a mitad de marzo y
tranbarria todo el año ezeto desde mitad de mayo asta mitad de junio para los ganados que entran a esquilar, y que con esto y con las deudas
que a la villa le deben y con las ganancias que azen de las carnizerias
y alondigas y estan echas al presente y con cargar a cada carga de leña
de las que se trahen de la sierra de yerga a miº Real se podra pagar
a su magd lo susodho aciendo md a esta villa de dar tpo para ello por
quatro o cinco aᵒˢ = conque las dhas sisas y adbitrios pasen adelante

el tpo que fuere nezesario asta en tanto que se quiten los censos que se tomaren para el consumo de los dhos rregimientos, y que esto le pareze que sera el menos daño y perjuicio de los v^{os} desta V^a que otro ninguno de los que se pueden tomar y esto es la verdad y lo que sabe y entiende para el jur° que tiene echo, e dixo ser de hedad de sesenta y un a^{os} poco mas o menos y que tiene un hermano rregidor, pero que por ello no a dexado de dezir berdad y no le ba ynteres en esta causa mas de mirar por el bien comun como un v°, e firmolo de su nombre Lope de Frias'.

Puntos de los testimonios de otros testigos.

Pasqual de Briones: 'aviendo orden para rresumyrse los dichos oficios a su parecer deste t° sera util y provechoso se rresuman en ocho rregidores añales o doze que se saquen de sus quadrillas que en esta villa ay, dos de cada quadrilla y que sean de los dos estados del comun e yjosdalgo, esto sera bien se aga aviendo de que saca ello sin que se vendan los propios ni se aga nyngun rrepartimy° entre v^{os} desta villa porque esto los v^{os} no lo consienten por ser libertada esta villa y que la causa y rraçon por que le parece a este t° se rresuman y quiten los dhos rregimientos perpetuos es porque en esta villa ay demasiados con los ocho o doze y sera bien gobernada y de otra manera lo tiene por confusion y que de donde se podra sacar dinero para rresumir los dhos rregimientos es hechando sisas en carnes y pescados y aceyte de vallena y vendiendo las yerbas de tranbarria y las viñas y si ay lugar que se arrienden corraliças en los montes y de algunos dineros que aya caydos de carnicerias y tiendas y de algunas deudas que se deban oy a el concejo por que desto es el menos daño y perjuicio de los v^{os} , y que no aviendo rrepartimiento aunque se tome de otra qualquier parte es util y provechoso que los dhos rregimyentos y alferazgo y depositaria se consuman y quiten y que los propios que esta villa tiene an montado asta agora asta mill y quinientos fanegas de trigo y trescientas mill mrs en dinero poco mas o menos, y que desto se paga el serbicio rreal que esta cargado sobre el propio de la cañada y asta siete mill y cien rreales que se pagan en cada un año a don diego de castejon de un rredito de un censo y los demas gastos ordinarios que se acen de los dhos propios y que siendo su mag sebido de dar prebilegio para el consumo de los dhos rregimientos como dicho tiene para que no se puedan vender otra vez sera vien se aga lo que tiene della rreferida y sino ubiere prebilegio su parecer es no se trate de ello por el daño que podria suceder en tornallos a vender'; 'y declaro ser de hedad de quarenta y tres años poco mas o menos, y que no es pariente de ninguna de las ptes, ny de nyngun rregidor, y aunque es v° no le ba ynteres mas de que desea se acierte, y lo firmo de su nonbre'.

Diego Rodríguez, escribano del número de la villa: 'que a el parezer deste t° para la quietud y buen gobierno desta villa sera bien se consuman los dhos rregimientos alferazgo y depositario porq algunos de los dhos rregidores perpetuos acen so color de sus oficios algunos hecesos ansi en materia de rriegos como en comerse con sus ganados los pastos y en otras cosas de que rresulta aver algun escandalo de que rresulta tener a la

27

gente pobre oprimida, todo lo qual cesaria rresumiendo los dhos oficios y
que fuesen añales porque desta forma la gente pobre y necesitada admi-
nistrarian mejor sus aciendas y podrian pedir los agrabios que se les yciesen...'; 'declaro ser de hedad de treynta años y que no es pariente de
nynguna de las ptes'.

Juan Garcés de los Fayos: 'que a el parecer deste t° sera grande
servicio a dios nro S⁰ʳ y de su magd y bien y utilidad desta rrepublica
y pobres della que los dichos rregimientos perpetuos se consuman y sean
añales porque este t° a oydo quejarse muchas veces a v⁰ᵃ desta villa de
que algunos de los dhos rregidores con la mano que tienen en gobierno
les açen muchos agravios y malos tratamientos y le pareze zesaria esto
con que los dhos rregimientos y oficios se rresumyesen y no fuesen perpetuos', 'y que no ubiese diputados por la mucha confusion que ay en
tantos botos'; 'y dixo ser de hedad de quarenta a⁰ᵃ poco mas o menos
tienpo, y que tiene un cuñado y otros parientes rregidores pero que por ello
no a dejado de decir la verdad por que a dho t° que le parece conbiene'.

Licenciado Francisco Garcés de los Fayos: 'que los daños que se siguen
de que sean perpetuos y aya tantos como ay a el pres¹ᵉ son muy grandes, en especial que /'algunos' tachado/ todos los dhos rregidores no se
conforman en las cosas tocantes a el vien comun y este t° lo a oydo
deçir muchas beces a los dhos rregidores y porque de ordinario save este
t° que los dhos rregidores por no se conformar no tienen el gobierno
desta villa como conviene y acen los daños contenidos en la rrelacion
de la dha rreal zedula en notable daño y perjuicio de esta villa y en particular de los pobres lo qual save este t° por la queja general que ay
en esta v⁰ᵃ y aver selo oydo decir a los mysmos rregidores y tiene por cierto este t° que rresumydos los dhos rregimyentos zesaran los dhos daños
y esta villa estara vien governada y no aria los malos hejemplos que de los
dhos daños y mala conformydad que entre ellos tienen se causa y que por
el favor que los dhos rregidores tienen con las justicias como no los
castigan se atreven a acer semejantes daños = '; 'y dijo ser de hedad
de treynta y ocho o quarenta a⁰ᵃ poco mas o menos tienpo y que es
deudo de algunos de los dhos rregidores, especialm¹ᵉ de Don Diego de
Frias rregidor en el quartu quinto grado pero que por esto no a dejado
de decir la verdad sino que desea que se biva bien y el bien publico'.

Juan Aznar, familiar del Santo Oficio: 'que para el servicio de dios y
de su magd y bien desta rrepublica le parece seria bien se rresumiesen
y fuesen añales' 'lo uno porque como son tantos y tienen ordinariam¹ᵉ
por rrazon de sus of⁰ˢ mucha mano con las justicias como en el gobierno
tienen oprimida a la probe jente y algunos de ellos tienen mucha mano en
comerse con sus ganados las yervas y canpos y viñas y ynpedir el riego
de las heredades a los labradores desta villa y regar las suyas, y porque
como son tantos y de diferentes opiniones y estados suele aver encuentros
entre ellos de que se siguie escandalo, y todo va a parar en perjuicio
de pobres'; era de edad de cincuenta y ocho años poco más o menos,
y tenia algunos deudos regidores.

Licenciado Martínez, magistral de la iglesia colegial de Alfaro: 'que de aber tantos rregidores y ser perpetuos se siguen muchos daños e ynconvenientes'; 'la conserbacion desta rrepublica depende de la conserbacion de sus terminos y canpos especialmente de la conservacion de las aguas por ser casi todo el termino de rregadio y de la conservacion de los frutos y es publico y publica voz y fama que los rregidores usan de la agua a su albedrio sin guardar la orden regando primero que les buenga su vez y que por esto no los denuncian ni castigan como a los demas que no son rregidores, y ansi mismo los rregidores que tienen ganados se comen con ellos los frutos entrando en las biñas y en las piezas antes que se saquen dellas los frutos todo lo qual es en detrimento de la rrepublica'; 'tan bien es publico y por tan sin /roto/ que no pagan las preserias ni prendaduras que les azen ni otros repartim^{los} que son comunes, como fuentes y calzadas y caminos'; 'es publico que por algunos disabrimientos que tienen con la gente pobre por que no les ayudan en sus aziendas o los sirven en otras cosas quando se nonbran soldados los echan soldados y les rreparten libros de preserias y otros rrepartimientos que tiene esta villa'; es de edad de 34 años poco más o menos, vecino y natural de Alfaro y pariente de algunos regidores.

Francisco Malimbres, clérigo: 'que con la mano que tienen alg^{os} de los dhos rregidores por sus off^{os} respeto de ser perpetuos muchos dellos se comen con sus ganados todas las yerbas bedades y biñas y panes y rriegan sus heredades sin guardar horden ni vez por lo qual viene a los v^{os} desta V^a muy oprimidos y la rrepublica mal governada'; es de 53 años poco más o menos, y no es pariente de ninguno de los dichos regidores, 'ni la va ynteres en esta causa mas del servicio de dios y el bien desta V^a por ver las cosas como pasan'.

Francisco de Acereda, clérigo y canónigo de la iglesia de Alfaro: los regidores perpetuos 'son muy señores en esta villa', 'y muchos de ellos con sus ganados se comen las vinas y pastos y dehesas boyadas y en el rregar acen ordenanzas muy escesivas para que los pobres no osen tomar el agua y ellos a vanderas desplegadas toman el agua, y demas desto dizen que los criados de los dhos rregidores cortan las carrascas de la sierra de Yerga...'; es de 62 años poco más o menos, y no es pariente de los dichos regidores.

Miguel de Rada, regidor del campo de Alfaro: los regidores perpetuos 'son muy señores y so color de que mucha cantidad de dus^o que son mas de diez mill dus^o los tenian a censo para el posito syn los aver menester entre ellos se tenian mucha cantidad por que el posito desta villa solamente a menester quatro myll y quis^o anegas de trigo poco mas o menos y son señores de las aguas syn dejar que rrieguen con ella los pobres sus heredades, y a este t^o le a sucedido este pres^{te} año siendo tal Regidor del canpo y llevando el agua para rregar por orden, y va a quitar por fuerça la dha agua uno de los dichos Regidores y otro rregidor rrego una viña dos veces en lo qual yço de daño a las viñas que estavan por rregar y sacar de barbecho mas de cien dus^o, y que los dichos rregidores teniendo binos de vender no dejan vender a otros, y de mas desto muchos de los dhos rregidores tienen vicio de comerse con sus ganados las vinas y heredades y pastos yerbas syn rresistencia todo lo qual sucede de ser rregidores perpetuos por que si fuesen añales no tendrian tanta mano con la Just^a por que si un año lo yciesen mal no los bolberian a hechar otros'; para pagar el consumo propone tomar censo sobre los propios y después ir sacando el dinero de sisas sobre carnes, pescado, congrio y aceite de ballena, y arrendando las yerbas de las viñas, Tranbarria y Sequerales, cobrando las ganancias de las carnicerias y pósito, haciendo corralizas en el monte y echando un cuartillo en cada carga de leña de la sierra de Yerga, 'todo lo qual es el menos daño y perjuicio que puede ser de los pobres porque todo ello o la mas cantidad an de pagar los rricos y no los pobres'; es de edad de 55 años poco más o menos, y es pariente de algunos de los regidores.

Vicente Vallés: 'save que con la mano que tienen rrespeto de sus oficios ansi con las justicias como en el gobierno de esta villa acen algunos agravios a los v^{os} de la dha V^a... y demas desto save que por ser tantos y aver demas de los dichos v^{to} rregidores y alferez y depositario general ay otros doze diputados .. nunca andan conformes en las cosas del buen gobierno desta villa antes son molestados los pobres y v^{os} desta villa e no se ace lo que conviene a el servicio de dios nro S^{or} '; propone sacar el dinero por censo y sisas y arrendamientos 'que esto casi todo lo bienen a pagar los rricos'; es de más de 50 años, y 'es deudo de algunos rregidores muy cercano'.

Hernando de Alfaro, regidor del campo: 'sera bien se aga porque como son tantos ay muchas discordias entre ellos y biene mucho daño a esta rrepublica de que aya tantos'; era de 44 años poco más o menos, no era pariente de ningún regidor, 'y no lo firmo por que dixo no sabia'.

Martín Ruiz, mayordomo de los propios de Alfaro: 'que le pareze a este t^o questa villa esta muy enpeñada y no puede con los propios ni sisas rresumir los dhos off^{os} . y le pareze que conbiene mas por agora tratar de quitar los zensos que tiene que no de rresumir los'; 'que le pareze a este t^o que si la villa estubiera desenpeñada y tubiera posibilidad para poder rresumir los dhos rregimientos estubiera mucho mejor gobernada con rregidores añales que no perpetuos, y que esta villa tiene de propios mill y quis^o anegas de tr^o y asta trezientos y quarenta mill mrs en dinero con su poco mas o menos, sobre los quales debe a don di^o de Cast^{on} asta treze mill dus^o que con facultad rreal tomo del a zenso, y ansimismo paga delos dhos propios el servicio hordinario y estrahordinario y los salarios hordinarios e que esto es lo que sabe y no otra cosa'; 'e dixo ser de hedad de mas de cinquenta años e no ser pariente de ninguno de los dhos rregidores e que este t^o no es ynteresado ni le ba yntere-res ni pasion en esta causa, e firmolo de su nonbre, y que demas de lo que dho tiene esta villa tiene muchos gastos en pleytos con los circunbezinos y sobre las aguas y otras cosas'.

Parecer del Juez.

'En la Villa de Ag^{da} a nueve dias del mes de Jullio de mill y seiscientos y dos años su md de Marcos de Orovio juez de comision susodho dando su parezer a la dha rreal cedula dixo que en su cunpli-
miento el fue a la dha villa de alfaro he yço juntar el concexo avierto a
canpana tañida segun por la dha rreal cedula se mandava en el qual
concexo se juntaron asta ducientas y nobenta personas poco mas o menos
y estando juntos m^{do} leer la dha rreal zedula y por mi el pres° escriv°
se leyo y aviendose leydo por las dhas personas que se allaron en el dho
q° se trato y confirio sobre lo contenido en la dha rreal zedula y se rres-
cibieron los botos y pareceres de las dhas personas y como por ellos parece tudos ellos unanimes y conformes vinieron en que se consumiesen los
rregimientos alferazgo y depositario, hecepto asta cinco personas que fueron
de direrente boto y parecer aunque tan poco dieron rraçones bastantes
p^a que se dejase de acer el dho consumo, antes consta por los dhos
botos y pareceres que se dieron en el dho q° ser muy cierta y verdadera la rrelacion que se yço p^a sacar la dha rreal cedula, y ansi dieron
poder p^a acer el dho consumo estando en el q°, y hecho esto se rrescivio
unf^{on} por la qual consta e pareçe que la dha villa de alfaro tiene asta
mill y docientos v^{os} poco mas o menos syn tener aldea ni otra jur^{on} y
que ay diez y ocho rregidores y un alferez y un depositario general perpetuos, y que los mas de los dhos rregidores tienen muy oprimidos y
molestados a los v^{os} de la dha villa aciendo les muchos agravios moles-
tias y vejaciones ansi en comerseles con sus ganados sus heredades como
no dejarselas rregar quando les viene su bez y no les dejan vender sus
binos buenos por bender ellos sus malos y otras cosas que de la ynf^{on}
y pareceres y botos del dho concexo consta y pareze a que se rrefiere,
y ansi dixo que le parece que sirbiendose su magt sera de mucho servicio a dios nro S' y suyo y de mucha utilidad y provecho a los v^{os} de la
dha villa de alfaro que los dhos oficios perpetuos se rresuman y consuman para que sean añales y en nyngun tpo se buelvan a vender, que desta suerte parece que la dha villa estara muy bien governada sacando y
nonbrando en cada un año ocho rregidores añales quatro de un estado
y quatro de otro, nonbrandose por las quadrillas que ay en la dha villa
nonbrando por cada una dos y que el uno quede y el otro salga por rregidor aqueel año de suerte que cada estado nonbre ocho y de ellos sal-
gan qtro por rregidores de aquel año, y que ansimismo se nonbre un
pr° general como y de la forma que asta aqui se a hecho, los quales
rrigan y gobiernen la dha V^a y sus v^{os} sin que aya diputados ni otro
ningun oficio de concexo, y ansi mismo parece por la dha ynf^{on} y quentas
que la dha villa de alfaro tiene asta tres mill dus° de propios en cada un
año y que sobre ellos tiene a censo con facultad rreal asta trece mill
dus° y que aciendose el dho consumo sera bien que su magd se sirva
de darles lic^a p^a tómar a censo sobre sus propios la cantidad que p^a ello
fuere necesario = y ansi mismo para hechar sisas en las carnes pescados y
aceyte de vallena en cada libra de carnero quatro mrs y en la libre de

XII

carne de varato dos mrs y en los pescados y libra de ballena otros dos
mrs y pª que puedan acer dehesas y cotos y bender las yerbas de las
vinas y heredades y trᵒ de Tranvarria y acer corraliças en los montes y
hechar en cada carga de leña de las sierras de Yerga un quartillo y tomar
otros adbitrios cargando a los menudos de las carnicerias y desta manera se
entiende se podran sacar en cada un año asta dos mill dᵒˢ y esto se podria
sacar a el menos daño y perjuicio de los vᵒˢ de la dha villa y con los
dhos adbitrios y deudas que dicen deven a la dha villa y con las ganancias que ay caydas y cayran en las carnicerias y alondigas se podria con
facilidad acer el dho consumo y pagar a su magt el dinero con que se
le aya de serbir por ello pasando las dhas sisas y cotos y dehesas adelante el tpo que fuere necesario asta que rrediman los censos que para
este hefecto se tomaren abiendo en todo ello quenta e rraçon y que el
dinero entre en una persona distinta del mayordomo de propios con libro
apˡᵒ para que aya quenta e rraçon pª que no se pueda gastar en otra
cosa, y esto es lo que le pareze conviene a la dha villa y sus vᵒˢ siendo
su magt de ello sebido, y lo firmo de su nonbre siendo tᵒˢ Gaspar Rujz
de Volloslada y Franᶜᵒ Guerra vᵒˢ de la dha villa.

Marcos de Orovio paso ante my Joan Frayle dela Cal'.

XIII

The Purchase of Nobility in Castile, 1552-1700

The sale of patents of nobility (*privilegios de hidalguía*) was one of the many arbitrary fiscal devices resorted to by the Habsburgs in their endless search for funds in the XVIth and XVIIth centuries. The fact of the sales is well known; their significance is more questionable. Most often the purchase of *hidalguía* is seen as an expression of an all-pervading ' lust for nobility ' and a reflection of a dominant, non-economic (even anti-economic) orientation in the Castilian mentality.[1] It is represented as a significant element both in the diversion of capital from productive investment and in the debourgeoisification of Castilian society,[2] drawing attention, incidentally, to the importance of

---

[1] ANTONIO DOMÍNGUEZ ORTIZ, "La desigualdad contributiva en Castilla durante el siglo xvii", *Anuario de Historia del Derecho Español*, 21-2 (1951-2), pp. 1262-3; J. H. ELLIOTT, *Imperial Spain 1469-1716* (1963), p. 305, writes of the ' universal hunger for titles of nobility', and p. 104, ' an object of universal desire '; JUAN REGLÁ, " Spain and her Empire ", *New Cambridge Modern History*, vol. 5 (1961), p. 370, and *Historia de España y América social y económica*, ed. J. Vicens Vives, vol. 3 (1961), pp. 53, 219, 244 (*HEASE*).

[2] Most recently, for example, by RALPH DAVIS, *The Rise of the Atlantic Economies* (1973), pp. 150-1, and JAN DE VRIES, *The Economy of Europe in an Age of Crisis 1600-1750* (1976), p. 218; REGLÁ, *HEASE* iii: 13, 53, 249; ANTONIO DOMÍNGUEZ ORTIZ, *Orto y Ocaso de Sevilla* (1946), p. 55.

state action and the impact of war (via the means required to finance it) in distorting the social structure and as agents of social mobility.[3] By exacerbating the gross disequilibrium in the burden of taxation between rich and poor, the sale of noble exemptions is said to have contributed to rural depopulation and the collapse of agricultural production.[4] The sale of nobility, therefore, by adding to the numbers, reinforcing the social and economic attitudes, and pandering to the universal appeal of the *hidalgo* has had to share part of a fundamental responsibility for Castile's economic decadence.[5]

This kind of view is based largely on the repeated but very generalized complaints of the Cortes about the number of *hidalguías* sold and the need for a consequential reallocation of taxation, and it has not been entirely endorsed by some of those most expert in the social and financial history of the period (Carande, Ulloa, Domínguez Ortiz). Even they, however, have lacked precise information on the chronology, the extent, the value and the beneficiaries of the sales, and it has, therefore, been impossible to make anything but an impressionistic assessment of their significance either as a fiscal device or as a social and economic phenomenon.

The evidence that would permit a detailed and reasonably exact resolution of these issues exists both in the general correspondence of the Councils of State and Finance and in the accounts of the royal treasury. What the purchaser actually bought was a patent, a *carta de privilegio*, according him the status and privi-

---

[3] RAMÓN CARANDE, *Carlos V y sus banqueros*, vol. 2 (1949), p. 503; DOMÍNGUEZ ORTIZ, *Desigualdad contributiva*, p. 1263; RUTH PIKE, *Aristocrats and Traders. Sevillian Society in the Sixteenth Century* (1972), p. 23.

[4] GONZALO ANES, *Las crisis agrarias en la España moderna* (1970), p. 109; De Vries, pp. 219, 217.

[5] ' El hidalgo es el responsable fundamental de la decadencia económica ', JOSÉ MARÍA DIEZ BORQUE, *Sociología de la comedia española del siglo xvii* (1976), p. 296; JOSEPH PEREZ, *L'Espagne du XVIe Siècle* (1973), p. 32; JAIME VICENS VIVES, *Historia económica de España* (3rd edit. 1964), pp. 380-1; Elliott, p. 305.

leges enjoyed by the customary and hereditary nobles of the realm (*hijosdalgo notorios de sangre y solar conocido*). The instrument opened with a recapitulation of the petition and statement of services and merits submitted by the recipient in justification of the grant. Here were set out the man's family history, the services to the Crown of himself and his predecessors and close relatives, the genealogy and origins of his house and its connections by blood and marriage with established noble lineages, together with any details of offices held, membership of confraternities, exemptions from taxes or levies, the existence of chapels, chantries or arms sculpted over the portals of the family home, and previous grants or court judgements that might support his claim to noble status. The justification was frankly propagandist and therefore has to be examined with considerable scepticism, but it does make possible at least a partial analysis of the kinds of persons who were buying *hidalguías*. The justification was followed by the formal grant of nobility by the king, expressed in a variety of legal formulae which in principle distinguished carefully between the creation of new nobility, the declaration of a nobility deemed already to exist, the ratification, restitution or confirmation of a previous grant or court judgement. The remaining sections of the document consisted of standard-form chapters setting out the detailed privileges and exemptions of *hidalguía*, dispensations and abrogations of the laws, guarantees against revocation, and instructions to the courts and local authorities to recognize and observe the rights to which the grantee was now entitled.

Theoretically, copies of all the *cartas de privilegio* should have been kept in the *contaduría de la razón* in order to maintain a central record of tax exemptions.[6] What copies there are, are now to be found in the section Dirección General del Tesoro, Inventario 5, of the Archivo General de Simancas, the first two *legajos* of which contain 154 patents issued in the XVIth and XVIIth

---

6 Archivo General de Simancas (AGS), Dirección General del Tesoro (DGT), Inventario 5, legajo 1, no. 1, RC Monzón, 6 Sept. 1552.

centuries.[7] This source is supplemented for the XVIIth century by two independent lists; one, an account drawn up in 1661 of the *hidalguías* sold since 1629 for which the purchasers had not yet proved full payment;[8] the other, a list dated 4 September 1710 of grants and confirmations of *hidalguía* issued by the *secretaría de la Cámara y Estado de Castilla* since 1623.[9]

Grants of nobility had been issued by the hundred by the Catholic Kings in the last quarter of the XVth century, but these had been made for military and personal services, not for money.[10] After 1495 these grants petered out, and though it has been argued that some *hidalguías* were sold at the start of Charles V's reign the evidence probably refers to a continuation of grants of patents by the Crown rather than sales.[11] In either event the practice was short lived, and successive instructions of Charles V to his regents forbade them to make grants of *hidalguía*, *caballería* and naturalization ' as I do not grant them, because they are greatly prejudicial to the kingdom '.[12] The possibility of putting

---

[7] AGS DGT 5, leg. 1, ff. 71 (71 for 1552-1600), leg. 2, ff. 84 (83 for 1600-99; f. 35 is missing). Subsequent references to specific patents and grantees will be designated CP 16 for legajo 1, CP 17 for legajo 2, followed by the folio number.

[8] AGS DGT Inventario 24, leg. 332, transcript of a statement given to the Consejo en Sala de Cobranças, 1661, ' de lo que por este libro constava en raçon de las hidalguias bendidas cuyos compradores no havian pressentado pagos de los precios dellas ', and ' Relacion de lo que se deve de Conpras de Hidalguias ', Madrid, June 1661.

[9] ' Documentos inéditos para la Historia Nobiliaria ', *Revista de Historia y de Genealogía Española*, vol. 1 (1912), pp. 40-3, 85-7, 133-5, 180-3, ' Relación de las hidalguías que se han despachado por la Secretaría de la Cámara y Estado de Castilla, como consta por los libros que hay en ella, desde el año de 1623 hasta la fecha de esta (4 Sept. 1710) en conformidad de la orden que S.M. se sirvió expedir para que se formase ' (henceforth ' Relación de 1710 '; the manuscript source is Real Academia de la Historia, Madrid, Colección de Grandezas, vol. 1). The fact that these patents were issued by the *Cámara* does not mean they were not sold. There is a considerable overlap among the three sources and 46 of the 116 patents listed here for 1625-1700 are known to have involved some direct, cash payment.

[10] MARIE-CLAUDE GERBET, ' Les guerres et l'accès à la noblesse en Espagne 1465 à 1592 ', *Mélanges de la Casa de Velázquez*, 8 (1972), pp. 295-326; Elliott, p. 104.

[11] Carande, II: 502-3.

[12] MANUEL FERNÁNDEZ ALVAREZ, ed., *Corpus Documental de Carlos V*, vol. 1 (1973), pp. 153, 416, 533, 544, vol. 3 (1977), pp. 29, 310.

hidalguías up for sale, however, was mooted as early as 1524,[13] and again in 1547,[14] but none seem actually to have been sold until the autumn of 1552 when, with preparations for the Metz campaign occupying all Charles V's resources in the north, the Council of Finance, faced with the cost of defending Spain and North Africa against the threat from the French and Turkish fleets, found all the Crown's ordinary revenues, the *servicios* of the Cortes, the rents of the Masterships of the Military Orders, the *cruzada* and the clerical subsidy mortgaged into 1555.[15] Five years later, in 1557, Philip II ordered 150 *hidalguías* to be sold in Castile in the hope of bringing three-quarters of a million ducats into the treasury;[16] but the expedient was a total failure. Only ten patents are known to have been sold between 1552 and July 1559 when Philip II called a halt to the sales. Two more are recorded prior to 1565 but the likelihood is that these were grants and not sales. Throughout the next decade, a decade that encompasses the relief of Malta, revolts in Granada and the Netherlands, Lepanto and the Holy League, and the third ' bankruptcy ' of the reign, sales were continuous, with no less than

---

[13] Charles V was said to be thinking of selling 500,000 ducats worth in 1524, Carande ii: 502.

[14] AGS Estado leg. 75, Philip to Charles V, 1 June 1547; *Corpus Documental*, vol. 2 (1975), p. 511.

[15] AGS Consejo y Juntas de Hacienda (CJH), leg. 13 (old number 23), f. 59, ' lo que parece al Consejo de la Hazienda que V. Alteza deve escrivir a Su Magt ' (1 Sept. 1552). FERNÁNDEZ ALVAREZ, *Corpus Documental* iii: 432, tentatively puts the date of the original decision in May 1552, but as it was taken in the presence of Don Juan Manrique just before his departure for the Netherlands, it must have been prior to 29 Mar. 1552 (Carande ii: 123). Copies of the royal orders authorizing the sales, dated Augsburg, 18 Sept. 1552, and Béthune, 1 Sept. 1554. are to be found in AGS DGT 5, leg. 1, no. 1. The measure was intended to raise 100,000 ducats, MODESTO ULLOA, *La hacienda real de Castilla en el reinado de Felipe II* (2nd edit. 1977), p. 95, and also *Corpus Documental* iii: 604, Charles V to Philip, 12 Aug. 1553, indicating that there had in fact been a previous attempt to sell *hidalguías* without much success, but it is not clear when that was.

[16] Carande iii: 450-1; AGS CJH leg. 23 (36), f. 205, Pedro Niño to Princess Juana, Toledo, 24 Mar. 1557. Carande's belief that 150 were to be sold in each province is symptomatic of the exaggerated importance attributed to the sales.

XIII

seventeen in 1567 alone, and another twenty by 1575. After 1575 no more were marketed until 1583, and, despite the recommendation of the *Junta Grande y de Arbitrios* and the Council of Finance late in 1591 to revive the sales,[17] only eight *hidalguías* are known to have been sold in the twenty-year period 1576-95. Another fourteen followed in 1596-1600, but, opposed by the Cortes and prohibited by the *millones* contract of 1618, only fourteen more were issued in the next twenty-eight years, a dozen of them by 1615. The sales were then revived as one of a number of emergency measures into which Olivares was driven by the loss of the plate fleet and the opening of the Mantuan war in 1628. In 1629 the Cortes was asked to lift the conditions of the *millones* to allow the king to sell 100 *hidalguías* at 4,000 ducats each.[18] A second 100 was proposed in 1635 as part of a grant by the Cortes of nine million ducats over three years, and another 100 in 1643, but neither proposal was given effect.[19] In the latter case the Cortes refused its consent, making a grant of 300,000 ducats instead, and further general sales were prohibited by the conditions attached to subsequent regrants of the *millones*.[20] However, the Cortes did permit individual grants to be made in contravention of these conditions on a number of occasions, and several *hidalguías* were issued to courtiers and officials for resale as *mercedes* or in settlement of debts and salaries.[21] In the

[17] AGS CJH 202 (292), *consulta* of Council of Finance, 5 July 1592; Instituto de Valencia de Don Juan (IVDJ), envío 43, f. 316, Junta en Valladolid, 10 July 1592.

[18] ANTONIO DOMÍNGUEZ ORTIZ, *Política y hacienda de Felipe IV* (1960), p. 43; AGS DGT 24, leg. 332, Philip IV to Council of Finance, 4 July 1630. DOMÍNGUEZ ORTIZ in *La sociedad española en el siglo XVII*, vol. 1 (1963), p. 182, says this issue was halted in 1632 at the request of the Cortes, but the records of the sales show this cannot have been so.

[19] MANUEL DANVILA, 'Nuevos datos para escribir la historia de las Cortes de Castilla en el reinado de Felipe IV', *Boletín de la Real Academia de la Historia (BRAH)*, 16 (1890), pp. 72, 88.

[20] *Actas de las Cortes de Castilla (ACC)*, vol. 55, pp. 297, 338; Danvila, *BRAH* 16: 86; FRANCISCO GALLARDO FERNÁNDEZ, *Origen, progresos y estado de las rentas de la Corona de España, su gobierno y administración*, vol. 1 (1805), pp. 184, 198.

[21] AGS DGT 24, leg. 332, the marchioness of Leganés was given three *privilegios*

reign of Charles II, *hidalguías* were again sold sporadically by the Crown, but, ostensibly at any rate, these were claimed to be still part of the 100 granted in 1629.

The total of the patents listed by the three sources is 272; 87 of them issued 1552-1615, 185 in 1625-1700.[22] The number actually sold was rather less than this, although the precise figure remains uncertain, partly because some of the term sales, which were the norm in the seventeenth century, may not have been completed, partly because it is not always clear whether a particular patent was sold or granted as a *merced*. Of these 272, 185 were certainly sold and the likely figure lies between 233 and 252.[23] When it is possible to check them against other documentary evidence, the figures compiled from the lists are generally slightly on the high side. A statement drawn up in 1629

---

in 1634 for her nominees, on account of 3,000 ducats a year pension granted to her as a *merced*; the secretary, Don Francisco de Calatayud, was given an *hidalguía* which he sold to Captain Lorenzo de Padilla González of Cieza in 1637, to cover 3,800 ducats owed him for five-years salary as secretary of the Junta de Competencias; ACC 55: 338, the Monastery of San Lorenzo el Real was granted two *hidalguías* for its nominees in 1638 to compensate it for the decline in its rents.

22 The 185 excludes two patents withdrawn and four 'ceremonial' *mercedes* to royal wet-nurses and on the occasion of the king's wedding. There were in all 301 male and five female recipients, together with all their dependent children, thirteen married or independent sons, six nephews, seven wives and two sisters. Five of the patents were legitimizations, and three others reissues, reconfirmations and restitutions of *hidalguía*.

23 For the purpose of analysis all grants apparently initiated from below have been included. Apart from the impossibility of drawing any meaningful distinction between direct, money 'services' and grants made for 'services' like the surrender of an *encomienda* in the Indies worth 1,000 *pesos* a year (CP 16, f. 52), the loan of 200,000 florins free of interest for a year (CP 16, ff. 47, 12, 13), or the free grant of *hidalguía* to Diego de Alburquerque of Seville soon after he had undertaken a large financial deal with the king (Ruth Pike, *Enterprise and Adventure. The Genoese in Seville and the opening of the New World* [1966], p. 96; CP 16, f. 6, 17 Mar. 1585), all the grantees had a common need for a royal declaration to establish a nobility which they had not been able to prove in any other way. None of the conclusions of this article would have been substantially different had analysis been limited to the minimum number of sales for which the evidence is unequivocal — the proportion of recipients presenting strong evidence of pre-existing nobility in their families, for example, would have been only about 5 per cent less, see below pp. 341-343.

from the registers of the *contaduría de la razón* lists only seventeen of the twenty-two sales made 1591-1609,[24] and in September 1637 only eighty *hidalguías* of the 100 granted in 1629 were said to have been sold,[25] against 87 shown in the lists. All in all, therefore, the maximum figure of 272 in 148 years is, if anything, likely to be a slight overestimate of the *hidalguías* sold in Castile during the Habsburg period.[26]

There was then no mass sale of nobility in Habsburg Castile. An average of less than two a year points, on the contrary, to a surprising slackness in the demand for *cartas de privilegio*. All the evidence indicates that, with the exception of the one year, 1567, it was very difficult to sell *hidalguías* in the XVIth century, and in some parts of the country virtually impossible. When the first *hidalguías* were put up for sale in 1552, only five were bought in one and a half years, realizing a quarter of the 100,000 ducats the Council of Finance had expected.[27] In March 1557, the king ordered the sale of another 150, but economic conditions were not favourable, in particular the bad harvests and high prices around 1557, and from practically all the cities the response was the same — ' no a hablado en ellas ' (Guadix), ' ninguna persona a tratado dellas ' (Murcia), ' no ay persona que ponga en precio ninguno de las ' (Toro), ' ninguno se mueva a dar un real por la hidalguia ni yo creo que avra persona en este lugar que le de ny trate deste negocio ' (Toledo); there was a possible buyer in Utrera, two in Granada, but nobody in Seville, nor in Palencia, Guadalajara or Málaga,[28] and in July 1559 Philip II

---

[24] AGS DGT 24, leg. 332, *relación* of *Contador* Tomás de Aguilar to President and Council of Finance, 27 Nov. 1629.

[25] AGS DGT, leg. 332, *Carta de privilegio* of Captain Lorenzo de Padilla González, 18 Sept. 1637.

[26] The uncertainties in the upper estimates of these figures can in part be offset against other known sales about which these sources are silent, the sale to Pedro Marcos of Getafe in 1618, for example, *ACC* xxxi: 247-8, 268, 298.

[27] Ulloa, p. 95; AGS CJH leg. 13 (23), f. 59; *Corpus Documental* iii: 629.

[28] AGS CJH leg. 55 (82), Don Iñigo de Córdoba to Philip II, Guadix, 29 Apr. 1557, and to Juan Vázquez de Molina, Guadix, 8 May 1557; AGS CJH leg. 23 (36),

ordered the sales to stop, 'since we have seen how little fruit and profit has resulted'.[29] Despite the complaints of the Cortes, which historians have too readily accepted at face value, the evidence fully supports the king in his reply to a petition of 1566 that 'few' patents of nobility had been issued to that date [30] — only sixteen in fact since 1552. Ironically, more were to be sold in 1567 than in the previous fifteen years; but it was impossible to maintain sales at that level and only twenty were disposed of in the next eight years. Thereafter there was never much confidence in official circles that there was a great deal to be got from *hidalguías*, as indeed there had not been on Charles V's part at the very beginning.[31]

Philip IV was somewhat more successful than his grandfather. Between 1629 and 1633 as many transactions were negotiated as in the whole of Philip II's reign. However, these *hidalguías* were being sold at a price little more than half of that demanded in the 1590s, and despite the reopening of the market after some twenty-five years during which there had been little opportunity for new men to buy their way into the nobility, demand was slow, got slower from 1633, and after 1640 largely dried up. As early as February 1630 the king had written to the *corregidores*, to whom, as in 1557, the negotiation of the sales had been entrusted, ordering them to try to get the money in more quickly than from the rather dilatory responses

---

f. 200 (Murcia), f. 206 (Toro), f. 205 (Toledo); AGS CJH leg. 21 (32), Ortega de Melgosa to Philip II, Seville, 25 June 1557 (Utrera and Seville); AGS CJH leg. 49 (74), Don Melchor de Guevara to Princess Juana, Guadalajara, 7 Apr. 1557; Carande iii: 450-1 (Granada, Palencia and Málaga); Ulloa, p. 95.

[29] AGS CJH leg. 23 (36), f. 157, Philip II to Council of Finance, Ghent, 23 July 1559.

[30] *ACC* ii: 434; see also petition 8 of 1558 Cortes, *Cortes de los Antiguos Reinos de León y de Castilla* (CLC), vol. 5, p. 743, and petition 57 of 1563 Cortes, ACC i: 336.

[31] IVDJ envío 43, f. 316, Philip II's apostil to Junta en Valladolid, 10 July 1592; CRISTÓBAL ESPEJO DE HINOJOSA, *El Consejo de Hacienda durante la presidencia del marqués de Poza* (1924), p. 36; *Corpus Documental* iii: 604, Charles V to Philip, 12 Aug. 1553, 'por lo passado tengo experiencia de quán poco se saca desto'.

that had hitherto been received, by persuading the cities and provincial capitals to accept a quota of sales for which they would take responsibility, in the meantime anticipating the returns by letting the king have the money straight away.[32] Many of the towns, however, were unable to dispose of their quotas and either paid the money in order that no *hidalguías* should be sold within their jurisdictions (Trujillo, Logroño, Salamanca), or had to bear the cost themselves out of communal revenues or taxation.[33] In Olmedo the best offer the town received was 31,000 *reales*, and it had to borrow the remaining 13,000 *reales* from the municipal granary. In Medina del Campo the town council could find no buyer at all (on account of its poverty, it claimed), and after raising the money to pay the king by an excise on meat, it had to get royal permission, ten years later, to hawk its *hidalguía* across the country; in the end, the *hidalguía* was passed on to the convent of Barefooted Carmelites of Santa Teresa de Avila who found a buyer in the town of Almendralejo, 200 miles away in Extremadura.[34] In the event, Philip IV probably got most of the 400,000 ducats he had intended to raise, but not by selling *hidalguías*, and when, in 1635, he proposed to put a second batch up for sale, the Council of Finance rejected the proposal as not worthy of consideration since the first 100 had not yet been disposed of despite all efforts.[35] Twenty still remained unsold in September 1637, and the Crown was apparently still selling off the 100 *hidalguías* of the 1629 grant in 1699, twenty-two of the forty-two issued during the reign of Charles II being attributed

---

[32] Details of these orders can be found in the authorization given to Medina del Campo, 1 May 1630, to raise the money by taxation, AGS DGT 24, leg. 332, and also in *Actas de las Juntas y Diputaciones del Principado de Asturias*, ed. Marcos G. Martínez, vol. 3 (1954), pp. 126-7.

[33] DOMÍNGUEZ ORTIZ, *Política y hacienda*, p. 46; *Actas de las Juntas... de Asturias*, vol. 5 (1955), p. 155.

[34] AGS DGT 24, leg. 332, *relaciones* of 1661.

[35] Danvila, *BRAH* 16: 72; DOMÍNGUEZ ORTIZ, *Política y hacienda*, p. 387; DOMÍNGUEZ ORTIZ, *Sociedad española en el siglo XVII*, vol. 1, p. 182.

to the 1629 grant,[36] either because some of the earlier sales had fallen through or as a crude constitutional subterfuge. How is this persistent lack of demand and the relatively small number of *hidalguías* sold to be explained in a society whose nobilomania has become a historiographical legend? One explanation lies in the widespread opposition to the creations and the ambivalence of royal policy which effectively restricted supply. The sale, and indeed the free grant, of *hidalguías* was vigorously and continuously opposed by the Cortes, by the town and village corporations, by the established nobility and by the *pechero* estate alike.[37] The repeated petitions of the Cortes to ban further sales on account of the harm done both to the reputation of the nobility by easy access and to the interests of the remaining taxpayers by granting exemptions to the wealthiest members of the community without any corresponding reduction in the total tax demand,[38] probably had little direct effect until the reign of Philip III when the prohibition was incorporated into the conditions of the *millones*, but the resistance of the Cortes was certainly responsible for holding back the number of *hidalguías* put on the market by Philip IV.[39] The town and village councils also had some influence, partly through their petitions to the Cortes, and partly through their willingness to buy out and suppress *cartas de privilegio* sold to their inhabitants,[40] the most striking case being the 50,000 ducats paid by the city of Seville

---

[36] In chronological order from 1669-99, CP 17, ff. 29, 39, 12, 19, 67, 80, 65, 45, 16, 33, 66, 73, 84, 34, 58, 83, 63, 20, 15, 61, 78, 42.

[37] *Corpus Documental* iii: 629, Philip to Charles V, 12 Nov. 1553.

[38] Petition 8, 1558, *CLC* v: 734; petition 57, 1563, *ACC* i: 336; petition 24, 1566, *ACC* ii: 434; petitions 16 and 78, 1570-71, *ACC* iii: 368, 412; petition 46, 1576, *ACC* v: 58-9; session 11 Aug. 1592, *ACC* xii: 176; session 10 July 1599, *ACC* xviii: 320; sessions 1 and 8 Feb. 1618, *ACC* xxxi: 247, 268.

[39] The Cortes withheld its consent to the sale of a further 100 *hidalguías* in April 1643 and granted 300,000 ducats instead, Danvila, *BRAH* 16: 86; DOMÍNGUEZ ORTIZ, *Sociedad española en el siglo XVII*, vol. 1, p. 182; Gallardo Fernández, vol. 1, p. 184.

[40] One of the measures Philip IV proposed in order to make the *hidalguías* more attractive was to make them immune from suppression in this way, Danvila, *BRAH* 16: 88 (2 Apr. 1643).

in 1584 in order that no more *hidalguías* be sold within her jurisdiction.[41]

Perhaps more important than the opposition of the country was the ambivalence of the Crown. Both Charles V and Philip II had the most serious reservations about selling *hidalguías*. They wanted the money, but neither to devalue nobility nor to increase the tax burden on the commons. All Charles V's Instructions (1529, 1535, 1537, 1538, 1548, 1551) forbade his regents in Castile from making grants of *hidalguía* ' because they are very much to the prejudice of the kingdom '.[42] It was from the Council of Finance in Castile that the pressure to sell *hidalguías* primarily came, and it was because of the reluctance of Charles V and Philip II that so few were actually sold.[43] Charles V forbade the sale of *hidalguía* to anybody guilty of public infamy, to sons of clerics, descendants of unpardoned *comuneros*, or to anybody with any trace of heretical or Jewish blood.[44] In practice some of these prohibitions had to be relaxed because they were so restrictive, but despite pressure from the Council of Finance Philip II was also concerned to exclude ' personas defectuosas '.[45] Acting as regent when the first *hidalguías* were put up for sale in 1552, he deliberately set the price so high that no more than a handful of people were prepared to pay it,[46] and in disregard of

---

[41] Ulloa, p. 426; PIKE, *Aristocrats and Traders*, p. 23, citing Montoto, gives the date as 1582.

[42] *Corpus Documental* i: 153, 416, 533, 544, iii: 29, 310. I have found no mention of *hidalguías* in the 1543 Instructions.

[43] AGS Estado leg. 75, Philip to Charles V, Guadalajara, 1 June 1547, ' En lo de las hidalguias aunque ha parescido lo mismo que a V.Md por los inconvenientes que en ello ay, todavia se ternia por menores que los que ay en lo del oro y plata de las yglesias en que ay tantas difficultades '; Carande ii: 503; *Corpus Documental* ii: 512, iii: 588, 604.

[44] *Corpus Documental* iii: 472-3 (18 Sept. 1552).

[45] *Corpus Documental* iii: 532, 569, 588, 629.

[46] AGS CJH leg. 13 (23), f. 59, Philip reported to Charles V, 1 Sept. 1552, that the sale of *hidalguías* and other measures ' an seido hasta agora de poco probecho, por que en lo de las hidalguias por ser en tanto perjuicio de los pecheros del reyno, yo he tenido fin a que se vendan las menos que ser puedan, y que los ricos y caudalosos

the advice of his ministers he never allowed any lowering of the threshold throughout his reign.[47] It was because he regarded it as a ' most hateful and prejudicial business ' that was in any case of little fiscal value that he ordered the sale of *hidalguías* to cease in July 1559.[48] It may be that the sales of 1567-75 reflect some relaxation of this attitude, but in 1592, when the *Junta Grande* and the Council of Finance proposed selling twelve or thirteen new *hidalguías* for upwards of 70,000 ducats, Philip II scotched the plan by arguing that some way had to be found of ' preventing the burden of exemptions falling on the poor, who in justice must be taken into account ', and refusing to issue any patents until a sufficient number had been sold to make the revenue they brought in worthwhile, a number he set at a level he knew full well was never likely to be reached.[49] It was to be four years before another *hidalguía* was sold. Indeed, in no less than nineteen of the 43 years of Philip II's reign there were no *hidalguías* issued

---

que las quisieren las paguen bien, y asi les puse precio de 5000 ducados cada una a todos los que tubieren de hazienda hasta L o LX M(il) ducados, y que si tubiesen mas hazienda se les pidiese mayor precio; y como tienen entendidas las necesidades, aunques cosa que mucho desean, an se detenido en venillas a conprar, esperando que verna alguna necesidad tan grande que para ella se vajara el precio, y asi no se an conprado hasta agora mas de quatro...' The price set by Philip was much higher than that proposed by Charles V — 2,000 ducats for individuals without children, or 10 per cent of the grantee's estimated wealth, *Corpus Documental* iii: 472-3 (18 Sept. 1552).

    [47] AGS CJH leg. 91 (135), Francisco Duarte, *Factor* of the Casa de Contratacion, to Philip II, Seville, 18 Sept. 1574, proposed that as prospective buyers thought the price was too high, ' si en esto se hiciese algun equibalencia, regulando la calidad y cantidad de los conpradores, creo se haria mas efeto ', but Philip replied tersely, ' el precio ha de ser de 5,000 ducados y que no tengan hijos casados '.

    [48] AGS CJH leg. 23 (36), f. 157, Philip II to Council of Finance, Ghent, 23 July 1559, ' lo de las hidalguias pues se a bisto el poco fruto e ynteres que desto a procedido y es negocio tan odioso y perjudicial, sera mejor que se dexe de husar deste arbitrio, y asi en lo que no estubiere ya effectuado hasta que otra cosa probeamos no se tratara '.

    [49] AGS CJH leg. 202 (292), *consulta* of Council of Finance, 21 June 1592; IVDJ *envío* 43, f. 316, Junta en Valladolid, 10 July 1592, ' que hasta que aya numero de cinquenta no se abra puerta a esto, y quando llegue lo avisen '; to which Philip II, underlining ' de cinquenta ', replied, ' basta decir 20, que 50 nunca se juntaran, ni aun creo que las 20 '.

at all. Philip III and Philip IV were perhaps less hostile in principle than their predecessors, and Philip IV, in particular, much less discriminating about who might buy from him,[50] but in the early years of the sales there is no doubt that the purchasers' fears of risking an examination into their backgrounds, on the one hand, and the high cost of the *hidalguías*, on the other, were powerful depressants of demand.[51]

What is clear is that the *hidalguías* were very much over-priced. The price varied with the particular conditions and special circumstances of each grant, the inclusion of married sons or sons living independently outside the paternal home, for example, but it was always a fixed and artificial charge, not a market price. From 1552 to 1575 the norm was set at 5,000 ducats in gold; from 1583 to 1609 it was 6,000 to 6,500 ducats; in the 1630s it was 4,000 ducats, silver if possible, but usually *vellón*.[52] The original price was deliberately designed to limit buyers to those with fortunes of 50 or 60,000 ducats; the equivalent figure at the end of the XVIth century would have been 60–80,000. The total market in Castile can hardly have been more than a few

---

[50] Philip III favoured the proposal of the Junta de Medios, 22 Nov. 1600, to sell *hidalguías*, as long as payment was made within six months, Espejo de Hinojosa, p. 36; and Philip IV personally pushed the measure against a reluctant Council of Finance, Danvila, *BRAH* 16: 88 (2 Apr. 1643), raising no social barriers against potential buyers and ordering the Council to sell 'a qualesquier personas que lleguen a comprar las', 4 July 1630, AGS DGT 24, leg. 332; see also RP to Governor of Villanueva de la Serena, 11 Dec. 1635, *ibid.*, 'siendo necessario venderse las dichas hidalguias a la persona o personas que las quisieren conprar de qualquier estado, calidad y condizion que sean, dando quenta particular en el dicho mi qonsejo de hazienda... os doy poder cunplida'.

[51] *Corpus Documental* iii: 629, Philip to Charles V, 12 Nov. 1553, 'De las hidalguías hay poca demanda porque no se han despachado sino çinco, como tengo scripto; dévelo causar que los que podrían pagar el precio de 5,000 ducados no se quieren avergonçar en examinar las calidades, ni en que se sepan sus máculas, y los otros que no las tienen, no se hallan en posibilidad para dar la dicha suma, y assí está parado este negocio...'.

[52] Twenty of 27 known prices 1552–75 fell between 5,000 and 5,300 ducats, 16 of 24 1583–1609 between 6,000 and 6,500 ducats, and 4,000 ducats was the standard in the 1630s but with a wide variety of conditions and credit terms.

thousands,[53] and even for many of those the price was regarded as excessive. It was the cost more than anything else that the *corregidores* thought explained the lack of interest in 1557.[54] Cut the price by four-fifths recommended the *corregidor* of Granada and there would be a thousand buyers.[55] Forty years later a Dr Castañeda thought 7,000 could be sold if they were priced at 2,000 ducats.[56] Yet when the price was halved in real terms in the XVIIth century, this did not happen. By 1629 the standard price had been dropped to 4,000 ducats *vellón* (the equivalent of 3,654 ducats silver)[57] with credit extended up to eight or nine years (compared with a year or eighteen months in the 1590s), and in the 1640s it was down to 2,000 ducats. Nonetheless, it took at least ten years to sell the hundred put on offer in 1629, if indeed they were ever sold in full during the Habsburg period.[58] Although prices recovered in the second half of the seventeenth century to average around 4,000 ducats again, the value of an *hidalguía*

---

[53] The distribution of wealth in Castile is something that can only be guessed at. Gerónimo de Salamanca, *procurador* for Burgos in 1596, estimated that there were 10,000 *vecinos* in Castile worth 20,000 ducats or more, *ACC* xv: 72, a figure DOMÍNGUEZ ORTIZ, *The Golden Age of Spain 1516-1659* (1971), p. 197, thinks optimistic. An income of 3,000 ducats a year, presupposing a capital of 40-60,000, was something worthy of historical record in such a medium-sized, New Castilian town as Casarrubios del Monte (650 *vecinos*), while anybody with a capital of 6,000 or 7,000 ducats was considered a rich man in the provinces. The wealthiest *vecinos* recorded in the *Relaciones* of Toledo and Ciudad Real in the 1570s were worth between 4,000 and 7,000 ducats, CARMELO VIÑAS and RAMÓN PAZ, *Relaciones de los Pueblos de España ordenadas por Felipe II: Reino de Toledo (primera parte)* [1951], pp. 259 (Casarrubios), 484 (Huecas, 5,000 ducats); *Ciudad Real* (1971), pp. 86 (Arenas, 4,000 ducats), 251 (Fuencaliente, 2-3,000 ducats), 269 (Herencia, 5,000 ducats), 431 (Quintanar de la Orden, 6,000 ducats), 498 (Terrinches, 7,000 ducats). BARTOLOMÉ BENNASSAR, *Valladolid au siècle d'or* (1967), pp. 134-5, can show no more than a handful of non-aristocratic fortunes in excess of 40,000 ducats, even in a city of 30-40,000 people.
[54] AGS CJH leg. 21 (32), Ortega de Melgosa, Seville, 25 June 1557; AGS CJH leg. 23 (36), f. 206, Toro, 2 Apr. 1557; AGS CJH leg. 49 (74), Don Melchior de Guevara to Princess Juana, Guadalajara, 7 Apr. 1557; and also Francisco Duarte to Philip II, Seville, 18 Sept. 1574, AGS CJH leg. 91 (135).
[55] Carande iii: 451.
[56] Espejo de Hinojosa, p. 36.
[57] 4,000 ducats seems to have been the asking price as early as 1618, *ACC* xxxi:247.
[58] The lists indicate that 100 *hidalguías* had been sold by 1640; but see above, p. 322.

had dropped continuously in real terms between the mid-sixteenth and the mid-seventeenth centuries. From an index of 100 in 1552, it stood at about 75 in 1600, about 40 in 1630, and about 20 in 1640. As over the same period the price of civic offices increased by about 50 per cent in real terms,[59] this decline cannot be explained as a simple reflection of a general impoverishment in the Castilian economy in the seventeenth century. The lust for honour was being satisfied in the seventeenth century less by movement into the nobility than by movement within it. With not only knighthoods of the Military Orders but also earldoms and marquisates now available for money, nobility was being cheapened all along the line,[60] and resources in the seventeenth century were diverted rather into office than into honour. In 1600 there was only one municipal *regimiento* that cost more than an *hidalguía*, that of Seville; by the 1630s there were no less than nineteen of them.[61] The *hidalguía de privilegio*, always difficult to sell, was clearly becoming even less attractive, and this can only be related to the nature of the commodity itself, and to the changing value of the benefits it conferred.

To buy an *hidalguía* was to buy a composite package of legal rights, financial privileges and social status. The *carta de privilegio* made, or declared (and the distinction was an important one), its recipient an *hidalgo*, and with him all his children under the age of twenty-five, unmarried and still in tutelage under the parental roof, together with their descendants in the male line, legitimate or illegitimate, for all time. They were thus entitled

---

[59] This calculation is based on work I have in progress on the sale of municipal offices in the sixteenth and seventeenth centuries.

[60] There were more *títulos* created by the Crown in the seventeenth century than *hidalguías* — 5 *vizcondes*, 128 *condes* and 296 *marqueses*, compared with 44 altogether in 1520-98, DOMÍNGUEZ ORTIZ, *Sociedad española en el siglo XVII*, vol. 1, p. 209; REGLÁ, *New Cambridge Modern History* v: 370.

[61] viz. Jerez de la Frontera, Murcia, Málaga, Granada, Jaén, Ecija, Córdoba, Cádiz, Seville, Antequera, Toledo, Madrid, Valladolid, Segovia, Salamanca, Plasencia, Badajoz, León, Burgos — though it is to be noted that the price of *regimientos* also fell markedly in the 1640s.

to all the 'honours, rewards, graces, freedoms, liberties and exemptions, preeminences, prerogatives, immunities and privileges to which by existing or future laws and statutes, or by use and custom, or in any other way, the *hijosdalgo notorios de sangre y solar conocido* were entitled to have and to enjoy'.[62] These were, principally, perpetual exemption from all royal or municipal taxes, excises and levies on property or the person from which the *hidalgos notorios de sangre* were exempt; the right to show arms on shields, plate, houses, chapels and tombs, to issue and accept challenges, to take the field and receive the surrender of castles and fortresses, to give and receive fealty and to participate in all the ceremonial acts of nobility. No *hidalgo* could be compelled to join the feudal host, or to parade in musters, or to serve public or municipal office. He was, on the other hand, to be admitted to *hidalgo* confraternities and assemblies and to offices customarily or by a formal 'mitad de oficios' statute given to *hidalgos*. He enjoyed immunity from arrest or imprisonment for civil debt and from judicial torture, as well as the privilege of special treatment if gaoled or punished for criminal offences.[63]

The question is, what were these privileges really worth? It is frequently asserted that it was to escape the heavy burden of taxation that anyone with a bit of money bought a patent of nobility,[64] but did the financial returns justify an investment of four, five or 6,000 ducats? The classic *pechos*, the payment of which defined social status, were those levied on the person, the *martiniega* (a feudal tax due to the lord on St Martin's day), the *moneda forera*, and the *servicios* granted every three years by the Cortes. The *martiniega* and the *moneda forera*, levied at a

---

[62] The example used here is the printed *privilegio* issued to Mateo de Angulo Vargas of El Arahal, 4 Dec. 1631, CP 17, f. 5.

[63] See DOMÍNGUEZ ORTIZ, *Sociedad española en el siglo XVII*, vol. 1, p. 180; NOEL SALOMON, *La campagne de Nouvelle Castille à la fin du XVIe siècle d'après les 'Relaciones topográficas'* (1964), p. 289 note 1.

[64] Elliott, p. 196; De Vries, p. 29; GONZALO ANES, *El Antiguo Régimen: los Borbones* (1975). p. 46, citing Pedro Antonio Sánchez, 1782.

rate of 12 or 16 *maravedís* per *pechero* every seven years, were of no financial significance.[65] The *servicios* were much more important, but even so in many places the *hidalgo's* exemption was irrelevant, either because no effective distinction of estates existed or because the entire community was exempt. It was this consideration that disinclined anybody in Toledo from offering anything for the *hidalguías* when they were put up for sale in 1557,[66] and many other important centres fell into one or other of these categories, including Burgos, Palencia, Salamanca, Granada, the entire Kingdom of Seville, Murcia and much of Andalusia.[67] The *servicios* were in any case after 1538 a fixed contribution of 400,000 ducats a year that was being rapidly devalued by inflation; comprising about 15 per cent of total domestic Crown revenue in 1559, they made up less than 5 per cent forty years later, entirely overshadowed by the *alcabalas* that were tripled during the reign of Philip II and the *millones*, first introduced in 1590. By the seventeenth century the *alcabalas* and the *millones* brought in more than ten times as much as the *servicios*, and from those the *hidalgo* could not escape. He was exempt from the *alcabala* only on the goods he sold, not on what he bought, and the *millones* were in theory levied indiscriminately on all consumption of the basic commodities, meat, wine, oil and vinegar. Clearly, then, everything depended on how taxes

---

[65] Carande II: 356-9; Ulloa, p. 493; DOMÍNGUEZ ORTIZ, *Política y hacienda*, pp. 203-4, 214; DOMÍNGUEZ ORTIZ, *Golden Age*, p. 157, on the *martiniega*; AGS CJH leg. 202 (292), Licenciado Paulo de Laguna to Philip II, 23 Aug. 1592, opposing permitting certain lords to levy the *moneda forera* because ' dase introduccion para que los Señores tengan mas mano en sus lugares de la que conviene haziendo hidalgos a su voluntad, por no cobrar de ellos esta moneda que es pecho de pecheros, con que adquieren posesion de hidalguia '.

[66] AGS CJH leg. 23 (36), f. 205; Ulloa, p. 95; ACC XIII: 72.

[67] ACC XIII: 71-2; Ulloa, pp. 469-71 and Carande II: 619 list a number of other places with such exemptions. In Poza (Burgos), where Don Juan González de Guzmán procured a *carta de privilegio* in 1691, the only direct tax paid by the *estado general* was 16 *maravedís* for the *moneda forera* every seven years; the *servicios* were paid from communal revenues, and the town was exempt from military levies and billeting because its residents were employed in the salt works, CP 17, f. 33.

were assessed and collected, and this varied from town to town. We know as yet far too little about the social incidence of taxation in Habsburg Castile to be able to generalize about the total value of the *hidalgo's* fiscal privileges. The few pieces of concrete evidence available suggest that they could not have provided much incentive for the purchase of an *hidalguía*. In 1631, Alonso Pantoja Correa bought an *hidalguía* but was denied recognition by the *alcaldes* of the town of Pinto, near Toledo, where he lived, on the grounds that he was the richest man in the place, with more property than 309 other *vecinos* put together and four times as much wealth as the next four richest residents; on top of which, they claimed, he had eight children to inherit his exemptions (he had in fact four sons and two daughters). The town offered 5,100 ducats, 100 ducats more than Pantoja had paid, for the patent to be withdrawn and for a promise that no other *vecino* of Pinto would ever be granted a similar exemption or *carta de privilegio*. Thereupon, Pantoja offered to make available 6,000 *reales* with which to buy *juros* sufficient to provide an annual income equal to his contribution to the services paid by the municipality. As *juros* secured on the *millones* gave a return of 5 per cent, Pantoja must have been assessed at 300 *reales* a year.[68] For his investment of 61,000 *reales* he could have procured an income in excess of 3,000 *reales*. If this was the case for a man in Pantoja's position, in a town which enjoyed no particular fiscal privileges, it is likely that the purchase of nobility made strictly economic sense only from a dynastic point of view. For a man with a number of sons whose exemption could multiply rapidly, it might be economically worthwhile in the long run;[69] otherwise, different considerations had to predominate.

---

[68] AGS DGT 24, leg. 332, *relaciones* of 1661 (23 Sept. 1634). In Fuente del Maestre (Badajoz), one particular exemption in 1530 was said to have been worth only 10-12 *reales*, CP 17, f. 72.

[69] AGS CJH leg. 91 (135), Francisco Duarte to Philip II, 18 Sept. 1574, 'entiendo que los que son Ricos y tienen muchos hijos no pararan en ello y las tomaran a este

Other benefits, the freedom from arrest for debt or from cooption as administrators of bankrupts, the exemption from billeting, purveyance, conscription and from service in the *caballería de cuantía* in Andalusia and Murcia, perhaps tended to bulk larger as the military pressures of the late sixteenth and seventeenth centuries resuscitated the traditional military obligations of the *hidalgo* precisely at the moment when the straight fiscal advantages were beginning to be eroded.[70] It is symptomatic that one of the concessions suggested by Philip IV to make *hidalguía* more attractive was to give new purchasers immunity for some years from being summoned to war.[71]

The concrete benefits weighed all the more because the *hidalguía de privilegio* was not in itself of much honorific value. It was very much a second-class nobility, much less respected than either the 'antigua y estimada nobleça de Castilla', the *hidalgos de solar conocido*, of ancient and renowned lineage, or the 'hidalgos notorios tenidos y estimados por tales', living nobly and held to be such.[72] Municipal councils whose membership was restricted to noblemen discriminated against the *hidalgos de privilegio* and their known descendants, and the purchasers of *privilegios* themselves did their best to obliterate the origins of their nobility, having any reference to payment written out of their patents, getting the grants to declare them to be *hidalgos de sangre*, and refusing to exhibit their titles when called upon

---

precio, pero otros que no tienen tanta hacienda ni tantos hijos se an de detener en el conprar'.

[70] See the reasons given by the Cortes in 1593 for the large number of *hidalguías* litigated in the *chancillerías* during the previous twenty years, *ACC* XIII: 74; DOMÍNGUEZ ORTIZ, *Desigualdad contributiva*, pp. 1262-3; Elliott, p. 332; HENRY KAMEN, *The Iron Century. Social Change in Europe 1550-1660* (1971), p. 160.

[71] Danvila, *BRAH* 16: 88; and 'Relación de 1710', grant to Juan Arias Pérez, 18 Feb. 1631, of the rights of *hidalguía* without any obligation to maintain arms and a horse.

[72] The classifications are those of the Conde Duque de Olivares, 'Papeles que Dio el Conde Duque a su Magd para el Gobierno de su Monarchia', British Library, Egerton Ms. 347, f. 258.

to prove their privileges so as not to prejudice the status of future generations.[73] Interest in the purchasing of nobility, therefore, seems to have been related to the degree of openness of access to the other, more prestigious forms of nobility.[74]

Apart from the grant of patents by the Crown, nobility was recognized either formally through the judgement of the courts, or informally through acceptance by one's peers and neighbours. The formal legal process involved a suit before the *alcaldes de los hijosdalgo* of the *chancillerías* of Valladolid or Granada for a declaration of nobility by virtue of direct descent in the male line from a family of established noble reputation. If after review and appeal judgement was found in favour of the litigant and against the Crown *fiscal* who challenged the action on behalf and at the expense of the local *concejo*, a *carta executoria* was issued declaring the suitor's nobility proved.[75] Nobility might also be recognized by common repute,[76] manifested normally by

---

[73] AGS DGT 24, leg. 319, 'traslado del acuerdo en que se mando despachar previlegio de Hidalguia para Antonio de Sant Millan, alcalde de las casas de la moneda y regidor de Segovia' (18 June 1596) — he was to pay 6,500 ducats in cash and the document was to be drawn up 'sin que en el previlegio se haga mencion de que sirve con la dicha cantidad'. It was normal to have separate copies made with and without payment clauses. *ACC* xii: 176, session 11 Aug. 1592; *ACC* iii: 412, petition 78 of 1570-71 Cortes, 'muchas personas que han comprado hidalguías en estos reynos, las esconden y encubren queriendo que se olviden y passen de la memoria para despues aprovecharse de la posession en que han estado, rehusando de mostrar el título con que la adquirieron...'.

[74] A similar process is apparent in eighteenth-century France with interest in the purchase of letters of ennoblement increasing as the possibility of acquiring nobility through the purchase of office declined, ELINOR G. BARBER, *The Bourgeoisie in 18th Century France* (1955), p. 117.

[75] The procedures are set out in *Novísima Recopilación*, vol. 5 (1805), *Libro XI, título* 26 'De los Juicios de hidalguía, y sus probanzas; y del modo de calificar la nobleza y limpieza', *leyes* 4, 12, 13, 17.

[76] *ACC* xiii: 73, session of 4 Nov. 1593; ANTONIO DOMÍNGUEZ ORTIZ, *La clase social de los conversos en Castilla en la Edad Moderna* (1955), p. 193, quoting Don Francisco de Amaya (1639), 'Es evidente que la pureza y la nobleza no es algo esencial, corpóreo, real y palpable, sino algo que consiste en la opinión humana, en la opinión del vulgo'.

the town council and the representatives of the commonalty accepting a man as noble and listing him in the *hidalgo* estate when tax rosters (*padrones*) were drawn up or allowing him to take part in elections for specifically *hidalgo* offices in the municipal corporation. Consequently, an alternative aid to social advancement lay in the purchase of a *regimiento* or municipal governing office from the Crown which enabled the venal *regidor* to have a hand in the manipulation of the *padrones* and in the control of municipal litigation.[77]

Neither the law nor office guaranteed success but they conferred a much more desirable status than purchase and in general they were very much cheaper. Any man who could afford to buy a *carta de privilegio* could almost certainly afford to take an action before the *alcaldes* of the *chancillerías*, and if he could afford that he stood a good chance of winning his case without opposition.[78] Only if the outcome of a court action was seriously in doubt and likely to be costly and inconvenient, perhaps because of the

---

[77] *ACC* xviii: 320, Don Gómez Fernández de Córdoba in session of 10 July 1599.

[78] Salomon, p. 300, cites the remarks in the Cortes, 11 Nov. 1624, that ' los oficiales de las villas y lugares no se atreven a empadronar a qualquiera que quiere litigar, aunque notoriamente sea pechero y le dejan reservado como si fuera hijodalgo, y con esto adquiere posesion de tal '. The problem is to know what the cost of such a *pleito* really was. It was said in the Cortes (13 July 1599) that it cost 30 ducats or so, *ACC* xviii: 327, but it is difficult to reconcile this figure with the Cortes' own complaints about both town councils and poor *hidalgos* being ruined by the expense of going to law, or with the standard declarations in the *cartas de privilegio* that the purchasers were paying 6,000 ducats or more in order to avoid the cost and inconvenience of litigation. On the other hand, if the 70,000 *reales* that one late eighteenth-century litigant claimed in costs had been normal, there could hardly have been as many court cases as there were, AGS DGT 5, leg. 3, f. 176. On the relative ease of convincing (or hoodwinking) the judges of the *chancillerías*, which led Philip II in 1593 to order a revision of all their judgements in the previous twenty years, see the recommendation of the king's inner cabinet in Valladolid, 13 Aug. 1592, ' por la mucha desorden que se oye dezir que ay en las chancillerias en librar cartas de hidalguias con mucha facilidad, se acuerda que es cosa en que se podria mandar mirar, y proceder con recato por el perjuizio que resulta, o a los derechos de Su Md o al estado de los pecheros, y assi se podria encargar a los Presidentes de las chancillerias que lo encomienden mucho a los fiscales y juezes ', and Philip II's reply, ' muy bien me parece esto, y muy necesario, pero mirese por donde y como ', IVDJ envío 43, f. 331.

absence of distant or defunct witnesses or the loss of documentary proofs, or if for some reason the interested party could not wait for the slow process of the law to take its course, perhaps because of age or to qualify for office or escape imprisonment for debt, did the purchase of *hidalguía* make sense,[79] for what the royal *privilegio* could ensure was speed and finality. It conferred the legal benefits of nobility, whatever they were worth, but more important it conferred them immediately and it also gave the quietus to litigation in train or pending. Whether nobility was based on a formal legal claim or on the acceptance of a customary right, the response of the local community was all important. If it opposed a claim or refused to implement a judgement, nobility was always at risk. Challenged in the courts generation after generation, a claimant and his successors might find themselves shackled to the irremovable irons of costly litigation and subjected in their home towns to victimization and violence. The attraction of the *carta de privilegio* was, therefore, in some ways greater to families who already had a claim to nobility, but whose status was in dispute, than to total upstarts. The threat to nobility, latent in the endemic hostility of the *estado llano* to *hidalgo* status and in the constant testing and sifting of *hidalguía* by *pechero* town councils,[80] arose most commonly when a man moved to a new area or a new town, or when some change took place in the political organization of the town government. It could be the introduction of the *mitad de oficios* (the formal division of offices between *hidalgos* and *pecheros*)[81] or the presence of personal

---

[79] For examples of such cases, CP 17, f. 17 (Pedro Díaz Coca of Utrera, 23 Sept. 1631, aged 70); CP 16, f. 12 (Don Diego de Bernuy y Barba of Burgos, 3 Nov. 1566, confirmation as Mariscal de Alcalá granted earlier in 1566, *Corpus Documental* iii: 618), f. 44 (Juan Martínez Herrera, 24o of Seville, 17 Mar. 1598), f. 4 (Antonio Alvarez de Alcocer of Toledo, 18 May 1572).

[80] See Salomon, pp. 295-9; *ACC* xiii: 77.

[81] CP 17, f. 12 (Don Francisco Carcelén y Vera of Tobarra, 19 Oct. 1672), f. 66 (Pedro Pérez Cañas de Oro of Hinojosa, 9 Mar. 1691), f. 58 (Pedro Ortiz Fernández Jara of Almendralejo, 30 Mar. 1694).

enemies in the town council [82] that made it necessary to define and make explicit a nobility that had previously been taken for granted, but which, in the transition to a more literate and more bureaucratic society with written records and formalized judicial procedures, now required the correct documents and statutory proofs.[83] Many of the purchases of *hidalguía* were in fact very circumstantial in nature, reflecting less the rise of new men out of the commons than the fragility and vulnerability of existing noble status. It is this that explains the many apparent anomalies in the purchase of nobility and the expenditure of several thousand ducats by men who claimed already to be enjoying all the privileges of nobility, and in one case by a man who was actually a Knight of Santiago.[84]

The *privilegio* could, of course, also establish a new family on the first rung of the noble ladder. Most important, it entitled the recipient to all the outward and visible signs of nobility, arms, tax exemptions, separate listing in the *padrones de hijosdalgo*, election to *hidalgo* offices, membership of *hidalgo* confraternities, and it facilitated socially advantageous marriages for sons and daughters. In due course the venal origins of the entitlement would be forgotten and nothing would remain but the visible signs. In three generations the *hidalgo de privilegio* would have become an *hidalgo notorio de sangre* in law as well,[85] and an acceptable candidate for a knighthood of one of the military orders, or better.[86]

---

[82] CP 16, f. 14 (Juan de Borja of Roa, 28 Mar. 1558), f. 26 (Pero Hernández de Andrada of Seville and Umbrete, 5 Oct. 1575).

[83] This is a consideration that arises in a number of justifications, e.g. CP 17, ff. 42, 63, 67, 83, 84.

[84] Licenciado Don Francisco Sánchez de Tena Sahabedra, Knight of Santiago, of Hornachos, AGS DGT 24, leg. 332, *relaciones* of 1661 (7 June 1630).

[85] Gerbet, p. 301.

[86] In 1733, Captain Don Juan Bautista Manuel Gómez Pardo, *natural* of Alfaro, procured a habit of Santiago, presenting a string of witnesses to testify that his parents and grandparents had been recognized as ' nobles hijosdalgo de sangre segun fuero y costumbre de España y no de prebilegio '; his grandfather, Don Alexandro Gómez Pardo, had in fact bought a ' carta de declaración de su hidalguía ' in 1669 (CP 17, f. 29), Archivo Histórico Nacional, Madrid, Pruebas de Santiago 3470. The Galiano Puches

The essential point, however, is that status was something deriving from the community and validated by the political voice of the community, the town council.[87] To try to impose status from the outside by an act of the royal will was itself the resort of the ' outsider ', the man who lacked roots in the community or influence on the council, or support from allies and relatives among the nobility. This is perhaps one explanation for the highly skewed geographical distribution of the purchasers of *hidalguías* (Table 2). Nearly four-fifths (78%) of the sales were made to residents of Castile south of the Tagus. The whole of Castile to the north of Toledo province, containing 55 per cent of the population, bought less than one fifth (19.2%) of the *hidalguías*. The five contiguous provinces of Toledo, Ciudad Real, Albacete, Badajoz and Sevilla,[88] in western Andalusia and the south of New Castile and Extremadura, with less than a fifth of the population, bought two-thirds of the patents. This is a distribution very reminiscent of that described by Gerbet for the grants made by the Catholic Kings between 1481 and 1516.[89] In broad terms it correlates inversely with the distribution of *hidalgos* within Castilian society as a whole.[90] Over 80 per cent of Castile's *hidalgos* resided north of the Tagus; the purchasers of nobility came predominantly from those areas of Castile where *hidalgos* were thinnest on the ground. None of the seven provinces with most sales per head lay in areas in which *hidalgos* made up any sizeable proportion of the population (4% or more); in León-Asturias where nearly half the population was *hidalgo*, no *hidalguías* were sold at all.[91] Tentatively one might suggest that in

---

bought an *hidalguía* in 1601, became knights of Santiago in the mid-seventeenth century, and marquises of Galiano in 1742, CP 17, f. 24.

[87] *ACC* xiii: 71.

[88] Sevilla here refers to the modern province; Seville to the city.

[89] Gerbet, *Les guerres et l'accès à la noblesse en Espagne 1465 à 1592*, p. 324.

[90] ANNIE MOLINIÉ-BERTRAND, ' Les " Hidalgos " dans le Royaume de Castille à la fin du XVIe siècle: Approche cartographique ', *Revue d'Histoire Economique et Sociale*, 52 (1974), pp. 51-82.

[91] Molinié-Bertrand, Table 1, p. 67, used sixteenth-century administrative divisions;

provinces where *hidalgos* were relatively common the aspirant
was more likely to be able to demonstrate the alliances and
relationships with other noble families or to buy the kind of
plausible testimony and specious genealogy that could prove his
case in the courts. The town council and the general public were
perhaps also less likely to be exercised by the addition of an
extra *hidalgo* to an already large number than they would have
been by a more egregious ennoblement. The south, on the other
hand, retained many of the characteristics of the frontier. It
was an area of resettlement and mobility in which the economy
of Seville and the opportunities of the New World had a considerable impact. There was, therefore, perhaps more new, individual
wealth, more conspicuous *arrivisme*, but also more difficulty in
proving affinity with established noble lines in distant home-
lands.[92]

The 272 patents of nobility issued 1552-1700, two-thirds of
them after 1629, averaged less than two a year and added an
insignificant 0.2 per cent to the 134,000 *hidalgo* families in Castile
at the end of the sixteenth century.[93] Even in Sevilla, the province
most affected, the sales increased the noble population by a mere
1½ per cent or so. Only 132 separate communities were affected.

---

the seven modern provinces correspond roughly with Toledo 20.7% (but only 9% of
those were outside the city of Toledo), Mesa Arzobispal de Toledo 2.1%, Ciudad
Real 6.9% (but all of them in the capital city), Campo de Calatrava 3.1%, Ocaña
3.2%, Alcaraz 2.5%, Campo de Montiel 3.07%, Provincia de León de la Orden de
Santiago 3.1%, Sevilla 3.9% (61% of them in the city).

[92] This explanation is valid only in very general terms. The whole S.E. corner
of Castile (Murcia, Granada, Córdoba and Jaén), with 12.8% of the population and
only one nobleman in every forty or so inhabitants, bought only 6.3% of the *hidalguías*. In Salamanca province, where only 3.2% of the population was noble, none
were bought at all. On the other hand, the provinces of Burgos and Logroño, where
nobles comprised one-fifth of the population, bought relatively more *hidalguías* than
Córdoba, where nobles were only one in 100, or Avila and Guadalajara, where they
were between one in forty and one in fifty. Interestingly, the Habsburg pattern did
not persist into the Bourbon period. In the eighteenth century the proportion of
hidalguías sold north of the Tagus is double that of the previous 150 years.

[93] Molinié-Bertrand, p. 62.

The biggest increments in individual towns were 37½ per cent in Utrera (Sevilla), 25 per cent in Manzanares (Ciudad Real), 24 per cent in Villarrobledo (Albacete), and there were four other towns, of the twenty-two in which three or more *hidalguías* were sold, with increments of over 10 per cent. In eighty-eight places there was only one new creation.[94]

Although the general impression is that the number of *hidalgos* in Castile was on the increase in the sixteenth century, there is no evidence that the *hidalgos de privilegio* contributed disproportionately to that increase or that their contribution was anything but marginal compared with that of the *hidalgos* who had won *cartas executorias* in the courts. We have no precise knowledge of the number of *cartas executorias* adjudicated by the *chancillerías* in the Habsburg period, but what fragmentary evidence there is suggests that we should be thinking in terms of several thousands, even perhaps in terms of five figures rather than four.[95] Whatever the exact number, there can be no doubt that the number of *hidalguías* proved in the courts was many times greater than, perhaps up to a hundred times as many as, those

---

[94] *Hidalgos* of known *vecindad* were distributed thus: Seville 29, Utrera 9, Ocaña, Villarrobledo 7, Almagro, Cáceres, Villanueva de los Infantes 6, Toledo, Zafra 5, Corral de Almaguer, Esquivias, Guadalcanal 4, Almansa, Almendralejo, El Arahal, Aroche, Burgos, Don Benito, Fuente del Maestre, Manzanares, Tobarra, Ubeda 3; twenty-two towns had two *hidalguías*, and eighty-eight had one.

[95] See ALFREDO BASANTA DE LA RIVA, *Archivo de la Real Chancillería de Valladolid. Sala de los Hijosdalgo*, 4 vols. (Valladolid, 1920-22), and ' Genealogía y Nobleza: quinientos documentos presentados como pruebas en la Sala de los Hijosdalgo de la Real Chancillería de Valladolid y estudiados ahora ', *BRAH* 78 (1921), pp. 437-56, 505-14; 79 (1921), pp. 42-57. 187-212, 434-48; 80 (1922), pp. 58-70, 137-45, 276-87, 340-68, 416-46. Scattered figures for individual towns give some idea of the extent of the litigation – in Alfaro, a city of 1,200 *vecinos*, there were sixty lawsuits over *hidalguía* pending in 1602 (AGS Cámara de Castilla, Oficios leg. 1, Agreda, f. 25, testimony of Pedro Martín, 25 June 1602), and in the 1570s there were thirteen pending in Aranda de Duero (c. 1,200 *vecinos*; AGS Guerra Antigua leg. 73, f. 8), eleven in Alcolea de Almodóvar (184 *vecinos*), five or six in Socuellamos (700 *vecinos*), and all forty *hidalgos* of Terrinches (150 *vecinos*) had been challenged and forced to appeal to the *alcaldes de los hijosdalgo* of Granada, VIÑAS and PAZ, *Relaciones de los Pueblos de España: Ciudad Real*, pp. 22, 475, 497. The last example underlines the point that many of the lawsuits were not about new *hidalguías* but the confirmation or reestablishment of the old.

which were sold. A partial comparison of the admittedly ambiguous categories of the *relaciones* of the 1570s with the census of 1591 suggests that the *hidalgo* population had grown about 5 per cent faster than the population as a whole. If this inference from a limited geographical area could be generalized, it would mean that the total number of *hidalgos* had increased by about 22,000, some 6,000 in excess of what could have been expected from the general trend of demographic growth, in a period during which only ten patents of nobility had been sold. In six towns of Toledo and Ciudad Real provinces for which a comparison is possible, the number of *hidalgos* increased from 170 *casas* to 204 without any *privilegios* having been bought there.[96] In Palencia, the number of *hidalgos* increased from three in 1530 to thirty-four in 1622, again without any sales there.[97]

The social impact of the new creations was perhaps even less than their absolute number. If the separate patents issued to brothers and cognates are taken into account, the number of families actually ennobled was only around 200. The same family names recur repeatedly. In the extreme case, fourteen recipients were linked by blood or marriage; nine of the twenty-seven *hidalguías* of Ciudad Real province came from a single six-family network, nineteen of the thirty-nine titles issued to residents of the Kingdom of Seville, outside the capital, went to members of three different family blocks, and at least eight of the *hidalgos* in the city itself were interrelated.

The purchasers of *hidalguías* were largely an urban group.

---

[96] For the 1570s, VIÑAS and PAZ, *Relaciones de los Pueblos de España: Ciudad Real*, pp. 73, 170, 231, 307, 590 (Almodóvar del Campo, Campo de Criptana, Daimiel, La Membrilla, Villanueva de los Infantes); *Toledo (primera parte)*, p. 509 (Lillo); and for 1591, Molinié-Bertrand, Table 3, pp. 71-4.

[97] *Pace* GUILLERMO HERRERO MARTÍNEZ DE AZCOITIA, 'La población palentina en los siglos XVI y XVII', "*Publicaciones*" *de la Institución* "*Tello Téllez de Meneses*", 21 (1961), p. 72, 'Este aumento sería debido, sin duda alguna, a la compra de hidalguías por parte de la gente adinerada'; there were three *hidalgos* in 1530, five in 1542, ten in 1562, twenty in 1614, and thirty-four in 1622.

Barely 15 per cent of them came from the 58.6 per cent of the population that lived in communities of 400 *vecinos* or less,[98] whereas nearly half came from towns and cities of over 1500 *vecinos*. However, as this was true of the *hidalgo* estate as a whole in those areas in which *hidalguías* were bought,[99] it says nothing about the new *hidalgos* which is not equally applicable to the old. An analysis of the information on the recipients' personal histories and family backgrounds presented in the patents goes further to suggest that the sale of *hidalguías* did not on the whole inject a new social dimension into the noble estate. One has to be careful about taking the claims of the grantees themselves at face value. None of them admitted to, let alone expressed any pride in, being self-made men. If they could not fabricate a genealogy going back to the Reconquista, they ignored their ancestry. Yet not all their claims can be set aside. A considerable number supplied hard evidence of the possession of nobility prior to the purchase of their patents. Of the 157 *cartas* which provide sufficient information for analysis, thirty-four contain convincing, concrete evidence of pre-existing *hidalguía* in the recipients' families. Antonio Alvarez de Alcocer's patent confirmed and ratified a *privilegio* of 1436 and a *carta executoria* of 1568;[100] Don Diego de Guzmán was the illegitimate son of a Commander of the Order of St John;[101] the great-grandfather of Juan de Sayago de Volaños was a knight of Santiago, and his own father had won a *carta executoria* in 1584 confirming his exemption from taxation;[102] the father of Don Grabiel de Torres del Salto had been freed from imprisonment for debt by the *audiencia* of Seville after proving his *hidalguía* in 1590;[103] Don Marcos de

---

[98] This is the criterion of urbanization employed by Molinié-Bertrand, *op. cit.*

[99] In eleven of the sixteen provinces south of Madrid, more than 70 per cent of the *hidalgos* lived in towns of 400 *vecinos* and over, Molinié-Bertrand, pp. 78-9.

[100] CP 16, f. 4 (18 May 1572).

[101] CP 16, f. 33 (5 June 1573).

[102] CP 17, f. 72 (15 Dec. 1608).

[103] CP 17, f. 81 (26 June 1610).

Flores Paredes, who paid 4,000 ducats for his *hidalguía* in 1633, had been appointed 'jurado en el estado de los caballeros hijos-dalgo' of Osuna in 1627 with the assent of the entire *cabildo*;[104] Fernando García Toledano y Lugo of Villamartín had been elected *alcalde de la hermandad* for the *hidalgo* estate with the approval of his town council;[105] Matías Lovera had contributed with money to the military obligations of the *hidalgos* in Alfaro, and was as well a member of the noble Confraternity of San Pablo;[106] Don Melchior Carrillo de Mora y Lerma, who bought an *hidalguía* for 50,000 *reales* in 1630, seems to have derived from the 'linage de los Carrillos' and the 'casa de Diego de Mora' which were listed among the *hidalgo* families of Daimiel in 1575;[107] Juan Antonio Corzo Vicentelo of Seville had proved noble descent in Corsica in 1568 — his daughter was later to marry the Count of Gelves with a dowry of 240,000 ducats.[108] Alcocer wanted his patent to escape imprisonment for debt; Guzmán wanted legitimization; Corso Vicentelo the naturalization of his Corsican nobility; Torres del Salto the restoration of the *blanca de la carne* collected from him in Seville because he had no *carta executoria*; Sayago de Volaños to resolve the lawsuit reopened by the *concejo* and *vecinos* of Fuente del Maestre; García Toledano to avoid the delays and the costs of litigation in the *chancillería*. In addition to these, eleven others (of twenty in all) claimed already to be enjoying the fiscal or legal privileges of nobility, and six more (of fourteen altogether) were actually in litigation with their town councils over their *hidalguías*. Another ten were the sons of Dons (including three who were the paternal grandsons of Dons), and thirty-three were themselves Dons, nine

---

[104] CP 17, f. 23 (8 Mar. 1633).
[105] CP 17, f. 27 (20 Nov. 1630).
[106] CP 17, f. 39 (31 Mar. 1669).
[107] AGS DGT 24, leg. 332, *relaciones* of 1661, and 'Relación de 1710' (22 Feb. 1630); VIÑAS and PAZ, *Relaciones de los Pueblos de España: Ciudad Real*, p. 231.
[108] CP 16, f. 23 (16 Apr. 1575); PIKE, *Aristocrats and Traders*, p. 116.

of whom did not fall into any of the previous categories. The title, Don, was not in itself a proof of nobility; it was rather, in both an active and a passive sense, an assumption of nobility. For the first three-quarters or so of the sixteenth century, its use was relatively rare and its absence meant very little, but from the end of the sixteenth century it became increasingly common, and by the later seventeenth century it was almost universal among the local elites.[109] This is reflected in our figures. Only 4.2 per cent of the seventy-two recipients of *hidalguías* 1552-99 were Dons; 20 per cent of the sixty 1600-59, and 64.3 per cent of the twenty-eight 1660-99.[110] As four of the nine Dons who had no other superior proof of prior nobility come from this last period, it is perhaps wise to treat their status with caution. On the other hand, three others had close relationships with knights of the Military Orders, and two were *veinticuatros* of Seville, an office for which nobility was a prerequisite.[111] In all, seventy-one of the 157 had a strong *prima facie* case for the possession of at least a disputed noble status independent of their patents.

Furthermore, as many as sixty-three others, with less positive justification, had already begun their assumption of noble manners and noble forms, claiming to be ' held and reputed to be noble ', or to be living nobly ' with servants, arms and horses ', or to be married into noble families (respectively ten, sixteen and fourteen in each category). The mothers of sixteen of them were Doñas (the Doña being a very much less exacting title

---

[109] Sebastián Covarrubias Orozco, *Tesoro de la Lengua Castellana* (Madrid, 1674), f. 220v, ' es título honorífico, que se dá al cavallero, y noble, y al constituydo en dignidad '; ' Muchas casas de señores han rehusado el don, y no se le ponen; y por estos pocos que le dexan le han tomado muchos, que no se les deve '. See also, Pedro Fernández Navarrete, *Conservación de Monarquías* (1625), Discurso X, Biblioteca de Autores Españoles, vol. 25 (1926), p. 472.

[110] The analyzable totals vary slightly with the information provided by the different sources.

[111] Pike, *Aristocrats and Traders*, p. 23; CP 17, ff. 1, 18; AGS DGT 24, leg. 332, *relaciones* of 1661 (Sebastián de Carrión Agraz, 8 June 1630); CP 16, f. 70 (Pedro de Villarreal, 20 Apr. 1567), f. 50 (Juan Núñez de Illescas, 19 Oct. 1567).

than the Don),[112] thirty-eight were married to Doñas, the sons
of sixteen of them had adopted the Don as a title, and in four
cases their daughters had married Dons. Excluding the seventeen
whose only claim derived from their wives and mothers, the
remaining forty-six might reasonably be put into a kind of pre-
noble category for whom the *carta de privilegio* stamped a formal
endorsement on their informally assumed status.[113] Only forty
of the 157 *hidalguías* for which we have information were granted
to recipients who either had no pretensions to prior nobility
or made no claim that was supported by anything more than
assertion. To the extent that these may have been 'new men',
they were heavily concentrated in the first decades of the sales.
Two-thirds of them date from before 1585, making up 45 per
cent of all patents issued by that year compared with only 13
per cent in the same category between 1585 and 1700.

There are far fewer clues to the economic origins of the buyers.
The justifications presented in the patents, somewhat surpri-
singly if one is to accept the traditional view of the importance
of employment in derogating from *hidalguía* in Castile, show
very little interest in the wealth of the applicant and none at
all in the way he made his money.[114] In not one single case
did an applicant consider it necessary to prove that he was not
engaged in any trade or 'oficio vil y mecánico' commonly regarded as derogating from nobility. In contrast to the assertions
of 'limpieza de sangre' made directly or indirectly in forty-two
of the patents,[115] the only information there is on occupation

---

112 Covarrubias Orozco, f. 220v, ' en las mugeres se admite con mas indulgencia,
y facilidad'.

113 Cf. Gerbet, p. 304, 'L'Hidalguia vient peut-être alors sanctionner une élévation
sociale datant du père?'.

114 In only nine cases was there any explicit emphasis on the petitioner's wealth,
although there were more oblique references in perhaps another thirty cases and in the
description of applicants as 'gente principal', living nobly with horses, arms and servants. On the signification of 'principal' as wealthy see BARTOLOMÉ BENNASSAR, *Los
Españoles, actitudes y mentalidades* (1976), p. 206.

115 Most frequently by the petitioner declaring himself (20 cases) or his father

or source of income comes as a by-product of the cataloguing of the applicant's services. What mattered was not private employment but public function. Forty-seven of the recipients held important posts in local government, *alguacil mayor, alférez mayor, regidor, jurado, alcalde, escribano, alcaíde*,[116] emphasizing the point that the new *hidalgos* were often men already prominent in the elites of their local societies, but also suggesting that municipal office was not always a complete instrument of social advance.

Also surprising, perhaps, is the small part that some of the boom careers of the sixteenth and seventeenth centuries seem to have played in the creation of the wealth of the new *hidalgos*. Only nine of them were lawyers or university graduates, or their sons, and no more than thirteen were, or had been, employees of

---

(12 cases) to be a ' familiar ' of the Inquisition, ' porque semejantes titulos y officios no se le an de dar ni dan sino a las personas que son limpias de sangre de su generacion ', CP 17, f. 71. There is also some evidence of *conversos* or New Christians among the recipients. Two confirmations of privileges were issued to descendants of converted Moors (CP 16, f. 69; CP 17, f. 22), and the status of nobility and *limpieza* was restored to a woman whose greatgrandparents had been condemned for heresy (' Relación de 1710 ', 3 Aug. 1629). It is possible also to link up to thirteen of the twenty-nine *hidalgos* of Seville to likely *converso* families, and two of the five Toledan *hidalgos* were probably *conversos* as well (JOSÉ GÓMEZ MENOR, *Cristianos nuevos y mercaderes de Toledo* [1970], p. 17 note 27 — Hernán Xuárez Franco, CP 16, f. 37, and p. xxxiii — Antonio Alvarez de Alcocer, CP 16, f. 4). The *hidalguía de privilegio* had the advantage of giving the New Christian the opportunity to justify his nobility on his own terms without the danger of public exposure and investigation; but in practice the channel that was opened was a narrow one. Until the reign of Philip IV, at least, the Crown did not welcome obvious *converso* applicants. Charles V actually prohibited them, and under Philip II and Philip III only five patents were issued with the cryptic ' supliendo qualquier defeto ' formula which may have concealed some disqualification or racial impurity (CP 16, f. 47, Don Juan Alonso and Don Francisco de La Mota, 20 Aug. 1565, and f. 12, Don Diego de Bernuy Barba, 3 Nov. 1566, of Burgos, ' y en caso que en la dicha posesion obiese avido algun defecto o quiebra por no tener todas las calidades que las prematicas destos reynos requieren... en vuestras personas o en las de vuestros predecesores, suplo todos e qualesquier defectos que pueden ynpedir la dicha posesion y propiedad '; CP 16, f. 71, Juan Zapata de Azuaga, 5 Feb. 1567; CP 16, f. 5, Licenciado Luis Alvarez, *regidor* of Guadalajara, 10 Nov. 1558; CP 17, f. 81, Don Grabiel de Torres del Salto of Seville, 26 June 1610).

116 *Alguaciles mayores* 2, *alféreces mayores* 3, *regidores* 31, *jurados* 3, *alcalde ordinario* 1, *escribanos del ayuntamiento* 2. *alcaídes* 5.

the royal household or administration, even in the lower eche-lons.[117] In four or five of these cases the *privilegio* may have been a royal grant rather than a proper sale,[118] but it is clear that in general the Habsburgs did not, or did not have to, reward their servants with *hidalguía*.

There is equally little evidence that the sale of *hidalguías* had any significant effect on the *desembourgeoisement* of the Ca-stilian, commercial middle-class. Although the purchasers of *hidalguías* were overwhelmingly an urban class, not many of them were residents of the great commercial centres of Castile. Burgos received three patents, all issued to the same La Mota-Bernuy family in 1565-6, and Toledo five (four of them in the years 1568-72), but it was not possible to sell any at all in Medina del Campo throughout the period, only one in each of Medina de Rioseco (1570), Villalón (1598), Segovia (1596), Guadalajara (1558), Cuenca (1640), Palencia (1699) and Valladolid (1699), and only two in Madrid (1572, 1641). In all the major Andalusian seaports there were only two sales, one in Málaga (1567) and one in Cadiz (1670); whereas the province with the second highest number of *privilegios*, with one in seven of all those issued, was

---

[117] Grants were made to Alonso de Mesa, ' mayordomo de la hazienda de Aranjuez, veedor y proveedor de sus obras', 25 Nov. 1567 (CP 16, f. 46), and to Contador Andrés de Almoguer, *alcaide* of the Casa del Bosque de Balsaín and *veedor* of buildings at Balsaín and of the *alcazares* of Segovia, 24 June 1572 (CP 16, f. 3). *Hidalguías* were also received by Francisco López de Almaguer, *contador* of the Council of Finance, and his brother, Antonio, sometime secretary of the viceroy of New Spain, for 3,500 ducats (CP 16, f. 40, 10 Jan. 1556), Pero Luis Torregrosa, ex magistrate and *factor* of the Casa de Contratación of Seville (CP 16, f. 68, 1 Oct. 1565), a royal *factor* in Peru (CP 16, f. 52), an inspector of mines (CP 16, f. 60), two attorneys of the royal councils (CP 17, ff. 20, 61), three *continos* and two others with some unspecified con-nection with the royal household (CP 16, ff. 1, 57, 71; CP 17, ff. 9, 23).

[118] The Mesa, Almoguer and Torregrosa grants probably (CP 16, ff. 46, 3, 68), the Ortega Valencia grant (CP 16, f. 52), and perhaps that to Albarado Riocavada (CP 16, f. .57). Discounted from this analysis are two *hidalguías* bestowed upon wet nurses of royal infants (' Relación de 1710 ', 26 July 1626, 17 Aug. 1632), aud two to residents of Navalcarnero for their services at the time of Philip IV's second mar-riage in 1649 (CP 17, f. 6; ' Relación de 1710 ', 5 Dec. 1649, 11 Dec. 1650).

Badajoz, one of the most rural and backward parts of Castile.[119] It was only in the city of Seville, with twenty-nine, or nearly 11 per cent of the *hidalguías*, that there was any reflection of the social transformations effected by the conquest ot the Americas and the growth of the economy in the sixteenth century. The Indies were the only area of Castilian enterprise to show up strongly in the patents. One quarter of all the titles issued 1552-1602 (19 of 77) were bought by men who themselves or whose fathers had spent part of their lives in the New World.[120] However, as the accounts they rendered of their services concentrated very much on their achievements in the Conquest and their contributions to military organization, we cannot take it for granted that even in this sector it was mercantile wealth rather than the prizes of war that went into nobility. What does emerge very clearly is the narrow chronological span within which the impact of the Indies was felt. Nineteen of the twenty-two patents with an American connection were issued between 1567 and 1602, while twenty-two of the twenty-nine granted to residents of Seville were dated between 1565 and 1585.[121] There was, of course, a considerable overlap; eleven of the twenty-two Indies titles went to residents of the city and four others to towns of the province of Seville. What is striking is the shift in the balance between capital and province before and after 1600. In the sixteenth century, of all sales in what are the present-day provinces of Sevilla, Huelva and Cadiz, 86 per cent were in the

---

[119] BENNASSAR, *Los Españoles*, p. 133.

[120] This is certainly a minimum figure to which at least three others should be added, although there is no mention made in their justifications: Luis Sánchez Dalvo, Rodrigo de Illescas and Juan Núñez de Illescas, all of Seville (CP 16, ff. 66, 34, 50); PIKE, *Aristocrats and Traders*, pp. 43-6, 127, and GUILLERMO LOHMANN VILLENA, *Les Espinosa, une famille d'hommes d'affaires en Espagne et aux Indes à l'époque de la colonisation* (1968), pp. 241-3.

[121] The prohibition of further sales in Seville in 1584 must have had some effect here, though it was never strictly adhered to; grants were made to *vecinos* of Seville in 1585, 1598 and 1610, 'no embargante el previlegio que la Ciudad de Sevilla tiene de que no se den cartas de ydalguia a ninguna persona de la dicha Ciudad' (CP 16, ff. 6, 44, 45; CP 17, f. 81).

capital city alone; in the seventeenth century, 87 per cent were in the provinces, indicative of the drift of the wealthy back to the land in the regressive phase of the economic cycle.

This same short chronological span also limits the period of specifically commercial and financial interest in the *hidalguías*. It has been possible to identify at least twenty-four *hidalguías* as connected either with administrators of local or royal revenues (8) [122] or with known banking and business families (16), like the Bernuys of Burgos, the Caballeros, the Illescas, Luis Sánchez Dalvo, Diego de la Torre, Pero Luis Torregrosa, Juan Antonio Corzo Vicentelo, and Diego de Alburquerque in Seville, Antonio Alvarez de Alcocer of Toledo, and Juan Xedler, the Fugger agent in Almagro.[123] Nineteen of these were sold before 1600; the other five in the seventeenth century.

The fact that two-thirds of all the patents issued were dated after 1629 should not, therefore, be taken to mean that the purchase of *hidalguías* represented anything like a flight of capital from commerce into status in the wake of the declining economic opportunities of the seventeenth century. What diversion of commercial wealth into nobility there was was a thing of the sixteenth not the seventeenth century. If one defines ' commer-

---

[122] García de León was *jurado* and *fiel executor* of Seville with long services in the financial administration of the Casa de Contratación (CP 16, f. 39, 7 Apr. 1567); Pedro de Ortega Valencia was royal *factor* for the province of Tierra Firme (CP 16, f. 52, 31 Dec. 1584), Fernando Rodríguez Ribas royal administrator of the rents and properties of Almodóvar del Campo (CP 17, f. 70, 18 Jan. 1631); Diego Vaíz of Peñaranda de Duero had twenty years' service in the treasury of royal rents of Santo Domingo de Silos (CP 16, f. 9, 27 Apr. 1592); Antonio de Sant Millán was *alcalde de las casas de la moneda* of Segovia (AGS DGT 24, leg. 319, *acuerdo* 21 Sept. 1596); Don Marcos de Flores Paredes's father was purveyor general of Potosí and treasurer of rents in Charcas (CP 17, f. 23, 8 Mar. 1633); Alejandro Gómez Pardo was *juez administrador* of the rents and properties of Alfaro (CP 17, f. 29, 31 Mar. 1669); Don Juan Martínez de Buxanda was *contador de visitas* of Ocaña (CP 17, f. 45, 22 Aug. 1682).

[123] A number of these were also involved in fiscal administration or tax farming, the Bernuys (with three patents, CP 16, ff. 12, 13, 47), Torregrosa (CP 16, f. 68), Alvarez de Alcocer (CP 16, f. 4), Sánchez Dalvo (CP 16, f. 66), Alburquerque (CP 16, f. 6); see Ulloa p. 43, and PIKE, *Enterprise and Adventure*, pp. 94, 96. There were undoubtedly others in this category that it has not been possible to identify.

cial wealth' broadly as including all the Seville and American purchasers as well, the combined titles issued to residents of Seville and to the American, commercial and revenue interests made up 54.3 per cent of analyzable titles pre 1600 (38 of 70), and 12 ½ per cent of those 1600-1700 (11 of 88). In general the market for *hidalguías* moved in step with and not against the overall trend of the economy. In the seventeenth century the price of *hidalguías* collapsed precisely as the economic depression deepened, and a number of buyers were forced to default on their contracts, despite the easy credit terms allowed, as they found their incomes overcommitted.[124] However, it is hard to see even the high sixteenth-century figure as of any general economic significance. The numbers were too few, the sums expended too small — perhaps 150,000 ducats from public and private sources in Seville in a twenty-year period 1565-85, less than 5 per cent of the private imports of bullion from the Indies in a single year. Nor should it be assumed that nobility was necessarily incompatible with commerce and finance. On the contrary, in some instances at least, nobility was purchased less for its own sake than for the furtherance of commercial interests. Antonio Alvarez de Alcocer bought an *hidalguía* in Toledo in 1572 in order to head off a prosecution for debt.[125] In March 1598, Juan Martínez Herrera bought an *hidalguía* for 6,600 ducats in order to qualify for taking up the *veinticuatría* of Seville that

---

[124] Petition of Alonso Díaz Guerrero of the town of Urda (Ciudad Real), who bought an *hidalguía* in 1629 for 4,000 ducats over nine years, but ' ya no estava en estado de poder tomarla por aver venido en mucha quiebra y desminucion de su hazienda y no tener con que pagarla '; he arranged for Andrés Nieto Patiño Castellanos to take it over for 38,500 *reales* in eight years, 14 Dec. 1637, but by 17 Mar. 1642 Nieto also found it impossible to continue payment ' a causa de la gran quiebra en que ha venido mi hazienda ', and he therefore contracted to pass it to Don Francisco Fernández Buenache, as Nieto, also a *regidor* of Villanueva de los Infantes, AGS DGT 24, leg. 332, *relaciones* of 1661.

[125] CP 16, f. 4; Hernando de Torres del Salto similarly procured his release from imprisonment for a debt of 2,714 *reales* of silver, owed for the purchase of Rouen linen and other cloths, by proving his *hidalguía* in Seville (CP 17, f. 81).

he had paid 7,800 ducats for the previous month, an office coveted among other things for the influence it gave over the control of trade and the administration of the customs system.[126] All in all, the 400,000-460,000 ducats that it can be estimated was diverted into *hidalguías* between 1552 and 1615, and the 650,000 or so during the rest of the seventeenth century can have taken only a tiny proportion of the investment resources of Castile. At least one hundred times as much went into government *juros* in the same period.[127]

As a fiscal expedient the sale of *hidalguías* was worth about 1¼ million ducats to the Crown over a century and a half in which royal revenues exceeded 2,000 million ducats.[128] In one totally exceptional year (1567) Philip II raised about 80,000 ducats, approximately 1 per cent of his income, and Philip IV sold some 300,000 ducats-worth in a four-year period (1630-33), but otherwise the contribution the *hidalguías* made to the treasury was barely noticeable. On the other hand, however small the sums involved, the sale of *hidalguías* was from the purely fiscal point of view an exceptionally good deal both for the Crown and, arguably and contrary to contemporary belief, for the country as well. It was a voluntary contribution, involving no alienation of revenue by the Crown, for the *hidalgo's* tax exemptions were not written off but absorbed into the allocation of the rest of the community. Furthermore, with the purchaser paying perhaps 200 years of tax obligations in one go, his re-

---

126 CP 16, f. 44 and AGS DGT 24, leg. 323 (24 Feb. 1598).

127 DOMÍNGUEZ ORTIZ, *Política y hacienda*, p. 164, gives the capital value of *juros* in 1657 as 133 million ducats.

128 These figures include the 50,000 ducats paid by Seville in 1584, and up to 100,000 ducats paid by the municipalities in 1630 over and above what they were able to recoup from sales. Ulloa, p. 650, prints a table of returns to the *Tesorería General* from the sale of *hidalguías* in the ten years 1567-70, 1572-5, 1596-7 showing 74,800 ducats for 1567 and a total of 107,506 for the remaining nine years. My own estimate is in the range 225-254,000 1552-75, 170-205,000 1583-1615 (plus 50,000 from Seville), and perhaps 650,000 1629-1700 (plus about 100,000 from the towns), see Table 1.

turn on capital invested ($\frac{1}{2}$ per cent in Pantoja Correa's case) was a very great deal less than it would have been had the Crown alienated revenues to him in *juros* at 5-7 per cent or sold him *alcabalas* and *tercias* at 2 $\frac{1}{2}$-3 per cent.[129] To the extent that the rest of the country was relieved of the need to raise the sums paid to the king by the purchasers of *hidalguías*, the community as a whole can be said to have been a net gainer. The fact that the great majority of the new *hidalgos* came from substantial centres of population (only five were bought in places of fewer than 200 *vecinos*) also meant that the impact of their exemptions was muffled by the number of taxpayers among whom the extra burden had to be shared. In Pantoja's case, and he was by a long way the wealthiest man in a town of over 3,000 people, this would have been about 13 *maravedís* per *pechero* per year, the equivalent of about one hour of labour. Other purchasers were not actually being taxed at all before their purchase (15 cases),[130] or were resident in places which did not separate *hidalgos* and *pecheros* for tax purposes (42 cases). Indeed, no less than one quarter of them came from the Kingdom of Seville where no significant fiscal distinctions existed,[131] and the total known to be in that category is over seventy. Only in the handful of cases in which there was a number of creations in the same small community, or when the initial exemption was multiplied rapidly by the growth of the grantee's family, could the fiscal impact have been of any importance. There were only twenty-two towns in which three or more *hidalguías* were sold; fifteen of them had populations in excess of 1,000 *vecinos*, and only one less than 400 (Esquivias, Toledo, with four sold 1630-79 in a

---

[129] SALVADOR DE MOXÓ, 'La venta de alcabalas en los reinados de Carlos I y Felipe II', *Anuario de Historia del Derecho Español*, 41 (1971), pp. 487-554.

[130] CP 16, ff. 5, 15, 4, 3; CP 17, ff. 72, 68, 7 mention *pechos* explicitly; CP 17, ff. 11, 41, 27, 3, 26, 23, 60, 39 refer to other privileges comprehending tax exemptions.

[131] *ACC* xiii: 71-2; DOMÍNGUEZ ORTIZ, *Orto y ocaso*, p. 50.

population of about 250 *vecinos*).[132]   Proliferation by natural increase was potentially a more serious problem. Contemporaries certainly believed that venal *hidalgos* tended to have a larger than average number of sons. In one case it was claimed that the original exemption had spread from three households to thirty or forty in the space of fourteen years.[133]   In La Membrilla (Ciudad Real), the *hidalguía* bought by Alvaro Cañuto in 1557 had spread to four Cañuto households by 1575; but his brother's, bought in Villanueva de los Infantes at the same time, was still the only one alongside thirty-nine *hidalguías de sangre*.[134] In fact, the average number of sons among the venal *hidalgos* at the time of purchase was only 2.56, and as many had no more than one son as had more than three.[135]   So, although in individual cases the belief of the Cortes and even of Philip II that the ennoblement of the richest members of a community imposed an intolerable burden on the rest may have been true, in general the sale of *hidalguías* had no such effect. When the *Junta Grande* and the Council of Finance discussed the problem in 1592, they decided that the harm to the poor was 'so little as not to be worth considering'.[136]   Even the Cortes, when, in 1599, it for once found itself on the other side, declared that the tax benefit was not worth what it cost a town to contest an *hidalguía* in the courts.[137]   If nothing else, the purchaser of a *carta de privilegio* saved the community the cost of litigation.

The evidence presented in this article calls for a substantial revision of the impact which the sale of patents of nobility is

---

[132] Of the twelve towns with four *hidalguías* or more, all except Esquivias had more than 1,000 vecinos.

[133] CP 17, f. 2.

[134] VIÑAS and PAZ, *Relaciones de los Pueblos de España: Ciudad Real*, p. 307; CP 16, f. 1.

[135] Of the 79 cases for which clear information is available, 3 had no sons, 17 had one, 22 had two, 17 had three, 14 had four, and 6 had five or more.

[136] AGS CJH leg. 202 (292), *consulta* of Council of Finance, 5 July 1592.

[137] ACC xviii: 329, session of 13 July 1599.

usually thought to have had on the economy and the social structure of Castile. It was very far from being the large-scale phenomenon that most historians have assumed. Nor is it true, as has been claimed, that the sale of *hidalguías* ' shattered the existing concept of nobility '.[138] Neither the absolute numbers sold, nor the social background of most of the purchasers, nor the probable sources of the wealth invested in nobility, nor the underlying ideals that validated the grants were such as to have had that effect. The essence of nobility continued to be, as it always had been, blood and war. Alongside the claims of lineage, the military services of the recipient and his ancestors and close relatives remained overwhelmingly the single most important criterion for ennoblement that the justifications put forward. Nine of the grantees had military rank, thirty-three others had served in person in war in Spain, Europe or the Indies, and a further seventy-two adduced the immediate or remote exploits, real or fictitious, of close relatives and distant ancestors back to the Reconquista. Nearly three-quarters of all the grantees made some claim to military service in their justifications.

The sale of *privilegios de hidalguía* was at odds with the concept of nobility as an essence transmitted by blood or by custom, not in its content but in its form. The *carta de privilegio* was a conspicuous act of the royal prerogative and an exercise of the absolute power of the king to *create* nobility where none had existed before. It involved both a particular abrogation and dispensation from all the laws of his predecessors made in the Cortes which prohibited such grants, and also an assertion of the ' poderío real absoluto ' over and against custom, on the one hand, and the purely declaratory judgement of the *chancillerías*, on the other. The disparagement of the *hidalguía de privilegio* was therefore implicitly a political statement, a denial of the superiority of the regalian authority over custom and tradition.

---

[138] Carande ii: 502; Salomon, p. 300.

It was also a recognition of the superiority of a corporate concept of honour (of a lineage, a region, a town) over personal nobility and an individualist ethos.[139] The sale of *hidalguías* in fact diminished the force of neither custom nor corporatism. On the contrary, the standard voluntarist formula of pure creation ('es my merced y voluntad que seais y os hago hijodalgo de sangre y de solar conocido... como si uvieredes nascido de padres e abuelos hijosdalgo notorios de sangre')[140] all but disappears after 1585, to be replaced by a primarily declaratory formula ('declaro a vos...y los hago a todos hijosdalgo notorios de sangre y solar conocido...tan cumplidamente come si en favor de vos...por mis Alcaldes de los Hijosdalgo de las mis Audiencias y Chancillerias por todas instancias fueran dadas sentencias en vista y en grado de revista'),[141] which made the royal decree a substitution of the judgement of the courts, not a supplementation of the grantee's deficiencies. At the same time, on the part of the petitioners, the genealogical reconstruction of lineages became even more extravagant in seventeenth-century patents than in the previous century. As long as traditional concepts remained unbroken in this way the purchase of nobility was in the strictest sense a contradiction in terms,[142] and hence something whose moral basis was suspect and whose attractiveness was limited.

---

[139] AGS CJH leg. 23 (36), f. 205, Pedro Niño to Princess Juana, Toledo, 24 Mar. 1557, 'yo e platicado con algunas personas diziendoles quan bien les estaria hazerse hidalgos ansi para sus personas como para las de sus hijos y decendientes. Responden que biviendo en Toledo no tienen necesidad de mas hidalgia que la que tienen por los previllegios y libertades que los Reyes pasados dieron a los vezinos desta cibdad que aqui biviesen. A esto yo les digo que les podian suzeder cosas que tuviesen necesidad de yr a poblar a otros lugares donde serian ellos y sus hijos pecheros y que no deven perder esta ocasio para ser libres para sienpre donde quiera que biviesen, y ni esta Razon ny otras muchas que les e dicho no an bastado a que ninguno se mueva a dar un real por la hidalguia, ni yo creo que avra persona en este lugar que le de ny trate deste negocio'.

[140] Quoted from CP 16, f. 17 (Alonso Cavallero of Seville, 20 Apr. 1567).

[141] Quoted from CP 17, f. 5 (Mateo de Angulo Bargas Catalán of El Arahal, 4 Dec. 1631), printed.

[142] ALBERT SICROFF, *Les controverses des Statuts de 'Pureté de Sang' en Espagne du XVe au XVIIe siècle* (1960), pp. 296-7; Gerbet, p. 301. Sicroff and Gerbet (p. 306)

The Purchase of Nobility in Castile, 1552-1700

The results of this investigation, then, are largely negative. It was only at moments of extreme financial need, provoked by the specific demands of war, that the Crown was prepared to tamper directly with the traditional structure of nobility, and then so reluctantly, with such diplomatic camouflage, and at such a high price that the overall social and economic effects were minimal. Any impact the sale of *hidalguías* had was largely concentrated within one city and a single decade, or at most a generation. To say this is, of course, to say nothing about *hidalguía* in general nor about the other ways of acquiring it. In Castile, as elsewhere, there were alternative and quantitatively much more important ways of becoming noble. Indeed, it may well be that the unimportance of the sale of *hidalguías* is itself an indication of the relative ease of social mobility and the openness of Castilian society in the sixteenth and seventeenth centuries.

What does seem certain, however, is that the direct interference of the Crown with the social order was much less in Spain under the Habsburgs than it was under the Trastámaras or the Bourbons,[143] or, in view of the proliferation of letters of ennoblement and ennobling offices sold from the time of Francis I and the enormous inflation of knighthoods by the first two Stuarts, than it was at the same time in either France or England.[144]

---

also draw attention to the current of feeling that recognized these attitudes to be both restrictive of royal authority and damaging to the nation, but it is obvious from such polemics that the traditional view remained very deeply rooted.

[143] Gerbet, *op. cit.*; ANTONIO DOMÍNGUEZ ORTIZ, *Sociedad y Estado en el siglo XVIII español* (1976), p. 349. AGS DGT 5, legs. 3 and 4, respectively 275 and 395 patents for 1700-99, of which 134 were Castilian titles; the ' Relación de 1710 ' lists 57 patents 1701-10.

[144] J. H. SHENNAN, *Government and Society in France 1461-1661* (1969), p. 26; R. J. KNECHT, *Francis I and Absolute Monarchy* (Historical Association, London, 1969), p. 12 — 183 letters of ennoblement were issued in the thirty-two years of Francis I's reign of which at least 153 were sold; DAVIS BITTON, *The French Nobility in Crisis* (1969), p. 95 — there were at least 1,000 ennoblements in Normandy alone 1550-1650; JEAN MEYER, *La Noblesse Bretonne au XVIIIe Siècle* (Flammarion, Paris, 1972), pp. 28, 135, after the revocation in 1598 of all *lettres de noblesse* granted since 1578, 500 were put up for sale in France in 1696 and a further 100 in 1704; *ibid*, pp. 155-7, the purchase

The same inflation of honours took place *within* the aristocracy, at the higher levels of *títulos* and knights of the Military Orders, but at the foundation of the nobility, the basic distinction between gentleman and commoner, the Spanish Crown was directly responsible for none of the scandalous ennoblements that marked the sale of knighthoods under James I. The Habsburgs issued less than 300 *hidalguías* in 150 years; the Stuarts created well over 3,000 knighthoods in forty years. The *hidalgo* in the early seventeenth century had to pay over 6,000 ducats, a sum which presupposed an estate of 60,000 ducats and an income of at least 3,000; the Jacobean knight paid perhaps £ 100 and needed no more than £ 40 a year in rent, the equivalent of about 150 ducats.[145] The Spanish Crown, therefore, did not contribute to the weakening of traditional concepts of nobility or to the undermining of respect for the social hierarchy (however much these may have been occurring in other ways) in the blatant manner that was happening in England and France. Nor, consequently, were the Habsburgs subjected to the same kind of bitter criticism from the Castilian equivalent of the ' gentry '. There was, of course, opposition to the sale and granting of *hidalguías* in the Cortes and in the country, but, significantly, whereas the opposition in France and England was on social grounds, in Castile it was primarily fiscal. The social complaints from the Cortes, to which the Crown was subjected both when it sold *hidalguías* and when it tried to make *hidalguía* more difficult

---

of office added about 2,000 new families to the French nobility in the eighteenth century, and in Brittany there were 303 new, noble families, 252 from office, 25 from the purchase of *lettres*.

For England, LAWRENCE STONE, *The Crisis of the Aristocracy 1558-1641* (1965), ch. 3, especially pp. 66-82, and ' The Inflation of Honours 1558-1641 ', *Past and Present*, no. 14 (November 1958), pp. 45-70.

145 The price of nobility was also cheaper in France than it was in Castile, though not to the same degree as in England; *lettres de noblesse* cost c. 300 *écus d'or* in the reign of Francis I (Knecht, p. 12), 6,000 *livres* in that of Louis XIV (Meyer, p. 135), the equivalents of less than 350 ducats in the earlier period and about 2,400 ducats in the later, although by then additional expenses raised the actual cost to 4,000 ducats or so.

to acquire, were both muted and secondary. At the same time, the grounds for fiscal complaint, in the light of the number and the impact of the *hidalguías* sold, were in real terms illusory. Not only, therefore, was the direct creation of nobility by the Crown a far less significant component of social mobility and a far less relevant factor in the economy under the Habsburgs than it was at either earlier or later periods, or than it was as the same time in either France or England, but politically it also contributed one ground less to that deep alienation from government that disturbed so many European states in the seventeenth century.

TABLE 1

INCOME FROM *HIDALGUÍAS* 1552-1700

issues		known income ducats	known sales	estimated income ducats	estimated sales
1552-8	10	42,500	9	47,222	10
1561-2	2				
1565-6	4			0-5,000	0-1
1567	17 ⎫	103,300	18	177,905-206,600	31-36
1568-75	20 ⎬				
1583-5	5	12,100	2	18,150	3
1591-2	3	18,700	3	18,700	3
1596-8	11	66,600	10	66,600	10
1600-2	5 ⎫	65,900	9	65,900	9
1605-9	4 ⎬				
1610-15	6			0-36,611	0-5
1625-9	4			0-12,000	0-3
1629-30	40	175,226	40	175,226	40
1631	20	67,887	17	71,880	18
1632	10	36,818	9	36,818	9
1633-9	34	48,699	13	123,620-127,366	33-34
1640-52	29 ⎫	14,323	8	46,550-57,292	26-32
1655-63	4 ⎬				
1655-73	12 ⎫				
1677-82	12 ⎬	35,044	8	118,274-175,220	27-40
1691-99	20 ⎭				
	272			966,845-1,120,585	219-53

TABLE 2

GEOGRAPHICAL DISTRIBUTION OF *PRIVILEGIOS*

modern provinces	population * in *vecinos*	*privilegios* 1552-1615	1625-99	total	%	priv.os % pop. % × 100
North	*743,293*	*20*	*29*	*49*	*19.22*	
Galicia, Asturias León, Salamanca	271,112	0	0	0		
Biscay	40,000	0	1	1	0.39	13
Santander	27,035	0	1	1	0.39	19
Logroño	25,217	1	4	5	1.96	104
Burgos	52,234	5	3	8	3.14	81
Palencia	36,799	1	2	3	1.18	43
Valladolid	48,498	2	5	7	2.75	76
Zamora	41,237	2	1	3	1.18	38
Avila	39,972	2	0	2	0.78	26
Segovia	30,571	1	0	1	0.39	17
Soria	25,792	1	1	2	0.78	40
Guadalajara	50,894	1	1	2	0.78	21
Madrid	53,932	4	10	14	5.49	136
South	*594,872*	*65*	*141*	*206*	*80.78*	
Cuenca	62,376	0	3	3	1.18	25
Albacete	17,574	2	15	17	6.27	509
Toledo	77,303	8	23	31	12.16	210
Ciudad Real	36,552	10	17	27	10.59	388
Cáceres	61,176	1	8	9	3.53	77
Badajoz	63,895	8	28	36	14.12	296
Sevilla	61,435	30	29	59	23.14	504
Huelva	22,989	0	5	5	1.96	114
Cádiz	20,021	0	3	3	1.18	79
Córdoba	48,554	1	5	6	2.35	65
Jaén	56,656	3	3	6	2.35	56
Granada, Málaga, Almería	48,021	2	1	3	1.18	33
Murcia	18,320	0	1	1	0.39	28
	1,338,165	85	170	255		

* Population is calculated from a re-working of the 1591 figures printed in Tomás González, *Censo de población de las provincias y partidos de la corona de Castilla en el siglo XVI* (Madrid, 1829).

The Purchase of Nobility in Castile, 1552-1700

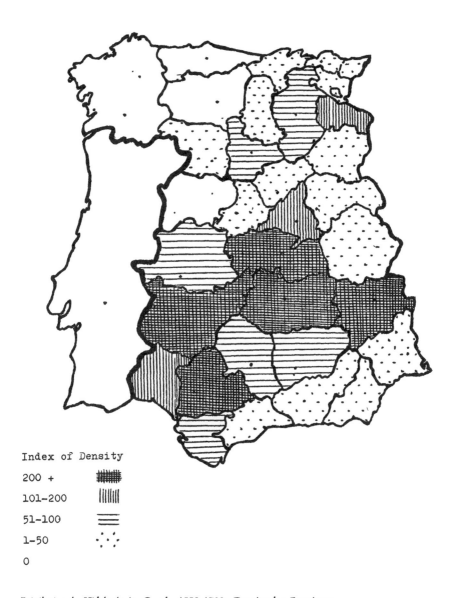

Index of Density

200 +

101–200

51–100

1–50

0

Privilegios de Hidalguía in Castile 1552-1700: Density by Provinces

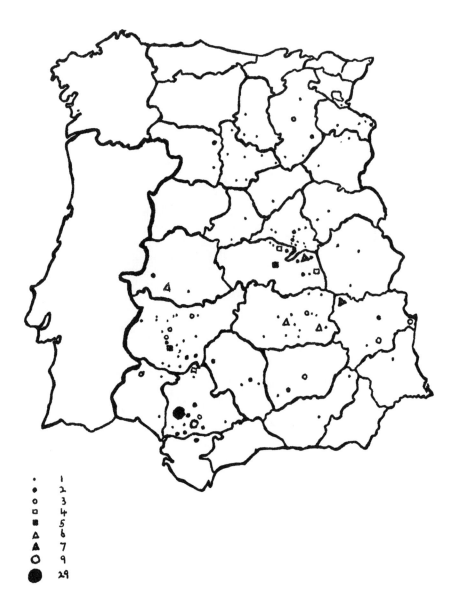

Geographical Origins of Purchasers of *Hidalguía* in Castile 1552–1700

XIV

Neo-noble Nobility:
Concepts of *hidalguía* in Early Modern Castile

The criteria by which a society defines its elites are among the clearest
expressions of the values of that society. This is a consideration of
particular relevance in a historiography which has related much of
the political, economic and cultural development of Spain and her empire
to social constructs and social thinking dominated by the ideals of *honor*,
hidalguía and *limpieza*. All these concepts have been extensively and
sometimes profoundly analysed by historians, but as is only too common
in the history of ideas, the study of ideals has been in the main the
study of idealization. The history of *hidalguía* has been quarried, on
the one hand, from a small number of doctrinals, theologies of status,
the treatises of Diego de Valera, Arce Otalora, Guardiola, García de
Saavedra, Moreno de Vargas, Peñalosa y Mondragón, the 'decálogo
del caballero' (Figueroa y Melgar), and others,[1] without regard for
their biographical or social contexts; and, on the other, from the
imaginative literature, in particular the drama, of the Golden Age, whose
themes undoubtedly reflected and perhaps also helped to form popular
stereotypes of the *hidalgo* and of noble-values, but whose connection
with actual behaviour is much more problematic.[2] The more positivist
approach to the definition of Spain's elites, drawing primarily on juridical
and notarial rather than literary evidence, has, however, produced its
own distortions. Its concern has been mainly sociological, a preoccupation
with social structure and mobility, with who became noble and how.
This concentration on the process of ennoblement inevitably makes for
a reliance on the external acts of the proving of nobility, namely the
lawsuits, the *pleitos de hidalguía* heard in the Chancillerías (the appeal
courts in Valladolid and Granada), and the investigations or *pruebas* for
admission into the Military Orders, both of which were designed to
demonstrate not that nobility was deserved but that it already existed.
This has led to a definition of *hidalguía* by its public manifestations,

fiscal exemptions, offices, life-style, common repute, family connections, membership of special fraternities or the Military Orders.[3] But what this adds up to is not a definition of *hidalguía* but a description of the *hidalgo*. The need is to do for the concept of *hidalguía* what is beginning to be done for the type of the *hidalgo*, namely to withdraw it from the history of literature and integrate it into the history of mentalities.

The purpose of this article is to contribute to the understanding of the contemporary meaning of *hidalguía* by examining a source which has hitherto escaped notice but which is unique in permitting a definition of *hidalguía* in terms of the perceptions of the *hidalgos* themselves, or more accurately in terms of the perceptions of *hidalguía* entertained by those aspirants to nobility who were required not so much to prove their status as to justify their claims to social promotion. These were the recipients of the several hundred royal patents of ennoblement granted during the course of the sixteenth, seventeenth and eighteenth centuries.[4] It has been possible to analyse some 150[5] of nearly 300 of these *cartas de privilegio* issued by the Crown between 1552 and 1700, according or confirming the status of nobility in return, for the most part, for a monetary service. Hundreds more were issued in the eighteenth century and the grants continued into the nineteenth century, but most of these were non-Castilian titles or other non-comparable patents, such as those granted to foreigners or to recipients of recent foreign extraction, or to the royal gynaecological staff.[6] No more than about 160 genuine Castilian *hidalguías* remain for the period 1720–99, and of these only one-fifth provide sufficient information for use in the present analysis. The discussion of *hidalguía* in the eighteenth century should, therefore, be regarded as based on an illustrative selection of data rather than on a statistical sample.

These *privilegios* followed a number of set formulae, but in all of them an essential component was the 'justification', a series of clauses which set out the genealogy and the past and present services of the recipient and his ancestors, as well as the various legal and circumstantial bases for the claim, previous royal grants, court judgements (*cartas ejecutorias*), municipal listings (*padrones*), tax exemptions, local offices held, membership of the Military Orders (*hábitos*) and noble fraternities family tombs and chapels, coats of arms, marriage alliances, style of life and public repute. These clauses, therefore, go beyond the more familiar 'proofs' of the *pleitos* and the Military Orders. They include these *proofs* but they also present a *justification* for nobility. These 'justifications' were the work of the grantees themselves. The patents incorporated the evidence that had been presented to the Council in their petitions for the grant and were clearly intended for public consumption. The *cartas de privilegio* had to be produced before the town councils in order to claim the exemptions and privileges of nobility, and they were appropriately doctored to conceal the stigma of venality and *arrivisme*. [7]

The 'justifications' are, therefore, uniquely valuable as expressions of what those seeking to impress their nobility on their fellows regarded as a convincing statement of noble qualities. The fact that the evidence covers a period of more than 250 years offers the further advantage of making possible a long-term history of the *hidalgo*-ideal and a dynamic analysis of the concept of *hidalguía* over a time-span which embraces the expansion, recession and recovery phases of the Monarchy's history and the entire sequence of conflicting ideological influences from Humanism and Counter-Reformation to Enlightenment.

I

The nobility of the *cartas de privilegio* was grounded on three criteria: inheritance, service and public recognition. Typically the 'justification' was concerned with all three. The *hidalgos de privilegio*, however parvenu, did not set themselves up as self-made men, nor did they stand for a nobility of virtue and merit as against the inherited nobility of lineage. The praise of self-advancement that is to be found in López Bravo, Moreno de Vargas and others, or the defence of personal as against inherited merit in Cervantes, Lope, Calderón, Ruiz de Alarcón, Bances Candamo and Peñalosa, gets no support from the new nobility. [8]

In the contemporary polemic about the nature and the source of nobility between those, like Arce Otalora, who defended the concept of a natural nobility, and the Bartolists, like Moreno de Vargas, who saw civil nobility as the creation of the sovereign will of the prince, the *hidalgos de privilegio* were in an anomalous position. The appeal to the Crown to create or confirm their *hidalguía* implied a Bartolist standpoint; yet their 'justifications', while accumulating as many grounds as were available to them, rested first and foremost on blood. In a significant number of cases no further justification was put forward. If possible, and it is irrelevant for our purposes whether their genealogies were spurious or not (indeed, the more spurious the more revealing), their lines were traced back or their family names were associated with some known, noble manor (*solar conocido*) of Vizcaya or the Montañas of Santander, Asturias, or León, or with an Aragonese or Galician source, where the blood of Tubal had been preserved untainted. Typically they had their ancestors descend from the north during the long wars of the Reconquista to resettle Extremadura or Andalusia, where with the passage of time and the vicissitudes of fortune the memory of their original nobility had become dimmed. Now they sought to relume the honour and lustre of the family name and to prove the nobility of their descent by adducing the evidence of coats of arms, escutcheoned portals, ornamented plate, family tombs and chapels, and earlier *pruebas* and *ejecutorias* won in the Chancillerías, linking them with their noble ancestors. All this, it must be emphasized, was presented as evidence not of life-style but of inheritance. The 'justifications' adhere totally to the traditional definition of *hidalguía* in the laws of the *Partidas*: 'fidalguía es nobleza que viene a los homes por manera de linage'.

Second only to blood, the nobility of the 'justifications' was a nobility of service. This was the criterion most directly linked to the Bartolist conception of nobility as a sovereign creation of the prince. Some, indeed, argued that it was the only proper basis of nobility, all hereditary nobility being in its origins a princely grace honouring a subject outstanding for his services.[9] However, although this was, no doubt, one implication of the emphasis on services, it was not the line actually taken in the 'justifications'. The Bartolist theory was blunted by the assertion that the nobility of the *cartas de privilegio* was recompense or repayment for services rendered and that these services were inheritable in the same way as blood.[10] The granting of nobility was not, therefore, a free act of the sovereign will but something akin to the fulfilment of a contractual obligation, an obligation that the king inherited from his predecessors, just as the grantee inherited the secular treasury of merits built up by his ancestors and relatives.[11] Furthermore, outstanding service could be envisaged not so much as a justification as a manifestation of nobility, the fruit by which the nobility of the family tree could be known.[12] In this way a gratuitous and essentially individualist concept of nobility was grafted back onto the trunk of the lineage. Even personal service in war was made familial where possible and its honorific merits reinforced by association with the clan, by referring to the accompaniment of relatives, friends, household and servants in that service.[13]

The criterion of service thus had little in common with the humanist concept of a nobility of virtue and individual worth. It was a nobility of service, not of merit, of remuneration rather than of desert, and whatever the nature of the services and however much they derived from the specific historical circumstances of the sixteenth and seventeenth centuries, the qualities they were supposed to reflect and the terms in which they were described remained thoroughly traditional. The *hidalgo's* services were not civic but vassalic, services to the person of the king and to his Crown. The model was the 'true vassal'. Fidelity and loyalty were the first requirements of the *hidalgo*.[14] Serving 'como bueno y fiel y leal vasallo' was the stock formula of the 'justifications', and 'fiel' and 'leal' by far the most usual qualifications of a service.[15] Even the official and the financier described their services in the language of vassalage and appropriated to themselves the qualities of the 'true vassal'.

The essence of the *hidalgo*'s service was selflessness and sacrifice, service undertaken voluntarily and without remuneration, risking life and property, undergoing hardship and danger, and suffering injury and loss in the king's service, the loss of property, of family, of blood. This element of personal danger and material loss, undertaken freely, without compulsion and at his own expense, was the crucial feature in the conception of *hidalguía* expressed in the 'justifications'.[16] These sacrifices were almost always associated with military services of one kind or another in defence of the Crown and the Faith. The military ideal of the *hidalgo* remained paramount. Of some 150 analysable *cartas de privilegio* issued before 1700, nearly three-quarters (73 per cent) appealed to the military services, real or fictitious, of the recipient or his family and ancestors. Even non-military services were militarized where possible. The financial 'services' which paid for the patents of nobility were represented as commutations of personal service in war, as the wages of a given number of soldiers, or speciously appropriated to specified military purposes.[17] The attributes of voluntariness and unpaid service were applied also to office in local government, and the merits of the warrior imputed to the administration of war. *Corregidores* cited their activities in checking border guerrillas and preventing the passage of contraband to the enemy, in levying troops and supervising fortification works.[18] *Regidores* on the town councils cited their membership of recruiting commissions and their co-operation in the dispatch of local levies or the establishment of city militias.[19] Significantly, they did not cite any of their other many activities in the regulation and policing of civic life. The ideal *hidalgo* of the sixteenth and seventeenth centuries remained the 'defensor', serving at his own expense, in person, with arms and horses, and capable of acts of signal valour and 'azañas memorables'.[20]

By comparison all other qualities were secondary. The concept of a 'nobleza de armas y letras' certainly existed[21] but, in contrast to the views propounded by the writers of treatises of nobility, 'letras' as such played little part in the new *hidalgo*'s self-profile. The mention of a university degree (and there were only seven *licenciado* recipients in the pre-1700 period) was either purely titular and descriptive, or designed to show that the applicant was already enjoying the exemptions (though not the status) of nobility.[22] Only two of the graduates even mentioned their university; none spoke anything of scholarship. One of the 'justifications' listed no fewer than seven relatives entitled *Licenciado*, but it is clear that what was important about them was not their learning but the evidence they provided of *nobleza* and *limpieza*; all were Knights of Santiago, five were clerics, and one a member of the Colegio del Rey at Salamanca.[23] The only case in which there is any hint of service through learning is that of Alfonso Botello of Toledo, in 1569, whose great-grandfather, a Doctor of Theology, had been an abbot in attendance at the Council of Basle.[24]

The services adduced in their 'justifications' by administrators, financiers, officers of the Royal Household and local government functionaries also called for qualities not derivable from the personal valour of the warrior, but, whilst the translation of civilian services into a military vocabulary undoubtedly had the effect of enabling honour to be extended to a wide range of non-military offices, new concepts of administrative and civilian virtue were not easily formulated or incorporated into the canon of *hidalguía*. Generalized references to 'servicios de paz y guerra' were common, but references to specific services within a particular office were either military, military-related, personal to the king, or financial.[25] Similarly, although services in local offices of government and justice (as *regidor, jurado, diputado, fiscal, administrador de propios, alguacil*, etc.) by the grantee or his relatives were frequently mentioned as in some general way meritable, the merit acquired through such services derived from the same qualities that were required of vassal service, 'fidelidad', 'lealtad', 'verdad', selflessness and unrequitedness.[26] Bureaucratic qualities, even where there was no taint of mercenariness, were much less commonly recognized. The only ones mentioned with any frequency (in perhaps one administrative service in ten) were 'diligencia' and 'cuidado'; 'industria', 'rectitud' and 'limpieza' (in the sense of probity) appear once or twice only.[27] A treasurer of taxes in Santo Domingo de Silos, commended for having given a good account of the offices he had held for over twenty years, was a unique case.[28] All these examples, it is worth noting, belong to the sixteenth century. In the seventeenth century what matters most is not the service but the office, the participation of the grantee or his relatives in 'cargos e negocios de calidad e importancia' and in 'oficios honrosos de la república'.[29] Office from being a source of service becomes, not so much a source of honour, as a mark of honour, a form of recognition associating the grantee with important and distinguished people and with functions which only important and distinguished people would be called upon to exercise.

The services of the *hidalgo* were to the king and his Crown. Rarely is there any suggestion of an obligation of nobility to the community as such. An official of Seville was one such case. His petition was given the active support of the city on account of 'the many benefits received from you, in that you have always attended personally and with great care to the many matters of major importance and quality that the community has entrusted to you, and as a result of your integrity and hard work ('fidelidad e industria') the citizens and residents of the city have been done great good ('utilidad')'. [30] Another man had saved eighty fellow passengers from death by an act of signal bravery, 'during which', the citation read, 'you underwent great travails, always in order to procure the well-being and preservation of those people, like an honoured and noble man'. [31] But public service, public works, public spirit are considerations in fewer than three cases in a hundred. 'Pious works', the foundation of a hospital, a chapel and a convent, are cited in only two 'justifications', and these are clearly presented as works of piety. [32] Not one chose to mention any work of charity, the founding of orphanages, schools, alms-giving, or the like. The notion that it was the part of the nobleman to devote himself to the common good was not unknown to the writers of treatises, [33] but it was not a dominant consideration among the aspiring nobility of the sixteenth and seventeenth centuries.

The third criterion, that of recognition, was postulated on a principle of authority different from and fundamentally at variance with either the naturalist or the voluntarist principles. Recognition came from the custom and acceptance of the community and the society of one's peers, and it was manifested in the public signs of that acceptance, omission from the *padrones* of taxpayers, tenure of *hidalgo* offices or acceptance into noble fraternities, legal submissions 'de un mismo acuerdo', [34] the unchallenged enjoyment of privileges and exemptions, and marriage alliances with established *hidalgo* families. All these were components of a noble reputation, signs of recognition not definitions of nobleness, and not infallible signs at that. Fiscal exemptions were enjoyed by non-noble privileged groups, *caballeros pardos*, graduates of Salamanca, Valladolid and Alcalá, the so-called 'hidalgos de bragueta'. [35] It is wrong to see fiscal privilege as the essence of *hidalguía*; it was a necessary adjunct, not a sufficient quality of nobility. Recognition by the community derived most obviously from birth, from the continuity of privilege over generations, but it also came to be accorded *de facto* to wealth and power.

The trappings of wealth enabled a man to 'live nobly', and (as in England) any man who could bear the port and charge of gentility and who was powerful enough to discourage open contention of his status was well on the way to being regarded by public repute as in fact noble. The 'justifications', therefore, commonly made reference to the material appurtenances that were evidence of living nobly: wealth, houses, servants, slaves, horses; yet they did so only tangentially, almost ritualistically. The concern with the port of nobility was largely reduced to a formula. There was almost no interest in real levels of wealth, in the actual number of servants, or slaves, or horses, or in specific sources of income. [36] Indeed, the material circumstances of the grantee were usually wrapped in language redolent of medieval knighthood. This is evidenced in the new formula which first became standard in the early 1590s: 'siempre os aveis tratado como gente principal, noble y rica, teniendo armas y cavallos, esclavos y criados y escuderos de vuestro servicio'. [37] The economic occupation of the petitioners was ignored in the 'justifications', even negatively as a defence against *derogación*. References to offices were almost always either purely descriptive or presented as evidence of service or of *limpieza*. None of the 'justifications' makes any mention of seigneurial revenues, the ownership of land, entails (*mayorazgos*), investments in public or private loans (*juros, censos*), or other sources of income indicative of an 'honourable leisure'; and the denial of any connection with 'vile and mechanical trades' is to be found not once in some 150 cases. [38] Nor do the 'justifications' put any value on dispendiousness, entertainment, or liberality. Conversely, they express no shame at poverty. Poverty was an explanation for having failed to maintain one's nobility unchallenged, or for having to resort to a royal patent; it was not a disqualification. [39] In this respect the 'justifications' are even weaker in the weight they place on 'accidentals' than contemporary theorists, who generally regarded wealth, if not as the life-blood, at the very least as a component and preservative of nobility. [40] Reflecting the attitudes of men able to spend 4,000 or 6,000 ducats for their patents, this studied indifference to material wealth, that was already seen as a traditional Castilian posture in the fifteenth century, [41] can only be regarded as a conscious refusal on the part of the power of money to challenge the prestige of arms and traditional concepts of honour. [42]

The composite profile that can be generalized from the credentials of the quasi- and neo-nobility of the later-sixteenth and seventeenth centuries is of interest both for the particular emphases it places on the four traditional justifications of *hidalguía* – 'Patria', 'Armas', 'Letras',

'Riqueza',[43] and also for what it leaves unsaid of the qualities that seemed so desirable to the men of letters whose doctrine of nobility historians have generally followed. 'El camino del saber' was not a path to nobility that even the *letrados* chose to follow, and 'el camino de la bondad de costumbres' was much straiter than in Moreno de Vargas's topography.[44] Sociability, the social graces, a social conscience had virtually no place. 'Generosidad de ánimo', magnanimity, moderation, wisdom, fairness, prudence, honesty, consideration, affability, liberality (Lope's 'a gentleman must be a bridge over which money can pass'), the protection of widows, orphans and the poor (Sánchez de Arévalo), and all the other components of 'nobleza social' were irrelevant to what the *hidalgo de privilegio* regarded as fitting for civil and political nobility. Although a somewhat ritualized conception of 'vivir noblemente' developed in the last decades of the sixteenth century, *hidalguía* was not, in the first instance, a way of life but a category of being.[45]

II

However, if the salient features of the *hidalgo*-profile remained recognizable throughout the early-modern period, its contours were far from static. It is one of the characteristics of the *cartas de privilegio* as a source that their serial nature can reveal more subtle changes and a more precise and continuous chronology of change than have hitherto been available to us. Important shifts of emphasis in the content of the *hidalguía* that informed the 'justifications' are clearly discernible within the 1550–1700 period, and even more significant ones during the eighteenth century.

A number of these shifts were of an exogenous nature. The heroic figure of the Conquistador receded and the contribution of the New World to the attainment of *hidalguía* declined as the age of conquest and settlement passed into a more stable colonialism.[46] At the same time there was an increased representation of administrative and quasi-administrative services in the field of local government adduced by ex-*corregidores* and by *regidores*, for the first time beginning to cite their voting records in the town councils,[47] a development associated with the new importance of the municipalities and the Cortes cities in administration and in the granting of taxation. These were, however, but two aspects of a much more fundamental change which becomes apparent from the 1580s, the trend towards the demilitarization of *hidalguía* in the seventeenth century. This was marked first and most clearly by the sharply declining proportion of *hidalgos de privilegio* with personal military services to their credit: 38.8 per cent of them in the period 1552–75, 25.3 per cent in 1583–1650, 11.5 per cent in 1665–99, less than a third of the mid-sixteenth-century figure. Initially this decline was offset by the more frequent appeal to the purported military services of relatives and ancestors, the proportion of 'justifications' adducing family military services to compensate for the absence of personal ones doubling between 1552–75 and 1583–1650 from 28.6 per cent to 58.2 per cent. As a result the 1583–1650 period was characterized by what would seem to be a heightened concern with the military virtues of the *hidalgo*,[48] no less than 83 per cent of all justifications representing military services of one kind or another.

The first half of the seventeenth century, therefore, appears as the high noon of the military ideal; but it was a false militarism dependent on ersatz exploits. By the end of the century the military ideal was in full retreat. Nearly half of all applicants for *hidalguía* in the 1665–99 period offered no military justification whatsoever, personal or ancestral, real or fictitious.[49] It is clear that what is reflected here is not simply a difference of circumstance but a fundamental alteration of values. Although at least one seventeenth-century writer claimed that with the defeat of the Moors and the ending of domestic strife there was less opportunity for deeds of martial prowess,[50] and the Reconquest of Granada, the Comunero rebellion and the two Alpujarran revolts had undoubtedly provided the occasion for many of the services adduced in the sixteenth-century 'justifications', it is difficult to argue that there was no place for the military virtues in Castile after the 1630s. The problem, as was universally recognized, was that there was no one prepared to exercise them,[51] and if this was in part a reflection of the changing nature of the nobility, it was perhaps even more a reflection of the changing nature of military service. The introduction of conscription, militia quotas and forced levies debased the soldiery and transformed war into an obligation of the taxpayer, the *pechero*. It was only then, after the middle of the seventeenth century, that the ideal – as opposed to the reality – of *hidalgo* military service went into retreat. The de-militarization of nobility was the natural consequence of the proletarianization of war.

The shift from the military exploits of the individual to those of the family between 1583 and 1650 was but one manifestation of the reinforcement of the idea of *hidalguía* as nobility of lineage that was the dominant current of the seventeenth century. One of the first indications of this change of emphasis was the adoption in the 1590s of a new format for the 'justifications', which now began not with the petitioner's *curriculum vitae* and the catalogue of his personal exploits and services, as they had from the 1550s to the 1580s, but with a full genealogical reconstruction of his ancestry, and the listing and naming of his wife and children, and their spouses and offspring. [52] In the seventeenth century the pretensions of the *hidalgos de privilegio* became more and more deeply rooted in the family, their genealogies more extravagant, their ancestral memories more remote. Prior to 1592 fewer than 14 per cent pretended to belong to a named lineage of recognized nobility or to have descended from a known, noble manor of the Montañas, a *solar conocido*; this figure rose to 68 per cent in 1596–1615, 95 per cent in 1629–50, and 85 per cent in 1665–99. Not one of the three-dozen recipients of *cartas de privilegio* granted in the seventeen years up to 1569 could trace his family-tree back beyond his grandfather (two generations); but the task became easier as time went on. The first naming of a great-grandfather (three generations) appeared in 1569, with twelve others by 1598, including one genealogy going back seven generations. Between 1598 and 1615 one-third of the genealogies went back four generations; between 1629 and 1650 four out of thirty-three went back five generations, and after 1665 one in seven reached back six generations or beyond, in one case eleven generations. [53]

The family histories related by the grantees show the same deepening awareness of their heritages. Only three of the first fifty-eight 'justifica-tions' (1552–90) referred to incidents that had occurred more than 100 years before, the exploits of ancestors in the wars of the Reconquista, for example, or the grant of ancient privileges and *ejecutorias*. But of the twenty-nine dating from 1591–1615 twelve made reference to events of the fifteenth century, three to the fourteenth, and two more to the thirteenth; and of sixty-five from the years 1629–99, no fewer than nine carried their memories back to the thirteenth century or beyond, and six others went back more than 200 years. [54]

All this was paralleled by a preoccupation with *limpieza de sangre* which also becomes apparent from the 1590s. Between 1552 and 1592 barely five per cent of the 'justifications' were concerned with *limpieza*; between 1592 and 1650 40 per cent sought to demonstrate *limpieza* in one way or another; and between 1665 and 1699 27 per cent did so. This increased concern was clearly a response to the spread of statutes of *limpieza* across a wide range of Spanish institutions from the mid-sixteenth century onwards and an attempt to inoculate *hidalguía* against the deep-rooted popular suspicion of impurity attaching to the *hidalgo* estate. [55] It was perhaps also a response to the Counter-Reformation's attack on a pagan worship of honour, a 'christianization' of *hidalguía* which has its parallels elsewhere in Europe at the same time.[56] In the process it added a further dimension to the predominance of the family over the individual.

Family, lineage, *limpieza* all attest to the triumph of the blood in the seventeenth-century conception of *hidalguía*. In great part this can be seen as a reaction to the apparent proliferation of *hidalgos* and the 'desvalorización social de la hidalguía' in the sixteenth and early seventeenth centuries, the debasement of nobility by its supposed openness to a reputedly vile and impure bourgeoisie, and the popular assumption that social position was acquired solely by money or favour.[57] One response was the symbolic exaggeration of social differentiation apparent in the seventeenth century, a dissatisfaction with 'mere' *hidalguía* and the garnishing of it with more patent distinctions, the title Don, knighthoods of the Military Orders, lordship over vassals. A more direct response was to seek to defend *hidalguía* by entrenching it behind the lineage. Even the 'fortuitous nobility' of ostentation and riches that had had some place in the 'justifications' of the later-sixteenth century becomes etherealized in the seventeenth century. The concept of 'living nobly' becomes vaguer and less concrete. The last direct reference to the material wealth, the 'bienes y hacienda', of a grantee dates from 1631.[58] Previously given some content by phrases like 'con decente ornato de casa y personas correspondiente a la calidad dellas',[59] it is expressed after about 1640 only by intangibles and tautologies – 'siempre os abiades tratado y portado con mucho lustre', 'tratado y portado como caballeros hijosdalgo', 'vivido con autoridad, honra y nobleza como gente principal', 'con el crédito y común estimación y correspondencia al lustre de su calidad y sangre'.[60] The more insubstantial the concept of 'living nobly' and the more it was confused with 'autoridad', 'honra' and 'el crédito y común estimación', the less important the 'fortuitous' component of nobility would be vis à vis the 'natural' and the customary.

There was also a political dimension to the changing perception of *hidalguía*. Implicit in the apotheosis of lineage was a challenge to the whole Bartolist conception of nobility and to the principle of princely voluntarism upon which it was based. The 'justifications' of the seventeenth century appeal overwhelmingly to alternative sources of authority, the natural law of inheritance and the custom and recognition of the community, visible in the emphasis now being placed on marriage alliances as evidence of acceptance by established *hidalgo* families. The Cantabrian origination of their lineages, the *solar conocido*, the claim to participation in the Reconquista, all helped to push nobility back far beyond any specific royal grant and elevated the consideration of service above the interests of any one prince. The Crown was even having to make its grants of privilege in the form of *hidalguías de sangre* in order to dispose of a commodity inherently unattractive simply as a royal grace. In practical terms the Bartolist conception of civil nobility was in retreat at the very moment when it was being most stoutly defended, by writers like Moreno de Vargas, Peñalosa, and Diego de Soto y Aguilar. This is most strikingly evidenced in the dramatic change that takes place in the formula of the royal grant itself from the 1580s. The strict voluntarist formula used in acts of pure creation ('es my merced y voluntad que seais y os hago hijodalgo de sangre y de solar conocido...como si uvieredes nascido de padres e abuelos hijosdalgo notorios de sangre...tan cumplidamente como si en favor de vos...por mis Alcaldes de los Hijosdalgo de las mis Audiencias y Chancillerías por todas instancias fueran dadas sentencias en vista y en grado de revista') virtually disappears after 1585, leaving a formula that is essentially declaratory ('declaro a vos...y os hago a todos hijosdalgo notorios de sangre y solar conocido...tan cumplidamente...' etc.). The royal decree had ceased to be a supplementation of the genetic deficiencies of the grantee by an act of the sovereign will; it was now simply a substitution for the judgement of the courts on the mere matter of fact. The 'reacción de la sociedad estamental' that has been seen as characteristic of the early seventeenth century cannot, therefore, be associated, as is often supposed, with the opening of a new phase of monarchical absolutism.[61] It was rather the opposite. Royal action tended, in principle, to open nobility not to close it, whereas the disparagement of the very notion of an *hidalguía de privilegio*, expressed in the common assertion that 'puede el rey fazer caballero mas no fijodalgo',[62] was inherently anti-absolutist. Given a climate of opinion that glorified lineage, de-emphasized service, and diminished state-voluntarism, it is not in the least surprising that direct intervention by the Crown to broaden the accepted criteria of nobility in the later seventeenth century, most notably by the celebrated pragmatic of 1682, should have had such little immediate effect.

III

The traditional justifications for nobility thus continued into the eighteenth century, but they were beginning to become less dominant. Something of an ideological vacuum was developing in the concept of *hidalguía* on the eve of the Enlightenment which facilitated, even necessitated, the adoption of new criteria of elite worth.

Taken as a whole the eighteenth century was marked by a turn against the cult of lineage and by the progressive demilitarization and defeudalization of the *hidalgo*. The proven nobility of one's ancestors (as established by *cartas ejecutorias*, membership of noble fraternities and election to offices in the noble estate) remained the principal justification in the post-1720 grants, but the family was ceasing to be of such overwhelming importance as in the seventeenth century. There were still those who traced their ancestry back to the Goths, and nearly one-third of the sample was able to compose genealogies going back five generations or more, actually a far higher proportion than in any preceding period. On the other hand, only one-quarter of them now claimed descent from a *solar conocido* of the Montañas, and one in three had no family claim to *hidalguía* whatsoever, a figure much more like the relatively open sixteenth century than the seventeenth, with its reactionary and sclerotic emphasis on blood and lineage. Symptomatic perhaps of the ambivalence of the eighteenth century, above all in Spain, was one area in which the importance of blood continued unabated, the preoccupation with *limpieza de sangre*, directly alluded to in just over 50 per cent of cases, a higher proportion even than 1596–1650, and one that was at least as high at the end of the century as it was at the beginning.

By contrast, the abandonment of the predominantly military definition of *hidalguía* was unambiguous and confirmed the pattern already discernible in the seventeenth century, and particularly in the last three decades of that century. Between 1720 and 1799 the direct military services of the grantee, his family, or his ancestors are referred to in less than 30 per cent of the sample (compared with 54 per cent in 1665–99), and there is not one with a claim to personal military services after 1740 (there had been four in 1720–40). Despite the persisting tendency to 'militarize' financial and administrative services, the petitioners specifying work in the organization of billeting, the transportation of materials and provisions for the royal dockyards, and loans made for the upkeep of the soldiery,[63] more than 60 per cent of the 'justifications' had no military services, direct or indirect, present or past, to record, a percentage higher than at any previous time.[64]

Furthermore, the feudal trappings of *hidalguía* had all but disappeared. I have come across only one reference to vassalage and fidelity in the eighteenth century, and that is dated only as late as 1740.[65] The feudal-military model of nobility was being modified by the growing acceptance of other criteria of merit and by purely civilian values. The feudalized vocabulary of service was largely replaced by the expression of 'bourgeois' virtues, 'diligencia', 'aplicación', 'celo', 'desvelo', 'trabajado incessantemente', 'acreditada conducta', 'exactitud', 'integridad'.[66] The traditional view of the *hidalgo* as someone who was willing to suffer loss and make personal sacrifices, to risk person and property and serve without pecuniary remuneration, persisted throughout the century,[67] but those qualities too were extended to magnify the services of state creditors, public granarists, carters, even schoolmasters, so that the ancient dichotomy of private gain and public merit ceased to hold any incompatibility. Though administrative service was actually relevant in only 20 per cent or 25 per cent of the cases, the function of an office had of itself become a sufficient qualification for nobility,[68] and such achievements were now considered worthy of merit as the carting of grain, salt and timber, or organizing the paving of streets, or getting top prices for the sale of community properties.[69]

The eighteenth century also brought reality to the concept of a nobility of learning, previously little more than the rhetoric of the men of letters. By the end of the eighteenth century there was an explicit feeling for education as an attainment befitting nobility and a recognition of services to education as particularly meritorious.[70]

Finally, the long campaign of ministers, reformers and moralists to honour achievement in manufacturing and commerce, which reached its climax in the celebrated decree of 18 March 1783, seems at last to have begun to win wider acceptance. Indicative was the growing recognition of wealth as a criterion of nobility, not merely in the rather oblique way that had been the case in the previous period, but overtly as a specific prerequisite necessary for the maintenance of an appropriate life-style. There appeared in the 1740s a euphemistic formula asserting that the petitioner and his family had the 'circunstancias correspondientes' to obtain and maintain this honour 'dignamente', but by the 1790s the possession of 'hacienda' and 'bienes de fortuna' had become an accepted part of the catalogue of *hidalgo* qualities, with grants being justified expressly 'por los bienes de fortuna que a vos y a ellos asisten para mantenerla'.[71] Furthermore, some of the new *hidalgos* in the later part of the century were prepared publicly to acknowledge their participation in commerce and manufacturing and to justify their ennoblement on the strength of a lifetime dedicated to business success ('en el que haveis tenido notables adelantamientos'), on the size of their establishments ('uno de los más opulentos de la dicha Ciudad', 'establecido con un comercio considerable'), and on the compatibility of business with honour ('que en este destino os abeis conserbado con el mayor honor').[72] The *hidalgo* of the seventeenth-century 'justifications' had had no economic existence. The recognition in the eighteenth century of noble-man as an economic being was indicative of the percolation of private, 'bourgeois' values into the notion of *hidalguía*, values almost totally absent in the previous century. Paradoxically, it also activated a more acute sensitivity to the taint of *dishonourable* economic activity and a repudiation of 'oficios viles y mecánicos' that had been similarly absent from the seventeenth-century 'justifications'.[73]

The attribution of virtue to non-traditional activities, to commercial success, educational achievement and administrative skill was a reflection of the social and economic changes of the eighteenth century and the intellectual influences of the Enlightenment, but also, and perhaps more importantly, of a fundamental transformation of political values. In the sixteenth and seventeenth centuries merit was acquired by service to the person of the king and in defence of his Crown and faith; in the eighteenth century a different principle of service was coming to be emphasized, the principle of utility and the public good. The idea of service as a personal contract between a vassal and his king was no longer the only one conceivable. From the last decades of the century classic expressions of the traditional concept of service ('ciegamente afectos y apasionados a el Rey...queriendo sacrificar sus vidas y hacienda en su servicio')[74] were being overtaken by transitional and hybrid formulations ('en servicio de la Monarquía', 'con utilidad de mi estado', 'haciéndome un gran servicio y a la causa pública', 'pruevas nada equíbocas del amor a mi Real Persona y a la Patria, y aun a vuestros convecinos').[75] The eighteenth century was transforming the vassal into the citizen; status in society was being justified by service to society. It is revealing to compare two analogous cases, one in 1720, the other in 1782. In the first instance, a *regidor* of Las Brozas was credited with tireless work in the provisioning of the town in years of disastrous harvests and the ravaging of contending armies, 'procurando con vuestra diligencia, crédito y hazienda mantener abastezida aquella villa para que sus abitadores estubiesen promptos a la defensa de Portugal'.[76] In the second, the son of a carter claimed credit for the efforts of his father and brother in getting supplies of salt through to Old Castile and Zamora despite floods, snow and the hardest of weathers, risking their animals and their capital, 'haciéndome un gran servicio y a la causa pública'.[77] Another grantee's merits were accumulated in Ocaña over the course of thirty years in the offices of *alcalde de la Santa Hermandad, diputado, regidor* and *procurador síndico general*, 'en los quales haveis servido al común de vecinos, procurándoles su maior alivio en sus abastos a espensas de vuestro celo, desvelo y apronto de vuestros caudales'. Particularly creditable were his initiative in organizing the paving of the greater part of the town and the planting of trees along the Valencia road and the public benefits derived from his periods of office as *diputado* and treasurer of charity funds, including the contributions he made with his own money for the relief of the poor and the good prices he got for the sale of the property of the Jesuit college of which he was administrator. [78] Yet another grantee, a silk manufacturer of Granada, presented as one of his services the employment and subsistence he had provided for a large number of the working population of the city. [79]

It is important to note, however, that this altering perception of *hidalguía* was a very late phenomenon in the eighteenth century. None of the new justifications for nobility is clearly apparent before the 1750s and none really makes its mark until the 1780s or 1790s. Of all the 'new' justifications seven out of ten date from the 1780s and 1790s. Furthermore, the new criteria of nobility grew up alongside and not in place of the old. Though the period 1720–99 taken as a whole experienced a falling away of the traditional justifications compared with the 120 years before 1700, there was no demonstrable difference between the later and the earlier parts of the eighteenth century in the number of times those traditional values were appealed to. The *solar conocido*, the genealogical tree, the family name and its *limpieza* were stressed as much, if not more, in the years 1769–99 as they had been in 1720–46. Almost as many recipients presented military services of some kind in the one period as in the other, and the concept of *hidalguía* as willing sacrifice continued undiminished. Neither was there any absolute social polarization between a promoted nobility based on traditional and a parvenu nobility based on modern criteria. Of all those recipients presenting novel modes of justification (riches, social services, education, commerce) only one in eight did not also claim traditional virtues acquired by inheritance and war. Even the almost naked commercial *hidalgos* of the 1790s made some pretence of wrapping what rags of family reputation, military service and financial sacrifice they could around the pudenda of trade. [80] Even at the end of the eighteenth century the *aggiornamento* of the *hidalgo*-ideal remained, if not entirely superficial, hesitant and incomplete. The underlying conservatism of the 'justifications' is, of course, no more than that of the generality of contemporary writers and social reformers. [81]

IV

The 'justifications' of the *cartas de privilegio* present a complete cycle in the ideology of the *hidalgo* from the mid-sixteenth to the late-eighteenth century. There is an initial phase from the 1550s to the 1570s of somewhat open promotion reflected in the lack of concern of the grantees with self-justification beyond that of monetary and personal services, and a preparedness to accept fully the parvenu status implicit in the Bartolist 'hago' formula of the patents. But from the last half of Philip II's reign and for the next 120 years the *privilegios* that were issued were predominantly *hidalguías de sangre y solar conocido*, the individual had been absorbed into the family, and an absolutist and voluntarist concept of civil nobility had retreated before the concept of a natural and customary nobility that could be declared but not created. In the eighteenth century, the acceptance of non-traditional criteria and de-traditionalized formulations to justify social promotion, the increasing (though still limited) preparedness of grantees to confess to honest but non-noble origins,[82] the reappearance of the 'hago' formula (found in at least one grant in three) were again associated with an assertion of the authority of the state over society. The long-term fluctuations in the history of the *hidalgo* ideal embraced by the ordinary *hidalgo de privilegio* seem to mirror the history of monarchical authority in Castile, as indeed they mirror the history of the Spanish Monarchy itself. The open and eclectic values of the mid-sixteenth and later eighteenth centuries coincide with periods of international success, economic opportunity and strong state authority; the narrower ideology of the seventeenth century coincides with a shrinking of Spain's political and economic horizons and with the erosion of central control in the years of 'decline'. The fixation on blood implied a closing of ranks, a freezing of nobility where it stood, the repudiation of merit as a sufficient criterion of social respect, the denial of personal advance. It meant a preference for past achievement over present, a *laudatio virtutis actae* that responded to a moment in the history of Castile when the greatness of the nation also seemed to lie in the past. It mirrored at the personal level the crisis of the Monarchy, the loss of confidence in the future, the obsession with 'conservación', the attribution of present disasters to the abandonment of the historic values on which the Monarchy had been built which was one of the most pervasive symptoms of the climacteric of the seventeenth century.[83]

This petrification of values did not, of course, have to coincide with social stasis, nor did it necessarily constrain the reality of social mobility. Unfortunately we just do not know enough at the moment to be able to plot that reality with any certainty, but the evidence of the *pleitos* in the Chancillerías, the complaints in the Cortes, the openings available through municipal office, the almost comic profusion of Dons, *caballeros* and *títulos*, and the very sluggishness of the market for the *cartas de privilegio* all suggest that the so-called 'fermeture de la noblesse' of the later sixteenth century was ideological rather than sociological.[84] The paradox that we seem to have in Castile of a relatively open nobility with caste-like ideals suggests that the sanguineous etiology of worth was primarily of symbolic importance, expressing not a 'principle of exclusion' (Maravall's 'principio de cierre')[85] but a 'principle of association'. What was in practice necessary was not so much to possess noble blood as, through the sophistries of the genealogist and the historian, to be able to profess it, and hence to subscribe to its creed.[86] Indeed, the very openness of nobility may have contributed to the reinforcement of that creed by inhibiting the development of an alternative self-sustaining 'bourgeois' consciousness or the implantation of a less archaic system of elite values.[87]

In effect, the emphasis on blood involved a compression of the rhetoric of prestige, a simplification of values coincident with the more restricted range of viable life-options available in seventeenth-century Castile. It was one aspect of a more general flight back to the land and from urban values to rural values characteristic of an economic 'B phase'. The effect was a homogenization of *hidalguía*. All nobility was conceived to be of one sort and of a common root. The assumption that the substance of nobility was radicated in a common genetic code and that variations of nurture and fortune were mere accidents meant that nobility was not thought of primarily as a behavioural category. It was not, therefore, fractured by the dichotomy of values between rich and poor, urban and rural, sword and robe that divided the second estate in France, for example. In Castile the ideological bonding of the noble-estate was stronger than the socio-economic differences within it, and this made for a unity of consciousnesss which contributed both to the internal mobility and to the broad political cohesiveness that existed across the different sectors of the Castilian dominant-elite after the mid-sixteenth century.[88]

Particularly striking is the disparity between 'elite' or literary *hidalguía*, at the theoretical level almost entirely the creation of Bartolist legists, and what (following Valera) one might call 'vulgar' *hidalguía*.[89] The latter was represented in the justifications as well as in the communal challenges to the pretensions of the justifications (also related in the *cartas de privilegio*), which of necessity defined nobility in terms of custom, heredity and acceptability, attributes which the community could judge, rather than in terms of personal virtue and service, which were matters for the royal grace alone. The relationship between Crown and community, the balance between royal authority and communal values, was crucial to the definition of elites in early modern Castile. The Crown could grant rights but it could not guarantee that they would be respected. Without the acceptance and recognition of the community of both *pecheros* and *hidalgos* to lubricate the machinery of proof (the *padrón*, the *prueba*, the *pleito*), the privileges of nobility could never be secure, and indeed might have to be fought for in the courts, and in the streets, over and over again.[90] It is for this reason that Maravall's argument that the emphasis on blood-virtue was an imposition of the values of the aristocratic elite, an instrument of exclusion, a new basis for justifying the dominance and the privileges of the nobility to compensate for the passing of its monopoly of the military virtues, is unacceptable.[91] The 'elite' principle of exclusion was of less importance in the definition of *hidalguía* than the 'vulgar' principle of enclosure. Standing on the frontier of social distinction, the *hidalgo* needed public validation as much as he needed elite acceptance. Least of all could a para-nobility of dubious status afford to get out of step with the accepted values of the community. The *cartas de privilegio* do not so much share the preoccupations of the elite with wealth, life-style and manners – filters for the controlled absorption of acceptable para-noble elements into the upper orders – as they do the 'vulgar' preoccupations with blood, lineage and *limpieza*, hurdles to prevent the escape of the wealthy from the ranks of the taxed.[92] It was deference to the conservatism of community sentiment, a sentiment which the convergence of the fiscal interests of the *pecheros* with the exclusivist interests of the *hidalgo* estate contrived to make narrowly restrictive, that made for the rejection of progressive definitions of worth and locked social promotion into a theory of nobility that belonged rather to the fifteenth than to the seventeenth century. The reality of social mobility for the individual could only be assured at the price of reinforcing and conserving the values of the traditional social order as seen from below. What was being sought was not so much new ways of justifying the privileges of a non-warrior nobility, as an attempt by new men to gain popular acceptance by conforming to the 'vulgar' stereotype. As a result honour in seventeenth-century Castile became neither 'individualized', nor 'nationalized' into the politics of the state (as it did in England and France);[93] neither letters, nor office, nor wealth were as important in transforming *hidalguía* in Castile as has sometimes been argued,[94] and the military ethos of *hidalguía* survived the de-militarization of the *hidalgo* by a hundred years or more.

It was not until the development of state absolutism in the eighteenth century made possible the socialization of service and personal virtue that the Bartolist and the 'vulgar' conceptions of *hidalguía* could be made to coalesce around such concepts as 'Patria', 'el bien público', 'el beneficio del público', or 'la causa pública'. The utilitarian imperative necessarily opened up new routes to public appreciation and civil honour, and in this respect the capture of the highest levels of government by the social critique of the Enlightenment was of crucial importance. It was only with the harmonization of service to the Crown and service to the community that the equation, *hidalgo* privilege = public detriment, could be confuted. No less important was the economic and demographic growth of the later eighteenth century. As long as the economy was in a zero-sum situation (as in the seventeenth century), the parvenu privileged, the *nouveau riche*, the self-achiever was inevitably diminishing everyone else; the richer and more successful he was, the bigger the burden his exemption from taxation would throw upon the rest of an increasingly impoverished and declining community. It needed conditions in which wealth was being *created* and fiscal privilege attenuated before the ennoblement of the self-made man could credibly be proposed to be for the common good.[95]

　　With the state asserting its authority over the processes of social promotion, the increasing tendency to equate aristocracy with title, and the decline in status and numbers of the mere *hidalguía* of custom and reputation,[96] noble-values were being transformed from above. At no previous time had there been such a consonance between the ideals of the writers and the justifications of the *hidalgos*. But at the same time, *hidalguía*, from being an assertion of custom and community values, was becoming increasingly cut off from its roots in popular sentiment.[97] However much the reformers may have been wanting to reinvigorate the society of orders rather than to dismember it, it was, ironically, precisely the internal modernization of the *hidalgo*-ideal in the eighteenth century that was to destroy the justification for a hereditary nobility altogether. The abandonment of the warrior-ethos and the reception into the canon of *hidalguía* of 'bourgeois' values, with their assumption of the compatibility of private interest with the public good and their promotion of 'decent', 'decorous' and 'educated' behaviour, left the old order on the eve of the Napoleonic invasion repudiating its historic military justification at the very moment when the functions of the *defensor* were most needed.[98]

400

Notes

1. Diego de Valera, *Espejo de verdadera nobleza* (c. 1441), Biblioteca de Autores Españoles, Vol. 116, 89–116; Juan de Arce Otalora, *De nobilitatis et immunitatis Hispaniae causis* (Granada 1553), Juan Benito Guardiola, *Tratado de nobleza* (Madrid 1591); Juan García de Saavedra, *Tractatis de hispanorum nobilitate et exemptione* (Alcalá de Henares 1597); Bernabé Moreno de Vargas, *Discursos de la nobleza de España* (Madrid 1622), Benito de Peñalosa y Mondragón, *Libro de las cinco excelencias del Español* (Pamplona 1629). There are of course a number of others less employed and less interesting. See, Alfonso de Figueroa y Melgar, 'Los prejuicios nobiliarios contra el trabajo y el comercio en la España del Antiguo Régimen', *Cuadernos de Investigación Histórica*, Vol. 3 (1979), 415–36, at 422.

2. Most notable among the studies based on a broad range of treatise and literary sources are, A. García Valdecasas, *El hidalgo y el honor* (Madrid 1948); J. A. Maravall, *Teatro y literatura en la sociedad barroca* (Madrid 1972); J M. Díez Borque, *Sociología de la comedia española del siglo XVII* (Madrid 1976); J. A Maravall, *Poder, honor y élites en el siglo XVII* (Madrid 1979)

3. Exemplary is the recent article by J Fayard and M-C Gerbet, 'Fermeture de la noblesse et pureté de sang en Castille à travers les procès de *hidalguía* au XVIème siècle', *Histoire, Economie et Société*, Vol. I (1982), 51–75.

4. See I. A A. Thompson, 'The purchase of nobility in Castile, 1552–1700', *The Journal of European Economic History*, Vol. 8 (1979), 313–60.

5. The number of analysable cases varies according to the quality and quantity of the information in each case. Of the 148 with the most detail 50 date from 1552–75, 33 from 1583–1615, 39 from 1629–50, and 26 from 1665–99.

6. Aragonese, Catalan and Valencian grants of various kinds are numerous in the eighteenth century and of great interest, but their tone and content differ markedly from the Castilian patents and, as I have no comparable data for the pre-1700 period, they have been excluded from the general discussion

7. Archivo General de Simancas, Dirección General del Tesoro, Inventario 5, *legajo* 2, folio 37 (this source cited subsequently by *leg.* and f. numbers only), *privilegio* of 14 March 1630 to Francisco Jiménez presented before a *concejo abierto* in the town of Esquivias (Toledo), and subsequently in Yales, Casarubias de Madrid and Madrid Antonio de Sant Millán paid 6,500 ducats for an *hidalguía* in 1595 with the condition that the *privilegio* be drawn up 'sin que en el previlegio se haga mención de que sirve con la dicha cantidad', AGS DGT Inventario 24, *leg.* 319, n.f. Moreno de Vargas also comments on this, op. cit., f. 34v.

8. H. Méchoulan, *Mateo López Bravo. Un socialista español del siglo XVII* (Madrid 1977), 254; Maravall, *Teatro y literatura*, 60; García Valdecasas, op. cit., 31–3; Guardiola, op. cit., f. 1; Moreno de Vargas, op. cit, ff. 8, 11; Peñalosa, op. cit., f. 96. The only hint of pride in self-improvement found in the pre-1700 'justifications' is in the *privilegio* of Juan Guerra Navarro Cordero in 1693, which refers to his father's promotion from 'soldado aventajado' to *alférez* in the course of eighteen years' service in the wars, *leg.* 2, f 34.

9. Valera, op. cit., 92, Moreno de Vargas, op cit., ff. 5, 8, 31v, Peñalosa, op. cit , f. 86; and the anonymous 'Floreto de anécdotas diversas' (c. 1575) cited by J I Gutiérrez

Nieto, 'Limpieza de sangre y anti-hidalguismo hacia 1600', in *Homenaje al Dr Juan Reglà Campistol* (Valencia 1975), vol. 1, 497–514.

10. *Privilegio* to D. Juan González de Guzmán as 'heredero de todos los servicios que hicieron en dicha Guerra. . . vuestros tíos carnales', *leg.* 2, f. 33 (1691). The formulistic justification of the grant 'en enmyenda y remuneración' of past services appears in over two dozen cases.

11. See the argument of the attorney for the Zambrano family in suit with the town of Fuente del Maestre, 1573–84, 'aún en caso que el privilegio no fuera en remuneración de los servizios que el dicho Albaro Rodríguez Çambrano avia fecho y ansi que no tuviera fuerça de contrato, sino que fuera mera gracia y liberalidad de príncipe, aún en aquel caso no avía sido nezesaria confirmación particular'; and again, 'su conçesión avía sido por méritos y servicios que avía fecho el Comendador Albaro Rodríguez Çambrano, padre y abuelo de sus partes, a nuestra corona real, que en efecto avía tenido fuerça de contrato y paga del servicio', *leg.* 2, f. 72. R. Boase, *The Troubadour Revival: a study of social change and traditionalism in late-medieval Spain* (London 1978), 42, draws attention to the development of this contractual view of the relationship between duties and privileges in the late Middle Ages.

12. Moreno de Vargas, op. cit., f. 40; Fernando Albía de Castro, *Memorial histórico por la Ciudad de Logroño*, ed. J. Simón Díaz (Logroño 1953), 133, citing Aristotle, 'ser la nobleza un congruente natural de una familia, o muchas, apta a produzir hombres hábiles, e idoneos a obrar conforme virtud, valor y prudencia'.

13. *Leg.* 1, ff. 19, 20, 39, 1, 38, 61, 31, 15, 27, 3, 33, 53, 25 (in chronological order).

14. García Valdecasas, op. cit., 72, with reference to Juan II, 1435.

15. The term 'vasallo' is used in twenty of the first 127 *privilegios*, 'fiel' in eighteen, 'leal' in twenty-three; but after being written into the printed-form *cartas de privilegio*, the last of which dates from 1638, the terms then rather fall out of use.

16. Stressed in at least twenty-six cases. On this concept see, Guardiola, op. cit., f. 32; Moreno de Vargas, op. cit., f. 11; García Valdecasas, op. cit., 43.

17. *Privilegio* of Alonso Rodríguez de Alcázar (14 May 1567), 'porque al presente a causa que no podeis servirnos con vuestra persona e yndustria por vuestra bejez y enfermedades como hasta aqui lo aveis hecho, nos aveis servido con seis myll ducados', *leg.* 1, f. 62, and ff. 63, 5, 13, 71, 52, 21; *leg.* 2, ff. 37, 82.

18. D. Juan Díez del Carpio, ex-*corregidor* of Béjar, *leg.* 2, f. 20 (10 March 1696); *Licenciado* D. Melchor Pardo, ex-*teniente de Asistente* of Seville and *corregidor* of Almería, *leg.* 2, f. 61 (5 July 1698).

19. *Leg.* 1, f. 54; *leg.* 2, ff. 51, 52, 24, 41, 60, 15.

20. Guardiola, op. cit., f. 51v, 'se alcança la verdadera nobleza por causa de hechos famosos'; and Fray Luis de Granada's comments on the importance contemporaries attached to 'bravery', J. Caro Baroja, 'Honour and Shame: A historical account of several conflicts', in J. G. Peristiany, ed., *Honour and Shame* (London 1965), 81–137, at p. 94; see also, Díez Borque, op. cit., 289; M. Herrero García, 'Ideología española del siglo XVII. La nobleza', *Revista de Filología Española*, Vol. 14 (1927), 33–58, 161–75, at p. 163.

21. For example, the *privilegio* of Antón Sánchez del Barco y Gasca (27 May 1631) refers to the *casa y solar de los Gasca* as one from which 'han salido nobles caballeros ansi en armas como en letras', *leg.* 2, f. 74.

22. *Licenciado* D. Juan Baillo de la Veldad (11 February 1631), 'y por haver algunos de vuestros pasados venidos de partes remotas y confundido y dexádose perder su nobleza, y tocaros la hidalguía por parte de hembra y estar impedidos los efectos della por este

camino, aunque gozais de las esempciones de hijodalgo por graduado de lizenciado en canones en la universidad de Alcalá de Henares', *leg.* 2, f. 7. The other *licenciados* are at *leg.* 1, ff. 5, 54; *leg.* 2, ff. 46, 61, 20; AGS DGT Inventario 24, *leg.* 332 (Tena Sahabedra).

23. Francisco Alcayde de Mudarra (17 November 1638), *leg.* 2, f. 1.

24. *Leg.* 1, f. 15.

25. Exceptions (or perhaps just different forms of financial service) were four cases involving the discovery, working, administration and supplying of gold, silver and mercury mines (*leg.* 1, ff. 36, 52, 60; *leg.* 2, f. 52) and one the incorporation of the *Maestrazgo* of Montesa into the royal domain in 1580 (*leg.* 1, f. 65).

26. *Leg.* 1, ff. 71, 17, 3, 6, 57; *leg.* 2, ff. 51, 52, 24, 60, 59.

27. 'Diligencia' and 'cuidado', *leg.* 1, ff. 71, 39, 17, 50, 3, 29, 48, 6; 'industria', *leg.* 1, ff. 36, 48; 'rectitud' and 'limpieza', *leg.* 1, f. 39, with the *residencias* of the office adduced in proof.

28. *Leg.* 1, f. 9 (27 April 1592).

29. *Leg.* 1, ff. 68, 12, 39; *leg.* 2, ff. 24 (1601), 9 (1608), 25 (1615), 93, 96, 70 (1630–1).

30. 'Considerando... los muchos beneficios que de vos a recevido en aver siempre acudido con gran cuydado con vuestra persona a los muchos negocios de gran importancia y calidad que aquella república os a cometido, de los quales, mediante vuestra fidelidad e industria a resultado notable utilidad a los vezinos y moradores della', Alonso Núñez, *jurado* of Seville (22 July 1583), *leg.* 1, f. 48. Seville also backed the application of Baltasar de Jaén (22 July 1583), 'por los muchos beneficios que de vos ha rescivido', *leg.* 1, f. 35.

31. 'Con lo qual padecistes grandes trabajos, procurando siempre el bien y sustento de aquella gente como hombre noble y honrrado', Alonso Moreno de Alva (9 November 1600), *leg.* 2, f. 52.

32. The uncle of Alonso Moreno de Alva was said to be the founder of the Monasterio de la Concepción in Mérida and of other 'obras pías', *leg.* 2, f. 52. Francisco de Cárdenas Carvajal was credited with 'muchas y piadosas obras' in the town of Los Santos, notably the foundation of the Hospital de la Limpia Concepción and the chapel of Nuestra Señora del Rosario, *leg.* 2, f. 11 (27 March 1602).

33. For example, Moreno de Vargas's insistence that the services of the *hidalgo* be 'útiles al Rey' or 'provechosos a la República', op. cit., f. 8. The piety and charity of the nobility was commonly exaggerated in the literature (no doubt for good didactic reasons), Díez Borque, op. cit., 278, but the idea of the mean and uncharitable *hidalgo* was also not unknown, see J. Silverman, 'Cultural backgrounds of Spanish imperialism as presented in Lope de Vega's play *San Diego de Alcalá*', *The Journal of San Diego History*, Winter 1978, 7–23, at p. 18.

34. Petitions to the Chancillería for confirmation of nobility which had the support of the *concejo* of the town concerned.

35. Moreno de Vargas, op. cit., ff. 16, 32. The case of the *Licenciado* Baillo de la Veldad cited at note 22 above, is much to the point here.

36. The *comedias* are similarly indifferent to noble economics, Díez Borque, op. cit., 283, but the culture as a whole was not entirely oblivious to specifics. A. Domínguez Ortiz, *La sociedad española en el siglo XVII*, Vol. 1 (Madrid 1963), 173, describes one defence of nobility in which the details of the *hidalgo*'s wealth were stipulated very precisely, and there are similar cases referred to by Fayard and Gerbet, op. cit., 69, though perhaps no more than two in a total of 255.

37. *Leg.* 1, f. 11 (21 September 1592). There were some anticipations of this sort of formula in earlier years, but they were few and irregular: *leg.* 1, f. 37 (19 February 1569)

– 'siempre aveys vivido. . .como personas nobles así en el trato de vuestras personas, casas y criados, como en todo lo demás'; f. 53 (2 October 1574) – 'teniendo muchos criados, cavallos y armas, y tratando sus personas como tales hijosdalgo notorios. . .y casándose con gente muy principal, hijosdalgo de sangre', and similarly f. 21 (9 October 1574); f. 59 (10 November 1591) – 'vivido con mucha autoridad y honra y nobleza como gente principal y nobles hijosdalgo, teniendo muchos criados, escuderos y cavallos, y emparentando con cavalleros hijosdalgo'. Contrast the observation of Fayard and Gerbet, op. cit., 68, that questions about arms and horses had become rare in the *pleitos* by the end of the sixteenth century.

38. On the marginality of 'oficios viles y mecánicos' for nobility in Spain see, Figueroa y Melgar, op. cit., 435; Marqués de Saltillo, 'La nobleza española en el siglo XVIII', *Revista de Archivos, Bibliotecas y Museos*, Vol. 60 pt. 2 (1954), 417–49, at 417 citing García de Saavedra, 'Nobilis nobilitate sanguinis per exercicium oficii vilioris nihi sibi nocet'; and Moreno de Vargas, op. cit., f. 50v, asserting, against 'algunos modernos', that in Spain 'por costumbre antiquíssima' nobility is not lost for this reason.

39. For example, *leg.* 2, f. 33 (6 December 1691), in which D. Juan González de Guzmán claimed his grandfather 'por sus cortos posibles se allanó a pechar'; but the expenses of litigation and the 'falta de medios' to undertake a legal resolution were the stock explanation for resorting to the purchase of a *carta de privilegio*, *leg.* 2, ff. 40, 69, 79, 82, 75, 77, 17, 4, 64, 65, 73, 84, 63, 61, 42.

40. Moreno de Vargas, op. cit., prologue, 'Las letras y las armas dan Nobleza, consérvala el valor y la riqueza', and ff. 29, 39v–44; Guardiola, op. cit., f. 66v; Peñalosa, op. cit., f. 85v; Díez Borque, op. cit., 282, 285; Herrero, op. cit., 170–1.

41. Américo Castro, *España en su Historia* (Buenos Aires 1948), 26, citing Alonso de Cartagena at the Council of Basle in 1434, 'Los castellanos no acostumbran tener en mucho las riquezas, mas la virtud; nin miden la honor por la quantidat del dinero, mas por la qualidad de las obras fermosas'.

42. *Pace* Caro Baroja, op. cit., 106.

43. Peñalosa, op. cit., f. 85v.

44. Moreno de Vargas, op. cit., f. 11.

45. Contrast the emphasis of Fayard and Gerbet, op. cit., 63, 68, 74–5, on the increasing importance of 'living nobly'.

46. Seventeen of the grantees in the period up to 1602 had personal (*leg.* 1, ff. 40, 70, 1, 55, 56, 16, 23, 35, 52, 60; *leg.* 2, f. 52) or family (*leg.* 1, ff. 39, 11; *leg.* 2, ff. 18, 11) connections with the Indies, only four in the rest of the seventeenth century (*leg.* 2, ff. 23, 55, 59, 84), only one personal.

47. *Leg.* 2, f. 15 (30 July 1696).

48. Contrast Fayard and Gerbet, op. cit., 70; Nieto, op. cit., 510.

49. 46 per cent; 12 per cent had personal services, 42 per cent family services. This was accompanied by the disappearance of the 'armas, caballos, criados' formula from the *privilegios* after 1640.

50. Peñalosa, op. cit., f. 95v.

51. A. Domínguez Ortiz, 'La mobilización de la nobleza castellana en 1640', *Anuario de Historia del Derecho Español*, Vol. 25 (1955), 799–825.

52. *Leg.* 1, f. 59 (10 November 1591). Fayard and Gerbet, op. cit., 71, also note an increased emphasis on relations with other nobles in their evidence.

404

53. Genealogical memory by generation (gtgdfather = 3)

	T	3	4	5	6	7	8	9	10	11
1569–98	35	12				1				
1600–15	15	7	4				1			
1629–50	33	8	9	4						
1665–99	26	8	3	2	2	1				1
1720–99	31	3	3	4	1	2		1		

Fayard and Gerbet, op. cit., 63, find a similar phenomenon, with 18 per cent of their cases going back to the great-grandfather before 1550, 40 per cent thereafter.
54. The Salas Ramírez de Arellano of Zafra (24 November 1693) claimed services back to the time of Don Rodrigo in the eighth century, *leg*. 2, f. 73.
55. Gutiérrez Nieto, op. cit., 505; Fayard and Gerbet, op. cit., 65, note a similar increase after 1560.
56. O. H. Green, *Spain and the Western Tradition* (Madison, Wisconsin, 1963), Vol. 1, 16–26; Herrero García, op. cit., 42; Maravall, *Poder, honor y élites*, 59. For the English parallel, M. James, *English Politics and the Concept of Honour 1485–1642*, Past and Present Supplement 3 (1978), 68.
57. Gutiérrez Nieto, op. cit., 509–11; Maravall, *Teatro y literatura*, 60.
58. *Leg*. 2, f. 74 (27 May 1631). The last direct description of a recipient's family as 'rica' is dated 1610, *leg*. 2, f. 14.
59. *Leg*. 2, f. 32 (15 December 1609).
60. *Leg*. 2, ff. 56 (1632), 42 (1699), 64 (1638), 47 (1694).
61. Maravall, *Teatro y literatura*, 39, 45, *Poder, honor y élites*, 131.
62. The dictum was cited as 'común proverbio' by Valera, op. cit., 100; Sánchez de Arévalo said much the same thing in his *Speculum vitae*, Boase, op. cit., 26; and Moreno de Vargas, op. cit., f. 31. Calderón in his *Alcalde de Zalamea* has Pedro Crespo ask rhetorically, 'Pues qué gano yo en comprarle una ejecutoria al rey, si no le compro la sangre?', cited by Herrero García, 'Ideologia', 175.
63. *Leg*. 4, f. 39; *leg*. 3, f. 98; *leg*, 4, ff. 285, 263–4, 149.
64. 21 of 34.
65. *Leg*. 3, f. 237 (19 June 1740), 'en que cunplisteis con la obligación de mi fiel vasallo'. The concept was already disappearing in the second half of the seventeenth century.
66. *Leg*. 3, ff. 72–3, 91; *leg*. 4, ff. 39, 125–6, 149, 89, 315.
67. 'Han sacrificado sus intereses en servicio de la Monarquía', *leg*. 3, ff. 72–3, *leg*. 4, ff. 125–6 (8 February 1791), and also *leg*. 3, f. 253, *leg*. 4, ff. 39, 79, 89, 285.
68. 'Bastarían los distinguidos empleos que disfrute...para que se os declarase la Nobleza', *leg*. 3, ff. 72–3, *leg*. 4, ff. 125–6.
69. *Leg*. 4, ff. 285, 79, 315.
70. The Fernández de León of Esparragosa de Lares (Badajoz) had a relative who, as *maestre escuela* of Caracas cathedral, had been one of the first, 'por su empleo, literatura y acreditado celo', to assist in the reform and reorganization of the university there, and the family had been raised 'con la decencia y educación correspondiente a la Nobleza' and 'han procurado dar a sus subcesores carrera correspondiente a sus circunstancias en Letras y en Armas', *leg*. 3, ff. 72–3, *leg*. 4, ff. 125–6 (1791).
71. *Leg*. 3, f. 119 (20 August 1743), f. 91 (18 April 1744); *leg*. 4, f 125–6 (24 December 1790). This growing materialism can also be seen in the high entry fees being imposed by the Maestranzas after the 1770s, R. Liehr, *Sozialgeschichte spanischer Adelskorporationen: die Maestranzas de Caballería, 1670–1808* (Wiesbaden 1981), 255. For this

renewed connection of nobility and wealth see also, M. García Pelayo, 'El estamento de la nobleza en el despotismo ilustrado español', *Moneda y Crédito*, Vol. 17 (1946), 57; V. Palacio Atard, *Los Españoles de la Ilustración* (Madrid 1964), 73; W. J. Callahan, *Honor, Commerce and Industry in Eighteenth-Century Spain* (Boston, Mass., 1972), 13.

72. D. Diego García Bravo had been *consul del comercio de Mexico*, *leg*. 3, f. 98 (21 October 1756); D. Raimundo de Onis y López had been consul in Bordeaux and *administrador general* of taxes in Cuba, *leg*. 4, f. 264 (1 April 1783); D. Manuel Galván y Bujidos was 'comerciante por mayor' of Medina de Rioseco, since his youth 'dedicado al ramo de comercio', in which he could boast 'notables adelantamientos' and in which two of his sons were also occupied, *leg*. 4, f. 149 (18 September 1796); D. Mariano Granja y Sayol had run for more than thirty years an 'establecimiento en el comercio y fábrica de sedas' which was one of the 'más opulentos' in the city of Granada, *leg*. 4, f. 176 (22 July 1799). Though none of these is appealing directly to the decree of 1783, the phraseology of the decree is lifted *verbatim* into the 'justifications' ('destino útil', 'con adelantamientos notables y utilidad al estado'). On the response of manufacturers to the decree see, 'Ennoblecimiento por el ejercicio del comercio y de la industria', *Hidalguía*, Vol. 9 (1961), 295–8.

73. All the predecessors of D. Bartolomé Sánchez de las Ramas were Old Christians, 'sin haver ynter006fervenido en vuestra Familia y Parentela más oficio que el de Labrador', *leg*. 3, f. 237 (19 June 1740); the Onis claimed nobility 'ya por no haver obtenido oficios viles ni mecánicos', *leg*. 4, ff. 263–4 (1 April 1783).

74. *Leg*. 4, f. 89 (7 April 1772).

75. *Leg*. 3, ff. 72–3 and *leg*. 4, ff. 125–6 (8 February 1791); *leg*. 4, f. 176 (22 July 1799), f. 285 (21 March 1782), f. 149 (18 September 1796).

76. D. Pedro Bravo, *leg*. 4, f. 39 (10 August 1720).

77. D. Juan Antonio de el Peral Duque of Camasobres, jurisdiction of Cervera de Rio Pisuerga, *leg*. 4, f. 285 (21 March 1782).

78. D. Manuel del Río, *leg*. 4, f. 315 (8 April 1783).

79. D. Mariano Granja, *leg*. 4, f. 176.

80. Galván's family claim amounted to a daughter-in-law who was the sister of two artillery colonels and a Caballero of the Order of Carlos III, *leg*. 4, f. 149.

81. On the ultimately 'conservative' nature of the debate over nobility see, in particular, the arguments of Callahan, op. cit., chapter 6, and J. Guillamón Alvarez, *Honor y honra en la España del siglo XVIII* (Madrid 1981), chapter 2.

82. *Leg*. 3, f. 237; *leg*. 4, f. 69, 'sois labrador de (Villada)...y que asi vos como vuestro padre y abuelo han sido y sois personas honradas y de buena reputación, aviendo servido todos los oficios honoríficos de república por vuestro estado general' (June 1757).

83. Herrero García, op. cit., 40, writes of this obsession with blood as 'obsesión de una vasta familia de perturbados', attacked by the dramatists, 46, and by many of the writers, including Peñalosa, op. cit., ff. 96, 98.

84. Peñalosa, op. cit., f. 107v, writes of 'las infinitas hidalguías y executorias de nobleça que cada día se litiga'; *Actas de las Cortes de Castilla*, Vol. 13, 63–82 (4 November 1593), Vol. 18, 325–30 (13 July 1599); M. Herrero García, 'Más sobre la nobleza española y su función política en el Teatro de Lope de Vega. II Los Títulos', *Escorial*, Vol. 20 (Madrid 1949), 13–60, on Lope's 'La Octava Maravilla'; Thompson, op. cit., 354.

85. Maravall, *Poder, honor y élites*, 79.

86. 'Procurad ser amigo de los historiadores y de los que escriben linajes', the bishop of Cuzco advised his nephew in November 1636, A. A. Sicroff, *Les controverses des Statuts de 'Pureté de Sang' en Espagne du XVe au XVIIe siècle* (Paris 1960), 267 n. 15. The fabrication of origins and genealogies was derided by Moreno de Vargas, op. cit., f. 10v.

87. B. Bennassar, *Los españoles, actitudes y mentalidades* (Barcelona 1976), 123. By contrast, the increasing difficulty of rising into the nobility in the eighteenth century coincided with a growing bourgeois sensibility.

88. On the unity of nobility in Castile, M-C. Gerbet, *La noblesse dans le royaume de Castille. Etude sur les structures sociales en Estremadure de 1454 à 1516* (Paris 1979), 142, 127.

89. Valera, op. cit., f. 91.

90. 'La diferencia del hidalgo viene a quedar en sola la voluntad del concejo', *Actas de las Cortes de Castilla*, Vol. 13, 71, and generally on the importance of 'la reputación común' the Cortes debates of 4 November 1593, ibid., 63–82, and 10 July 1599, Vol. 18, 319–31. 'Es evidente que la pureza y la nobleza no es algo esencial, corpóreo, real y palpable, sino algo que consiste en la opinión humana, en la opinión del vulgo', D. Francisco de Amaya in 1639, cited by A. Domínguez Ortiz, *La clase social de los conversos en Castilla en la Edad Moderna* (Madrid 1955), 193. For concrete examples of the constant need to defend one's *hidalguía, leg.* 4, f. 210, D. Agustín Francisco de Puerto Maheda (17 April 1738) – challenges in 1698, 1710, 1737; *leg.* 4, f. 176, D. Antonio Josef Martín de Oliva (21 September 1792) – 1739, 1785, 1788, 1790, despite *cartas executorias* going back to 1460 and 1532.

91. Maravall, *Poder, honor y élites*, 201, 205.

92. Moreno de Vargas, op. cit., f. 31, reported it as the common view that 'los hijosdalgo de sangre son los verdaderos hijosdalgo'; on the common hostility to wealth and indifference to 'letras' or 'ciencia', Díez Borque, op. cit., 246–7, Herrero García, 'Ideología', 166, 173.

93. James, op. cit., 68.

94. Maravall, *Poder, honor y élites*, 220; Fayard and Gerbet, op. cit., 63, 68, 70; Gerbet, op. cit., 133.

95. It is significant that there is barely a mention of fiscal exemptions in the eighteenth-century 'justifications', either as evidence for or as a consequence of *hidalguía*.

96. G. Anes, *El Antiguo Régimen: los Borbones* (Madrid 1975), 48, 56; A. Domínguez Ortiz, *Sociedad y estado en el siglo XVIII español* (Madrid 1976), 349.

97. 'Las ideas se han mudado, es verdad, mas solo entre los escritores. . .mas el pueblo subsiste siempre inmutable', wrote Capmany, cited by Palacio Atard, op. cit., 59; 'llamar al socorro la voz del Soberano' was for Pedro Antonio Sánchez, writing in 1781, the only corrective for the fact that 'todo el mal reside en la persuasión vulgar', Guillamón Alvarez, op. cit., 108–9; and Callahan, op. cit., 26.

98. See the excellent piece by A. Lazo Díaz, 'La lucha contra los privilegios estamentales en las Cortes de Cádiz', *Atlántida*, Vol. 9, no. 49 (1971), 53–61.

I. A. A. Thompson

is Senior Lecturer in History at the University of Keele. His publications include *War and Government in Habsburg Spain 1560–1620* (1976) and 'Crown and Cortes in Castile 1590–1665', in *Parliaments, Estates and Representation* (1982). His current interests are the Cortes of Castile and public office in Castile during the sixteenth and seventeenth centuries.

Hidalgo and pechero: the language of 'estates' and 'classes' in early-modern Castile

Formal descriptions of society in Castile from the Middle Ages through to the eighteenth century were set, as they were everywhere in the West, within the framework of a tripartite structure inspired and sanctioned by the divine order of the heavens.[1] Those parts were spoken of usually as 'estados', sometimes as 'brazos', very occasionally as 'clases'. The language reflected three models of society coexisting in contemporary beliefs: the medieval concept of a society ordered by functions (*oratores*, *defensores*, *laboratores*); the organic concept of society as a *corpus mysticum*; and the Aristotelian concept of a society ordered by quality, power, and wealth (*mayores/ricos*, *medianos*, *menores/pobres*). Changes in the language of social description in Castile reflected the changing balance within the status system of those three principles of social classification: function, lineage, and wealth.

'Clase' was already in use as a term of stratification in Castile in the sixteenth century, much earlier, it seems, than in England. It is found both in a simple categorical sense,[2] and in the classical sense, as used by Servius Tullius for an ad hoc grouping of the population according to wealth for fiscal purposes.[3] But it also existed as a straightforward

---

[1] R. Pérez Bustamante (ed.), *La Villa de Santillana: estudios y documentos* (Santillana del Mar, 1984), p. 287, RC 8 Aug. 1445.

[2] A. González Palencia (ed.), *La Junta de Reformación* (*Archivo Histórico Español*, vol. 5, Madrid, 1932), pp. 245–7.

[3] Instituto de Valencia de Don Juan, envío 45, caja 59, f. 453, Junta Grande, 20.2.1591: resolved on *empréstito* to 'repartir en tres clases todo el Reino, una de los grandes, prelados y Señores y cabildos eclesiásticos y ciudades; otra de

alternative to 'brazo' or 'estado'. Olivares in his *Gran Memorial* of 1624, having surveyed in turn the politics of the clergy, the various ranks of the nobility, and the 'people', concluded, 'having given Your Majesty an account of the classes of which these kingdoms are composed and of the manner in which Your Majesty should deal with each of them.'[4] This use of 'clase' may, however, have had a more specific, if latent, social connotation. Cobarruvias in his 1611 dictionary suggests that it was primarily an affectation of Latinists who 'divide peoples into three classes, "menores", "medianos" and "mayores".'[5] This Aristotelian division of society into 'mayores', 'medianos', and 'menores' was pervasive. It was already enshrined in the late-thirteenth-century *Partidas* of Alfonso the Wise, and expressed a view of the social order which, well before the end of the Middle Ages, was not specifically functional, and which was open to the application of general political, economic, and intellectual criteria to social stratification.[6]

The use of 'brazo' (literally 'arm', better rendered as 'member') was most often found in general considerations of the political system. This is the way Olivares used it in the *Gran Memorial*, for example.[7] Its importance lay in its metaphorical force. The analogy with the human body, so much more current in Spain as a theory of relationships than the Great Chain of Being, served to reinforce an organic and genetic, rather than a hierarchical, vision of the social order and to promote an

---

los caballeros y mayorazgos, y clérigos y hombres ricos; y otra de la demás gente del pueblo.' For the division of the population of Rome into tax bands by Servius Tullius, see P. Calvert, *The Concept of Class: an historical introduction* (Hutchinson, London, 1982), p. 13.

[4] 'Habiendo hecho relación a V. Majd. de las clases de que se componen estos reinos y del modo con que V. Majd. se debe gobernar con cada una': J. H. Elliott and F. de la Peña, *Memoriales y Cartas del Conde Duque de Olivares* (Madrid, 1978), vol. 1, p. 63.

[5] Sebastián de Cobarruvias, *Tesoro de la Lengua Castellana o Española* (1611), in modern edn (Madrid, 1979).

[6] E. Elorduy, *La idea del imperio en el pensamiento español* (Madrid, 1944), p. 466, 'Pueblo llaman el ayuntamiento de todos los omes comunalmente, de los mayores, e de los medianos, e de los menores. Ca todos son menester, e non se puede escusar, porque se han de ayudar unos a otros, porque puedan bien bivir, e ser guardados, e mantenidos': *Partidas*, II, 10, 1; Pérez Bustamante (ed.), *La Villa de Santillana*, p. 286.

[7] Elliott and de la Peña, *Memoriales y Cartas*, vol. 1, pp. 49–63: 'El brazo eclesiástico, que puede considerarse por la piedad de religión por el primero' (uses only 'brazo' for clergy); 'este brazo de la nobleza', p. 60; 'este brazo de la república', p. 61; 'los otros brazos', 'este brazo' (*sc.* 'el pueblo'), p. 61.

ideology of social harmony based on a functional network of reciprocal obligations and expectations.[8]

Neither 'clase' nor 'brazo' was in common use. Overwhelmingly, the preponderant idiom of social description was that of 'estados'. The language of 'estates' was ambivalent, however. Even by the early fourteenth century, when Don Juan Manuel's *Libro de los Estados* gave it its first, classic formulation, it had both an ordinal and an occupational sense, defining men not only in the mass ('all the estates in the world are comprised in three'), but also individually ('there are as many estates as there are men in this world').[9] Because of this ambivalence, the use of 'estates' was protean and imprecise. In its primary sense, 'estado' denoted a functional order with its own distinct way of life. It marked off the fundamental divisions of civil society into one or other of which a man must necessarily fall, 'since', as Moreno de Vargas put it, 'it would be an absurdity for one and the same person to be in two contrary estates.'[10]

Although the traditional, tripartite system of 'sacerdote', 'caballero', and 'labrador' survived in the literature of the sixteenth and seventeenth centuries and even into the eighteenth,[11] already during the later Middle Ages it was coming under increasing pressure from alternative perceptions of society deriving from the secular, social analysis of revived Aristotelianism and from the realities of economic and political change. With the growth of the market, urban culture, the legal profession, and a proto-bureaucracy, the language of 'estados' was having to be adapted to accommodate the development of more complex social formations than the simple functional presuppositions of the old society of orders could easily comprehend. One response was to make the functional system of the society of orders itself more complex. Enrique de Villena

[8] Closest to the idea of a 'Great Chain of Being', though very late (1781), is Antonio Javier Pérez y López: 'la sociedad es una cadena y no todos los eslabones deben ser iguales en consideración, pero los menores son dignos . . . y necesarios para la subsistencia del todo': see P. Molas, *La burguesía mercantil en la España del Antiguo Régimen* (Madrid, 1985), p. 143.

[9] 'Digovos que todos los estados del mundo se encierran en tres: al uno llaman defensores et al otro oradores et al otro labradores' (92); 'tantos son los estados que homes viven en este mundo' (83): from J. R. Araluce Cuenca, *El Libro de los Estados: Don Juan Manuel y la sociedad de su tiempo* (Madrid, 1976), pp. 54–5.

[10] J-M. Pelorson, *Les 'Letrados' juristes castillans sous Philippe III* (Le Puy-en-Velay, 1980), p. 224.

[11] J. A. Maravall, *Estado moderno y mentalidad social* (2 vols, Madrid, 1972), vol. 2, pp. 14–15.

in the fifteenth century conceived of society as divided into twelve 'estados', and in Diego Tovar y Valderrama (1645) there are not three basic social functions, but eight: those of the clergy, magistracy, army, nobility, agriculture, commerce, and the liberal and industrial professions.[12] Cobarruvias, in 1611, interposed the 'ciudadano' – 'he who lives in the city, and lives off his own capital, income, or property' – as 'an estate in the middle, between *caballero* or *hidalgo* and the artisan', which included 'the *letrados*, and those professing letters and the liberal arts.' In a number of places in the previous century an 'estado de ciudadanos', or 'mercaderes', actually existed as a separate estate of local government.[13]

Others responded by retaining the language of the three estates while depriving it of its traditional functional content, speaking, for example, of 'el estado de los medianos', 'el estado de la medianía', 'el mediano estado',[14] or, like Fernando Alvarez de Toledo in 1602, regarding the estates simply as degrees of wealth: 'There are considered to be three estates in the commonwealth: one of the rich, one of the poor, and one of those who have moderate wealth to get by on.'[15]

Both the 'ricos/medianos/pobres' schema and the Aristotelian 'mayores/medianos/menores' represent a more overtly hierarchical view of society than the traditional 'sacerdote/caballero/labrador' or the vulgar

[12] Ibid., vol. 2, p. 19: 'ca el mundo es partido de doze estados principales e más señalados, so los quales todos los otros se entienden': J. A. Maravall, *La philosophie politique espagnole au XVIIe siècle* (Paris, 1955), pp. 109, 92. The 'cuerpo místico' concept was also particularly useful in permitting both greater complexity and imaginative flexibility in the description of social relationships. See, e.g., Juan Pablo Mártir Rizo, *Norte de Príncipes* (1626), ed. J. A. Maravall (Madrid, 1988), p. 18: 'Y porque toda República o comunidad es un cuerpo . . . podemos decir, y con razón, que el príncipe es la cabeza, los hombres sabios y prudentes, los ojos; los magistrados, jueces y otros ministros son los oídos que reciben las leyes, las constituciones del Señor, y las ejecutan. La lengua y boca, los letrados y abogados; las manos, la nobleza; los labradores, los pies, de quien se sirve este cuerpo así distribuido.'

[13] In Logroño, the three estates were 'hidalgos', 'labradores cristianos viejos', and 'ciudadanos': 'Nobiliario Riojano', *Berceo*, 2 (1947), p. 307. Of Herrera de Rio Pisuerga it was said in 1616, 'en la dicha villa hasta de algunos años a esta parte había tres estados, uno de hidalgos, otro de labradores, y otro de ruanos y mercaderes'; for which see Pelorson, *'Letrados' juristes*, p. 231.

[14] Gónzales Palencia (ed.), *La Junta de Reformación*, pp. 246, 247, 255.

[15] 'Tres estados se consideran en la República: el uno de ricos, el otro de pobres, y el otro de los que tienen moderado caudal con que pasar': J. L. Sureda Carrión, *La hacienda castellana y los economistas del siglo XVII* (Madrid, 1949), p. 165.

employment of 'estado' as a simple occupational category that one finds in village surveys: 'here there are people of all estates, farmers, *hidalgos*, artisans and labourers.'[16] The language of social description seems in general to have been less insistently vertical in Castile than it was elsewhere. Castilians spoke neither of first, second, and third estates;[17] nor did they oppose 'upper' to 'lower' in their general social classifications as commonly as the English. 'Upper' is little used. There are examples of generalized uses of 'bajo' or low – Cobarruvias, for example, defines 'Plebeyo' as 'el hombre baxo de la república que ni es cavallero, ni hidalgo, ni ciudadano' but 'lower' was usually applied more discriminatingly to specific individuals, groups, and occupations, rather than to the totality of the non-noble. However, Castilian social vocabulary was far from being entirely horizontal. Social mobility was usually described in terms of 'upwardness' (though less often in terms of 'downwardness'), and the natural/anthropological model was readily amenable to combining the ideals of harmony and interdependence with distinctions of quality and importance between the various members of the body.[18]

At the level of ordinary usage (as opposed to the theoretical formulations of the treatises) the impression is of a complete absence of coherence in the vocabulary of social description. Olivares, for example, uses 'brazo', 'estado', 'clase', 'lugar', 'jerarquía', 'grado', 'linaje' apparently indiscriminately to mean the same and different things. The nobility is spoken of variously as 'brazo', and 'clase'; but sub-groups within the nobility are also termed 'brazos' ('grandes') 'estados' ('los demás estados', 'tres estados' of *hidalgos*), 'clases' ('la cuarta clase de la nobleza'; 'divido también los caballeros en dos clases'), or they are a 'jerarquía de personas' (*señores titulados, caballeros*), a 'lugar' or station ('el segundo lugar de la nobleza', 'el tercer lugar de la nobleza'), a 'grado' or rank ('los hidalgos es el grado primero de la nobleza de Castilla'), or, in the case of the

---

[16] 'Hay de todos estados de gentes, labradores, hidalgos, oficiales e jornaleros': C. Viñas and R. Paz (eds), *Relaciones de los pueblos de España ordenadas por Felipe II: Ciudad Real* (Madrid, 1971), p. 580 (Villamayor).

[17] It is interesting that J. Lalinde in a recent contribution in J. Lalinde Abadía et al., *El Estado Español en su dimensión histórica* (Madrid, 1984), p. 43, translates Sieyès' 'tiers état' as 'estado llano'. Nevertheless, Olivares did use ordinal language in his *Gran Memorial*: 'El brazo eclesiástico, que puede considerarse por la piedad de religión por el primero' (p. 49), and 'El pueblo, señor, tiene el lugar tercero y inferior' (p. 61).

[18] Hierónimo Merola, *República Original sacada del cuerpo humano* (1587), 'tiene naturaleza partes viles y bajas cuyas partes son obedecer,' in P. de Vega (ed.), *Antología de escritores políticos del Siglo de Oro* (Madrid, 1966), p. 100.

'pueblo', 'este linaje de gente'.[19] This terminological promiscuity suggests that the words themselves were not particularly heavy with meaning, and that by this time the ordinary vocabulary of social description had become detached from its original associations.

The division of society into 'estados' did not, therefore, presuppose any particular scheme of social stratification: *eclesiástico/caballero/labrador*, *hidalgo/pechero*, *mayor/mediano/menor*, *rico/pobre*. Functional, economic, and legal definitions were frequently confused. An 'estado' could be an order, a status, an occupation, or a category of wealth. It merely denoted a distinct grouping of men with a way of life defined by some distinguishing feature which could be genetic or legal or functional or material – 'there are various estates in the community . . . gentlemen, burghers, craftsmen, husbandmen . . . each estate and way of life with its order and limits' (Cobarruvias) – and which varied from writer to writer and from place to place.[20] The use of 'estado' did not, by itself, make any statement about the nature of society; it did not necessarily connote the relational values of the society of orders; nor did it presume any consistent principle of status distinction.

Perhaps because of its flexibility, its conceptual ambivalence, its emphasis on function or occupation and on difference rather than hierarchy, the general vocabulary of social description in Castile does not seem to have responded very directly to changes in society. The language of 'estados' is the predominant idiom throughout the sixteenth and seventeenth centuries; and, despite increasing competition from alternative expressions in the eighteenth century, it remains so even at the end of our period. The changing balance within the status system of those three principles of social classification, function, lineage, and wealth, is reflected less in changing terminology than in changes in the meaning and the content of the words themselves. Those changes are best examined by

---

[19] 'El brazo eclesiástico' (p. 49), but also 'los otros estados más nobles' (p. 61); 'este brazo de la nobleza' (¿*hidalgos*? – not clear from text), 'los demás estados' (p. 60), 'este brazo de la república' (again not clear whether this is *nobleza* as a whole or *hidalgos*); references, to 'El pueblo, señor, tiene el lugar tercero y inferior' (p. 61), 'los otros brazos', 'este brazo', 'los otros estados más nobles' (p. 61), 'este linaje de gente' (p. 62); and quotation in fn 4 above: see Elliott and de la Peña, *Memoriales y Cartas*, vol. 1 pp. 49–63.

[20] In Villacastín (Segovia), for example, the graziers claimed to be 'el estado de señores de ganados': A. García Sanz, *Desarrollo y crisis del Antiguo Régimen en Castilla la Vieja* (Madrid, 1986), p. 366. In Bargas (Toledo) there was an 'estado de vecinos de Toledo' with its own reserved offices: C. Viñas and R. Paz (eds), *Relaciones de los pueblos de España ordenadas por Felipe II: Reino de Toledo*, pt 1 (Madrid, 1951), p. 122.

concentrating on one set of words, those which expressed the basic
division within early-modern society, that between the noble and the
non-noble.

There is no great problem in analysing what the learned have to say
about society. More difficult to catch are the perceptions of those who
lived the categories the learned thought. In this respect Spanish historians
are supremely fortunate. Because of the peculiar importance of the
lawcourts and the Military Orders as arbiters of nobility, they have
available an exceptional body of materials expressive of the language of
the ordinary, unlettered noble or commoner. The investigations for the
Military Orders, entry into which required proof of nobility and purity
of Christian blood on both sides for three generations, and the 'executive
letters' (*cartas ejecutorias*) issued by the high courts of Valladolid and
Granada in resolution of cases of disputed nobility between claimants
and the towns and villages which challenged them generated a huge mass
of documentation consisting largely of depositions of witnesses from all
levels of society. No less than 30,000 'executive letters' survive in Valladolid alone. To these records can be added the justifications presented
by the recipients of the hundreds of patents of nobility (*cartas de
privilegio*) granted or sold by the Crown between the sixteenth and the
nineteenth centuries and the responses to two national surveys, the so-
called 'Topographical Relations' carried out in New Castile in the 1570s
and the remarkable Ensenada *Catastro* of 1751/2 which runs to tens of
thousands of manuscript volumes.[21] These unique records are only just
beginning to be systematically exploited for the study of social history.
Nevertheless, something can be said, albeit tentatively, about the
social grammar of the 'vulgar', from whichever order of society they
came, a grammar which is in many respects very different from that
of the writers whose constructs have been relied upon rather too
easily.

[21] See E. Postigo Castellanos, *Honor y privilegio en la Corona de Castilla: El
Consejo de las Ordenes y los Caballeros de Hábito en el siglo XVII* (Junta de
Castilla y León, 1988); A. Basanta de la Riva, *Archivo de la Real Chancillería
de Valladolid. Sala de los Hijosdalgo: catálogo de todos sus pleitos, expedientes
y probanzas* (4 vols, Valladolid, 1920); J. Fayard and M-C. Gerbet, 'Fermeture
de la noblesse et pureté de sang en Castille à travers les procés de *hidalguía* au
XVIe siècle', *Histoire, Economie et Société*, 1 (1982), pp. 51–75; I. A. A.
Thompson, 'The purchase of nobility in Castile, 1552–1700', *Journal of European
Economic History*, 8 (1979), pp. 313–60; idem, 'Neo-noble nobility: concepts
of *hidalguía* in early-modern Castile', *European History Quarterly*, 15 (1985),
pp. 379–406; N. Salomon, *La campagne de Nouvelle Castille à la fin du XVIe*
d'après les 'Relaciones topográficas' (Paris, 1964).

The responses of the small-town and village elders to the questionnaires of the 'Topographical Relations' are probably the closest we can get to a coherent view of popular perceptions of the social order.[22] For them, too, society was divided into estates; on the one hand, 'el estado de los hijosdalgo' (the terms *noble* or *caballero* are not so commonly found) and on the other, a multiplicity of expressions, the most usual being 'el estado de pecheros', 'los hombres buenos pecheros', 'labradores, hombres buenos pecheros', 'hombres llanos pecheros'. What in the terminology of the 'Topographical Relations' distinguishes noble from non-noble is the *pecho*, personal taxation. The commoner was the taxpayer, the *pechero*; the *hidalgo* was the privileged, exempt from his share of the fiscal burdens of the community. To express the distinction noble/non-noble in the terms *hidalgo/pechero* was to highlight the fundamental conflict between *hidalguía* and the fiscal interests of the community ('they do not want to pay tax nor to contribute as the other householders do').[23] Ennoblement, therefore, was something to which the community was naturally hostile and resistant.[24]

Thus *hidalguía* in the 'Topographical Relations' was not defined by function, wealth, power, or lifestyle. The dichotomies rich–poor, powerful–weak, leisured–labouring existed, of course, and there are sometimes hints of their equation with status; but as often as not, the *hidalgo–pechero* axis bisected those poles. It is almost as if *hidalguía* in many communities was a social irrelevance. Indeed, when tax exemption was not at issue, communities were often indifferent to *hidalguía*, and might neither know nor care who was *hidalgo* and who was not.[25] In

---

[22] The surveys that survive have been published in C. Viñas and R. Paz (eds), *Relaciones histórico-geográfico-estadísticas de los pueblos de España, hechas por iniciativa de Felipe II: Provincia de Madrid* (Madrid, 1949); idem, . . . *Reino de Toledo* (3 parts, Madrid, 1951–63); idem, . . . *Ciudad Real* (Madrid, 1971); J. Zarco Cuevas, *Relaciones de pueblos del obispado de Cuenca* (Cuenca, 1983); J. Catalina and M. Pérez Villamil, 'Relaciones topográficas de España', *Memorial Histórico Español*, vols. 41–3, 45–6 (Province of Guadalajara).

[23] Zarco Cuevas, *Relaciones de Cuenca*, p. 512 (Tarazona de la Mancha).

[24] J. M. Diez Borque, *Sociología de la comedia española del siglo XVII* (Madrid, 1976), pp. 256–7.

[25] Viñas and Paz (eds), *Relaciones de Toledo*, p. 51: 'hay algunos vecinos de la villa de Talavera que viven en este lugar y pechan y contribuyen en la villa de Talavera y no se sabe si son hidalgos o no' (Alcaudete); p. 57: 'tres o cuatro están en este lugar en posesion de hidalgo, aunque no tienen ejecutoria, ni ellos saben si son hidalgos, ni si no' (Aldeanueva de Balbarroya); Alcántara, 15 Apr. 1570: 'por ser esta villa libre de pechos . . . y no ser por esta causa del todo conocidos los hijosdalgo', AGS GA 73, f. 14; Valladolid, 18 Apr. 1570: 'el

Pastrana (Guadalajara), the respondents in 1575 did not know how many *hidalgos* there were in the town nor who they were, 'nor has it been of concern, as has, and still is, purity of blood, which is much esteemed. Hence the custom has been that no *converso* [of Jewish blood], nor anyone of Moorish race, be allowed as an official or deputy in its government.'[26] Equally, individuals might be content with their exemptions and indifferent to their status. When the *Corregidor* of Toledo tried to sell patents of nobility in the city, those he approached replied, 'that as they live in Toledo they have no need of any *hidalguía* beyond that bestowed by the privileges and liberties that past kings have granted to the householders living here in this city.'[27] The *hidalguía* of the 'Topographical Relations' was first and last a legal status that had little connection with any other scheme of values, and the language in which it was described was the language of the law. *Hidalguía* was spoken of as a property ('en propiedad y posesión de hidalgos', 'gozan de posesión') and as a legal right ('derecho adquirido'); and nobles were ranked not as *hidalgos* or *caballeros*, nor by 'sangre' or 'solar conocido' (although there are instances of such classifications), but by the judicial basis of their status – that is to say, whether they were accounted *hidalgo* by a judgement of the courts ('por executoria'), convention ('por posesión'), or royal patent ('por privilegio'), or whether their claims were still doubtful or in litigation ('dudosos', 'pretendientes'). It is the language of litigiousness and contention, in which *hidalguía* was often uncertain, subject to repeated challenge, and sustainable only so long as it could be successfully defended in the courts.

If the primary division was between noble and commoner, *hidalgo* and *pechero*, the dualism rich–poor was no less prominent in the 'Topographical Relations'. The fusion of status and wealth and the mass ennoblement of the rich has been seen by many historians as the central dynamic of the social history of the sixteenth and seventeenth centuries.[28]

---

pueblo es grande y libre, con dificultad se puede saber el que es hijodalgo, o no', AGS GA 73, f. 24.

[26] N. Salomon, *Recherches sur le thème paysan dans la 'Comedia' au temps de Lope de Vega* (Bordeaux, 1965), p. 82.

[27] 'Que biviendo en Toledo no tienen necesidad de más hidalguía que la que tienen por los previllegios y libertades que los Reyes pasados dieron a los vezinos desta cibdad que aqui biviesen': AGS CJH 23, f. 205, 24 Mar. 1557.

[28] M.-C. Gerbet, *La noblesse dans le royaume de Castille: étude sur ses structures sociales en Estrémadure de 1454 à 1516* (Paris, 1979), p. 132; A. Domínguez Ortiz, *La sociedad española en el siglo XVII*, vol. 1 (Madrid, 1964), pt 2, ch. 3; J. A. Maravall, *Poder, honor y élites en el siglo XVII* (Madrid, 1979).

62

The profits of growth and the financial problems of government enabled the rich, by buying offices, lands, and jurisdictions, to seize control of political and economic power in the communities and to engineer their own social elevation. It is not accidental that contemporaries used 'ricos y poderosos' as if they were one word; and it is undoubtedly true that wealth facilitated upward mobility, while poverty made difficult the preservation of status. As one speaker stated in the Cortes in 1624:

> The officials of the towns and villages will not dare list anyone in the tax rolls who is prepared to go to litigation, however notorious a *pechero* he is. Thus he is left exempted as if he were an *hidalgo*, and so becomes one. Contrariwise, if they list an *hidalgo* who is poor, he cannot litigate and loses his *hidalguía*.[29]

There was, of course, absolutely nothing unique about this challenge to the traditional system of orders from the pressure of new wealth in the early-modern period. Complaints about the devaluing of nobility by the power of money can be found in the fourteenth and fifteenth centuries no less than in the sixteenth and seventeenth. Moreover, the theoretical relationship between nobility and wealth was an ambivalent one. Almost all writers thought wealth an essential adjunct of nobility, while at the same time deploring the ennoblement of the rich. The difficulties of trying to reconcile socio-economic change with the traditional tripartite structure of society can be seen in an anonymous paper of the early 1620s which bemoaned the breakdown of the balance between 'the poor', 'the middling' ('medianos'), and 'the truly rich', these last being equated with 'señores de título', 'caballeros', 'hidalgos', and 'nobles'. By taking from both 'ricos' and 'medianos' and by means of mortgages (*censos*), entails, and dowries, some men

> have become a special estate and separate kind [*género*] of person, neither of the rich, nor of the poor, nor of the middling, and have brought our society to the state of disorder that we see. In their ambition, those who would not have been out of place among the middling have wanted to join the rich, and others have become *caballeros* and *nobles* who would have been better in the business and the occupations that their fathers followed in their trades and *medianía*.

His solution to the diminution of the middling kind and to the rise of many low persons was to prevent access to 'el estado equestre' to anybody with less than the very considerable income of 4,000,000 *maravedís*; the rest could remain 'ciudadanos' or 'plebeyos'. Wealth could

---

[29] Salomon, *Campagne de Nouvelle Castille*, p. 300.

thus be made a quality of nobility precisely in order to check the ennoblement of the well-to-do.[30]

In effect, whatever social changes may have been taking place, the ideology of nobility was reluctant to accommodate the claims of the *nouveaux riches*. Conventionally, historians portray a noble hierarchy in Castile of *grandes, títulos, caballeros*, and *hidalgos*, graded by wealth. In general terms it was probably true that the average *grande* was richer than the average *título*, and so on; but there was no presumption in the language of status that this should be so. To be recognized as an *hidalgo* implied nothing about one's economic position – the 'Topographical Relations' abound in both poor and well-off *hidalgos*. Nor were contemporaries at all consistent in distinguishing *caballeros* from *hidalgos*, least of all in understanding the *caballero* to be a superior and wealthier kind of nobleman.

Just to take one example, in an account of 1570 a local official listed 142 'cavalleros hijosdalgo' in the town and district of Montanches (Extremadura), all of them 'poor, as are the people of this district in general.'[31] There was an economic difference between *caballero* and *hidalgo*, as Peñalosa wrote; for 'now, incorrectly, we call "caballeros" those noted *hidalgos* of ancient house and distinguished name who are of a more eminent and wealthy estate than other *hidalgos*.'[32] But the difference was not simply, or even principally, economic, but a difference of 'quality and estimation'. The epithets most characteristically associated with 'caballero' were not 'rico', nor even 'honrado', which were also applied at times to the *hidalgo*, the *labrador*, and the *mercader*, but 'principal', 'particular', 'calificado', 'noble'. In the city of Cáceres in the seventeenth century, when tax rolls were compiled, the 'caballeros notorios' and their descendants were noted as 'caballero hijodalgo', other nobles simply as 'hijodalgo'; and this was done 'as a clearer distinction and designation of the quality of each individual'.[33] Mme D'Aulnoy, though sometimes rather overcoloured in her descriptions of later-

---

[30] Gónzalez Palencia (ed.), *Junta de Reformación*, pp. 245–7.

[31] AGS GA 73, f. 46; at the same time, in Santo Domingo de la Calzada and the Merindad de Rioja no less than 942 'caballeros hijosdalgo' were listed, AGS GA 73, f. 60.

[32] Benito de Peñalosa y Mondragón, *Libro de las Cinco Excelencias del Español* (Pamplona, 1629), f. 87v.

[33] AHN Ordenes Militares, Calatrava, 1901, f. 23v., Calificación de la nobleza de D. Diego Antonio de Ovando, Cáceres, 26 June 1623: 'lo qual parece se haze para mayor distincion y declaracion de la calidad de cada uno.'

seventeenth-century Castile, got the tone right when she wrote, 'here it is not enough to be rich; it is necessary also to be of quality.'[34]

The language of the 'Topographical Relations' described the distinguishing marks of nobility; but it had nothing to say of its essence nor of the criteria by which the legal judgement of nobility was reached. *Hidalguía*, the generic term for nobility in Castile, was defined in the Middle Ages as 'the nobility which descends to men through their lineage.' It was not synonymous with knighthood (*caballería*). *Caballero*, at that time, was a functional term which did not necessarily denote hereditary nobility at all, but rather the personal grant of the privileges of nobility to townsmen of a certain level of substance, conditional on the maintenance of a horse and arms. During the fourteenth and fifteenth centuries, the tendency was for this 'caballería villana' of wealthy, sometimes *converso*, urban oligarchs to transform itself into hereditary *hidalguía*; and by the sixteenth century the semantic hierarchy had been reversed. The *hidalgo* had become the broad, base level of nobility, often rural and semi-proletarianized, and a new composite was emerging, the *caballero hijodalgo*, the term itself giving verbal expression to the fusion of lineage, wealth, and personal service to the king in war.[35]

The absorption of *caballería* into *hidalguía* had the effect of intensifying the militarist resonances of the language of nobility in the sixteenth century. Yet, at the same time, with the ending of the wars of the *Reconquista*, it was ceasing to be generally possible to move into the nobility through the half-way house of 'caballería villana'. The reign of Ferdinand and Isabella saw the last mass ennoblement in Castile for military service.[36] Ennoblement in the sixteenth century was overwhelmingly a civilian process effected through the courts and the phoney militarism of the Military Orders. More and more, nobility was being acquired by administrators, lawyers, financiers, and men for whom war was remote and foreign. There was a growing tension, therefore, as the sixteenth century progressed, between the social reality of the noble estate and the functional presuppositions of the society of orders.

Yet a functional view of nobility as the order of *defensores* persisted. It underlay the reimposition of military service on all *hidalgos* and

---

[34] Diez Borque, *Sociología de la comedia*, p. 201.

[35] Roger Boase, *The Troubadour Revival: a study of social change and traditionalism in late medieval Spain* (Routledge, London, 1978), pt 1; Gerbet, *La noblesse dans le royaume de Castille*, pp. 95, 125, 134.

[36] M-C. Gerbet, 'Les guerres et l'accès à la noblesse en Espagne de 1463 à 1592', *Mélanges de la Casa de Velázquez*, 8 (1972), pp. 295–326.

knights of the Military Orders in the mid-seventeenth century, as well as, for example, the opposition of the town of Fuente el Maestre to the exemptions of the Zambrano family on the grounds that such grants 'are always made for great and signal services in wars and battles, which neither they nor their father have ever done.'[37] The parvenu noble, therefore, compensated for his personal military deficiencies by an exaggerated adherence to a feudal-military ethos, translating his own administrative or financial services into the language of war and vassalage, and conjuring up deeds of valour by his family and forebears. A striking illustration of this sort of totemism is to be found in the complaint of two attorneys of Ubeda in 1600 against being listed as 'caballeros cuantiosos' and therefore required to present themselves at musters with horse and arms:

> They should not be obliged to maintain arms and a horse to go to the war when they are engaged in advocacy which is also fighting [*milicia*], for attorneys are justly called soldiers, and those who are actually practising that career and noble office, so necessary for Your Majesty's service and the good government of the commonwealth, have the same privileges, liberties and exemptions.[38]

More than four out of five of the justifications adduced for the grants of nobility sold in the seventy years after 1580 represented military services of one kind or another, but 70 per cent of those were surrogates, attributable to ancestors or relatives.[39]

The *hidalgo* ideal expressed in those justifications remained the 'defensor'. Yet the gap between the ideal and the reality, both in terms of social mobility (fewer and fewer of the new *hidalgos* had military services of their own) and in terms of the sociology of the military profession (which was proletarianized by conscription and deserted by the nobility), suggests that it is not enough to see the persistence of the language of the 'defensor' simply as a conservative force, buttressing an archaic, feudal ethos at the expense of progressive, 'bourgeois' attitudes. The petition of the Ubeda attorneys shows how conservatism of language could be used as a means of grafting groups with different values and backgrounds onto the stem of a historically sanctioned, and hence popularly accepted, status system without the need to compromise or deny those values, while at the same time holding together an elite of disparate origins under a common, unifying, ideological umbrella.

---

[37] AGS DGT Inventario 5, leg. 2, f. 72.
[38] Pelorson, '*Letrados*' *juristes*, p. 238.
[39] For the above, see Thompson, 'Neo-noble nobility', pp. 388–91.

With no reputable route to nobility by personal service alone, ennoblement in practice became almost exclusively a legal process of proving that one was already noble. To do that, it was necessary to prove affiliation in the male line to a recognized noble lineage, at least back to the grand-father, or a reputation as noble within the community by acceptance into the society of one's peers, through marriage, membership of noble confraternities, and a shared lifestyle. Until well into the seventeenth century, this took claimants back to a world of aural record, in which proof depended on the testimony of witnesses to their personal and hearsay knowledge of fact and repute, and in which the vulgar opinion of the community was the all in all. In effect, it was the community which was the arbiter of nobility. The endemic hostility of the community towards social promotion was, therefore, crucial in the definition of nobility in early-modern Castile. Nobility was defined as much by the concern to prevent escape from below as by the reluctance to allow access from above. What the community recognized, therefore, was not the accidentals of personal merit, virtue, learning, office, wealth, liberality, charity, and all the qualities so vaunted by philosophers and moralists, but the unchanging essence, blood and lineage. 'God forbid that I should be the vassal of someone baser than me,' expostulated one resident of Villalobón when he heard that Philip II's secretary of war was planning to buy the town.[40]

Elite designations of the commons frequently had connotations which were morally or politically pejorative: 'la gente común', 'el plebeyo', 'el vulgo', 'villanía'.[41] Most often the commons were defined in terms of qualities which were the antitheses of noble virtues: vicious, grasping, intemperate, inconstant, irrational, and cowardly.[42] The elite found it easier to maintain a unified vision of society and to hold nobility and commonalty within a single continuum of values. 'Since the beginning of the world there have always been some good and noble, and others evil and base,' wrote the Andalusian patrician Ferrand Mexia in 1477.[43] Against the

[40] AHN Pruebas de Santiago, exp. 2426, f. 10.

[41] 'Suena tan mal el nombre de labrador que es lo mismo que pechero, villano, grossero, malicioso', from Peñalosa, *Libro de las Cinco Excelencias del Español*; cited in L. Pfandl, *Cultura y costumbres del pueblo español de los siglos XVI y XVII* (Barcelona, 1929), p. 116.

[42] Cosme de Aldana's 1,000-line 'Invectiva contra el vulgo y su maledicencia' (1591), which begins 'Tramposo, desleal, Gente abatida,/ Gente manjar de horca, y de cuchillo./ Hambrienta Arpia, cruel fiera homicida,/ Hydra immortal . . . ,' is a nice example.

[43] *Nobiliario Vero*, bk 1, ch. 40, facsimile edn (Madrid, 1974). Mexia was a city councillor of Jaén and of an ancient noble family. His social attitudes were

tripartism of the formal models of society and the multiplication of estates in the late medieval and early-modern period, there was a counter-tendency to a polarization and a reduction to a unified scale of social values in which the dichotomies *noble–plebeyo*, *hidalgo–pechero*, rich–poor, *limpio–notado*, good–bad, handsome–plain, powerful–weak, ruler–ruled, would coalesce into the two poles of a single spectrum of honour and esteem.[44] The seventeenth-century mania for knighthoods of the Military Orders stemmed precisely from the fact that they were seen as demonstration of 'limpieza' in all four categories: lineage, office, race, and religion. Even in local government, those earlier instances of a third estate of 'mercaderes' or 'ciudadanos' seem to have disappeared. In the writing of the later sixteenth and seventeenth centuries, *noble–mayor–rico* were coming to be fused.

Conversely, the insistence on the particularity of 'estados' as referring to specific distinctions, as well as to a general partition of society, and the primacy of the purely legal *hidalgo–pechero* divide served to prevent the exclusion of the 'plebeyo' from the honour system. When the *hidalgo* graziers of Villacastín (Segovia) claimed the right to a half of all local offices as 'el estado de señores de ganado', they were denied by the town council on the grounds that

> sheep baron is not an estate with standing in the law, for there are also merchants, farmers and craftsmen, besides other occupations and ways of living, which are not 'estados' for the allocation of offices. . . . There are other townsmen who do not own sheep who are merchants, very rich and honourable men, very zealous for the public good . . . and they have no separate status nor personal distinctions amongst them.[45]

---

no doubt related to his bitter opposition to the favourite of Enrique IV, the populist upstart, the *Condestable* Miguel Lucas de Iranzo.

[44] Diez Borque, *Sociología de la comedia*, p. 261; B. Moreno de Vargas, *Discursos de la Nobleza de España* (Madrid, 1659), f. 42, cites the dictum 'no aver más de dos linajes en el mundo, que son ricos y pobres, juzgando aquellos por nobles, y a estos por plebeyos'; Merola, 'los plebeyos . . . como rudos, y de quien les mande como hombres cuyas partes son obedecer solamente,' in Vega (ed.), *Antología*, p. 105; *Actas de las Cortes de Castilla*, vol. 13, p. 78, 'está dispuesto aún por derecho divino que los nobles tengan el mando de los lugares, y los plebeyos los obedezcan, y se ocupen solo en servir para la provisión dellos' (4 Nov. 1593).

[45] 'Señores de ganado no es estado considerable en derecho, pues hay también mercaderes, labradores y oficiales, y otrosi dichos tratos y maneras de vivir, que no son estados para oficios . . . los demás vecinos que no tienen ganado son mercaderes, personas muy ricas y honradas y muy celosas del bien público . . .

The uniquely Spanish concept of 'limpieza de sangre' had something of the same function. The distinction between the 'limpio' and the 'notado', the pure and the impure of blood, was perhaps as fundamental a division of Spanish society as that between the noble and the commoner.[46] Indeed, in some ways 'limpieza' was the nobility of the commoner. According to an anonymous early seventeenth-century source:

> There are two kinds of nobility in Spain, a greater, which is *hidalguía*, and a lesser, which is *limpieza*, by which we mean 'Old Christian'. And although to have the former, *hidalguía*, is more honourable, it is more shameful to be without the latter, because in Spain we hold in more esteem a *pechero* who is *limpio* than an *hidalgo* who is not.[47]

'Limpieza de sangre', therefore, was at the same time a form of non-noble lineage honour, which the simple peasant 'labrador', uncorrupted by contact with the suspect urban civilization of the Moor and the Jew, enjoyed by virtue of the very anonymity of his ancestry, and a challenge to the honour of the noble lineage. Until the middle of the sixteenth century, when statutes requiring 'limpieza' spread throughout many of the most important institutions of Spanish society, *hidalguía* and *limpieza* had not necessarily been associated. The nobility, therefore, because of the very fame of its lineage, was vulnerable to the accusation of being tainted with Jewish blood. According to Jerónimo de Zevallos, writing *c.* 1635:

> by these means lowly men have set themselves against [the nobles], wanting through the investigation of their *limpieza* not merely to put themselves on the same plane but even to exceed them. . . . This so puffs them up with pride and arrogance that there is not a gentleman, noble, or lord whom they dare not try to discredit and defame as not *limpio*.[48]

---

y no hay diferencia de estados entre ellos ni cosa por la que hacer diferencia en las personas': García Sanz, *Desarrollo y crisis*, p. 367.

[46] The classic account of 'limpieza' is Albert A. Sicroff, *Les controverses des Statuts de 'Pureté de Sang' en Espagne du XVe au XVIIe siècle* (Paris, 1960). The centrality of 'limpieza' is stressed in contrary directions by J. I. Gutiérrez Nieto, as a form of class struggle of nobility versus bourgeoisie, in 'La estructura castizo-estamental de la sociedad castellana del siglo XVI', *Hispania*, 33 (1973), pp. 519–63, at p. 559; and as a form of anti-nobility, in 'Limpieza de sangre y antihidalguismo hacia 1600', in *Homenaje al Dr D. Juan Reglà Campistol* (Univ. of Valencia, Valencia, 1975), pp. 497–514. For J. A. Maravall, on the other hand, it is merely another barrier to the acquisition of nobility: *Poder, honor y élites*, p. 119.

[47] A. Domínguez Ortiz, *La clase social de los conversos en Castilla en la edad moderna* (Madrid, 1955), p. 229.

[48] 'Se han opuesto y oponen [a los nobles] por este medio los hombres bajos, queriendo no sólo igualarse pero aventajarse a ellos con un acto de limpieza, . . . y éste les llena de tanta soberbia y vanidad que ni hay caballero, noble ni

Limpieza was thus a form of anti-*hidalguismo*, a means by which the peasant could avenge himself on the pretensions of noble and urban wealth, and a form of compensation, a way for the *labrador* to counter his own social baseness. The *hidalgo*, in danger of being demeaned by his very status, was forced to react; and from the second half of the sixteenth century, *limpieza* too became an increasingly necessary prerequisite for nobility.[49]

The fact that the terminology of social description in Castile leant towards horizontality rather than verticality – that is employed a language that was not manifestly hierarchical in its categorization of the different social orders – may also have contributed to a sense of a common participation in the honour system. That the non-noble was not spoken of in the mass as the third estate, or the lower orders, but as 'el estado llano', 'el estado común', 'los hombres buenos', 'el estado de los pecheros', may have had something to do with what struck so many contemporary observers, right through the *ancien régime*, as the extraordinary social presumption of the Castilian commons, that punctilious lack of deference which persists still, and the relatively muted nature of social conflict in early-modern Castile, compared with other European societies.[50] The Frenchman Jean Muret, travelling in Spain in 1666, had imagined that the Spaniard's hypersensitive self-respect was only an amusing something that he had read about in *Don Quixote*:

> but I would never have believed that universally every Spaniard would have affected this ridiculous concern for his honour. It comes, sir, from that pride which is so natural to him and which makes them believe that all the other nations are as nothing in comparison with theirs. Indeed, you cannot see the meanest tramp who does not wear a sword. They imagine that to be Spanish is to be noble, as long as one does not descend from a moor, a jew, or a heretic.[51]

Castile seems to have been the only country in Europe in which the theatre did not portray honour as exclusive to the nobility, but allowed the ordinary peasant a genuine claim to honour and to the respect of the upper orders.[52]

---

señor a quien no se atrevan a desacreditar e infamar de no limpio': cited in Gutiérrez Nieto, 'Limpieza de sangre y antihidalguismo', p. 514, n. 37.

[49] Fayard and Gerbet, 'Fermeture de la noblesse', p. 65.

[50] For example, Bartolomé Joly (1603–4), Antonio de Brunel (1665), J. García Mercadal (ed.), *Viajes de Extranjeros por España y Portugal* (3 vols, Madrid, 1952), vol. 2, pp. 124, 412.

[51] Ibid., vol. 2, p. 717.

[52] D. R. Larson, *The Honor Plays of Lope de Vega* (Harvard University Press, Cambridge, Mass., 1977), p. 71.

For 300 years the 'executive letters' and the 'letters of privilege' are unwavering in deriving *hidalguía* first and foremost from the proven inheritance of a recognized, noble blood-line, a derivation encapsulated in the formula 'hidalgo notorio de sangre y solar conocido'. The assumptions of the claimants to nobility, of their witnesses, and, in so far as it is possible to judge, of the ordinary man adhered totally to the traditional definition of *hidalguía* as 'the nobility which descends to men through their lineage'. Indeed, although from the last decades of the sixteenth century, important changes are beginning to be visible in the language and the idioms of the 'executive letters' and the 'letters of privilege', they are changes that are tending to reinforce, rather than undermine, traditional values. Social differentiation itself becomes more extreme, more insistent, more verbalized. It is necessary to distinguish and to be distinguished. The title 'Don', once relatively uncommon, though beginning to be abused in the late sixteenth century, by the seventeenth century is sported by almost everyone of any social pretension whatsoever. City corporations, where in the sixteenth century, not one in five of the councillors would have been 'Don', are full – almost without exception – of 'Dons', knights of the Military Orders, *señores de vasallos*, even *títulos*.

Furthermore, nobility becomes more and more exclusively hereditary. The genetic language of blood, breeding, lineage, roots, trunks, branches ('sangre', 'casta', 'generación', 'raíz', 'tronco', 'rama') becomes more pervasive. The concept of purity of blood, unconnected with *hidalguía* in the earlier sixteenth century, becomes very much tied up with it by about 1570. That in turn brought the maternal line into the forefront of genealogical investigation. The genealogies, the ancestral memories, the family histories related in the proofs become longer, more remote, more glorious. Lineage connections are enshrined in a cascade of family names. In 1631, Juan Pérez Moreno de Mesa, the son of Juan Pérez Moreno de Mesa Cárdenas Alvarez Boorques y Gimeno and Doña Isabel de Montoya Palma y Marín, applied for *hidalguía*, and traced every single one of his parental lines.[53] The language of nobility becomes more profuse, more 'baroque'. Mere *hidalgo* is not enough; it has to be 'hombre noble caballero hijodalgo'. There is a proliferation of titles and of ranks; the *vizconde* appears, and three grades of grandeeship. There is a riffling turnover of titles as men rise from *señor* to *vizconde* to *conde*

[53] AGS DGT Inventario 5, leg. 2, f. 68.

to *marqués* and, not satisified with one title, must become *Cardenal-Duque*, *Conde-Duque*, *Duque-Duque-Conde*.[54]

It is as if society was being de-individualized, the self dissolved into the family, the lineage, and the title, and personal characteristics erased by status. Graduates, who in the sixteenth century would always have called themselves *licenciado*, are in the seventeenth commonly using only the 'Don', and there are even army captains not using their titles. Wealth and poverty – mere accidents – seem also to be regarded with increasing indifference in the seventeenth century. This obsession with blood and lineage has been seen by historians as an aspect of 'refeudalization', a 'reaction of the society of orders' to a period of rapid social mobility and what has been called 'the social devaluation of *hidalguía*'.[55] It has been seen variously as an instrument of social exclusiveness, a 'closing of nobility', an attempt to shore up the social order by constructing a new justification for a demilitarized and unmilitary aristocracy, and the consequence of the collapse of the 'bourgeois alternative' in the sixteenth century.[56] It may also be related to the economic and moral crisis of Castile, one manifestation of a loss of confidence in the present and a flight back to past glories and traditional values. It could not have occurred, however, without the documentary revolution which took place from the middle of the sixteenth century or so. The reconstruction of ancient lineages became possible only when families could overcome the limitations of memory. The preservation of records of baptisms and marriages, notarial deeds of entail, marriage settlements and wills, the accumulation of 'executive letters', and the plethora of local and family histories and genealogies made it possible to prove affiliation documentarily and hence to escape the stranglehold of collective memory and public repute. Once fixed in the documents, the cult of lineage could overcome the vagaries of vulgar recognition and community acceptance; but it could do so only because it was itself the complete apotheosis of 'vulgar' values (Diego de Valera).[57]

By the end of the seventeenth century this hypertension is showing

---

[54] A. Cánovas del Castillo, *Estudios del reinado de Felipe IV* (2 vols, Madrid, 1888–9), vol. 2, p. 372, of Medina de las Torres.

[55] Maravall, *Poder, honor y élites*, p. 73; Gutiérrez Nieto, 'Limpieza de sangre y antihidalguismo', p. 509.

[56] Fayard and Gerbet, 'Fermeture de la noblesse', p. 75; Maravall, *Poder, honor y élites*, pp. 102, 216; B. Bennassar, *Los Españoles, actitudes y mentalidad* (Barcelona, 1976), p. 123.

[57] 'Espejo de Verdadera Nobleza', *Biblioteca de Autores Españoles*, vol. 116, p. 100.

signs of subsiding, and in the eighteenth century a new and radically different social vocabulary begins to emerge.[58] First of all, the need to seek justification for *hidalguía* in feats of arms and service in war ceases to be so pressing. By the last third of the seventeenth century, nearly half of all applicants for *hidalguía* grants do not mention any military services at all; and after 1720, less than one in three offers any sort of military justification. Going too was the feudal language of the 'good and loyal vassal' that had characterized service until the mid-seventeenth century. Personal services to the king and his crown were no longer the only ones being used to justify ennoblement. In the eighteenth century it was also beginning to be possible to escape the obsession with blood and lineage. Whereas in the mid-seventeenth century, over 90 per cent had claimed association with a known, noble manor of the mountains of Cantabria ('solar conocido'), only one-quarter were doing so after 1720, and one-third made no pretence of any family connection with nobility whatsoever. The gaps left by the erosion of traditional values had to be filled by new values and new idioms, the 'bourgeois' virtues of 'unceasing work', 'diligence', 'application', 'integrity', education, and a new utilitarian ideology of service to the public ('la causa pública'), to one's neighbours and to the local community, manifested in public works, the provision of employment, or the paving of the streets and the planting of trees along the Valencia road that Don Manuel del Rio of Ocaña adduced in support of his ennoblement in 1783.[59] 'Utility' was the universal yardstick, measuring noble and commoner alike on a single scale of value; the census-takers of Arnedo in mid-century, for example, estimated that the *vecinos* of their city 'comprise, on the best judgement, the useful [*los útiles*], some 132½; the useless and day-labourers [*los ynútiles y brazeros*], some 500.'[60]

Changes were also taking place in the relationship between the 'estados'. The polarity *hidalgo–pechero* seems to have faded. Instead, the *Catastro* and other censuses of the late eighteenth century and the 'cartas de privilegio' refer to 'el estado noble' on the one hand and to 'el estado general' or 'el estado de los hombres buenos' on the other. Not only is 'el estado pechero' relatively uncommon, but the emphasis on fiscal privilege and exemption from *pechos* as the distinguishing mark of the nobleman, though not entirely disappeared, is very much less prominent. Nobility was no longer being represented in terms that opposed it to

[58] For all that follows, see Thompson, 'Neo-noble nobility', pp. 392–5.
[59] AGS DGT Inventario 5, leg. 4, f. 315.
[60] F. Abad León, *Radiografía de Arnedo en el siglo XVIII* (Logroño, 1972), p. 65.

the interests of the community as a whole, and the ennoblement of the rich was no longer, almost by definition, a moral outrage. The correlative of this was the open acceptance of 'bienes de fortuna' as an explicit qualification for ennoblement in the last decades of the century. The wealthy, rather than being oblique and circumlocutory about their money, as in the seventeenth century, were now not ashamed to advertise their riches as a positive merit, and even to put hard figures on their incomes, thus bringing Castilian practice into line with what had been the norm in the Crown of Aragon even in the sixteenth century. Alongside that, it became possible, encouraged by royal legislation in 1783, to declare commerce and manufacturing as activities compatible with honour and as contributions to the public good worthy of honouring. Conditions of economic growth in the eighteenth century could enable the rich man to be seen not as anti-social but as a public benefactor.

The tendency to polarize society into rich and poor was, of course, nothing new to the eighteenth century, though eighteenth-century expressions of that polarization seem to be exceptionally stark – 'the rich are the masters and the poor the slaves.'[61] What is different in these years, in comparison with the predominant feeling of the previous 200 years, is the concern to increase the numbers of the nobility and the conviction that, for political and economic reasons, new wealth ought to be rewarded with noble status.[62]

In the eighteenth century, one has a sense of a realignment of social relationships. On the one hand, there is a rise in the status of the commons, recognized politically in the local government reforms of the 1760s and socially in the willingness of some new *hidalgos* to admit to 'honrado' and Old Christian, 'labrador' origins. On the other, there is a bridging of the gulf between *hidalguía* and 'el estado general' as

[61] Diego de Bohorquez to Campomanes, Granada, 27 Jan. 1766: 'estando en España tan mal repartidos los bienes con que Dios enriqueció la tierra, nos hemos vuelto unos polacos, que los ricos son los amos y los pobres los esclavos,' in M. Aviles Fernández and J. Cejudo López (eds), *Pedro Rodriguez de Campomanes: Epistolario, tomo 1 (1747–77)* (Madrid, 1983), p. 140.

[62] Ibid., p. 383, Rodrigo Ponce: 'Proyecto para multiplicar el número de gente noble en España,' 14 Sept. 1772; p. 385, Miguel de Muzquiz to Campomanes, 10 Oct. 1772; p. 401, Campomanes to Muzquiz, 26 Oct. 1772: 'Nunca conviene cerrar la puerta a la concesión de algunas hidalguías, porque hay hombres tan acaudalados en los pueblos, que conviene honrarlos, para que se establezcan solidamente y fomenten en ellos su industrial . . . Cuando una familia enriquece demasiado, posee un mayorazgo cuantioso y se halla con muchos renteros y colonos, no es fácil contener en la condición de los plebeyos a semejantes personas en una Monarquía, ni en una República Aristocrática.'

theoretically immutable distinctions of blood and lineage give room to individual achievement and purely personal criteria. In the personal listings of the *Catastro*, for instance, the courtesy title 'Don' is divorced from *hidalguía*; there are Dons who are not *hidalgos*, and many *hidalgos* (in some places a majority) who are not Dons. At the same time the language of 'estados' is beginning to weaken. It is difficult to draw up an accurate balance-sheet or a precise chronology, but there seems to be, first, an increasing use of historically neutral terms, such as *condición* ('condition'), and *calidad* ('quality' or literally 'sort'), and then, by the last quarter of the eighteenth century, a widespread use of 'clase'. Most often 'clase' was employed merely as a substitute for 'estado' or to designate a sub-grouping within an 'estado'; 'la clase de notorios hijosdal-go' (1774), 'la clase de caballeros' (1788), 'el estado y clase de ciudadanos' (1778), 'las clases llanas del vecindario' (1793), distinguishing 'comerciantes en grueso' from 'las demás clases de plebeyos' (Puig); or, as when Melchor de Macanaz demanded in the reign of Philip V, 'that every man dress according to his class, so that one's dress proclaim one's profession and nobles not be confused with plebeians, nor the great with the middling'; or when Ramón Lázaro de Dou wrote in 1800, that 'In all times there has been debate about the compatibility of certain professions or activities with the estate of nobility which, in order to preserve the dignity which should pertain to persons of higher class [*clase superior*], has seemed to require that those who are in that class should abstain from sordid occupations.'[63] In the third edition of the influential *Diccionario de la Lengua Castellana*, published by the Royal Spanish Academy in 1791, 'estado' and 'clase' were defined almost interchangeably: 'estado' as 'El órden, clase, gerarquía y calidad de las personas que componen un reino, una república ó un pueblo; como el eclesiástico, el de nobles, el de plebeyos, etc.'; 'clase' as 'Orden ó número de personas del mismo grado, calidad ú oficio; como: la clase de los grandes, de los títulos, de los nobles, &.'[64]

---

[63] AGS DGT Inventario 5, leg. 4, f. 127, 18 Dec. 1774; f. 112, 6 Nov. 1788; f. 94, 25 Oct. 1778; Molas *Burguesía mercantil*, p. 160 (1793), p. 142 (Puig), p. 173 (Macanaz: 'que cada uno viste según su clase para que el vestido diga la profesión y no se confundan los nobles con los plebeyos, ni los grandes con los medianos'), p. 146 (Dou: 'En todos tiempos se ha disputado de algunas profesiones o exercicios si podían compadecerse con el estado de la nobleza, la qual, para conservar el decoro en que deben estar las personas de clase superior, ha parecido exigir que los que se hallen en dicha clase se abstengan de ministerios sórdidos').
[64] It is interesting to see how definitions had changed since the first edition of the *Diccionario* some sixty years earlier: 'classe' (vol. 2, 1729) – 1. 'Orden

In all these cases, 'clase' introduces no new principle of stratification. On the contrary, 'clase' is frequently associated with quality or birth, as in 'the renown and class of those of our family name' (1778); 'some who are distinguished from the rest by their class and by the fortune of birth' (1801); 'there would be nothing more beneficial than a levelling of all classes and conditions, the result would be that no man would be accorded more virtue than is his due' (1786); 'Of what use is the illustrious class, a high descent, without virtue?' (Jovellanos).[65] It remains essentially a designation of status ('maintaining ourselves . . . with the honour, decency, and form appropriate to our class').[66] But by the end of the century it is beginning to be something more than that. In the 1790s, the enlightened reformer and civil servant Gaspar Melchor de Jovellanos, for one, is applying the term 'clase' to a binary social system based on relationship to the means of production:

> I shall divide the population into two classes: one which labours and the other which is leisured [these he later calls 'the opulent classes, who live of their own and are always at leisure']; I shall include in the former all

---

escogida en alguna materia en que hai diferentes individuos'; 2. 'Orden distinto de personas, que resulta de la division que se hace en las vecindades de alguna Ciudad, Villa o Poblacion, para el gobierno y conocimiento de los individuos, y vecinos que la componen'; 3. 'el grado o calidad que corresponde a la esphera de algunos individuos: como la classe de los Nobles, Hijosdalgo, Doctores, Maestros, Sabios, Politicos, &.'; 4. 'En las Universidades y Estudios se llama el Aula u orden en que se dividen los Estudiantes'; 'estado' (vol. 3, 1732) – 'Vale tambien comunmente la especie, calidad, grado y orden de cada cosa; y por esso en las Repúblicas se distinguen, conocen y hai diversos estados, unos seculares y otros Eclesiásticos, y destos los unos Clérigos y los otros Religiosos, y de los Seculares proprios de la República, unos Nobles y Caballeros, otros Ciudadanos, unos Oficiales, otros Labradores, &, y cada uno en su estado y modo de vivir tiene orden, reglas y leyes para su régimen.' By 1791, 'estado', though still retaining something of the broader sense of the genus (of which the 'clase' was the species), was explicitly conflated with 'clase', and had lost the connotation of a legally ordered way of life, distinguished by formal rules of conduct and prescriptions of the law.

[65] 'La buena memoria, y clase de los de nuestro apellido' (1778); 'algunos que distinguiéndose de los demás por su clase y por la casualidad del nacimiento' (1801); 'nada habría tan favorable como una igualación a nivel de todas las clases y condiciones, de donde resultaría que a ningún hombre se diese más valor que el que tuviera por si mismo' (1786); '¿De qué sirve La clase ilustre, una alta descendencia Sin la virtud?' (Jovellanos): AGS DGT Inventario 5, leg. 4, f. 94; Molas, *Burguesía mercantil*, p. 148; A. Dominguez Ortiz, *Sociedad y Estado en el siglo XVIII Español* (Madrid, 1976), p. 355.

[66] 'Manteniéndonos . . . con honor, decencia, y conveniencia correspondientes a nuestra clase': AGS DGT Inventario 5, leg. 4, f. 94.

the professions which live by the product of their daily work, and in the latter those which live by their rents or their safe investments . . . . It is true there will still be many people in the middle, but they will always belong to one class or the other, depending on whether their situation tends more or less towards occupation or idleness.[67]

Jovellanos's model of society is a long way from that of Cobarruvias, whose 'ciudadano' estate also lived off its rents, but which included the 'professions' and was distinguished as an 'estado medio', not only from 'los oficios mecánicos', but also from the 'caballeros' and 'hijosdalgo'. Jovellanos, much influenced by the writings of Cantillon, Turgot, Condillac, and, above all, Adam Smith, may be exceptional.[68] Given the general lack of new content in the word, it is uncertain what significance should be given to the adoption of the new idiom of 'clase'. The phenomenon has not been studied to my knowledge, or even noted. It may not be much more than a modish imitation of the French or the English. It is perhaps best, therefore, to take it to mark not so much a clear perception of a new social order as a mental retreat from the old. It is none the less interesting that the same terminological development occurred at much the same time in England, France, and Spain, societies of a very different nature which were undergoing very different experiences of economic and social change. The movement away from the language of 'estados' and 'brazos' was sometimes part of, sometimes merely the concomitant of, a radical critique of a social order that had been based on the ideal of a harmonious, organic community of interdependent, hereditary functions, distinguishing men in honour and respect by virtue of birth and lineage and embodying their status in legal rights and privileges. That society had never really been like that, never static nor closed to merit and mobility, did not mean that the new terminology was not part of a process of releasing individualist, competitive, self-made values from homage to the social ideals that the traditional vocabulary had enshrined.

What is not clear is how far and how quickly these linguistic changes

---

[67] 'Memoria para el arreglo de la policía de los espectáculos y diversiones públicas' (1790/96), in G. M. de Jovellanos, *Espectáculos y Diversiones Públicas Informe sobre la Ley Agraria*, ed. J. Lage (Cátedra, Madrid, 1977), pp. 117, 123.

[68] Gaspar Melchor de Jovellanos (1744–1811) was one of the most notable figures of the Spanish Enlightenment. An ecclesiastic, he was born of an ancient Asturian family with a modest estate, and followed a university and legal career as a high-court judge in Seville and Madrid, where he was closely associated with a team of enlightened aristocratic reformers in the government of Charles III, especially Campomanes and Floridablanca.

penetrated the society they were describing. There may well be regional and strata differences which it is not possible at the moment to identify. It is striking that many, though not all, the users of 'clase' are Valencian and Catalan. In the backwaters, away from the mainstream of industrial and commercial activity, society, values, and language may have been more resistant to change. That certainly was the opinion of the reformers themselves. The 'modernization' of honour was essentially a movement engineered from above by reformers and a reforming government intent on constructing a new social harmony, based on utilitarian functions to replace the natural harmony of the now largely defunct *corpus mysticum*.[69] The imposition of new values from above and the redrawing of the economic lines of social division upwards plutocratized nobility, and turned the entire institution of nobility into something alien to the traditional values of the community.

As the reformers themselves realized, the regeneration of Castile through the transformation of social values could not proceed against the conservatism of popular sentiment. 'The whole evil lies in the persuasion of the vulgar,' one complained in 1781.[70] 'Ideas have changed, it is true,' wrote another a few years later, 'but only among the writers . . . the people remains always immutable.'[71] In one sense, then, the failure of social reform, perhaps even the inconsistency with which it was pursued, was simply a recognition of the ineradicability of the 'vulgar' and populist conviction that regalist writers had been trying to combat for centuries: 'The king may make knights, but he cannot make gentlemen.'[72]

Clearly language is not something entirely divorced from its social context; but, equally clearly, words have lives of their own. For 500 years, and despite all the political, economic, and social changes that took place between the last centuries of the *Reconquista* and the ending of the *ancien régime*, the language of 'estates' remained the dominant idiom of social description in Castile. The language of 'class', lacking the residual, normative resonances of 'estados' and denoting a more

---

[69] Richard Herr, *The Eighteenth-Century Revolution in Spain* (Princeton University Press, Princeton, 1958), is still the fullest and best general English-language account of the reformers and reform in eighteenth-century Spain. Specifically on attitudes to nobility, W. J. Callahan, *Honor, Commerce and Industry in Eighteenth-Century Spain* (Harvard Graduate School of Business Administration, Boston, 1972) is particularly informative.

[70] J. Guillamón Alvarez, *Honor y honra en la España del siglo XVIII* (Madrid, 1981), p. 162, quoting Pedro Antonio Sánchez.

[71] V. Palacio Atard, *Los españoles de la Ilustración* (Madrid, 1964), p. 59.

[72] Valera, 'Espejo', p. 100.

XV

material objectivity of classification, carried greater potential for the description of post-*ancien-régime* society, in the same way that 'caballero' survived the abolition of the legal privileges of nobility, whereas 'hidalgo', which was too specifically a legal concept, did not. Yet the rise of 'clase' antedated the decisive change in the nature of Castilian society, and did not initially carry the distinctive sense of a particular relationship to the means of production that it was to acquire. To put it another way, changing social realities did not so much create a new social vocabulary as expand the content of the vocabulary that already existed. Both 'estado' and 'clase' were able to contain different social circumstances through an expansion of meaning. Yet, at the same time, both were tied to the string of meanings they trailed behind them – hence the imprecision in their use but, at the same time, their adaptability and their survivability.

INDEX

Acuña Vela, Don Juan de: VI 357; VII 72, 74, 78, 79, 80, 81
administración: IV 21–3; state investment II 10, 17, 20
Agreda (Soria): XII 4
Albert, Archduke: X 5
Alburquerque, duke of: IX 77
alcabala: II 1, 6
Alcalá Zamora, J.: IV 15
Alfaro (Logroño): XIII 342; municipal offices XII 2–3, 18; municipal finances XII 10–11, 12, 17–18; population XII 2, 7
Alfonso XI: XII 1
Aljarafe (Sevilla): II 16
Allen, Cardinal William: X 5
Almendralejo (Badajoz): XIII 322
Almodóvar del Campo (Ciudad Real): II 16
Alva, Fernando Alvarez de Toledo, 3rd duke of: V 209
Alva, Andrés de: IX 76
Alvarez de Alcocer, Antonio: XIII 341, 348, 349
Alvarez de Toledo, Fernando: XV 56
Amiens, cloth production in: III 263
Amsterdam: III 264
Andalucía: III 266, 268; IV 17; V 210, 212, 216; IX 73, 76–7, 81, 87; XI 256, 257, 262, 266; XIII 330, 337; commissariat, expenditure in II 13–19, 21
Antequera: II 15, 16
Antwerp: III 264, 270
Aquitaine: III 261
Aragon: IX 87, 261; XI 257–8; military contributions I 17; IV 9
Aragonese constitutionalism: X 4
Arana, Martín de, shipbuilder: IV 3, 23
arbitristas: XI 244, 261
Arce Otalora, Juan de: XIV 379, 381
Aristotle, concept of society: XV 53, 55, 56
Armada: III 261; objectives V 200–6, 213; VIII 18–19; plans VIII 5–6, 13; diplomacy V 199, 201; VIII 3; English diplomacy and V 201; consequences of VIII 18–19

— composition of VIII 4; cost and financing of V 202, 209; VIII 8, 9–10; preparations and organization of V 204; VIII 6; IX 78, 91–2; logistics of IX 76–7, 81–3, 93; supply problems, rations VIII 11; armaments VIII 7; gunpowder VIII 9, 16–17
— seamen V 210; VIII 6; soldiers V 210; VIII 6–7, 10–13; conscripts VIII 13; morale VIII 15
— guns VI 362, 364; VII 70, 75–7; VIII 15; comparison with English VIII 16; battle range VI 356; VII 69
— squadrons, Oquendo of Guipúzcoa VI 358; *urcas* VII 70; *pataches* VII 70; galleys V 207; VIII 14
— ships VIII 8, 14–15; Ragusan IX 89; named VII 76–7; 'Florencia' VI 358; 'Gran Grifón' VI 357; 'Gran Grín' VIII 10; IX 82; 'Nuestra Señora del Rosario' (flagship of Andalusian Squadron) VI 357, 358; VIII 11; IX 82; 'San Juan' (*almiranta* of Portugal Squadron) VI 356, 358; 'San Martín' (flagship of Portugal Squadron) VI 360; 'San Salvador' (Guipúzcoa) VI 357, 364; VIII 4; 'Santiago' (Portugal) VI 360; 'San Mateo' (Portugal) VIII 17
Armada de la Guarda de la Carrera de Indias: IV 4; VIII 2, 8; IX 71, 73, 80, 86
Armada del Mar Océano: IV 4; IX 85
Armada Proclamation of 1597: X 3, 6
armaments: *see* munitions
artisan: XV 56–7
Arundel, earl of: X 2
Aulnoy, Mme d': XV 63
Auñón, Melchor de Herrera, marquis of: VIII 9
Austria, Don Juan de: V 198
Avila: III 274
Ayamonte (Huelva): II 15
Azores, campaign 1583: IX 73

For Product Safety Concerns and Information please contact
our EU representative GPSR@taylorandfrancis.com Taylor & Francis
Verlag GmbH, Kaufingerstraße 24, 80331 München, Germany

T - #0044 - 160425 - C0 - 224/150/20 [22] - CB - 9780860783282 - Gloss Lamination